Seeking Śākyamuni

Buddhism and Modernity
A series edited by Donald S. Lopez Jr.

Seeking Śākyamuni

South Asia in the Formation of
Modern Japanese Buddhism

RICHARD M. JAFFE

The University of Chicago Press
Chicago and London

The University of Chicago Press, Chicago 60637
The University of Chicago Press, Ltd., London
© 2019 by The University of Chicago
All rights reserved. No part of this book may be used or reproduced in any manner
whatsoever without written permission, except in the case of brief quotations in
critical articles and reviews. For more information, contact the University of Chicago
Press, 1427 E. 60th St., Chicago, IL 60637.
Published 2019
Printed in the United States of America

28 27 26 25 24 23 22 21 20 19   1 2 3 4 5

ISBN-13: 978-0-226-39114-4 (cloth)
ISBN-13: 978-0-226-39115-1 (paper)
ISBN-13: 978-0-226-62823-3 (e-book)
DOI: https://doi.org/10.7208/chicago/9780226628233.001.0001

Library of Congress Cataloging-in-Publication Data

Names: Jaffe, Richard M., 1954– author.
Title: Seeking Śākyamuni : South Asia in the formation of modern Japanese
    Buddhism / Richard M. Jaffe.
Other titles: Buddhism and modernity.
Description: Chicago ; London : The University of Chicago Press, 2019. |
    Series: Buddhism and modernity | Includes bibliographical references and index.
Identifiers: LCCN 2018043832 | ISBN 9780226391144 (cloth : alk. paper) |
    ISBN 9780226391151 (pbk. : alk. paper) | ISBN 9780226628233 (e-book)
Subjects: LCSH: Buddhism—Japan—History—1868–1945. | Buddhists—Travel—South
    Asia—History—19th century. | Buddhists—Travel—South Asia—History—20th
    century. | Japanese—Travel—South Asia—History—19th century. | Japanese—
    Travel—South Asia—History—20th century. | Japan—Relations—South Asia. |
    South Asia—Relations—Japan.
Classification: LCC BQ691 .J34 2019 | DDC 294.30952—dc23
LC record available at https://lccn.loc.gov/2018043832

♾ This paper meets the requirements of ANSI/NISO Z39.48–1992
(Permanence of Paper).

For Elaine

Contents

Acknowledgments

Numerous people and institutions provided support that enabled me to complete this book. Duke University is a congenial home for humanities scholarship. I am grateful for the research funds, superb library resources, sabbatical leaves, and the numerous opportunities for scholarly conversations that supported this project. Thanks go as well to the National Endowment for the Humanities and National Humanities Center, for fellowships that provided me with additional leave time to concentrate on the book.

Research for this book required gaining access to a wide array of documents, temples, buildings, photographs, and artworks. It also necessitated working with a variety of languages and scripts. The list of languages includes Chinese, Japanese, Sanskrit, Pali, Tibetan, Brāhmī, Devanagiri, and Sinhala. Many people and institutions around the world helped me see, photograph, and interpret these materials. I am grateful to those who staff the Aichi Prefectural Library, Buddhist Publication Society, Entsūji, Jōzaiji, Kasuisai, Kobe Betsuin, Komazawa University, Manpukuji, Matsugaoka Bunko, Nittaiji, Otani University, Ryūkoku University, Sanneji, Shinpukuji, Tōkeiji, Unshōji, Tōhoku University, and the University of Tokyo. I particularly want to express my gratitude to Aikawa Tenshin, Aikawa Yasumichi, Andō Sonjin, Ehara Ryōsen, Sumi Kōyō, Suzuki Hiroyuki, and Unno Ninshō, all of whom allowed me access to the archival materials they oversaw. Without their graciousness and generosity, I would not have discovered many of the documents and images that formed the lineaments of this book.

My friends and colleagues in Japan and around the globe also provided invaluable assistance to me. They helped me use the libraries at their institutions, provided introductions to many of the temples mentioned above, pointed me toward new sources, and helped me interpret what I uncovered in my research. I thank Annaka Naofumi, Ban Katsuyo, Ishii Kōsei, Ishii Seijun, Ishii Shūdō, Kumamoto Einin, Moriya Tomoe, Ogawa Takashi, Okuyama Naoji, Orion Klautau, Sasaki Shunsuke, Sueki Fumihiko, Tanaka Chisei, Tatsuguchi Myōsei, and Yoshinaga Shin'ichi for helping make my numerous visits to Japan while working on this project productive and pleasant. For decades, a number of wonderful friends in Japan have made it a second home for me. Thank you, Eshū, Hakushū, Keiko, Kiyoshi, Kyoko, Tomoko, Ryūken, Myōsei, Takatoshi, and Yukiko for many years of warm friendship.

I also owe a debt to Anne Blackburn, Jonathan Silk, Justin McDaniel, Bhikkhu Nyanatusita, and Shimada Akira for coming to my aid by reading the Indic and Tibetan scripts on the polylingual calligraphy or tracking down information about South-Southeast Asian individuals who figured in the episodes I have traced. In addition, I am thankful to Bhikkhu Soorakkulame Pemaratana, Douglas Ober, Dr. Janaka Goonetilleke, Ramachandra Guha, and Kevin Trainor for sharing their insights with me.

My colleagues at Duke also aided this research in a number of ways. I am grateful to Kristina Troost, Hwansoo Kim, David Morgan, Leela Prasad, Elizabeth Clark, Simon Partner, Gennifer Weisenfeld, and Prasenjit Duara for their suggestions, assistance, and encouragement. I also thank the graduate students in the Graduate Program in Religion at Duke, Susannah Duerr and Rebecca Mendelson, who helped me in various ways prepare the manuscript for publication.

I have had the good fortune of working with fine editors at the University of Chicago Press, Alan Thomas and Kyle Wagner, as well as Donald Lopez, the editor of the series that this book now joins. I am indebted to them for their patience and advice over the years. In addition, I thank two anonymous readers of the manuscript and the copyeditor for this project, Jo Ann Kiser, for helping me to improve the manuscript. Portions of several chapters of this book first were published in journals. I acknowledge the gratis permissions to draw on my own work from the *Journal of Japanese Studies* and *Material Religion*, and the Japanese journal *Shisō*. I thank James Dobbins, David Morgan, and Sueki Fumihiko for helping me place these articles in the above journals: "Shakuson o sagashite: Kindai Nihon Bukkyō no tanjō to sekai ryokō," trans. Maeda Ken'ichi, *Shisō* 943 (2002); "Seeking Śākyamuni: Travel and the Reconstruction of Japanese Buddhism," *Journal of Japanese Studies* 30, no. 1 (2004); and "Buddhist Material Culture, Indianism, and the Construction of Pan-Asian Buddhism in Pre-War Japan," *Material Religion* 2, no. 3 (2006).

A number of people who assisted me in Japan, several of them in their eighties or nineties when we met, died before I completed this book. I posthumously acknowledge Furuta Shōkin, Inoue Zenjō, Shaku Shinshō, and

Unebe Toshiya for generously sharing their time, resources, and knowledge with me. Diagnosed with advanced Stage III multiple myeloma in July 2010, I too would not have lived to bring the book to this stage were it not for the amazing medical team at the Duke Cancer Center, especially Drs. Louis Diehl and Joseph Moore, who patched me back together again. With great skill, Dr. Cristina Gasparetto, as well as a platoon of nurses and physician assistants, especially Anderson Garrett-Hicks and Scott Winkle, at the Adult Bone Marrow Transplant Clinic, carefully saw me the rest of the way to recovery. Eight years later, thanks to them all, I can write that for the time being, apart from having multiple myeloma, I am perfectly healthy.

Thanks to my family—Pam, Susan, Michael, Bernie, Bonnie, Rose, and Gloria—for lovingly supporting me every step of the way as I brought this book to completion. They continue to help me keep everything in proper perspective. My spirits have been buoyed by watching Zina and her partner, Christopher, launch themselves on their careers. I am deeply grateful to Elaine for the steady encouragement, good humor, insight, and affection that sustained me in countless ways as I completed this project. She believed I would complete the book, even when I could not imagine doing so.

Conventions

In the book I have used the Revised Hepburn and pinyin transcription systems for the Romanization of Japanese and Chinese terms, respectively. Tibetan transliterations follow the Wylie system. For cognate forms of names and terms, I have used the abbreviations C., P., and S. to identify the Chinese, Pali, and Sanskrit alternate forms. I have designated unattested Pali or Sanskrit titles of texts with an asterisk in front of the title. For Japanese, Chinese, and Korean persons, I have followed the East Asian convention of giving the family name first. When a person has written a book or article in English, however, I have written the given name before the family name in the footnotes or, in the bibliography, with a comma separating the family name from the given name. Pre-titles (as opposed to subtitles) of Japanese works are designated with angle brackets, as in <Mokusen Zenji> Nangoku junrei ki or <Shin'yaku> Shaku Sōen Saiyū nikki.

Abbreviations

AHZ *Akegarasu Haya zenshū*
BB *Bibliography on Buddhism*
HAC *Hirakawa Akira chosakushū*
IBJ *Iwanami Bukkyō jiten*
KECS *Kawaguchi Ekai chosakushū*
MNB *Meiji no Bukkyōsha*
NBCS *Nanjō Bun'yū chosaku senshū*
NBJ *Nihon Bukkyō jinmei jiten*
OBDJ *Bukkyō daijiten*
PDB *Princeton Dictionary of Buddhism*
SBJ *Studies on Buddhism in Japan*
SSS *Shinshū shiryō shūsei*
SUS *Shaku Unshō*
T *Taishō shinshū daizōkyō*
YE *Young East*
ZGDJ *Zengaku daijiten*

Introduction

Locating Tenjiku

In March 1881, having made it to England, Nanjō Bun'yū was two years deep into his study of Sanskrit with Max Müller at Oxford. Nanjō already had published a series of works that would earn him fame and he looked forward to another four years of study overseas. Most fervently, he desired to visit India, writing a poem that expressed his long-standing but yet unfulfilled desire to travel to Śākyamuni Buddha's homeland.

> I, man of the East, do not yet try to travel through the five (ancient) parts of India,
> But have only a few Sanskrit books and clothes for my journey;
> There is a tree of knowledge [Bodhi tree], which I think of and long for even from the distance of 10,000 li;
> There is a forest of the "firm" trees [Sāla grove where Buddha died] where the footprint of a traveller (such as Hiouenthsang [Xuanzang]) might have vanished a thousand years ago.
> Fate was so bad the (Japanese) prince [Prince Shinnyo] died in a remote country region;
> Time was so different (from ours), that the eminent priest [Hōtan] grew old in his home country:
> Now my stay and study here are already above my desert;
> So, I hope, that the tale [*sic*] of a snake will not join with the head of a dragon.[1]

Among the very first Japanese Buddhists to spend an extended period of time studying in Europe, Nanjō Bun'yū (1849–1927) had been sent to England in 1876 by the head of his denomination, the Jōdo Shinshū Higashi Honganji

---

1. F. Max Müller, *Biographical Essays* (London: Longmans Green, 1884), 205–10. I have interpolated information from Nanjō's footnotes on the poem in brackets.

(Ōtani-ha). Accompanied by Shin cleric Kasahara Kenju (1852–83), Nanjō was part of a wave of early Buddhist travelers to Europe and the United States. Like other members of the Ōtani and Nishi Honganji branches of Jōdo Shin, the two young men were following in the wake of the Iwakura Mission, which had been sent around the globe in search of knowledge to help Japanese respond to the turmoil sparked by their encounter with Americans and Europeans in the second half of the nineteenth century.

After gaining facility in English, Nanjō and Kasahara embarked on the study of Sanskrit with Max Müller at Oxford University. According to Müller, both became accomplished in Sanskrit, thus allowing them to "read the canonical books of Buddhism in the original." Imagining the possibility of traveling to the land of the Buddha's birth, in 1881 Nanjō wrote the above Sino-Japanese poem (kanshi) and appended it to a brief autobiography he had written for Müller while in residence at Oxford. The very next year, his friend Kasahara was forced to cut short his study abroad because of an increasingly severe case of tuberculosis. Even in his weakened condition, however, Kasahara during his return journey to Japan managed to spend more than three weeks in Ceylon, where he toured the Temple of the Tooth, which supposedly enshrines a tooth of Śākyamuni Buddha, and Anurādhapura, the ancient Sinhala capital. Also while in Ceylon, Kasahara met with the renowned Buddhist monk Hikkaḍuvē Sumaṅgala and other Ceylonese bhikkhu. Finally arriving in Japan in late November 1882, Kasahara was dead from his disease within a year.

Like Kasahara, Nanjō found himself forced to return to Japan earlier than he had hoped. Though he had planned to work with Müller until 1885, Nanjō's adoptive mother fell ill in 1884, and his biological mother, widowed in late 1883, requested that their son return home.[2] Promptly complying with his family's wishes, Nanjō returned to Japan in 1884. In his autobiographical essay written for Müller, Nanjō freely lamented that his overseas studies had been curtailed and regretted that he would be unable to travel to India, unlike even his ailing friend, Kasahara, who had toured Ceylon. Having failed to make it to India, it appears that Nanjō saw his mission abroad as incomplete.[3]

In the poem, Nanjō imagines Bodh Gayā, the seat of Śākyamuni's awakening, and sadly recalls his predecessors, the Heian-era Shingon cleric Shinnyo (Prince Takaoka; Takaoka Shinnō; 799–865) and the Edo-era Kegon

2. The practice of adoption of an adult or adolescent male son as an heir (yōshi) was a common practice among elite families during the late nineteenth and early twentieth centuries. The adoptive child would, as in Nanjō's case, sometimes maintain ties with his natal family as well.

3. Müller, Biographical Essays, 202–3.

cleric Hōtan (1659–1738), who, like Nanjō, had longed to reach the land of the Buddha. Elaborating upon the lineage of Japanese Indophiles decades later, Takakusu Junjirō (1866–1945), who studied with Müller after Nanjō, described how Shinnyo died en route from China to India, in Luoyue (J. Ra'etsu; possibly Singapore), and Hōtan consoled himself "by bathing his feet in the seawater at a beach in the province of Kii, while indulging in the thought that the water extended to the shore of the motherland of Buddhism," where Śākyamuni had lived.[4] Having begun his time abroad in grand fashion—like the head of a dragon—studying with Max Müller at Oxford, Nanjō vows not to conclude his journey disappointingly—the tail of a snake—as had his predecessors, who failed to reach the land of the Bodhi tree and the sala groves.

In an era when travel to India remained difficult and out of reach for most Japanese, Nanjō expressed the persistent importance of India in the minds of Japanese Buddhists. Although many scholars have viewed Oxford as the endpoint of Nanjō's journey, his own verse illustrates the extent to which, even in traveling to the "West," Japanese Buddhists like Nanjō were also heading to the "East"—that is, to India–South Asia—to recover the supposedly original Buddhism that served as the foundation for the tradition in Japan. In this manner, both the journey to Europe and the journey to India were essential parts of Japanese Buddhism's modernization.

Back in Japan, Nanjō worked to support the interest in Indian travel, providing Sanskrit and Pali language training for several in the first wave of Japanese Buddhists who headed to South Asia. Three years later, in 1887, Nanjō did finally manage to reach India and other locations in South Asia, a journey he records in his travel diary, *Indo kikō*.[5] In that account, Nanjō mentions that while he was in Benares his interest in pursuing further Sanskrit studies in India was squelched by the German head of Benares Sanskrit College. He writes that the German warned him about great difficulties for non-Brahmins studying Sanskrit in Benares and the scarcity of teachers in the city who could actually teach Buddhist Sanskrit.[6] While Nanjō spent only two months in India and Ceylon, for the rest of his career he corresponded about Buddhist

---

4. Junjiro Takakusu, "India and Japan," *Young East* 1, no. 2 (1925): 35–39. (Hereafter YE.) On Shinnyo, see Robert E. Morrell, "Passage to India Denied: Zeami's Kasuga Ryūjin," *Monumenta Nipponica* 37, no. 2 (Summer 1982): 180, note 3.

5. Nanjō Bun'yū, *Indo kikō* (Kyoto: Sano Masamichi, 1887).

6. Nanjō, *Indo kikō*, 32. As mentioned by Micah L. Auerback, *A Storied Sage: Canon and Creation in the Making of a Japanese Buddha*. Buddhism and Modernity. (Chicago: University of Chicago Press, 2016), 183, Nanjō later recalled that the principal of the college warned him that India was "unhealthy." This information is based on Nanjō's 1927 reflections, *Kaikyūroku*, in *Nanjō Bun'yū chosaku senshū* (hereafter, NBCS) 8: 278.

texts and practices with those Japanese who dared, despite the dangers, to spend extended periods in South Asia, and he also served with regularity as an intermediary for many South and Southeast Asian Buddhists who came to Japan.

As for numerous other Japanese Buddhists from the start of the Meiji period, travel to India and the surrounding regions of South Asia—a geographic area roughly encapsulated by the rather vague Sino-Japanese term Tenjiku (C., Tianzhu), a transliteration of "Sindhu"—stood as an indispensable part of Nanjō and Kasahara's Buddhist education and maturation as clerics. Prior to their return journeys to Japan, their predecessors in global travel, for example, Akamatsu Renjō (1841–1919), Ishikawa Shuntai (1842–1931), Ōtani Kōei (1852–1923), Umegami Takuyū (1835–1907), Shimaji Mokurai (1838–1911), and Kitabatake Dōryū (1820–1907), each managed to make a stop in India, Ceylon, or both, to tour Buddhist sites. (See chapter 1.) Kitabatake, to much acclaim, even succeeded in reaching Bodh Gayā in late 1883, making him the first-known Japanese to do so. These ventures into South Asian hinterlands by early Japanese Buddhist travelers were not just opportunistic tourist junkets undertaken at convenient entrepôts en route to Japan from Europe. The sometimes risky early ventures by Japanese Buddhists instead demonstrate how Shinnyo and Hōtan's dream of reaching Tenjiku was revived after the Japanese opened their country to foreign travel in the second half of the nineteenth century. That the Japanese would bother with these perilous South Asian pilgrimages to Buddhist sites—a number of Japanese Buddhists subsequently died making the journey—underscores the growing importance that South Asia would play in Japanese Buddhist life in the late nineteenth and twentieth centuries. Although it is common to see Nanjō, Kasahara, and Takakusu's periods of study in Europe as another example of the "Westernization" of Japanese Buddhism in the modern era, their journey to Europe and acquisition of Indic language facility enabled them to reach South Asia, where they could encounter directly the "Buddhism of the Southwest," to use the appellation of one early Japanese traveler to the region.

To date, most scholars have understood the rise of Indian Buddhist and Sanskrit studies in Japan as the result of the importation of European and American scholarship into Japan. Many of the changes in Japanese Buddhism, particularly in Buddhist studies, from the Meiji period onward, thus are understood as a product of "Westernization." Makoto Hayashi, for example, in a series of articles on the rise of Buddhist universities and religious studies in Japan mentions how departments of Indian philosophy " served to introduce to Japan the methods of Western Buddhology, though the primary goal of Buddhist universities was to train priests. While at imperial universities the study of Buddhism involved learning Pali and Sanskrit and most affiliated scholars focused on early Buddhism, research at sectarian universities was centered on Chinese translations of Mahāyāna sutras and the writings of their sect founders."[7] Although this is partially true, in this book I will show that the sectarian universities partook in the trend toward Indic studies, but many who assumed those chairs in Sanskrit, Pali, and Indian philosophy trained in South Asia rather than in Europe or the United States. For Japanese Buddhists who, as a matter of self-survival, strove to embrace nineteenth- and twentieth-century standards of scholarship and models of religious practice hegemonic in Europe and the United States, coming to terms with Japanese Buddhism's South Asian Buddhist roots was a central pillar in reconceptualizing Buddhism in the modern era in Japan, that is, in the period that approximately began in the mid-nineteenth century.[8] Much of this process occurred in South Asia, not Europe and the United States, and involved many South Asian voices in addition to the far better-known American and European ones.

The education the Japanese received in India certainly was beholden to British colonial institutions of higher learning in India. Most of their teachers, however, were not Europeans, but Indian pandits, many of whom continued to emphasize precolonial pedagogical practices and traditional religious perspectives. This, too, counts as modern education but it is uncertain how "Western" it is. As Michael Dodson and Brian Hatcher suggest in their edited volume on "transcolonial modernities" in South Asia, modernity for the Indians in the nineteenth and twentieth centuries was not simply something forced upon them by European colonialists. Rather than being monolithic and globally uniform, in South Asia we see "that modernity, far from being imposed wholesale from without, was always partial and subjected to reinterpretation and negotiation."[9] Thus, the pandits did not merely transmit colonial European and American scholarship unchanged to the Japanese.

7. Makoto Hayashi, "The Birth of Buddhist Universities," *Japanese Religions* 39, nos. 1 & 2 (Spring & Fall 2014): 20.

8. I am following the conventional periodization of Japanese history as seen in Walker, for example, who writes of Japan's entry into the modern period in the mid-nineteenth century. See Brett L. Walker, *A Concise History of Japan*, Cambridge Concise Histories (Cambridge: Cambridge University Press, 2015), 124. Gordon similarly describes events from 1868–1905 as the "modern revolution" and the period covered by his survey history as " an era we call modern." Andrew Gordon, *A Modern History of Japan: From Tokugawa Times to the Present*, third ed. (Oxford: Oxford University Press, 2014), xi; 60.

9. Michael S. Dodson and Brian A. Hatcher, *Trans-Colonial Modernities in South Asia* (New York: Routledge, 2012), 2, Kindle.

They offered their version of that scholarship as well as their own indigenous approaches to the study of Indic languages and Buddhism. As I will demonstrate, the construction of Japanese Buddhist "modernity" involved a sustained encounter with South Asia as well as with the "West." That is, for many Japanese Buddhists, as for many other Asians, becoming modern meant embracing, interpreting, and adapting the dimensions characteristic of European and American modernity, including science, objective history, industrialization, nationalism, and empire. At the same time, however, an indispensable aspect of forging Japanese Buddhist modernity in the late nineteenth and early twentieth centuries also entailed connecting Japanese Buddhism to South Asia, interpersonally, scholastically, spiritually, and artistically. The main actors to construct these connections with South and Southeast Asian Buddhism were educated clerics and laity who had the resources and education required for travel to South Asia and the appropriation of what they encountered there. Through the public display of South and Southeast Asian relics, images, artwork, and texts these travelers brought back and the arrival of Buddhists from those regions in Japan, they helped spread this new understanding of Buddhism among large numbers of the laity as well.

Some of the Buddhists and other actors to be discussed in this book bear the features, at least in part, of the modernist Buddhists whom Donald Lopez aptly characterizes as eschewing ritual, magic, monasticism, and hierarchy in favor of a rational, lay, text-oriented "Protestant" form of Buddhism that aspires to recapture the true spirit of the Buddha's teachings.[10] This group includes such individuals as Shaku Sōen, Sakurai Gichō, Itō Chūta, Kawaguchi Ekai, and some of the architectural correspondents I will describe in chapter 4. These individuals self-reflexively describe themselves as creating a modern or new Buddhism in Japan, which, in contrast to earlier forms of the tradition, was better suited for the twentieth century. Other Buddhists I analyze in the pages that follow, however, for example, Ōtani Kōzui, Ōtani Son'yu, and Kuruma Takudō, consciously and explicitly chased the "modern" as much as the aforementioned modernist Buddhists, viewing engagement with South and Southeast Asia as integral to constructing a Japanese Buddhism suitable for the twentieth century, even as they continued to embrace monasticism, hierarchy, and ritual, as well as image and relic veneration. They thus accepted many of the features of established Buddhist denominations that were called into question by the new Buddhists. A third and smaller

10. Donald S. Lopez, *A Modern Buddhist Bible: Essential Readings from East and West* (Boston: Beacon Press, 2002), ix–x. Lopez refers to them as "modern Buddhists," but for clarity, I have designated them "modernist."

group of traditionalists, some of whom Winston Davis long ago classified as "praxis masters," including Shaku Unshō, Shaku Kōzen, and their disciples, did not view their efforts at reform as specifically modern.[11] Instead, following in the footsteps of their Edo-period predecessors, they conceived of their travels in and exchanges with South and Southeast Asian Buddhists primarily as a search for the true practices and precept lineage of the Buddha. Although these latter two groups might be considered "traditionalists," their traditionalism in late nineteenth and early twentieth-century Japan was shaped by many of the same factors, including global capitalism and new forms of technology, that stimulated various iterations of Buddhist modernism across Asia. We thus should bear in mind, as Nile Green cautioned concerning the competing forms of Islam in the nineteenth- and twentieth-century Indian Ocean region, that the disenchanted, modernist forms of religion are not more "modern" than the enchanted ones. In the case of Japan, modernist Buddhism was produced by the same forces and competed for adherents on the same stage as the Buddhisms promoted by the most conservative traditionalists.[12] In this sense all of the Japanese Buddhists detailed in these pages were equally "modern," even if they were not all self-consciously "modernist" in the manner that Lopez delineated. I therefore have used the term "modern Japanese Buddhism" in a capacious sense to describe the tradition in Japan from the mid-nineteenth to the end of the twentieth century.

For most of the premodern period, Japanese direct contact with India was extremely rare. The distance and difficulty of travel to India made it all but impossible for Japanese Buddhists to make the journey, even when motivated by intense longing. Although a number of Japanese dreamed of traveling to the land of Śākyamuni, none successfully made the trip. In one of the few recorded instances of direct contact with South Asian Buddhism, the Indian monk Bodhisena (Bodaisenna; 704–60), came to Japan in 736 at the invitation of Emperor Shōmu (r. 724–49). Bodhisena presided at the 752 "eye-opening" (*kaigen*) ceremony of the Great Buddha at Tōdaiji and played a role in establishing the study of Kegon (C. Huayan) teachings in Japan. Like Shinnyo, who was mentioned in Nanjō's poem, Myōe Kōben (1173–1272), a Shingon cleric, expressed a deep yearning to make the pilgrimage to India, so he could be closer to the land where Śākyamuni had taught. In his two

11. Winston Davis, *Japanese Religion and Society: Paradigms of Structure and Change* (Albany: State University of New York Press, 1992), 161–63.

12. Nile Green, *Bombay Islam: The Religious Economy of the West Indian Ocean, 1840–1915* (Cambridge: Cambridge University Press, 2013), 10, Kindle. Green uses the language of a "religious economy" or religious marketplace to describe the competing forms of a tradition.

attempts to head to India, a series of dreams, oracles, and signs revealed to Myōe that he should not make the trip, however. Coming to an understanding of the *Kegongyō* would enable Myōe to enter the world of the Buddha and remembrance of the Buddha (*nenbutsu*) was a way to meet him. These visions made clear that the *kami* (deities) were manifestations of the buddhas and bodhisattvas of India, including the Kasuga *kami*, who was a manifestation of Śākyamuni.[13] The acceptance of *honji suijaku* (manifestation from the original state) thought that viewed indigenous deities as manifestations of Indian buddhas and bodhisattvas, to some degree displaced the desire for actual travel to India among Japanese Buddhists. The imagined presence of India in Japan thus made travel to India unnecessary.[14]

The role of Tenjiku changed in the Japanese Buddhist imagination during the centuries of Tokugawa rule, as Japanese Buddhists embraced a Sino- or even Japan-centric view of the world. This involved a shift from what Fabio Rambelli deftly has described as the old Sangoku model of the Buddhist world, in which emphasis was placed on Buddhism's transmission from India, China, and Japan, to a "Ka-I" (China-barbarian) one, in which the realm of Sinitic civilization was contraposed with that of the "barbarians," including the denizens of Tenjiku. According to Rambelli, as a result of this shift in thinking, South Asia came to hold a diminished place in the Japanese Buddhist imagination for much of the Tokugawa era.[15]

Nonetheless, dreams of travel to Tenjiku and scrutiny of the Indian origins of Japanese Buddhist practices did not die completely, even amidst the new Ka-I understanding of Japan's place in the world. With the formation of the Buddhist sectarian academies fostered by the Tokugawa authority's stress on educating the clergy, Japanese Buddhists, like Japanese Confucians, began an intensive scrutiny of Buddhist history as portrayed in the key denominational sources of their schools. These efforts resulted in an efflorescence of textual analysis, including a search for the Indian roots of Japanese Buddhist practices. Tōrei Enji (1721–92), an important Rinzai cleric and disciple of Hakuin,

---

13. George J. Tanabe Jr., *Myōe the Dreamkeeper: Fantasy and Knowledge in Early Kamakura Buddhism* (Cambridge, MA: Harvard University Press: 1992), 38; 66–72; Myōe's efforts to journey to India are discussed in detail in Morrell, "Passage to India Denied," 179–200. The story of his second failed attempt to make the pilgrimage was dramatized in Zeami's fifteenth-century Noh drama *Kasuga Ryūjin*, which is translated in Morrell, "Passage to India Denied," 190–200.

14. Fabio Rambelli, "The Idea of Tenjiku (India) in Pre-Modern Japan: Issues of Signification and Representation in the Buddhist Translation of Cultures," in *Buddhism across Asia: Networks of Material, Intellectual, and Cultural Exchange*, ed. Tansen Sen (Singapore: Institute of Southeast Asian Studies, 2014), 260–61.

15. Rambelli, "The Idea of Tenjiku," 279–83.

sought to find the Indian underpinnings of Zen meditation techniques, which he conjectured had been brought to China by the Indian patriarch Bodhidharma. Tōrei's 1784 commentary, *Darumatara zenkyō settsū kōsho*, on the *Damoduoluo chan jing* was an effort to better understand what Tōrei believed were the Indian sources of Zen. A harbinger of deepening concern with Zen's ties to Buddhist South Asia in the Meiji era, Tōrei's commentary was republished in 1893 with a preface by Kōgaku Sōen (Shaku; 1860–1919), the first recorded Zen cleric in the nineteenth century to reach South Asia.[16]

In the eighteenth century, Shingon cleric Jiun Onkō (1718–1804) also used textual scholarship to study Siddham script and Sanskrit grammar in his effort to reveal Japanese Buddhism's Indian foundations. Jiun argued for the primacy of the Sanskrit Buddhist texts that were the basis for the Chinese translations in the canon. Piecing together grammatical information that was scattered across Chinese Buddhist texts, Jiun compiled several guides for understanding Sanskrit texts, including the one-thousand-fascicle *Bongaku shinryō* (Guide to Sanskrit Studies). In an effort to ferret out proper Buddhist precept practice and clerical deportment, Jiun also examined carefully the descriptions of such early Buddhist travelers to South Asia as Yijing (635–713) in his South Asian travel account, *Nanhai jigui neifa zhuan*, writing a detailed commentary on the text, the *Nankai kiki naihōden geransho*.[17] The emphasis on precept authenticity and revival in Shingon made some of the school's clerics a receptive audience for the information about South Asian Buddhism that would flow into Japan after the start of the Meiji era. Although Jiun had to content himself with combing Buddhist texts for information about Sanskrit and the practices described by Yijing, his successors in the Shingon denomination, for example, Shaku Unshō and Shaku Kōzen (see chapter 1), hearing of Ceylonese and Siamese precept lineages that differed from those they used in Japan, endeavored to travel to South Asia to witness firsthand Buddhist practice there.

In addition, as geographical information from Europe flowed into Japan during the Edo period, Japanese Buddhists sought to reconcile traditional

16. Michel Mohr, "Imagining Indian Zen: Tōrei's Commentary on the *Ta-Mo-to-Lo Ching* and the Rediscovery of Meditation Techniques during the Tokugawa Era," in *Zen Classics: Formative Texts in the History of Zen Buddhism*, ed. Steven Heine and Dale S. Wright (New York: Oxford University Press, 2006), 215–46. The usual reading of the commentary's title is *Datsumatara zenkyō settsū kōsho*, but Mohr, following Tōrei's view that the text is by Bodhidharma, reads the title as *Darumatara*.

17. Paul Brooks Watt, "Jiun Sonja (1718–1804): Life and Thought" (PhD diss., Columbia University, 1982), 109–19. Rambelli, "The Idea of Tenjiku," 283. Jiun Onkō. "Nankai kiki naihōden geransho," in *Jiun Sonja zenshū*, ed. Hase Hōshū (Kyoto: Shibunkaku, 1974), 441–580.

Buddhist cosmological maps with imported ones. Hōtan, for example, who was mentioned in Nanjō's poem, immersed himself in the study of non-Buddhist materials available in Nagasaki, including, apparently, maps that had been brought to Japan by Jesuits. Hōtan planned a journey to India, as mentioned above, that was unsuccessful. He subsequently worked to harmonize the traditional Buddhist maps with Jambudvīpa, the India-shaped "Rose-apple" island at their center, and early modern European depictions of the world, creating in 1710 a map placing Europe and Japan in relationship to the continent of Jambudvīpa (J. Enbudai; Nan'enbudai). This sort of effort among Japanese Buddhists continued through the Edo period, with such cosmographers as the Tendai cleric Entsū (1754–1834) creating a world map in 1810 that added, in addition to Europe, Africa, America, Australia, and Antarctica to a map that still had Jambudvīpa as its central geographical feature.[18]

In the first decades of the Meiji period other factors foreign and domestic further stoked Japanese Buddhist attention to South Asia. Long-simmering interest, like Jiun's, among Japanese Buddhists in finding the most orthodox practices, particularly in South Asia, was heightened as new European and American scholarship on Buddhism emphasizing the South Asian origins of the tradition flooded into Japan.[19] Japanese translations of tracts by such European and American Buddhist sympathizers as Henry Steel Olcott and Edwin Arnold drew Japanese attention to Buddhism in South Asia. Dharmapāla and Olcott also highlighted the plight of Buddhists under European colonial domination in Asia, rallying Japanese Buddhists to join them in their struggles. While also interested in the sorts of Buddhist practice that survived in South and Southeast Asia, such Buddhists as Nanjō and Takakusu responded to calls from Müller and other European scholars to search for Sanskrit and Pali manuscripts in South and Southeast Asia. In response to the growing body of European and American works on Buddhism—many quickly translated into Japanese—Japanese Buddhists like Shaku Sōen and Oda Tokunō headed southwest to explore "Southern Buddhism" (*Nanpō Bukkyō*) to discern its relationship with their "Northern Buddhism" (*Hokuhō Bukkyō*) and the overlap of these forms with such traditional Buddhist classificatory categories as Mahayana Buddhism (*Daijō Bukkyō*) and Hinayana Buddhism (*Shōjō Bukkyō*).[20] As scholars and Buddhists argued about the filiation of

18. Masahiko Okada, "Vision and Reality: Buddhist Cosmographic Discourse in Nineteenth-Century Japan" (PhD diss., Stanford University, 1997), 99–100.

19. On the importation of European and American scholarship concerning Buddhism in Japan during the Meiji era, see Auerback, *A Storied Sage*, 182–93.

20. I have followed Oda, reading the characters as Hokuhō, rather than the more common *Hoppō*. See Oda's *Bukkyō daijiten* (hereafter OBDJ), 1587.

various forms of Buddhism across Asia, Japanese who had encountered the Buddhism of Ceylon, India, Siam, and elsewhere in South-Southeast Asia defended the legitimacy and, at times, superiority of Japanese Buddhism around the globe, in public speeches as well as in print in multiple languages. The systematization of Buddhist sectarian academies and their transformation into universities in the early 1920s provided further impetus to Japanese Buddhists for study in South Asia, where they learned Sanskrit and Pali from a host of Indian and Ceylonese scholars and *bhikkhu* before returning to staff new positions in Indian studies back home. The sudden efflorescence in South Asian interest among Japanese Buddhists during the second decade of the Meiji era calls into question Rambelli's assertion that, "in the early Meiji period, we can see that the newly discovered India could have only the slightest attraction for contemporary Japanese."[21]

Far from diminishing interest in Buddhism in Japan and elsewhere in Asia, such new technologies as steamships, textile mills, inexpensive mass printing, reinforced concrete construction, and photography heightened the availability of information and cultural artifacts Japanese Buddhist travelers brought back from South Asia. Nile Green cogently demonstrated how in nineteenth- and early twentieth-century Bombay and elsewhere in the Indian Ocean region, "industrialization fueled new forms of religious productivity" by Muslims rather than leading to a disenchantment of their world.[22] In much the same way new technologies contributed to an expanding awareness of Japanese Buddhism's ties to India, Ceylon, Siam, and elsewhere across South Asia. Events initiated by politicians, for example, the gifting of Śākyamuni's relics by the Siamese king Chulalongkorn to Japan, attracted large numbers of Japanese to novel nodes for gathering—railway hubs—while newly formed periodicals recorded the movement of the relics around the globe and across Japan. Japanese Buddhist travelers to South Asia brought back to Japan Buddhist sculptures, Indic texts, and other artifacts via railways and steamships. Exhibitions of these items were advertised by postcards sent through Japan's new postal system and in newspapers, thus exposing a broad swath of the Japanese public to Japanese Buddhism's ties to Southern Buddhism.

Evolving political and economic concerns also facilitated growing Japanese Buddhist interest in South Asia. Japanese government officials, seeking to broaden contacts in South and Southeast Asia, frequently served as conduits for contact with South and Southeast Asian Buddhists and those in Japan. The rise of pan-Asianism that linked Japan to Asians not only in the

21. Rambelli, "The Idea of Tenjiku," 284.
22. Green, *Bombay Islam*, 235.

Far East but along the Asian continent's southern tier among Japanese intellectuals also intensified interest in the sorts of travels, study abroad, and exchanges that I detail in this volume. Technological and economic forces also played a significant role in facilitating these contacts while heightening the importance of South-Southeast Asia, particularly India, for the Japanese. The growth of the global textile trade, especially cotton, contributed to increased shipping between Japan and India, while the expanding web of railways on the Indian subcontinent facilitated travel from the major port cities to regions in the hinterlands that were dotted with Buddhist religious sites recently uncovered by teams of British and Indian archaeologists. As prices dropped and conveyances across Asia became more reliable, the Japanese were able to reach India in greater numbers than ever before.

The geographical terms and Buddhist sectarian categories we now use as convenient shorthand were being coined during the years covered in this volume, which focuses on events between the mid-Meiji era and the start of all-out hostilities between Japan and the Allied forces in the Pacific in 1941. Particularly in the late nineteenth century, the Japanese used a variety of terms to describe the various regions and countries in South and Southeast Asia. Eri Hotta observes that from the Meiji period through the Fifteen Years' War years ending in 1945 that the boundaries of what was included in Asia (*Ajia*), itself a historical construct, were constantly shifting both in the understanding of Europeans and Americans and among the so-called "Asians" themselves.[23] To a lesser extent, Tenjiku as a geographical term was used in a variety of ways, at times referring to India, at others to all of South Asia, and, on occasion, an even broader swath of territory that included what we now call Southeast Asia. Even the characters for writing Tenjiku were unsettled. Although commonly written 天竺, toward the end of the Tokugawa era, the characters for Western regions, *Saiiki* 西域, were sometimes glossed with the pronunciation "Tenjiku," as can be seen in Kawanabe Kyōsai's woodblock print of the elephant brought to Japan in 1863, which was entitled *Tenjiku hakurai daizō no shashin* 西域舶来大象之写真.[24] The shifting terminology reveals the amorphous, vague understanding of the region when Japanese first began traveling to South Asia.

Accounts from 1884 to 1885 of Kitabatake Dōryū's travels that culminate

23. Eri Hotta, *Pan-Asianism and Japan's War 1931–1945* (New York: Palgrave Macmillan, 2007), 23.

24. Oikawa Shigeru. "Kore Zo Kyōsai! Ten," ed. Bunkamura Museum of Art, Kochi Museum of Art, Museum "Eki" Kyoto, Ishikawa Prefectural Museum of Art and Tokyo Shimbun (Tokyo: Tokyo Shimbun, 2017), 97.

in his 1883 visit to Bodh Gayā are variously named *Kitabatake Dōryū Shi Indo kikō* (Master Kitabatake Dōryū's India Travels) and *Tenjiku kōroji shoken* (Things Seen En Route to India), using both Tenjiku and Indo to refer to South Asia. Shaku Sōen, who spent years in Ceylon and a brief period in Siam (since 1939, Thailand), although clearly identifying his main destination as Ceylon (*Seiron*), opted for the broader geographical designations for the two works about his travels, entitling one "A Diary of a Western Journey" (*Saiyū nikki*) and another, analyzing Ceylonese Buddhism, "The Buddhism of the Southwest" (*Seinan no Bukkyō*).[25] Throughout these two works, Sōen was remarkably inconsistent in the names he used for various countries and the orthography selected to render the words. In the course of the two works, he refers to the region as both Tenjiku and India (Indo), inconsistently writing the latter designation as 印度 in the diary and 印土 in *Seinan no Bukkyō*. By contrast, Oda Tokunō, who spent three years in Siam contemporaneously with Sōen's residence in Ceylon, was more precise. In his book "The State of Siamese Buddhism" (*Shamu Bukkyō jijō*) he uses more exact and now familiar place names like Siam (*Shamuro*), Burma (*Biruma*), and Asia (*Ajia*). By the twentieth century most Japanese travelers to South and Southeast Asia adopt the terms in use today, for example, "Indo," "Biruma," Shamu/Shamuro, etcetera. Even into the 1920s, however, authors continue to use "Tenjiku" in the titles of their travel accounts, for example in Seki Seisetsu's 1922 *Tenjiku angya* (Indian Pilgrimage), thereby enhancing the Buddhist connotations of their travels.

In order to exercise some consistency in geographical terminology, I primarily have used contemporaneous names for the regions under consideration in this book. For present-day Thailand I use the name of Siam for events prior to 1939, when the leaders of that nation adopted the current name, Thailand. In most of the travel accounts and books I discuss, the Japanese authors use colonial Anglicized names for Indian regions and cities. For consistency I too have used those colonial-era names, for example, Benares, Bombay, Calcutta, Ceylon, and Madras, instead of the names more recently employed, for example, Kāśī, Mumbai, Kolkata, Chennai, and Sri Lanka.

The terminology used to describe various streams of Asian Buddhism also was evolving rapidly during the period covered in this study. Todd Perreira, in his important essay on the use of the word "Theravāda" as a blanket term for the Pali-centric Buddhism practiced across much of South and Southeast Asia, points out that the word was not used in that sense until 1907. The term "Theravāda," according to Perreira, was not widely used until it was adopted

25. For details about these works, see chap. 1.

as the official designation by Buddhists following the practices preserved in Pali until 1950 at the First Conference of World Fellowship of Buddhists.[26] The writings by Japanese Buddhists from the period examined in this volume mostly confirm Perreira's conclusion. Shaku Kōzen, a Shingon cleric who lived in Ceylon in the 1880s, uses the phrase "Tathāgata's Pure Transmission of the Elders" (Nyorai junsei Jōza denshō) to describe the orthodox transmission of the precepts.[27] Yamakami Sōgen makes a brief reference to the "Ceylonese Buddhism, which loves to style itself Theravāda (S. Sthavira=P. Thera)," but again the term appears to refer to a precept lineage rather than a school of Buddhism that extends across South and Southeast Asia.[28] Nonetheless, one can detect in the Ceylonese usage as reported by Yamakami the later hints of the broader understanding of "Theravāda" as a pan-Asian school of Buddhism that has predominated since the mid-twentieth century. In Oda Tokunō's posthumously published 1917 Buddhist dictionary the term Jōzabu is employed when he describes the filiation of the various early Buddhist schools, but he does not provide the Sanskrit or Pali cognates.[29] Apart from those passing references I have not encountered the terms "Theravāda" and Jōzabu used as general terms for the Buddhism of Ceylon, Burma, Siam, etcetera, in any of the works examined. Instead, during the period under scrutiny in this book, the Japanese mostly referred to Southern Buddhism (Nanpō Bukkyō) and Northern Buddhism (Hokuhō Bukkyō), frequently treating the two terms as isomorphic with Hinayana and Mahayana Buddhism respectively. In their 1890 history of Buddhism in India, China, and Japan, Shimaji Mokurai and Oda Tokunō delineate three basic geographical divisions for Buddhism: Southern (Nanbu)—Ceylon and Siam; Northern (Hokubu)—Tibet, Mongolia, Manchuria, and Xinjiang; and Eastern (Tōbu), with the last category referring primarily to Japan, but including China and Korea.[30] Although avoiding the use of Theravāda as a generic term can be cumbersome,

26. Todd LeRoy Perreira, "Whence Theravāda? The Modern Genealogy of an Ancient Term," in How Theravāda Is Theravāda? Exploring Buddhist Identities, ed. Peter Skilling et al. (Chiang Mai, Thailand: Silkworm Books, 2012), 443–571. See esp. 449–51, 549–51; Princeton Dictionary of Buddhism, 904–5 (Princeton, NJ: Princeton University Press, 2014) (hereafter, PDB).

27. Shaku Kōzen, Sanneji jihō narabi kyōyō ninka kisoku (Kanagawa: Sanneji, 1908), 3.

28. Sōgen Yamakami, Systems of Buddhistic Thought (Calcutta: University of Calcutta, 1912), 100. Yamakami, following European Buddhologists, equates Theravāda with the unattested Sanskrit term, *Sthaviravāda.

29. OBDJ, 966. I have not been able to consult the original 1917 edition of his dictionary.

30. Shimaji Mokurai and Oda Tokunō, Sangoku Bukkyō ryakushi (Tokyo: Kōmeisha, 1890), 4r–5v.

I have opted to use the contemporaneous terms used for the various forms of Buddhism.

This book focuses on the conversations that took place between the Japanese and South and Southeast Asian Buddhists that largely have gone unnoticed by scholars, particularly outside of Japan. Although there were frequent, important exchanges that occurred between Japanese Buddhists and other Buddhists in Korea, China, and elsewhere in the sphere of Sinitic Buddhism, those sorts of conversations and cultural flows have received far more scrutiny by scholars. In this book, I have chosen to focus on the crucial but frequently overlooked role that South and, to a far lesser extent, Southeast Asia played in shaping how Japanese Buddhists thought about their tradition in the twentieth century. Of particular significance for Japanese Buddhists, particularly those in the leadership of the main denominations and the growing number of scholar clerics staffing the sectarian universities, placing their interpretations of Buddhism in the context of their distant Indian roots, Indic-language sources, archaeological sites, and the forms of practice still extant across South and Southeast Asia, became an important task. With the rapid uncovering and renovation of Buddhist archaeological sites, South Asia drew the attention of Japanese Buddhist pilgrims. In addition, because of the Anglophone academic culture, presence of British-style higher educational institutions, and what by the 1920s became a rather developed infrastructure of Japanese business and government offices in India, South Asia became an attractive location for overseas travel and study by Japanese Buddhists. By the 1930s, pilgrimage to India had become an important marker of Buddhist devotion, Japanese Buddhist scholars trained in India were teaching in many of the Buddhist sectarian universities, and ties between Japanese Buddhism and its Indian precursors were highlighted in a variety of ways. Although the majority of Japanese lay Buddhists could not travel to South or Southeast Asia, such events as the transfer of Śākyamuni's relics from Siam to Japan, the importation of Indian Buddhist images, and creation of Indian-inflected temples made Japanese Buddhism's Indian origins and surviving ties with Buddhists in South and Southeast Asia widely visible.

For the most part, I have focused my research on the numerous flows of people, objects, texts, and scholarship that took place between South Asia and Japan. Without taking those phenomena into account, it is difficult to understand the ways that Japanese Buddhism was reconfigured in the late nineteenth and twentieth centuries. For Japanese Buddhists, it was South Asia, especially India, with its increasingly available historical Buddhist sites, sophisticated Anglophone system of higher education, numerous pandits well versed in Sanskrit, and a Buddhist revival movement of its own that was particularly compelling. Japanese Buddhist engagement with India grew in intensity through the 1920s, accompanying India's growing economic importance to Japan. For these reasons, Japanese Buddhist engagement with South Asia far overshadowed that with Southeast Asia until the height of the Fifteen Years' War in the 1940s. Japanese travelers nonetheless were drawn into a larger Buddhist network that extended across the Indian Ocean region, connecting South Asian Buddhists, particularly in Ceylon, with those in Burma, Siam, and the rest of Southeast Asia.[31] The Japanese availed themselves of these ties, particularly those with Buddhists in Siam, which for the period under scrutiny remained the only country in Asia apart from Japan to escape European colonization. I therefore touch on Japanese Buddhist interactions with their coreligionists in Siam, especially when the actors or events also involve the Japanese engagement with South Asia. A prominent example of this connection discussed in the book involves the sequential transfer of Śākyamuni's newly discovered relics from the British Raj to the Siamese court and, from there to the Japanese. The gifting of the relics resulted in the creation of the temple Nissenji, the Japan-Siam temple, as I discuss in chapter 4. Although an important symbol of Japanese-Siamese comity, the presence of the relics tied the site to India as well as Siam. In addition, many Japanese travelers and students who spent time in Ceylon or India also visited Siam, where Siamese officials at times were generous hosts. When tensions with Great Britain heightened in the 1930s, Japanese Buddhist travel and study in South Asia was curtailed. At the same time, as the Japanese turned their planning to alliance with and conquest of Southeast Asia, Japanese Buddhists were drawn into that effort and dispatched to Southeast Asia. Although I touch on that topic at the end of the book, I do not delve into it in great detail, but Ōsawa Kōji provides a detailed examination of the role Japanese Buddhists played in the war effort on the southern Asian front.[32]

Like a number of Japanese intellectuals and artists of the period, Japanese Buddhist travelers to South Asia were active participants in the formation of pan-Asianist thought in Japan. Their contributions in this regard frequently are overlooked or overshadowed by such better-known pan-Asianist thinkers as Okakura Tenshin/Kakuzō (1862–1913) and Ōkawa Shūmei (1886–1957). As I will show, however, Japanese Buddhists traveling to South Asia were among

31. Blackburn provides a detailed description of this network in Anne M. Blackburn, *Locations of Buddhism: Colonialism and Modernity in Sri Lanka* (Chicago: University of Chicago Press, 2010), 143–96.

32. Ōsawa Kōji, *Senjika no Nihon Bukkyō to Nanpō chiiki* (Kyoto: Hōzōkan, 2015).

the early voices expressing a transnational sense of solidarity with other Asians. In the early twentieth century, Japanese Buddhist resident students in South Asia had some of the most extensive direct interactions with South Asians of any Japanese. Some of these long-term overseas students, for example, Kawaguchi Ekai and Kimura Nichiki, possessed a command of classical and vernacular Indic languages that was amongst the best in Japan. Their interchanges with such Indian independence advocates as Rash Behari Bose, Rabrindranath Tagore, Aurobindo Ghose, and Annie Besant, among others, predisposed them toward anticolonial attitudes that they helped weave into the fabric of Japanese pan-Asianism. Their recognition of shared religious heritage with South and Southeast Asians also provided part of the foundation for Japanese pan-Asianist thinking. Japanese Buddhists in South Asia befriended leaders like Tagore and Bose, helping them during their visits and assisting them while they were in exile in Japan. The material culture Japanese Buddhists transmitted from South Asia to Japan and their support for South Asian–inflected temple architecture also provided tangible touchstones for the pan-Asian theorizing that swirled through Japanese twentieth-century intellectual and political realms.

As was the case with Japanese pan-Asianists more generally, Japanese Buddhist travelers to South Asia expressed a complex, not always logically coherent, variety of attitudes toward South Asia and pan-Asianism. In her helpful overview of pan-Asianism's role in the Fifteen Years' War, Eri Hotta teases out a number of distinct threads falling under the umbrella term of pan-Asianism that was variously known as *han Ajia shugi*, *Ajia shugi*, and *Dai Ajia shugi*. The varieties of pan-Asianism embraced by Japanese engaged with South Asia include what Hotta labels "Teaist pan-Asianism," an approach made well-known by Okakura Kakuzō in the *Book of Tea* and *Ideals of the East*. Advocates of this type of pan-Asianism emphasized the importance of spiritual values among all Asians, counterposing them to the materially oriented Europeans and Americans. For pan-Asianists such as Okakura, "the most fundamental questions of—who exactly was an Asian and what constituted the territorial and 'racial' limits of Asia—were left undefined. The concept of Asian unity here allowed for elusive and shifting boundaries that amounted to a loose cluster of extensive but only vaguely generalizable attitudes toward life on the part of non-Western, nonwhite people."[33]

The second strand of pan-Asianist thought voiced by Japanese Buddhist travelers to South and Southeast Asia is what Hotta describes as "Meishuron pan-Asianism," in which Japan was seen as the rightful, indispensable leader

---

33. Hotta, *Pan-Asianism and Japan's War*, 36.

of an alliance of Asian nations in a struggle against European and American colonial powers. For advocates of this type of pan-Asianism, Japan, because of her successful modernization, military might, and cultural sophistication, was the only nation capable of leading other Asians in their struggle with Europe and the United States. In this sense, Japan represented the culmination of Asian civilization. Echoes of this attitude are visible in frequent Japanese Buddhist statements that Japanese Buddhism stood at the apex of Buddhist evolution in Asia. Due to their debt to India, China, Korea, and elsewhere for Buddhism, Japanese Buddhists had a responsibility to reinvigorate Buddhism, which was in decline across Asia. *Meishuron* pan-Asianism would become the dominant stream in Japan in the period of the Fifteen Years' War, although never to the complete exclusion of other forms of pan-Asianist thought. Even in the earliest stages of the Japanese encounter with South Asia this type of pan-Asianism is visible. For many Japanese Buddhist travelers to South Asia, as we will see, the chauvinistic pan-Asianist attitude coexisted with the more egalitarian Teaist type, even though the two approaches stood in tension with each other.[34] Okakura's writings demonstrate this sort of contradiction. While writing of the shared civilizational values among Indians, Chinese, and Japanese, Okakura also contended that Japan's position at the historical and geographical endpoint of Asian development allowed it to synthesize the multiple strands of Asian cultural achievement in a unique fashion, thus making it superior to India and China. Hotta points out that pan-Asianist thinking would remain heterogeneous even in the 1930s, despite the growing emphasis among Japanese that Japan had a responsibility to lead other Asians to liberation.

The flows of people, objects, texts, and ideas detailed in the chapters that follow reveal what a number of recent scholars, particularly global historians, increasingly are describing as the "entangled" or "circulatory" nature of historical processes. The story of the Japanese Buddhist engagement with South Asia highlights many of the features of global history. Sebastian Conrad observes that in this approach to history "its core concerns are with mobility and exchange, with processes that transcend borders and boundaries. It takes the interconnected world as its point of departure, and the circulation and exchange of things, people, ideas, and institutions are among its key subjects."[35]

34. Hotta describes a third strand of pan-Asianism, which she calls "Sinic" pan-Asianism. The third variety, which is not of central concern for this book; in arguing for East Asian pan-Asian unity, this strand emphasizes the shared cultural and language bonds with other Sinic cultures across East Asia. See Hotta, *Pan-Asianism and Japan's War*, 37–44.

35. Sebastian Conrad, *What Is Global History?* (Princeton, NJ: Princeton University Press, 2016), 5.

For Japanese Buddhists, South Asia served as a crucial nexus for the exchange of people, scholarship, artifacts, and texts. During the late nineteenth century and first third of the twentieth century, Indian pandits adapted colonial scholarship to their native environment, while Japanese Buddhists who studied with them began producing Buddhist scholarship and religious tracts in English and Japanese in India as well as elsewhere. Indian institutions thus provided Japanese Buddhists with an important outlet for shaping the understanding of Buddhism in India and around the globe. Each of the actors involved in the stories that follow emerged from an environment in which Buddhism was undergoing rapid change, while at the same time they entered contexts in which the local Buddhism also was in flux. While international trade, technological change, and colonialism transformed the world, American and European actors, from scholars to religious activists like Annie Besant, Henry Olcott, Nyanatiloka (a.k.a. Anton Gueth), traveled around the globe, transmitting ideas and interacting with Buddhists in India, Ceylon, America, Europe, and Japan. The result was a remarkably complex network in which, to cite a few examples to be discussed, Japanese clerics lectured on Mahayana Buddhism in India, Ceylonese Buddhists translated Chinese Buddhist texts into English in western Japan, and American architects built Indian-inflected Japanese Buddhist temples in Hawaii, thus adding a global dimension to the face of twentieth-century Japanese Buddhism.

1

South Asian Encounters: Kitabatake Dōryū, Shaku Kōzen, Shaku Sōen, and the First Generation of Japanese Buddhists in South Asia

Much in the history of the late Edo period and the early Meiji (1868–1912) years impelled Japanese Buddhists to reconsider their tradition and to travel abroad. From the mid-nineteenth century until the mid-1870s, the collapse of the Tokugawa regime and the restoration of imperial rule had triggered the most violent suppression of Buddhism in Japanese history. Although the Tokugawa regime had regarded the Buddhist clergy as a crucial aide in the maintenance of religious and social order, nativists, Shintoists, and many members of the new Meiji regime demonized them as un-Japanese, parasitic, and corrupt. Government leaders subjected Buddhist institutions to a series of harsh measures that led to the widespread laicization of the clergy and the closure or destruction of numerous temples. By 1872 the most violent of these attacks on Buddhism had ended, but the Buddhist clergy found themselves struggling to return to the position of power and influence that they once held.

Several areas of concern led members of the Buddhist clergy to look to Europe, the United States, and other parts of Asia as they sought to reconstruct a Buddhism that would thrive in the emerging new order in Japan. Responding to the imperative of the Charter Oath (*Gokajō no Goseimon*) to seek knowledge throughout the world, the Meiji regime sent official delegations like the Iwakura Mission (1871–73) overseas to survey the economic, government, military, and other institutions of the Western powers that threatened Japan's independent existence. Following in the wake of those missions, the leaders of both of the largest Jōdo Shin branches dispatched delegations of clerics to circle the world collecting information on religious life in the United States and Europe.

The leadership of the powerful and wealthy Honganji branch of Jōdo Shin was one of the most active promoters of overseas clerical travel, sending at least three different clerical missions abroad between 1870 and 1880.[1] As two of the largest and wealthiest denominations in the late Edo and early Meiji periods, the Nishi and Higashi Honganji establishments were probably best prepared to fund extended travel overseas for their representatives. Following the example of the Iwakura Mission, which was sent on behalf of the government to survey government and nongovernment institutions in Europe and the United States, Ōtani Kōson (1850–1903) and the Nishi Honganji institution leadership dispatched a number of clerics overseas to survey state-religion relations as well as the state of religious scholarship in Europe and the United States. Included in the 1872 mission were Kōson's brother, Ōtani Kōei (1852–1923); Umegami Takuyū (1835–1907); as well as such prominent clerics as Akamatsu Renjō, Shimaji Mokurai, Ishikawa Shuntai (1842–1931), and the lesser-known Mitsuda Tamenari (dates unknown).[2] Impressed by what they witnessed, upon their return to Japan these leaders sent more groups of clerics and scholars to collect information about US and European state-church relations and to survey the new Buddhist scholarship overseas.[3] Impressed by the thriving state of orientalist scholarship in Europe, particularly the use of Indic texts of important Buddhist sutras, Japanese Buddhist leaders dispatched students overseas to learn Sanskrit and Pali, as well as to master modern European scholarly methods.

Interest within the Japanese Buddhist community in travel to Buddhist sites in other parts of Asia also increased during the first decades of the Meiji era, building on the investigations into Sanskrit, the precepts, and geography that had been sustained through the Edo period, despite the limited access to information and lack of direct contact. As commercial shipping between the ports of European colonies in Asia and Japan increased and

---

1. *Shinshū shiryō shūsei* 12: 39–45. (Hereafter SSS.)

2. A fine account of the first Nishi Honganji mission is provided in Hans Martin Krämer, *Shimaji Mokurai and the Reconception of Religion and the Secular in Modern Japan* (Honolulu: University of Hawai'i Press, 2015), 88–113. For information concerning the Japanese Buddhist clerics and scholars studying in Europe between 1872 and 1882, see Ryōichi Horiguchi, "Léon de Rosny et les premières missions Bouddhiques Japonaises en Occident," *Cipango* 4 (1995): 121–39. A detailed study of interactions between Japanese scholars and Max Müller and Sylvain Lévi is Maejima Shinji, *Indogaku no akebono* (Tokyo: Sekai Seiten Kankō Kyōkai, 1985). Just how the over-representation of Jōdo Shin clerics in early exchanges with European and American scholars of Buddhism skewed the perceptions of Buddhism of such collaborators as Müller and Lévi is an important question. The significance of this issue has been noted by Jonathan A. Silk in "The Victorian Creation of Buddhism: Review of the British Discovery of Buddhism by Philip C. Almond," *Journal of Indian Philosophy* 22, no. 1 (1994): 194, n 6.

3. Krämer, *Shimaji Mokurai*, 89–92.

colonial and naval interests in those regions grew, private travel from Japan to China, Korea, India, Ceylon, and other Asian countries became possible in unprecedented ways.[4] European scholarly attention to Buddhist archaeological sites in India and elsewhere in Asia also contributed to a growing interest in Buddhist travel to those regions. In addition, reports of brief stops by Japanese travelers—for example, the visits by Akamatsu Renjō to Ceylon and Shimaji Mokurai to India—further piqued the interest of the Japanese Buddhist community in Buddhist pilgrimage sites and the practice of Buddhism in what, from the Japanese perspective, were heretofore unexplored parts of Asia.

One of the last clerics to embark in this first wave of Nishi Honganji–sponsored overseas missions was the adventurer Kitabatake Dōryū (1820–1907). A rather eccentric figure, Kitabatake was the son of a Jōdo Shin cleric and had studied for a number of years at the academy at the Nishi Honganji. Kitabatake left the clergy for a time, engaging in a variety of military and educational efforts that included martial arts training, fighting on the side of shogunate forces, studying German language and military science, and opening a school in Tokyo for legal studies. After becoming a confidant of Ōtani Kōson, the head of the denomination, Kitabatake reentered the clergy. In order to adapt the Nishi Honganji denomination to the rapidly changing circumstances of the Meiji era, Kōson sought to revolutionize denominational education, regulations, and relations with the central government, enlisting Kitabatake as his point person in the endeavor. Kōson and Kitabatake engaged in a failed attempt to move the administrative office of the Nishi Honganji from Kyoto to Tokyo and carry out a series of other reforms of the denomination, including separating the liturgical and religious role of chief prelate (*hosshu*) from that of chief administrative incumbent (*kanchō*). They also launched an attack on some of the new positions concerning the relationship between Shin Buddhism, the Doctrinal Instructor (Kyōdōshoku) system, and the Meiji state that were promoted by Shimaji Mokurai and Akamatsu Renjō, placing themselves at loggerheads with those two prominent denominational leaders. In the end, Shimaji and other members of the opposition, many of whom hailed from the Chōshū region, prevailed upon Itō Hirobumi, who was from the same region, to force Kōson

4. For a description of the growth of transnational exchanges along these trade routes in South and Southeast Asia see Mark Frost, "'Wider Opportunities': Religious Revival, Nationalist Awakening and the Global Dimension in Colombo, 1870–1920," *Modern Asian Studies* 36, no. 4 (2002): 937–68.

and Kitabatake to desist. As a result, the administrative headquarters for the denomination remained in Kyoto and many of the other proposed reforms were abandoned.[5]

Following the collapse of Kōson's reform effort, perhaps in part to mollify Kitabatake, in 1881 Kōson sent him on a study mission, like that of Akamatsu, Shimaji, and others, to Europe and the United States. For the next three years, Kitabatake traveled westward through much of Europe, to the United States, and then back again to Japan via Europe and India, returning to Japan in 1884. His itinerary in Europe was ambitious, including stops in France, Russia, Poland, Bavaria, Austria, and England. Kitabatake then crossed the Atlantic to New York City, where he arrived in time to attend the opening of the Brooklyn Bridge in 1883. Following his stay in the United States he then returned to Europe and subsequently traveled back to Japan after making stops in Turkey, Greece, and Rome, before heading to Bombay. While in Europe and the United States, Kitabatake visited a number of scholars of Asia and Asian religions, including Hermann Oldenberg in Germany and Max Müller in London. He also visited with such notable figures as the first British consul general in Japan, Rutherford Alcock (1809–97), and the Swedish explorer of the Arctic, Adolf Erik Nordenskiöld (1832–1901). The greatest amount of time in Europe was spent in Austria on his return trip, where over the course of the summer of 1883, Kitabatake regularly met with an Austrian scholar, Lorenz von Stein (1815–90), to discuss Buddhism and European religious institutions and history. Stein, who taught political economy at the University of Vienna, was a specialist in political science, sociology, and public administration. He worked in such diverse fields as constitutional law and education policy. When Itō Hirobumi was in Vienna, he had also met with Stein, who is credited in part for imparting to Itō a good deal of information concerning constitutional law and national studies, thus eventually influencing the shape of the Meiji constitution. For much of the summer of 1883, Stein and Kitabatake held daily conversations on a range of topics. During the day, Stein would expound on religion and politics. In turn, in the evenings, Kitabatake would explain Indian philosophy (perhaps Buddhism?) and Confucianism to Stein.[6] According to Kitabatake, in the course of their conversations, Stein also passed on information concerning Buddhist archaeology, Buddhist stud-

5. Tsunemitsu, *Meiji no Bukkyōsha* 1: 206–9. (Hereafter MNB.)

6. Uehara Sadao. "Kitabatake Dōryū ni okeru L. V. Shutain to no shisō kōryū: omo ni shūkyō to seiji, shūkyō to kyōiku no mondai ni kakawatte," *Gifu Seitoku Gakuen Daigaku Kyōiku Gakubu Gaikokugo Gakubu kiyō* 37 (1999): 133–56.

ies, and India, thus shaping the cleric's journey to the subcontinent on his return to Japan from Europe.

At least three versions of Kitabatake's travel accounts were published soon after his return to Japan. The earliest, *Sekai shūyū tabi nikki—ichimei Shakamuni Butsu funbo no yurai* (A Travel Diary of a World Tour: The History of Śākyamuni's Tomb), was published in March 1884 only a little more than one month after Kitabatake's return to Japan at the end of January that same year.[7] The same month, in what appears to have been an attempt to advertise his adventures widely, Kitabatake also published a one-page broadside, *Kitabatake Dōryū Shi Indo kikō* (Master Kitabatake Dōryū's India Travels), summarizing his pilgrimage to what he repeatedly called Śākyamuni's "tomb" (*funbo*), that is, the Mahābodhi Temple at Bodh Gayā.[8] In 1886, a detailed version of Kitabatake's account was published as *Tenjiku kōroji shoken* (Things Seen En Route to India).[9] Although Kitabatake traveled abroad for three years, his time in India comprised just one month at the very end of his journey. Nonetheless, the titles of all three works emphasize the India portion of his trip, including the successful journey to Bodh Gayā. Even the title of the lengthy full travel account, *Tenjiku kōroji shoken*, two-thirds of which details Kitabatake's travels in Europe and the United States, depicts India as the ultimate destination of his journey. At the heart of all versions of his chronicles is Kitabatake's claim to have been the first Japanese to have traveled to the important Buddhist pilgrimage site of Bodh Gayā and, most important, his claim to have visited the "tomb" of Śākyamuni Buddha, an achievement that stands as the apotheosis of the three-year journey. Just as Nanjō Bun'yū when he departed from Oxford depicted his travels as only partially successful because of his failure to reach Bodh Gayā, the land of Śākyamuni loomed large in Kitabatake's accounts as the ultimate end of his global journey.

Kitabatake had good reason for emphasizing the India portion of his trip, particularly the pilgrimage to Bodh Gayā, which was the most remarkable aspect of his journey. The European and the American portions of Kitabatake's journey had been preceded by a similar trip undertaken by his bitter opponents in Jōdo Shin reform politics, Akamatsu Renjō and Shimaji Mokurai, a decade earlier. Like Kitabatake, the pair of clerics had already surveyed the religio-political scene in the United States and Europe and had brought back

7. Akiyama Tokusaburō, *Sekai shūyū tabi nikki: ichimei Shakamunibutsu funbo no yurai* (Tokyo: Kyūshunsha, 1884), 84.

8. Emoto Ryūzō, *Kitabatake Dōryū shi Indo kikō* (Tokyo: Emoto Ryūzō, 1884).

9. Kitabatake Dōryū, *Tenjiku kōroji shoken* (Tokyo: Aranami Heijirō, 1886). Also in SSS 12: 287–373.

a considerable amount of information from those countries for the denomi-national leadership to use as reference for its own modernization efforts. Akamatsu and Shimaji also played a crucial role in the denomination's rejec-tion of the reform agenda advocated by Kitabatake and Ōtani. Shimaji also had managed only to make a fairly brief, but impressive visit to India in the summer of 1873 on his return from Europe. After arriving in Bombay, Shimaji visited Delhi, Allahabad, Patna, and Bengal, stopping at numerous Buddhist sites while en route to Calcutta, making him the first recorded Japanese Bud-dhist to visit India.[10] Thus a good deal of Kitabatake's long, three-year global journey and encounters with American and European scholars repeated Shimaji's exploits from a decade earlier. Unlike the Japanese Buddhists like Shimaji and others who had preceded him to Europe, Kitabatake and his fellow traveler Kurosaki Yūji, an overseas Japanese studying commerce that Kitabatake met while visiting England, made a one-month trip into the in-terior of India that culminated in their visit to Bodh Gayā, making them the first Japanese to reach the site of Śākyamuni Buddha's awakening. It was this unique achievement that Kitabatake chose to emphasize in his various travel accounts. Even before leaving Japan, details of Kitabatake's proposed route through India had circulated in Japan. Hearing of the planned trip, Kitazawa Masanari gave Kitabatake an article he authored concerning the search for the location of Shinnyo's death—Luoyue. He asked Kitabatake to see whether any traces of Shinnyo remained along Kitabatake's planned route through South Asia. The lingering memory and fragmentary record of Shinnyo's failed trip to Tenjiku, provided another stimulus to Kitabatake to make a foray into the interior of the subcontinent.[11]

A marked shift in the language and tone of the most complete version of his 1886 travel account, *Tenjiku kōroji shoken*, occurs when Kitabatake turns his attention from his experiences in Europe and the United States to his ex-cursions in India. Whereas Kitabatake seemingly looked up to the various scholars, officials, and experts he met in Europe and the United States as he investigated the history of church-state relations and the state of Buddhist studies in each country, once he arrived in India, his language became impe-rious in tone. While in Europe Kitabatake had inquired on several occasions about general conditions in India and the state of Buddhist sites there. In the 1884 account of his trip to India, *Sekai shūyū tabi nikki*, the author records

10. Murakami Mamoru, *Shimaji Mokurai den: ken o taishita itan no hijiri* (Kyoto: Mineruva Shobō, 2011), 177

11. Isamu Shimizu, "Takaoka, Priest Imperial Prince Shinnyo," *Transactions of the Asiatic Society of Japan*, Third Series 5 (1957): 23.

Stein relating to Kitabatake that India was "the most dangerous place in the world" where "not only do wild beasts and poison snakes endanger and injure people, but barbarian, obstinate people threaten and rob [others] at will."[12] Reflecting on the scene from the train he took from Bombay, Kitabatake remarked on the poverty of the homes he saw and declared that even the homes of Japan's poorest mountain hamlets were greatly superior. For the first time during the whole trip, Kitabatake wrote, he felt that Japan was better than some other place, a sentiment that would be expressed by Japanese travelers to India who would follow.[13]

Kitabatake vacillated between scorn for the poverty and backwardness of India and sympathy for the plight of the Indians who suffered at the hands of their British rulers. Like other Buddhist travelers in Asia during the late nineteenth century, Kitabatake viewed India's modern history as a cautionary tale for the Japanese—if they failed to compete with Europe and the United States successfully, they would suffer a similar fate. At the end of his earliest account of the journey to Bodh Gayā, Kitabatake entered into a lengthy description of what he considered a brutally oppressive British colonial regime in India. Observing the regressive nature of the British salt act that levied a tax on salt for all Indians, hurting the poorest Indians the most, Kitabatake concluded that the brutal British colonial policy was hypocritical and shameful. In the final sentence of the book, Kitabatake warned that "there was nothing more extremely unfortunate for the Indians or the whole Asian region than this."[14]

Most important, though, Kitabatake felt that rather than simply receiving knowledge, as he had in Europe, in India he could search for that which he contended had been lost—the tomb of Śākyamuni—the significance of which only a Buddhist could fully appreciate. Kitabatake emphasized that while in Europe he had asked various scholars, including Oldenberg, Stein, and Müller, about the whereabouts of Śākyamuni's tomb (*Shakashi no funbo/Shakuson no bosho*), but they each had been unclear about its exact location.[15] This seems somewhat odd given that H. H. Wilson in 1854 and Alexander Cunningham in 1861–62 had each tentatively identified the site of Śākyamuni's death, Kuśīnagarī, with the village of Kasia in the Gorakhpur region. By 1876 Cunningham's assistant, A. C. L. Carlleyle, had unearthed a large stupa and a reclining statue of Śākyamuni depicting the "Great Decease" at the site. Cun-

12. Akiyama, *Sekai shūyū*, 10–11.

13. SSS 12: 345. I cite the more readily available version of *Tenjiku kōroji shoken* that is anthologized in Volume 12 of the *Shinshū shiryō shūsei*.

14. Akiyama, *Sekai shūyū*, 84.

15. Kitabatake Dōryū Kenshō Kai, *Gōsō Kitabatake Dōryū* (Wakayama, Japan: Kitabatake Dōryū Kenshō Kai, 1956), 76–77; Akiyama, *Sekai shūyū*, 10–11.

ningham's conjectures were published as early as 1871, but detailed accounts of Carlleyle's discoveries were not published until 1883.[16] Although debate over the accuracy of Cunningham's identification continued until the early twentieth century, it seems unlikely that someone as concerned with the biography of Śākyamuni as Oldenburg would have not known of the earliest of these archaeological discoveries by the time Kitabatake came to Europe in the early 1880s. Stein had mentioned some speculation concerning the whereabouts of the tomb to Kitabatake, although he could not confirm the veracity of what he had heard, but it was with that vague information in hand that Kitabatake and his companion, Kurosaki, set out to find Śākyamuni's tomb.

On the return trip to Japan in the autumn of 1883, Kitabatake and Kurosaki sailed from Italy to Bombay, arriving on November 4, 1883. After almost a week in Bombay, the pair boarded a train bound for eastern India, stopping for a time in Benares (Kāśī), where they arrived on November 22 and spent time with an Indian guide they engaged until they headed to Patna on November 29. Identified in *Tenjiku kōroji shoken* as Rainbu Channeru Baneruzē, the guide, responding to Kitabatake's query, stated that he had seen something in a Benares paper about the discovery of the tomb. Unfortunately for Kitabatake, however, the exact location of the site was not made clear in the article, although apparently the tomb was at some remove from Benares in central India.[17] After a week in Benares, the Japanese traveled by train to Patna and then, lest they pass their goal on a train, by oxcart toward Gayā.

As in much imperial travel literature, the inhabitants of India are rendered almost mute and invisible in Kitabatake's descriptions. Kitabatake derisively referred to the natives as *kokudo/kuronbo* (blacks) and portrayed them as nearly naked, that is, uncivilized.[18] Much to their dismay, the Japanese found that once they left Patna, not only did the people they encounter not speak Japanese, but also they could not even understand English, French, or Chinese.[19] After several difficult days of travel, forced to resort to hand gestures and pictures to make themselves understood, given their primitive method of communication, while scrounging food and lodging as best they could, the two travelers finally stumbled upon Bodh Gayā. There Kitabatake and Kurosaki found a group of Indian workers excavating in the vicinity of the

16. D. R. Patil, *Kuśīnagara* (New Delhi: Archaeological Survey of India, 1981), 13–14, briefly describes the British efforts to locate Kuśīnagarī.

17. SSS 12: 350–51. For a summary description of European attempts to locate sites associated with the narrative biography of Śākyamuni, see Janice Leoshko, *Sacred Traces: British Explorations of Buddhism in South Asia* (Aldershot: Ashgate, 2003), 30–60.

18. For example, Akiyama, *Sekai shūyū*, 15.

19. Akiyama, *Sekai shūyū*, 12.

Mahābodhi Temple, the site of Śākyamuni's awakening. Only after encountering the site foreman did Kitabatake discover that they had indeed made it to Bodh Gayā. In an extended conversation with three English-speaking Indians directing the dig, Kitabatake and Kurosaki learned that the disrepair of Bodh Gayā was due to the ascendance of "Brahmanism" some 1,800 years ago. The Indians, according to Kitabatake's account, also informed the Japanese of the history of the discovery of "Śākyamuni's tomb" at the site some ten years earlier and of the current efforts to fully excavate it. One of the foremen explained that the two Japanese were extremely fortunate to have come upon the site when they did. Had they arrived earlier, he explained, they would have been unable to see the then-unexcavated tomb. In the first 1884 account, the foreman attributed both the preservation of the tomb and the good fortune of the clerics to the power of the Buddha, who had led Kitabatake and Kurosaki to the site. The foreman then urged the Japanese to go to the tomb and offer thanks to Śākyamuni for having ensured the preservation of the tomb and for leading the men to it just as it was uncovered.[20] The portrayal of the preservation of the tomb and its discovery by Kitabatake and Kurosaki suggests that the Japanese were destined to arrive at the site just as the structure was being unearthed.

By December 4, 1883, when Kitabatake and Kurosaki arrived in Bodh Gayā, archaeologists and Buddhist pilgrims increasingly were studying the Mahābodhi Temple and its surroundings. In 1878, Rajendralal Mitra (1824–91), one of the pioneers of Buddhist studies in Bengal, published a book about Bodh Gayā, and a number of British turned their attention to the site, due to its apparent age and the international character of the remains, some of which bore Chinese and Burmese inscriptions.[21] The king of Burma also began a well-funded effort to restore the Mahābodhi Temple in 1877. The British colonial authorities, however, became deeply dissatisfied with the work being done by the Burmese. As a result, the Burmese workers had been replaced by a Government of India–sponsored effort to restore Bodh Gayā, led by Alexander Cunningham and Rajendralal Mitra.[22] By 1885, with the outbreak of the Third Anglo-Burmese War, the Burmese presence at the site came to an end. Kitabatake and Kurosaki arrived at Bodh Gayā while the British-led repairs were underway. The two photographs of the temple brought back to

20. Akiyama, *Sekai shūyū*, 18.

21. Leoshko, *Sacred Traces*, 83–89. On Mitra, see Douglas Fairchild Ober, "Reinventing Buddhism: Conversations and Encounters in Modern India, 1839–1956" (PhD diss., University of British Columbia, 2016), 66–67.

22. Dipak Kumar Barua, *Buddha Gaya Temple: Its History* (Buddha Gaya: Buddha Gaya Temple Management Committee, 1981), 77–78.

Japan by Kitabatake and published in *Tenjiku kōroji shoken* show in one image the Mahābodhi Temple enveloped in scaffolding and in the other bearing a ladder perched above the entryway for repairs.[23] The various descriptions of the temple in Kitabatake's travelogues describe statues and other features that are not found at Bodh Gayā today. Inside the temple, for example, the travelers found a statue of Śākyamuni, in front of which was a large cavity, covered with an iron plate. Inside the cavity, the visitors were told, was the "golden coffin" of Śākyamuni (*Shakuson no kinkan*). Whether they understood correctly what they were told is uncertain, but Kitabatake and those who later chronicled his trip were convinced he had arrived at the tomb of Śākyamuni.

Once it became clear they had reached their goal, Kitabatake shed his explorer's clothing for Buddhist robes. According to the account in *Sekai shūyū tabi nikki*, taking a copy of the Three Pure Land Sutras (*Sanbukyō*) that had been presented to him by the head of the Honganji when he departed Japan and grasping his prayer beads, Kitabatake stood before the image, which is described as a golden, standing statue of Śākyamuni. Kitabatake loosened the cords to open the Japanese accordion-style (*orihon*) sutra book, and performed a "turning reading" (*tendoku*) of the text. He then performed a series of prostrations before the image. Once the ritual was completed, Kitabatake then ascended from the site of the tomb along with Kurosaki and the Indians who had gathered around him and then left the temple.[24] Kitabatake then commissioned one of the stonemasons working at the site to carve a stele (*sekihi*) to commemorate his visit. Although many aspects of Kitabatake's account cannot be confirmed, several later Japanese travelers reported that the stele was still standing at Bodh Gayā in the early 1930s (see fig. 1.1). Izumi Hōkei mentions seeing the marker in a 1933 article and Amanuma Shun'ichi, during a 1936 visit to Bodh Gayā, provides a photograph of the stele, which actually had a somewhat different form than the artist's rendering of the stele in Akiyama's 1884 account. The picture of the stele found in the *Tenjiku kōroji shoken* more closely resembles the photograph of the actual stele provided by Amanuma. The inscription read, "Dōryū, the first Japanese to make a pilgrimage to the tomb of Śākyamuni, December 4, 1883."[25]

Kitabatake's account of his discovery is curious, for, as I have mentioned, the pair had made their way not to the site of Śākyamuni's tomb, but to the

---

23. SSS 12: 360–61.

24. Akiyama, *Sekai shūyū*, 20.

25. Akiyama, *Sekai shūyū*, 1; SSS 12: 365; Izumi Hōkei, "Meiji jidai ni okeru toin no Bukkyōto," *Gendai Bukkyō* 105 (1933): 163; Amanuma Shun'ichi, <*Teisei zōho*> *Indo Buttō junrei ki*, 2 vols. (Osaka: Akitaya, 1944), 1: 267.

FIGURE 1.1. Kitabatake's stele at Bodh Gayā. From Akiyama Tokusaburō, *Sekai shūyū tabi nikki.*

place of his awakening. Strangely, at no point does Kitabatake connect Bodh Gayā with Śākyamuni's enlightenment. The closest thing to the excavation of Śākyamuni's tomb may have been the excavations that took place in the late 1870s at Kuśīnagarī, the site of Śākyamuni's death, which was hundreds of miles away near Gorakhpur in the vicinity of the India-Nepal border. That Kitabatake could be so wrong about Indian geography is not hard to understand. That he seemingly was so ignorant of the details of Śākyamuni's biography as to consider Bodh Gayā the site of the sage's tomb may indicate how little was known in Japan about the geographical details of Śākyamuni's life

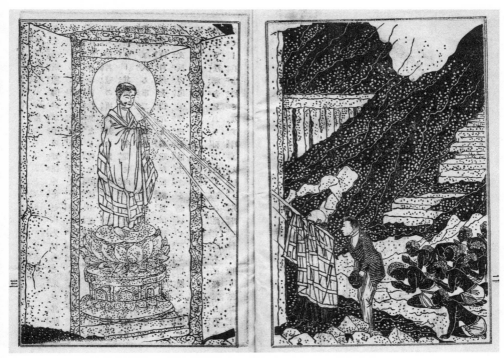

FIGURE 1.2. Kitabatake Dōryū at Śākyamuni's "tomb." From Akiyama Tokusaburō, *Sekai shūyū tabi nikki.*

in Japan during the mid-Meiji period, even among high-ranking Buddhist clerics.[26]

Despite this error, Kitabatake's pilgrimage to sites associated with the life of Śākyamuni held great significance for him and had great potency as a symbol for Japanese Buddhists. The woodblock illustration of the event that is contained in the earliest published account of Kitabatake's travels provides a glimpse of how his actions were construed by one artist who read this account and, perhaps, how it was viewed by a wider Japanese audience. (See fig. 1.2.) The illustration conflates the standing image of Śākyamuni with common images of Amida (Amitābha) Buddha, the central object of veneration for Kitabatake's Jōdo Shin denomination. In the print Śākyamuni, although an Indian himself, is depicted as light-skinned as Kitabatake and Kurosaki. As in many traditional Japanese depictions, humans are connected to the Buddha by rays of light that stream forth from him. In this particular rendering of the

26. Izumi Hōkei and Tsunemitsu Kōnen also have noted with curiosity Kitabatake's error. See Izumi, "Meiji jidai," 163; MNB 1: 209–10.

events, Kitabatake is shown in full Buddhist clerical garb and stands erect, receiving Śākyamuni's light for all others present. Portions of the *orihon* Three Pure Land Sutras flutter in the air, as Kitabatake "turns" the sutra. The sutra book and the Amida-like image serve to link the Amitābha-centered Jōdo Shin teaching to the reality of Śākyamuni's sacred geography. The Japanese cleric serves as an intermediary not only for other Japanese—here depicted as the half-erect Kurosaki in European-style clothing, that is, the vestments of civilization—but also for the dark-skinned, almost-naked and, thus, uncivilized, kneeling Indians. The literate, English-speaking Indians directing the excavation are absent from the picture. Kitabatake, the Japanese Buddhist cleric, in timeless robes that echo those worn by Śākyamuni himself, delivers the "Light of Asia" to the Japanese, halfway to civilization and enlightenment, and to other Asians, who lag behind on the road to modernity.

The woodblock illustration thus clearly demonstrates the superiority of the Japanese both as Buddhists and as successful modernizers in comparison with the Indian workers. At the same time, the portrayal does not reject out of hand solidarity with Japan's less-advanced Asian compatriots, who, at the very least, share a Buddhist past with the Japanese, as evidenced by their participation in the rites for Śākyamuni officiated by Kitabatake. In this way the illustration differs from the sorts of contemporaneous pictorial and journalistic representations of such other Asian groups as the Taiwanese aborigines, who were depicted as being clearly hostile to the Japanese civilizing influence and, therefore, justifiable targets of Japan's colonial aspirations.[27] At the same time, the image of the encounter reveals the dilemma that increasingly faced Jōdo Shin Buddhists in Japan—how should a tradition centered on a nonhistorical buddha, Amida, incorporate the growing body of historical and archaeological information concerning the historical Buddha, Śākyamuni. George Tanabe has suggested that perhaps Kitabatake was venerating Śākyamuni as the source of the Pure Land Sutras, thus merging the

---

27. Robert Eskildsen (402) has noted how in the case of the Taiwanese aborigines these portrayals "increased the perceived cultural distance that separated the Japanese from the aborigines. In the context of the 1870s, a larger cultural distance helped both to validate Japanese claims for higher status in the Western-dominated international order and to eliminate a middle ground between civilization and savagery that might trap the Japanese in a less than salutary solidarity with other East Asian peoples." See Robert Eskildsen, "Of Civilization and Savages: The Mimetic Imperialism of Japan's 1874 Expedition to Taiwan," *American Historical Review* 107, no. 2 (2002): 388–418. The relationship between Japanese Buddhist travelers in South and Southeast Asia and the natives of those regions was far more ambiguous. Nonetheless, Kitabatake and Sōen's accounts of their travels contain hints of the same sort of colonial attitudes described by Eskildsen.

mythical Śākyamuni with the historical one.[28] As I will show in chapters 3 and 4, well into the twentieth century Jōdo Shin Buddhists would continue reconceptualizing doctrinally and artistically the relationship between Amida and Śākyamuni in light of the growing body of archaeological evidence about the latter Buddha.

Along with Shimaji and Akamatsu Renjō, Kitabatake was one of the first of what soon became a steady stream of Japanese travelers to visit important Buddhist sites in South and Southeast Asia. Following his return from India in January 1884, Kitabatake lectured to the public about his travels in Europe, the United States, and India. His travel accounts, the most extensive of which included several photographs of Bodh Gayā, also made available information concerning Buddhist sites in India.[29] Kitabatake's post-travel publications and lectures made him one of the more prominent religious leaders in the mid-1880s. In a May 1885 reader survey conducted by the *Konnichi shinbun* of the most popular leaders in ten different fields, ranging from military affairs to painting, Kitabatake was the most popular Buddhist preacher (*kyōhōka*), receiving 486 votes.[30]

Interest in the South Asian region also was fueled by the steadily growing trade with the region, particularly with British India. As I have described in the Introduction, cotton manufacturing was of growing importance from the end of the nineteenth until well into the twentieth century. With the growing demand for raw cotton, the Japanese reliance on India as a major source of that material also increased. In the short period between 1877 and 1886, Japanese imports from British India grew in value from ¥191,000 to ¥3,561,000, an amount that would continue to grow rapidly well into the twentieth century.[31] Cargo shipping between the Indian Ocean region and Japan expanded to transport the materials, making travel across the region more accessible as well.

Around the same time that Shimaji, Kitabatake, and others were spreading news about Buddhist sites in India, increased shipping between South

28. I thank George Tanabe for pointing this out in a reference to my article "Seeking Śākyamuni," in his presentation: George Tanabe, "Śākyamuni for Modern Japan, Hawai'i, and California," paper presented at *When Modernity Hits Hard: Buddhism's Search for a New Identity in Meiji-Taishō-Early Shōwa Japan* (Berkeley, CA, 2015), 13.

29. *Tenji kōroji shoken*, SSS 12: 360–61.

30. The survey is cited in Kitabatake Dōryū Kenshō Kai, *Gōsō Kitabatake Dōryū*, 79–80. I have not been able to consult the original newspaper survey to confirm the information in this source.

31. Department of Finance, ed. *Returns of the Foreign Trade of the Empire of Japan for the Thirty-two Years from 1868 to 1899 Inclusive* (Tokyo: Department of Finance, 1901), 27.

Asia and Japan brought Buddhists from that region and growing numbers of European and American Buddhist sympathizers to Japan. Even prior to the high-profile visit of Henry Steel Olcott and Dharmapāla to Japan in 1889, South Asian Buddhists gave lectures to Japanese audiences concerning the revival of Buddhism in their region, thus helping to stoke interest in travel to India, Ceylon, and Siam. One extremely prominent cleric, Shaku Unshō (1827–1909), responded with resolve to the information about South Asian Buddhism that was becoming ever more available in Japan. A Shingon cleric noted for his advocacy of strict precept observance, Unshō had been ordained with both the Dharmaguptaka Vinaya (*Shibunritsu*) as well as the lesser-known *Mūlasarvāstivāda Vinaya* (*Konponsetsu Issaiubu binaya*).[32] Unshō founded the Jūzenkai (Ten Good Precepts Society), a popular, long-lived organization devoted to the preservation of the precepts. Unshō attracted a well-connected and prominent following, interacting with such government officials as Yamagata Aritomo (1838–1922), Itō Hirobumi (1841–1909), Ōkuma Shigenobu (1838–1922), Hayashi Tadasu (1850–1913), and others, all of whom are listed as having taken the Buddhist refuges with Unshō around 1890 as members of the Jūzenkai.[33] He also was visited regularly by non-Japanese interested in Buddhism, for example, Edwin Arnold (1832–1904), Ernest M. Bowden (?), and Charles William Pfoundes (1840–1907), especially in the early 1890s.[34]

When at a lecture around the same time, Shaku Unshō heard an "Indian" visitor speak about the decrepit state of Bodh Gayā, he resolved to help. Unshō's interest in Ceylon and India was further stoked by a conversation he had with Akamatsu Renjō, whom Unshō happened to meet while traveling by steamship from Yokohama to Kobe. Akamatsu, who had stopped in Ceylon on the way back to Japan from Europe, mentioned to Unshō that he had met a prominent *bhikkhu*, Bulatgama Dhammālaṅkāra Siri Sumanatissa (1795–1891), who wore three-part robes similar in color and form to those of Unshō. According to Noguchi Fukudō's 1920 lecture on Kōzen, this further solidified Unshō's resolve to find out more about the practice and condition of Buddhism in South Asia.[35] As Shayne Clarke notes, Unshō was one of a number of Shingon clerics deeply concerned with the fine points of Vinaya prac-

32. Shayne Clarke, "Miscellaneous Musings on Mūlasarvāstivāda Monks: The *Mūlasarvāstivāda Vinaya* Revival in Tokugawa Japan," *Japanese Journal of Religious Studies* 33, no. 1 (2006): 32–40.
33. Kusanagi, *Shaku Unshō* 1: 122–25. (Hereafter SUS.)
34. Clarke, "Miscellaneous Musings," 35.
35. Noguchi Fukudō, *Shaku Kōzen to Shakuson Shōfū Kai* (Kanagawa, Japan: Sanneji, 1920), 5–6.

tice, having undertaken ordination with two different sets of Vinaya rules, the Dharmaguptaka and the Mūlasarvāstivāda.[36] Unshō thus demonstrates the continued importance of the Vinaya for some clerics during the Meiji era. Given his interest in the practice of the Vinaya regulations, Akamatsu's description of Siri Sumanatissa's robes must have intrigued Unshō. However, Unshō, who was fifty-nine years old at the time, felt unable to travel to South Asia. Instead, he requested that his nephew and fellow Shingon cleric, Shaku Kōzen (1849–1924), travel to Ceylon and India.[37] Unshō also requested that Kōzen study the Buddhist precepts used in Ceylon and Buddhist customs of the region before returning to Japan.[38]

Both Kōzen and Sōen had heard of Kitabatake prior to embarking on their own journeys to South Asia. According to Noguchi Fukudō, after resolving to travel to South Asia, Kōzen attempted to meet with Kitabatake. When that was unsuccessful, Kōzen then turned for advice from Dogi Hōryū, another prominent Shingon cleric, and also began studying Sanskrit with Nanjō Bun'yū.[39] In addition, Sōen, while a student at Fukuzawa Yukichi's Keiō Gijuku in Tokyo from 1885 to 1886, expressed admiration for Kitabatake's compelling exposition of the Buddhist teaching, particularly in the context of a growing Christian presence in the Kantō region.[40]

Buddhist travelers like Shimaji, Akamatsu, and Kitabatake who traveled to Europe and back had availed themselves of the stops in Bombay, Calcutta, and Colombo on either outbound or return trips. Government officials and business people also became more familiar with India and other stopover points along the steamship line routes from Europe to the Middle East to South and Southeast Asia. When Hayashi Tadasu, an early minister to Great Britain and architect of the Anglo-Japanese Alliance of 1902, accompanied Prince Arisugawa Taruhito (1835–95) on a diplomatic mission overseas to Russia in 1882–83, he also visited Ceylon. Hayashi had a growing interest in Buddhism, having forged connections with such prominent Japanese Buddhists

---

36. Clarke, "Miscellaneous Musings,"

37. Noguchi, *Shaku Kōzen to Shakuson Shōfū Kai*, 5–6. See also, Okuyama Naoji, "Nihon Bukkyō to Seiron Bukkyō to no deai: Shaku Kōzen no ryūgaku o chūshin ni," *Contact Zone* 2: 23–36.

38. MNB 1: 372–73. Although technically not Unshō's disciple, Kōzen seems to have treated his uncle as a teacher. The two worked closely together, although they came to hold different views concerning the legitimacy of Mahayana Buddhism and the validity of Japanese ordinations. For example, one of Kōzen's own disciples, Shaku Kaiyū, described Kōzen as Unshō's "distinguished disciple" (*kōtei*).

39. Noguchi, *Shaku Kōzen to Shakuson Shōfū Kai*, 6.

40. See Inoue Zenjō , *Shaku Sōen den* (Kyoto: Zenbunka Kenkyūsho, 2000), 41, 47.

as Akamatsu Renjō and Shimaji Mokurai, whom he had met while traveling in London during the 1870s.[41] During the stopover in Ceylon, Hayashi met with Conrad Peter Dias Bandaranayaka, who was a Mahā Mudaliyar, that is, a high-ranking native colonial official, and other Lankans, including Don David Jayatilleke Gooneratne (Guṇaratna), the father of Edmund Rowland Gooneratne (1845–1914).[42] According to the account of Janaka Goonetilleke, Hayashi commented that like Ceylon, Japan was a Buddhist country and requested that Japan be allowed to send some clerics to Ceylon to study Buddhism. In 1885, Don David Gooneratne forwarded a letter to Hayashi from his son, E. R. Gooneratne, who expressed an interest in visiting Japan, where he understood Buddhism was flourishing. He also raised a number of questions about Buddhism, asking that someone knowledgeable about the subject respond. Hayashi then passed the letter on to Nanjō Bun'yū, initiating a two-year exchange of letters between E. R. Gooneratne, Nanjō, and, on one occasion, Kōdāgoḍē Paññāsekhara, the *bhikkhu* who would become Shaku Sōen's main preceptor in Ceylon. In the letter, as noted by Okuyama, Paññāsekhara asked from which country Buddhism had spread to Japan and whether this occurred during the time of the Buddha or during Aśoka's reign. It thus revealed curiosity coupled with a lack of concrete knowledge about the nature of Japanese Buddhism among many Ceylonese.[43] Given the dearth of English-language accounts of Japanese Buddhism and the almost total lack of prior exchanges between Ceylonese and Japanese Buddhists, the crude level of Paññāsekhara's understanding is not surprising. In addition, Nanjō translated some detailed questions about Ceylonese precept practice from Shaku Unshō that he sent to Gooneratne. Gooneratne invited Japanese Buddhists to study in Ceylon, promising to support them financially and provide them with introductions to appropriate teachers during their sojourns on the island. Gooneratne's plans to visit Japan and return with Japanese clerics to Ceylon were scuttled when he fell ill in Siam, so Unshō dispatched Shaku Kōzen, his nephew, who had been studying with Nanjō to prepare for an eventual journey to South Asia and Ceylon, in 1886.[44]

---

41. Satō Tetsurō, *Daiajia shisō katsugeki: Bukkyō ga musunda, mō hitotsu no kindai shi* (Tokyo: Saṃgha. 2008), 215–16; MNB, 1: 373–74.

42. In most instances, I have used the more commonly seen spelling Gooneratne rather than the more precise romanization of the Sinhala name, Guṇaratna, for the family surname.

43. Okuyama Naoji, "Nihon Bukkyō to Seiron Bukkyō to no deai, 29–32. Although much of the correspondence was in English, the nineteenth-century Japanese journals that published the letters seem to have translated them into Japanese. Okuyama provides all quotations from the letters in his article in Japanese.

44. Okuyama, "Nihon Bukkyō to Seiron Bukkyō no deai," 32.

Edmund Rowland Gooneratne, the nephew of Bandaranayaka, was the son of a high-ranking official in Galle.[45] E. R. Gooneratne was a lay supporter of Buddhism with ties to one of the most prominent *bhikkhu* in late nineteenth-century Ceylon, Hikkaḍuvē Sumaṅgala (1826–1911).[46] Sumaṅgala tutored E. R. Gooneratne in Pali and Sanskrit and received donations from Gooneratne, although the Gooneratne family attended services at a Christian church. E. R. Gooneratne was actively involved with the work of the Pali Text Society beginning in the mid-1880s, serving as secretary for the organization in Ceylon. His publications with the Society include annotated English translations of the *Dhātuvaṃsa*, *Dhātukathā*, and *Aṅguttaranikāya*. E. R. Gooneratne also visited Bodh Gayā in 1894, donating, along with another Ceylonese Buddhist, Fredrika Ilangakoon, a marble platform for flower offerings at the site.[47] A generous patron of Buddhist institutions, E. R. Gooneratne provided financial support for the Gooneratne Mudalindarama Buddhist Academy (*piriveṇa*) in Matara and a second academy, the Gooneratne Mudalindarama, on the grounds of his estate in Galle, the Atapattu Walawwa. When, several years later, Japanese clerics arrived in Ceylon to train and study, Hayashi and E. R. Gooneratne help sponsor at least several of them, including Shaku Kōzen and Shaku Sōen (1860–1919). Kōzen, when he received the full Ceylonese monastic ordination, was connected enough to E. R. Gooneratne that he received the eponymous Theravāda ordination name, Guṇaratna, in honor of his patron.

Unlike Kitabatake, who spent little over one month in India, Sōen and Kōzen practiced for extended periods of time in Buddhist monasteries in Ceylon, which was then a British colony.[48] These two clerics also differed from Kitabatake in that they came from two primarily monastic denominations of

---

45. A detailed source of information about E. R. Gooneratne is Janaka Goonetilleke, ed., *Atapattu Walawwa: Residence of the Gooneratne and Dias Abeyesinghe Families of Galle* (Galle, Sri Lanka: Atapattu Walawwa, 2012). Specific information about Hayashi's visit to Ceylon is found on page 153. Japanese sources indicate that Hayashi returned to Japan in 1883, not 1884, however. I thank Dr. Janaka Goonetilleke for sharing his book and research with me. I have used the spelling in Goonetilleke's book rather than the more precise "Guṇaratna."

46. Information about Sumaṅgala is found in Blackburn, *Locations of Buddhism*, 79–81.

47. Goonetilleke, *Atapattu Walawwa*, 149–53.

48. Biographical information about Shaku Kōzen comes from MNB 1: 371–82; Noguchi, *Shaku Kōzen*; Higashimoto Tarō, "Gunaratana Shaku Kōzen Wajō den," *Kaigai Bukkyō jijō* 10, no. 3 (1944): 1–13; and the very useful Itō Hiromi, ed., *Unshō/Kōzen iboku shū* (Tokyo: Bunka Shobō Hakubun Sha 1974). I have encountered two different readings of Shaku Kōzen's name. Shingon sources and Tsunemitsu read his name Shaku Kōnen. However, Sōen writes the name Shaku Kōzen in roman letters in the front of his diary, *Saiyū nikki* (Kamakura: Tōkeiji, 1941), and Unshō, in an English-language letter to Sumaṅgala, also refers to Kōnen as Kōzen. Following

Buddhism—Zen and Shingon respectively, rather than the nonmonastic Jōdo
Shin denomination. Like Kitabatake, their contact with Buddhism in South
Asia and with ideas flowing from Europe and the United States through Ceylon led them to reassess the importance of Śākyamuni Buddha for Japanese
Buddhism. It is thus fitting that when, in the early 1870s, the Meiji regime
forced all Buddhist clerics to assume surnames, both men had chosen the
name Shaku, the shortened Japanese transliteration of Śākyamuni.

The two Shakus traveled to Ceylon within one year of each other, with
Shaku Kōzen heading to the island first in 1886.[49] Kōzen remained in South
Asia for seven years before returning to Japan in 1893. Sōen, ten years Kōzen's
junior, traveled to Ceylon in 1887 to complete his Zen training, to study Sanskrit and Pali, and to survey the state of Buddhism in Ceylon. Sōen had been
given an additional push to head to Ceylon by Fukuzawa Yukichi (1834–1901),
who urged him to go to the island to study the "origins of Buddhism," as well
as Torio Tokuan (a.k.a. Torio Koyata; 1847–1905), a conservative politician
interested in Zen who had advised Sōen about entering Keiō Gijuku.[50] He
also stoked Sōen's interest in South Asia, a region Torio had visited en route
home to Japan from his tour of European countries.[51] One of Sōen's seniors
notes in a farewell letter to the cleric that Sōen "had decided to sail to India's
Ceylon in order to experience first hand the conditions of Buddhism there
and later help revive the decaying teaching of this country."[52] Sōen left Ceylon

what I assume to have been the contemporaneous pronunciation of his name, I shall refer to him
throughout the book as Shaku Kōzen.

49. Unfortunately a record of Kōzen's stay in Ceylon does not appear to be extant—the cur-
rent incumbent of Kōzen's temple, Andō Sonjin, told me that there is no diary of his stay at the
Sanneji. However, the first two-thirds of Sōen's record of his three-year stay in Ceylon does exist.
The first volume, covering the period from his departure from Yokohama on March 8, 1887 to
February 28, 1888, was reissued in a facsimile edition and a modern Japanese translation. See
Inoue Zenjō, Masaki Akira, and Yamada Tomonobu, eds., <Shin'yaku> Shaku Sōen "Saiyū nikki"
(Tokyo: Daihōrinkaku, 2001); and Shaku Sōen, Saiyū nikki (Kamakura: Kamakura Matsugaoka
Tōkeiji, 1941).

50. Tsunemitsu mentions Fukuzawa's advice to Sōen about Ceylon in MNB 1: 214. On Torio's
advice to Sōen about Keiō see Janine Anderson Sawada, Practical Pursuits: Religion, Politics,
and Personal Cultivation in Nineteenth-Century Japan (Honolulu: University of Hawai'i Press,
2004), 139.

51. See the Afterword, 3, by Itō Naozō, in Shaku Sōen, Seinan no Bukkyō (Tokyo: Hakubunkan, 1889).

52. Shaku Sōen, Saiyū nikki, "Nantei Kōgaku Oshō o okuru kotoba" 難弟洪嶽和尚ヲ送
ル詞 (Page numbers are not given in this portion of the original text, but a modern Japanese
rendering is found in Inoue, Shaku Sōen "Saiyū nikki," 34–35.)

on June 13, 1889, returning to Japan in October of that year after first visiting Siam and China.

Official contacts made by Hayashi with Ceylonese officials facilitated Kōzen and Sōen's trips to Ceylon. Sōen also mentions in his travel diary that he brought with him a letter of introduction from Hayashi that he presented to his lay patron in Ceylon, E. R. Gooneratne, upon arriving on the island.[53] Through Kōzen's connections both studied under the same Ceylonese master, Kōdāgoḍē Paññāsekhara, a close associate of the learned clerical leader Hikkaḍuvē Sumaṅgala, although Kōzen also studied with Paññāsekhara's teacher Bulatgama Siri Sumanatissa, from whom he received the Five Precepts. Ultimately Kōzen received the full monastic (*upasampadā*) ordination from Sumaṅgala.[54] Kōzen thus received the lay precepts and his full *bhikkhu* ordination from teachers in different monastic fraternities (*nikāya*), as Sumanatissa belonged to the Amarapura Nikāya and Sumaṅgala to the Siyam Nikāya. For some reason, Kōzen was not troubled by this multiple ordination identity, whereas Sōen would find it bothersome enough that he eventually sought full ordination—unsuccessfully—in Siam rather than choosing one or the other of the two Ceylonese *nikāya*.

Both Sumanatissa and Sumaṅgala were deeply involved in the Buddhist revival and anti-Christian activities on the island. Sumanatissa oversaw the founding in Galle in 1862 of the second Buddhist printing press established in Ceylon, Laṃkopakāra Press. Established at Kataluwa Ranweli Vihāra, the press received support from not only within Ceylon but also from King Mongkut of Siam.[55] By the early 1890s the Kataluwa Ranweli Vihāra was headed by Bulatgama's student, Paññāsekhara, who also published some of his tracts with the press. In the 1860s Laṃkopakāra Press also printed a number of works by Sumaṅgala, many of them part of the debate between Ceylonese Buddhists and Christian missionaries.[56] Sumaṅgala was a cosmopolitan monk who, in addition to his efforts to strengthen monastic practice on the island, nurtured contact not only with such foreigners as Henry Steel Olcott but also,

---

53. Inoue, *Shaku Sōen "Saiyū nikki,"* 78.

54. An album of photographs from Sōen's temple, Tōkeiji, contains a photograph of K. Paññāsekhara, who in all likelihood is the well-known *bhikkhu* Kōdāgoḍē Paññāsekhara.

55. Kitsiri Malalgoda, *Buddhism in Sinhalese Society, 1750–1900: A Study of Religious Revival and Change* (Berkeley: University of California Press, 1976), 219–20; Soorakkulame Pemaratana, "Promotion of the Ritual of Venerating the Buddha in Colonial Sri Lanka," paper presented at *Buddhism in the Global Eye: Beyond East and West* (University of British Columbia, 2016). I thank Venerable Pemaratana for sharing this unpublished conference presentation with me.

56. Malalgoda, *Buddhism in Sinhalese Society*, 221.

through correspondence, with clerics in Burma, Siam, and Japan. Sumaṅgala also was one of Thomas Rhys Davids's teachers in Ceylon.[57] Interested in reviving Buddhist practice throughout Asia, Sumaṅgala facilitated the Ceylonese sojourns of numerous Japanese clerics and corresponded with foreigners interested in Buddhism.[58] Although Sumaṅgala served for a number of years as the head of the Buddhist Theosophical Society's clerical division, at times he disagreed strongly with Olcott, at one point even threatening to resign his position over what he considered unorthodox interpretations of nirvana in Olcott's *A Buddhist Catechism* and for Olcott's questioning the authenticity of the Tooth Relic, which devout Ceylonese contended was Śākyamuni's tooth.[59] As mentioned above, E. R. Gooneratne, one of Sumaṅgala's strong supporters, also had worked with T. W. Rhys Davids and the Pali Text Society, publishing a number of translations of Pali texts, for example, the first part of the *Aṅguttara Nikāya*, with the Society and serving as its Ceylonese secretary.[60]

Thus the sponsorship of E. R. Gooneratne placed the Japanese clerics at one of the epicenters of Buddhist activity in Ceylon, Galle, where Kōzen and Sōen were exposed to orientalist, Theosophical, and Buddhist revivalist activities. In Galle, studying with Bulatgama, Sumaṅgala, and Paññāsekhara, the Japanese came into contact with Ceylonese, Southeast Asian Buddhists, Europeans, and Americans playing pivotal roles in the academic and religious revival of Buddhism. From Galle, translations and texts were shipped to Europe, while the Buddhist printing press churned out works critiquing Christianity and promoting Buddhism. As manuscripts, ideas, linguistic skills, translations, and, most crucially, people crisscrossed the globe, the flow of "influence" became correspondingly complex, with its starting points similarly diffused. Tracing this concatenation of connections provides us with a glimpse of what Charles Hallisey calls "intercultural mimesis" in action. As Hallisey has cautioned, understanding the back-and-forth exchange of ideas of intercultural mimesis enables us to "avoid a Manichean division between East and West and remind us that cultures are not only different but connected."[61] Kōzen and Sōen were part of the rich intercultural exchanges

57. Goonetilleke, *Atapattu Walawwa*, 150.

58. See, for example, the English-language letters exchanged between Sumaṅgala and Shaku Unshō, J. H. Barrows, and the Thai king, Chulalongkorn, in Yagirala Śrī Prajñānanda, *Śrī Sumaṅgala Caritaya dvitīya bhāgaya* (Colombo: Lake House Publishing, 1947), 768–69; 774–76. I am grateful to Anne Blackburn for providing me with copies of this correspondence.

59. Stephen R. Prothero, *The White Buddhist: The Asian Odyssey of Henry Steel Olcott* (Bloomington: Indiana University Press, 1996), 167–68.

60. Goonetilleke, *Atapattu Walawwa*, 149–52.

61. Charles Hallisey. "Roads Taken and Not Taken in the Study of Theravāda Buddhism,"

that were taking place in late nineteenth-century Ceylon, where Europeans, Americans, Japanese, Siamese, and Ceylonese interested in Buddhist revival and scholarship interacted.

The two Japanese clerics had gone to Ceylon seeking a pure, original Buddhism with which they could inform their practice in Japan. What they discovered in nineteenth-century Ceylon was a tradition that, like their own, was undergoing radical change. In colonial Ceylon Buddhism was being transformed against a background of widespread Christian missionary activity, the solidification of the English colonial administration, and, ironically, a new emphasis among Ceylonese Buddhists themselves in reviving their tradition.[62] For decades scholars have viewed the changes taking place in Ceylonese Buddhism during the turn of the century largely as a response to European Protestant Christian influence and changes wrought by centuries of Portuguese and British colonialism. In this new "Protestant Buddhism" we see, for example, the growth of lay practice, increased emphasis on Buddhist texts, and rejection of "superstitious" beliefs. Recently, however, scholars have offered correctives to the contention that the transformations taking place in Ceylonese Buddhism were solely a product of native responses to American and European patterns of social and religious organization. Anne Blackburn, in particular, in several important monographs has observed that the responses by Ceylonese Buddhists to these challenges were far more complex than the simple bipolar challenge-response "Protestant Buddhism" model suggests.[63] According to Blackburn's critique, portraying the shifts in Ceylonese Buddhism as simply a response to the West denies agency to the Ceylonese Buddhists and fails to take into account reformist trajectories well underway prior to the nineteenth century. She observes that

---

in *Curators of the Buddha: The Study of Buddhism under Colonialism*, ed. Donald S. Lopez Jr. (Chicago: University of Chicago Press, 1995), 33.

62. The nineteenth-century Buddhist revival in Ceylon is examined in detail in several works, including George Doherty Bond, *The Buddhist Revival in Sri Lanka: Religious Tradition, Reinterpretation, and Response* (Columbia: University of South Carolina Press, 1988); Richard Francis Gombrich and Gananath Obeyesekere, *Buddhism Transformed: Religious Change in Sri Lanka* (Princeton, NJ: Princeton University Press, 1988); and Malalgoda, *Buddhism in Sinhalese Society*. The international interests of the Ceylonese Buddhists, especially in South and Southeast Asia, are explored by Mark Frost in "'Wider Opportunities.'" Although commonly referred to as "Protestant Buddhism," the usefulness of this characterization in Ceylon has been called into question by several authors in recent years.

63. See Anne M. Blackburn, *Buddhist Learning and Textual Practice in Eighteenth-Century Lankan Monastic Culture* (Princeton, NJ: Princeton University Press, 2001), 200–203; and *Locations of Buddhism*, ix–xv; 197–217.

looking closely at the life and work of Hikkaḍuvē Sumaṅgala, one of the most central figures in British-period Lankan Buddhism and the island's wider society, we see that new imported discourses and forms of social identification did not always displace those which had existed previously, whether among residents of Laṅkā or in the wider southern Asian Buddhist region. Rather, in Hikkaḍuvē's case, many deeply historical perceptions of affiliation and social responsibility, intellectual styles, and ways of navigating the highly competitive world of monastic life held steady.[64]

Rather than adopting Protestant Christian practices and values wholesale, Buddhist intellectuals and leaders like Sumaṅgala varied the ways in which they utilized new forms and intellectual standards depending upon the context. When dealing with the colonial administration, they conformed to expectations by employing British standards and religious language. By contrast, when working within the confines of the monastic establishment and newly formed Buddhist academies, however, Ceylonese Buddhists would freely employ elements drawn from the religious and academic armamentaria of the British in a manner that was consonant with long-standing Buddhist modes of argumentation.[65] As was the case in Japan, where Buddhists responded to the opening of the country to foreigners and the growing presence of Christian missionaries in a variety of ways that escape characterization as mere mimicry, so, too, did the Ceylonese creatively stitch together new modes of Buddhist expression in manners consonant with ongoing, precolonial trends. As I will show in chapter 2, the encounter of Japanese Buddhists with Indian pandits followed the same pattern, with the Japanese arriving while Indian scholarship and practice was being transformed in a multiplicity of ways in reaction to British colonial scholarship and the presence of Christian missionaries.

In addition to the response within the Buddhist Sangha to colonialism, the Theosophist Henry Steel Olcott (1832–1907) and Anagārika Dharmapāla (1864–1933), who founded the Mahābodhi Society in 1891, through their international connections drew worldwide attention to the struggles of South Asian Buddhists to oppose the Christianization of the populace by missionaries and restore South Asian Buddhist heritage sites, most prominently at Bodh Gayā.[66] For a time on the island, the two men worked together closely

64. Blackburn, *Locations of Buddhism*, xii–xiii.

65. Blackburn, *Locations of Buddhism*, xiii.

66. These efforts are described in detail in Steven Kemper, *Rescued from the Nation: Anagarika Dharmapala and the Buddhist World* (Chicago: University of Chicago Press, 2015). Anne Blackburn points out that the alliance between such Ceylonese Buddhist leaders as Sumaṅgala and Ol-

in an effort to unify Ceylonese Buddhists in their efforts to resist Christian influence. These efforts of the two men, who both held what Kemper has characterized as "universalist" sentiments, soon drew attention from a number of Japanese Buddhists. Sōen's diary makes clear that while in Ceylon, he and Kōzen were aware of activities being undertaken by Dharmapāla and Olcott. The two clerics paid a visit to Dharmapāla, according to Sōen's diary entry for June 27, 1887, while Sōen was visiting Kōzen at the Vidyodaya Piriveṇa in Colombo, traveling to Dharmapāla's home and Olcott's private Buddhist school that was next door to Dharmapāla's residence. The diary does not go into detail about the visit, however, merely stating that "we visited the home of H. Don David (Theosophical Society). Next door was the private school of the American, Mr. Olcott."[67] As we will see below, from 1890 Kōzen worked closely with Dharmapāla in an effort to free Bodh Gayā from Hindu control.

Sōen also was clearly aware of Olcott's book, *A Buddhist Catechism*, first published in 1881, as he made use of the book to practice his English. To that end, at first, in April 1887, Sōen copied such aphorisms as "Honesty is the best policy," "Where there is a will, there is a way," and "Many men, many minds" in each of the daily entries.[68] Just one month later, on April 29, however, he notes that he will begin using Olcott's *A Buddhist Catechism* instead for his exercises, beginning with the quotation, "(Q) Of what religion are you? (A) The Buddhist. (Q)What is a Buddhist? (A) One who professes to be a follower of our Lord Buddha and accepts his doctrine." Working through the section on Śākyamuni, Sōen wrote out such passages as "Is Buddha a god? No"; "Was he a man? In form, but internally not like other men"; and "Where was Kapilavastu? In India, 100 miles northeast of the Benares, and about forty miles from the Himalaya mountains."[69]

Olcott's *A Buddhist Catechism* (1881), which mimicked the primers used by Christian missionaries, presented Buddhism as a textual, rational, scientific religion centered on the founder, Śākyamuni.[70] Olcott's approach turned Buddhism into "one religion among many. And this reified 'ism' was imme-

---

cott although strategically useful was uneasy at best, as they had vastly different understandings of Buddhist practice. See Blackburn, *Locations of Buddhism*, 104–42.

67. Shaku Sōen, *Saiyū nikki*, 75 verso.

68. Shaku Sōen, *Saiyū nikki*, 43 recto–52 verso. (Hereafter, recto and verso pages in the diary will be abbreviated "r" and "v.")

69. Shaku Sōen, *Saiyū nikki*, 56r; 57v; 61r–62v. Sōen may well have seen the Japanese translation of *A Buddhist Catechism*, *Bukkyō mondō*, which was published in April 1886.

70. Olcott, Henry Steel, and Hikkaduve Sri Sumangala. *A Buddhist Catechism According to the Canon of the Southern Church* (Colombo, Ceylon: Theosophical Society, Buddhist Section, 1881). The citations to the text are to Henry Steel Olcott and Elliott Coues, *A Buddhist Catechism*,

diately reduced to the beliefs of the ancient Buddha."[71] Olcott's work, which was reissued in successive editions, quickly garnered the attention of Buddhists in Japan. In November 1882, just one year after the publication of the *Catechism*, Mizutani Jinkai, a Jōdo Shin cleric, had written to Olcott, seeking permission to translate the book into Japanese. A few months later, Mizutani received permission to produce a Japanese translation. By 1886, a year prior to Sōen's departure for Ceylon, the Japanese translation, *Bukkyō mondō*, was published, bearing a title calligraphed by the incumbent of the Jōdo denomination head temple, Chion'in, and a preface by Akamatsu Renjō.[72] The book was thus a joint production by a range of prominent Kyoto Buddhists, who soon collectively invited Olcott to Japan.

Sōen writes little about the passages he copied for practicing his English, but his reading of the text may have played a role in several decisions he made concerning how best to present Buddhism to Americans, Europeans, and to Meiji- and Taishō-generation Japanese. When invited to serve as a member of the Japanese delegation to the World's Parliament of Religions, Sōen chose to deliver his address on the "Law of Cause and Effect As Taught by Buddha," one of the topics also covered by Olcott in *A Buddhist Catechism*, in which he claims that Buddhism is consonant with modern science, precisely because it is a doctrine of cause and effect.[73]

The Ceylonese seem to have celebrated the visiting Japanese clerics as comrades in the struggle against the missionaries and the English colonial order. Although we do not have any account of popular reaction to Kōzen's ordination, Sōen's diary details the festivities that accompanied his own. Just as crowds all over the island lauded Henry Steel Olcott and Helen Blavatsky as European Buddhists when the pair arrived on the island in 1880, Ceylonese treated Sōen's ordination as a novice monk (*sāmaṇera*) as a highly auspicious event. According to Sōen's diary, he took the ten *sāmaṇera* vows on May 7, 1887. The precept master (*upajjhāya*; J. *kaishi*) for the event was Siri Sumanatissa. Paññāsekhara was in attendance as Sōen's teacher (*ācariya*; J. *ajari*), a role he would continue to hold for the more than two years Sōen was in Ceylon. Following the ordination, Sōen was greeted by a boisterous crowd of more than a thousand people, who celebrated the event with fireworks and

---

According to the Canon of the Southern Church. "The Biogen Series," No 3, 1st American ed. (Boston,: Estes and Lauriat, 1887). This is the American edition of the work.

71. Prothero, *White Buddhist*, 102–3.

72. Satō, *Daiajia shisō katsugeki*, 30–33; Toshio Akai, "Theosophical Accounts in Japanese Buddhist Publications of the Late Nineteenth Century: An Introduction and Select Bibliography," *Japanese Religions* 34, no. 2 (2009): 188–89.

73. Olcott, *A Buddhist Catechism*, 34.

European-style Buddhist hymns. The geopolitical implications of the event were clearly on the mind of at least one member of the crowd. A Ceylonese layman in attendance told Sōen that there had not been such a grand event since the English had colonized the island. The man elaborated that this celebration expressed the islanders' gratitude to the Buddha, Japanese-Ceylonese Buddhist solidarity, and, finally, congratulations to Sōen for receiving his monastic vows. Sōen wrote that from that day forward he wore Ceylonese-style *bhikkhu*'s robes while on the island.[74] On the twenty-fourth of the same month, Sōen notes that he received the name Pannākètu from Paññāsekhara, thus sharing the first portion of the name with his Ceylonese master.[75]

Despite the warm welcome Sōen received in Ceylon and his immersion in local monastic life, Sōen found some Ceylonese customs repugnant. He also was not totally enamored with the Buddhist practice on the island. Writing early in his stay, Sōen described his difficulty pronouncing Sinhala and adapting to such customs as eating with one's fingers, walking barefoot on the hot ground, washing his behind with water after defecating, and blowing his nose with his hand.[76] Sōen also continued to consider the Buddhism in Ceylon as "Hinayana" (*Shōjō*), that is, the "Lesser Vehicle," viewing it as the first stage of Buddhism and extremely shallow in terms of its teachings. In addition, Sōen wrote, some of the *bhikkhu* were dismally ignorant regarding Buddhist doctrine. One individual, for example, explained to Sōen that consciousness (*shinshiki*) was extinguished at death with the dissolution of the Four Elements and told Sōen that the notion that it persisted following death was a heterodox teaching. Sōen commented that this was such a gross misunderstanding that he could not hide his surprise. Lacking the linguistic facility to explain the true Buddhist view of consciousness, Sōen states that the conversation ended at that point. He does not raise the possibility, given the poor communication with the *bhikkhu*, that, perhaps, he had misunderstood what he was being told, however.[77] Sōen also criticized the lack of balance in Ceylonese Buddhist practice. Noting that Buddhist training required equal attention to each of the three learnings (*sangaku*), morality, meditation, and

---

74. Shaku Sōen, *Saiyū nikki*, 47r–49v.

75. Shaku Sōen, *Saiyū nikki*, 54v. Sōen writes in the diary that the name (in katakana) is *Pannyakētsu*, meaning "peak of wisdom" (*chihō*). On the inside cover of *Saiyū nikki* Sōen spells the name Pannaketū. The spelling Pannākètu is found on Sōen's 1889 official Certificate (of practice) that bears his teacher's seal. See Umezawa Megumi and Tokura Takeyuki, eds. *Shaku Sōen to kindai Nihon—wakaki Zensō, sekai o kakeru*. (Kita-Kamakura: Engakuji, 2018), 84.

76. Shaku Sōen, *Saiyū nikki*, 41r–41v.

77. Shaku Sōen, *Saiyū nikki*, Kan 2: 7r. (The diary was divided into to two volumes, with pagination starting over in Kan 2.)

wisdom, Sōen wrote that in Ceylon the monks had totally ignored meditative practice in favor of unreflective textual study. Paying careful attention to the monastic rules (Vinaya) while lacking meditative attainment was as pointless as "a monkey donning a cap," Sōen concluded.[78]

While in Ceylon Sōen wrote one of the earliest Japanese-language works on South Asian Buddhism. The book, *Seinan no Bukkyō* (The Buddhism of the Southwest) was completed in August 1888 and was published in Japan in January 1889, while Sōen was residing in Ceylon.[79] In this work Sōen's familiarity with Olcott and Dharmapāla's reform Buddhism, Euro-American literature concerning Buddhism, and Ceylonese monastic life are clearly evident. In discussing Ceylonese Buddhism, Sōen cites such authors writing about Ceylonese Buddhism as James De Alwis, Spence Hardy, Max Müller, and Robert C. Childers. Sōen completed the book in the era prior to the use of the word Theravāda (in Japanese, Jōzabu) as a term to designate as a group the various regional Buddhisms found in Ceylon, Burma, Siam, Laos, Cambodia, and elsewhere in South and Southeast Asia.[80] As indicated by the title, which points to the Buddhism practiced in the region southwest of Japan, these forms of Buddhism were defined regionally and, as made clear in the book, defined in contrast with Sinitic forms of Buddhism. In the course of the book, Sōen primarily refers to southwestern Buddhism (*Seinan no Bukkyō*) and southwestern Buddhists (*Seinan no Bukkyōsha*), although on occasion he employs the broad categories of Hinayana (Shōjō) and Mahayana (Daijō) Buddhism instead. At times Sōen includes within the category of Southwestern Buddhism the forms of the religion found in Tibet, India, Burma, Ceylon, Siam, and Annam.[81]

Having directly witnessed Hong Kong and Ceylon under British rule and only recently learning of Britain's full conquest of Burma, Sōen graphically described the plight of Buddhism in Asia: "At the front door the wolf of Christianity opens its jaws; at the back door the tiger of Islam sharpens its claws."[82] The situation, however, was not entirely hopeless. Sōen saw the emergence of

78. Shaku Sōen, *Saiyū nikki*, 40v–41r.

79. Shaku Sōen, *Seinan No Bukkyō*. Sōen published a second more general book about Ceylon shortly after his return to Japan. In that work, Sōen included information about Ceylonese history and the caste system, as well as a more general view of Ceylonese religion, including Buddhism. See Shaku Sōen, *Seirontō shi* (Tokyo: Gukyō Shoin, 1890).

80. For a superb history of the use of Theravāda as a term to embrace the various Buddhisms of Southeast Asia, see Perreira, "Whence Theravāda?" A cogent analysis of the term also is found in PDB, 904–5.

81. See, for example, *Seinan no Bukkyō*, 84–86.

82. Shaku Sōen, *Seinan no Bukkyō*, 86.

the Theosophical Society in Europe and the United States as a sign of growing interest in Buddhism. To nurture this nascent sprout of the tradition and thereby ensure the future flourishing of Buddhism, Sōen urged Southern and Northern Buddhist clerics to unite and actively proselytize in the "West."[83] Sōen, at the start of 1889, when *Seinan no Bukkyō* was published, was delivering a timely message from Ceylon. Just one month after the publication of *Seinan no Bukkyō*, Olcott and Dharmapāla arrived in Japan, where Olcott would urge Southern and Northern Buddhists to unite around a common set of principles in the interest of sparking a Buddhist renaissance across Asia.[84]

In the chapter entitled "The Gist of Buddhism" (Bukkyō no taii), Sōen takes up a number of topics that overlap with those touched on by Olcott in *A Buddhist Catechism*. Sōen discusses in short order the origins and nature of image worship—idolatry (*gūzō raihai*) in Buddhism, the nonexistence of a creator god and a soul, the nature of nirvana, and the central importance of the Twelve-fold Chain of Conditioned Coproduction (*jyūni innen*; S. *pratītyasamutpāda*).

Much like Olcott, Sōen rejected the claim that Buddhism originally involved the practice of idolatry, writing, "Although image worship was not one of the original principles of Buddhism, I am not one who aims to eliminate the practice. I just hope that however they understand the reason for worshiping the image, they will strive to pay reverential obeisance."[85] Sōen then noted important differences that existed in the practice of image veneration between the Buddhists of Northeast Asia (*Tōhoku no Bukkyōsha*) and those of South-Southeast Asia (literally 'Southwest'; *Seinan no Bukkyōsha*). Whereas for the most part Buddhists of Ceylon and other South-Southeast Asian countries venerated only Śākyamuni, Buddhists of Northeast Asia venerated a host of different deities, bodhisattvas, and buddhas.

Sōen's sojourn in Ceylon coincided with attempts by Buddhists on the island to promote the practice of *Buddha-vandanā*, that is, venerating Śākyamuni by chanting, performing prostrations, and offering incense, flowers, and light. With the rise of Buddhist printing presses, texts detailing this practice and urging its performance by monastics and laity alike were printed beginning by at least 1887. Sōen's teacher, Paññāsekhara, was part of this movement, publishing *Buddha Meheya* (Service to the Buddha), advocating the veneration of Śākyamuni, in 1888. The work proved popular enough to warrant its republication in 1893 in a printing of 1,500 copies and by the turn of

83. Shaku Sōen, *Seinan no Bukkyō*, 87–88.
84. Prothero, *The White Buddhist*, 124–27; Kemper, *Rescued from the Nation*, 134–44.
85. Shaku Sōen, *Seinan no Bukkyō*, 39. See Olcott, *A Buddhist Catechism*, 58–60.

the century, tracts of this type, some of them for free distribution, were being printed in editions of 8,000–10,000 copies.[86] The widespread dissemination of these texts on Buddha veneration is an example of how the new technology of the printing press aided the promotion of the traditional Buddhist practice of Buddha veneration, which served as a weapon for defending Buddhism against Christianity.[87]

Sōen saw the great diversity in images of worship as a problem for Japanese Buddhists, particularly during the period of crisis in which they found themselves. Without a sense of unity, a moral renaissance would be impossible for Buddhism. Sōen had no illusions about the difficulty in achieving this for all Buddhists, however. For this reason he argued that Buddhists in Japan should begin by choosing one figure of veneration for their own denomination of Buddhism. Members of the Jōdo Shinshū, for example, uniformly worshipped Amida, which gave their denomination a unity that was exceptional. For his own Rinzai denomination, Sōen argued that Śākyamuni should be made the central image of veneration. Not only would this unify the Zen school, it would also provide common ground with the Buddhists of Southeast Asia and with people familiar with Buddhism in Europe and the United States.

> When we ask which Buddha is most appropriate as the main image of veneration I believe that it is Śākyamuni Buddha. (This does not apply to denominations that, like Jōdo Shinshū, already have a designated image of veneration.) That is because Śākyamuni is our Great Master to whom we are indebted for the Teaching, that is, he is the Teacher for the current cosmic age. . . . What is more, today Śākyamuni's name is not valued just in Buddhist countries, it is known in all the countries of Europe and the United States. People who do not know the names of other buddhas are numerous not only in the West, of course, but also in other Buddhist countries of Asia (*Tōyō*). In Southwest [*Seinan* i.e., "Southeast"] Asia those who do not even know the names of the seven past buddhas are numerous. Śākyamuni is the image of veneration that is karmically connected with the civilized world of the twentieth century.[88]

Sōen was not the only Japanese struck by the contrast between the heterogeneity of image veneration in Japan and the almost exclusive devotion

86. Soorakkulame Pemaratana, "Bringing the Buddha Closer: The Role of Venerating the Buddha in the Modernization of Buddhism in Sri Lanka," (PhD diss., University of Pittsburgh, 2017), 32; 35; 87. I thank Pemaratana for sharing the dissertation and the translation of the title *Buddha Meheya*. See also Malalgoda, *Buddhism in Sinhalese Society*, 221.

87. On the ways in which new technologies, particularly printing, promote traditional religious practices, see Niles Green, *Bombay Islam*.

88. Shaku Sōen, *Seinan no Bukkyō*, 46.

to Śākyamuni that was visible among South and Southeast Asian Buddhists. Shortly after Sōen departed Japan for Ceylon, Oda Tokunō (1860–1911), an Ōtani branch Jōdo Shin cleric, headed to Siam in order to survey Siamese Buddhism in order to compare the "Southern and Eastern sects" (*Tōnan nibu no Bukkyō o taishō sen*).[89] Accompanied by several other clerics from various sects of the Jōdo Shin denomination, Oda remained in Siam from March 1888 to June 1890. Like Sōen, Oda remarked on the unity of Siamese Buddhists with regard to their image of worship, which was exclusively Śākyamuni Buddha: "In temples the only image enshrined is the Venerable Śākyamuni, occasionally accompanied by images of the attendants Śāriputra and Mahāmaudgalyāyana." He also observed that "furthermore, only temples enshrine a buddha image; one does not see this in the homes of the laity." Although this meant that when *bhikkhu* visited lay residences they sat cross-legged in a line and chanted sutras without an image of the buddha present, Oda concluded that despite the absence of buddha images in lay households or, perhaps, because of it, the Southern Hinayanists (Nanpō Shōjōsha) were even more fervent in their reverence than the Northern Mahayanists (Hokuhō Daijōsha).[90]

Following the discussion of the appropriate image of worship for Buddhists, Sōen turned his attention to the ultimate goal of Buddhism, nirvana, and the arising of existence from causes and conditions. In this portion of "The Gist of Buddhism," Sōen demonstrates his familiarity with the works of European Buddhologists and scholars of Asian religions, citing Max Müller's definition of nirvana as "annihilation of existence" and Robert C. Childers's "free from human passion," as well as referring to the lengthy description of nirvana found in Childers's *Dictionary of Pāli Language*, which had been published in 1875.[91] Perhaps Sōen had taken note of these works prior to heading to Ceylon, but it is more likely that he became acquainted with them during his stay on the island. Sōen, a Zen master through and through, stresses the ultimately nondualistic nature of awakening. "The nirvana of our Buddhism, unlike the nirvana of the various heterodox paths (*sho gedō no nehan*), is the elimination of the defilements (*bonnō*). When one attains nirvana there are no defilements. We speak of defilements and nirvana, however, the thought of the delusion and awakening of self-nature (*jishō meigo no ichinen*) exists

89. "Ikuta Tokunō jiden" 生田得能自伝 in Oda Tokunō, *Shamu Bukkyō jijō* (Tokyo: Shinshū Hōwa Shūppan, 1891), 11–13.

90. Oda Tokunō, *Shamu Bukkyō jijō*, 46–50.

91. Robert Cæsar Childers, *A Dictionary of the Pali Language* (London: Trubner & Co., 1875).

in our heads. If we seek it apart from ourselves, this would be to mar the transcendent jewel. The old poem [reads], 'Until yesterday, [I] saw the sky scraping mountains!/Today, the cloud-treading [narrow mountain] road in Kiso'" (*Kinō made sora takaku nomi mishi yama mo kyō wa kumo fumu Kiso no kakehashi*).[92]

The discussion of the nature of nirvana and death gave Sōen the opportunity to reflect on the differences in funeral procedures, particularly the role of the Buddhist clergy in them, in Ceylon and Japan. Looking at funeral practices from his widened pan-Asian Buddhist perspective, Sōen mentions how in Ceylon the Buddhist *bhikkhu* do not conduct an involved funeral or regular memorial services for the deceased as is done in Japan. Instead, Sōen observed, the *bhikkhu* merely recited a brief verse concerning the impermanence of all compounded things and praising the quiescence of nirvana. Following the recitation of the verse three times, Sōen writes, the *bhikkhu* gives a terse sermon to soothe the sorrow of the family. Sōen contrasts this to the involved funerals and ongoing memorial services conducted in Japan, which, he concludes, "mostly are adopted from Chinese Confucian ritual" (*taitei Shina no Jurei o saiyō shitaru mono*).[93] This section thus reveals how the experience of Ceylonese Buddhist practice catalyzed Sōen's rethinking of Buddhism as a pan-Asian tradition that is separable from its various cultural inflections, in this case, Confucian ritual. The "gist of Buddhism" that Sōen is describing is that which transcends these regional differences and, therefore, is foundational to the tradition.

Sōen then examined the fundamental aim of Buddhism, nirvana, which is the goal of all Śākyamuni's teachings and is permanent and unchanging (*jōjū fuhen*), and he gave an account of how deluded consciousness arises in the world based on conditioned coproduction. In discussing this subject, Sōen stresses that he is not substituting the Hinayana perspective for the Mahayana one, as there is only one Buddhist truth. Sōen dismisses as false the assertions of other traditions like Christianity and Hinduism that consciousness, which Christians call soul (*sōru*) is something endowed to us by the Creator or Brahma. In place of the creator, Buddhists advocate the notion of non-self (*muga*), a body composed of the five elements and consciousness arising due to fundamental ignorance and the forgetting of the original, awakened state of being. Turning away from innate awakening, ignorant consciousness arises: this a fundamental law of the universe. The thorough examination of the Twelve-fold Chain of Conditioned Coproduction, writes Sōen, allows one

92. Shaku Sōen, *Seinan no Bukkyō*, 48.
93. Shaku Sōen, *Seinan no Bukkyō*, 50.

to achieve the nirvana of the pratyekabuddha vehicle (*engakujō no nehan*), noting parenthetically that Southeast Asian Buddhists do not discuss either the Buddha vehicle or the bodhisattva vehicle. Sōen then provides a detailed elaboration of the twelve links in the Twelve-fold Chain, the circulation of which gives rise to the three periods, past, present, and future. Sōen concludes that "to pursue the three times apart from the law of cause and effect (*inga*) is not the true Buddhist teaching."[94] The key to achieving nirvana, at least from the perspective of Southeast Asian Buddhism, is to reverse the chain of causation beginning with the extinguishing of ignorance. Through this reverse course, the practitioner is able to free himself from all defilements and karmic hindrances, thereby attaining nirvana. Sōen adds the caveat that in Ceylonese Buddhism the heart of the teaching is the Three Marks of Existence, that is, suffering, impermanence, and nonself but the goal arrived at is one solely of self-benefit without any attention to teaching others (*jiri ni tomarite keta ni oyobazu*). In this the teachings of Ceylonese Buddhism resemble those of Laozi and Zhuangzi, Sōen adds.[95] By contrast, Mahayana consists of comprehending the Three Bodies of the Buddha, the Four Wisdoms, the Six Perfections, and the myriad dharma gates (*sanjin shichi rokudo mangyō muryō no hōmon*). As in other portions of the text, Sōen was quick to distinguish Ceylonese Buddhist teachings concerning the path from those of Japanese Mahayana.[96]

On June 13, 1889, Sōen left Ceylon for Siam, where he hoped to receive the full *bhikkhu* ordination. In a contemporaneous letter sent to the Buddhist journal *Meikyō shinshi*, Sōen explained that he was heading to Siam with a letter of introduction from his teacher, Paññāsekhara, in order to receive an ordination into the Dhammayuttika Nikāya. In the communication to the journal, Sōen mentioned that originally the ordination lineage in Ceylon was pure, but because it had to be restored from Siam and Burma during the medieval period, it was an offshoot of the lineage in those two countries. In addition, the lineage in Ceylon had now split, making it inconvenient for a foreigner to receive the *bhikkhu* ordination from one of the groups.[97] For that reason Sōen proposed that he and Kōzen travel to Siam to receive their full ordination. As Blackburn has described, the split of the Kalyāṇi Nikāya from the Siyam Nikāya had roiled the Sangha in Ceylon. In an effort to reunite the

94. Shaku Sōen, *Seinan no Bukkyō*, 58.
95. Shaku Sōen, *Seinan no Bukkyō*, 59.
96. Shaku Sōen, *Seinan no Bukkyō*, 60.
97. Okuyama Naoji, "Rankā no hassō: Meiji nijyū nendai zenhan no Indo ryūgakusō no jiseki," in *Indogaku shoshisō to sono shūen: Bukkyō Bunka Gakkai jisshūnen Hōjō Kenzō Hakushi koki kinen ronbunshū*, ed. Bukkyō Bunka Gakkai (Tokyo: Sankibō Busshorin, 2004), 92–93.

Sangha, some leading *bhikkhu* hoped to have the Siamese conduct a Dhammayuttika ordination on the island, but the plans did not succeed.[98] Sōen was aware of the tensions between the various lineages in Ceylon and hoped to avoid the problem of becoming associated with one group or another through his *upasampadā* ordination. Sōen asked Kōzen to accompany him to Siam, but Kōzen declined to go for health reasons. Sōen arrived in Siam on July 10, 1889, but, despite bearing a letter of introduction from Paññāsekhara, Sōen, for unknown reasons, was denied permission to take the full ordination in Siam.[99] After failing to attain his goal, Sōen returned to Japan in October 1889.

Although both Kitabatake and Sōen were ambivalent about what they saw in South Asia, Shaku Kōzen embraced the Buddhism of Ceylon as the purest, truest form of the tradition, becoming, for all intents and purposes, a convert. Born in Izumo in Shimane Prefecture in 1849, Kōzen came from an extended family with five members who were Buddhist clerics. Kōzen's mother, Itagaki Iyo (born as Watanabe), was an elder sister of the famed Shingon master Shaku Unshō. Kōzen was ordained at the age of ten by his maternal uncle, Watanabe Senmyō, who was Unshō's elder brother as well as the incumbent of an Izumo Shingon temple, Iwayadera, where years before his uncle, Unshō, also had been ordained. Kōzen rose through the ranks of the Shingon denomination, completing the four initiations (*shido kegyō*), then training on Mt. Kōya. An earnest and talented student, Kōzen became a doctrinal instructor for the Ministry of Doctrine (Kyōbushō) and incumbent of the Kanagawa Prefecture Shingon temple Sanneji, which controlled thirty-two branch temples, in 1882.[100] (See fig. 1.3.)

When Unshō became determined to assess the situation of Buddhism in South Asia, as mentioned above, he turned to his nephew Kōzen to go on his behalf. Letters from Unshō sent to Kōzen throughout the latter's stay in Ceylon make clear Unshō's reasons for dispatching his nephew to South Asia. In correspondence written in November and December of 1886, Unshō expressed deep interest in the state of precept practice on the island and in touring the eight great Buddhist pilgrimage sites (literally "Eight Great Stupa"; Hachi Daitō) in India.[101] His interest stoked by Kōzen's successful entry into the Ceylonese Buddhist order and progress in studying Pali and Sanskrit, Unshō wrote of his determination to follow Kōzen to South Asia in the fall

98. Blackburn, *Locations of Buddhism*, 144–50.

99. Okuyama, "Rankā no hassō," 92–93; Inoue, *Shaku Sōen den*, 58.

100. MNB 1: 371–72; Noguchi, *Shaku Kōzen*, 2–3.

101. The eight sites include Lumbinī, Bodh Gayā, Sārnāth, Śrāvastī, Saṃkāśya, "settling of disputes stupa," Capālācaitya, Kusinigarī. See PDB, 1081–82.

FIGURE 1.3. Shaku Kōzen in *bhikkhu* robes, n.d. Courtesy of Tōkeiji.

of 1888. Unshō's ambitions included receiving ordination in Ceylon, studying Indic Buddhist languages, and, in the fall of 1889, traveling in north India as well as Tibet before returning to Japan. Although those aspirations were never realized, Unshō makes clear his longing for ordination in an unbroken precept lineage that had been transmitted by precept-upholding *bhikkhu*. Unshō also was keen to determine a number of fine points concerning Ceylonese Buddhist precepts and practice. For example, Unshō inquired about which image of worship, if any, was enshrined in monastic dining halls; the rituals performed during meals and bathing, and the number and size of alms bowls used by the *bhikkhu*. Unshō also sought Kōzen's opinion concerning the educational level of the monastic population.[102]

Kōzen remained in South Asia for seven years, departing Japan in September 1886 and returning from Ceylon in September 1893. In Ceylon, Kōzen studied and practiced under Paññāsekhara and other teachers and visited a variety of Buddhist sites in India. Soon after his arrival in Ceylon, Kōzen moved to Galle, where he first was hosted by E. R. Gooneratne. For much of his sojourn in South Asia, Kōzen received money collected by Unshō from a number of lay supporters and sent to Kōzen via E. R. Gooneratne.[103] Although initially able to understand hardly a word of Sinhalese or Pali, Kōzen got by with the help of a dictionary. He followed the precepts he had received as a Shingon cleric strictly, which soon earned him the admiration of the laity in the area. He took the Three Refuges and Five Precepts from Bulatgama Dhammālaṅkāra Siri Sumanatissa, the *bhikkhu* that Akamatsu had encountered, before undertaking study of the precepts with Paññāsekhara, Siri Sumanatissa's disciple.[104] Whereas Sōen lived in the port town of Galle for most of his time on the island, Kōzen studied at the monastic training college Vidyodaya Piriveṇa, in Colombo, where Sumaṅgala served as principal, although Kōzen returned to Galle from time to time, visiting Sōen on occasion, for example.[105] Founded in August 1873, the college, according to an 1876 newspaper account, trained students in such subjects as "Pali grammar, Pali reading, Sanskrit grammar, Sanskrit reading, Sinhalese grammar, Sinhalese reading, medicine, and mathematics (*sāstric* rather than European)."[106] By the time Kōzen left Ceylon in 1893, there were, according to Blackburn, 147 students enrolled in the college, many of them drawn from Sumaṅgala's Siyam Nikāya (lineage/group).

Four years after his arrival on the island, Kōzen received the full *bhikkhu* ordination from Sumaṅgala on June 9, 1890, in Kandy. Kōzen was one of eight *bhikkhu* ordinands participating in the ceremony, receiving the full *bhikkhu* precepts with three others at the ordination platform at Malwatta Mahavihara (Kaen Kaidan). (The others received the precepts at a second temple.) Dur-

102. SUS 2: 31–41.

103. See, for example, letters sent to Kōzen from Unshō dated March 11, 1889, and October 18, 1889, in SUS 2: 83–84; 117–21.

104. MNB 1: 374.

105. Shaku, Sōen, *Saiyū nikki*, 55r, for example.

106. *Overland Examiner*, January 18, 1877, cited in Blackburn, *Locations of Buddhism*, 47. Blackburn gives a detailed account of the school's curriculum, activities, and demographics in *ibid.*, 46–54.

ing the ceremony, Kōzen visited the Temple of the Tooth Relic, the Dalada Maligawa, then traveled mounted, along with one other ordinand, on the first of a procession of four elephants to the Malwatta Mahavihara, where the ceremony took place. This made him, according to Noguchi, the first recorded Japanese to become a *bhikkhu*, in the strictest sense of the term.[107] Soon after Kōzen's *bhikkhu* ordination, in a letter to Dogi Hōryū (1854–1923), Unshō reported that Kōzen hoped to return to Japan along with Sumaṅgala and four additional *bhikkhu* in order to conduct ordinations based on the Southern precept lineage (*Nanpō sōshō no kairitsu*) in Japan. His letters to Kōzen from this period reveal that Unshō was excited by this prospect, which he believed might enable Southern Buddhist precept ordinations to take place in Japan. In return, the Japanese could convey the limitless precept teachings that had been delivered by the Tathāgata when he presented the *Kegongyō*.[108] The exchange between Northern and Southern Buddhism, Unshō wrote to Dogi that same day, would benefit Buddhist countries and the Japanese state.[109] Despite his keen interest in receiving ordination in the precept lineage of Sumaṅgala, Unshō neither traveled to Ceylon, nor did Sumaṅgala come to Japan with a contingent of *bhikkhu*. Kōzen remained in South Asia until 1893 and, following his return to Japan, continued attempting, unsuccessfully, to establish the Southern precept lineage in Japan.

Judging from Sōen's diary entries, as well as correspondence between Unshō and Kōzen while the latter was in Ceylon, Kōzen was actively involved with several of the activists that headed the opposition to the Christian missionaries in Ceylon while seeking to bolster Buddhism on the island. Kōzen worked closely with Olcott and Dharmapāla, traveling to Adyar, India, a suburb of Madras (Chennai), in December 1890 with the Nishi-Honganji Shin cleric, Tokuzawa Chiezō (1871–1908), as Japanese representatives at the Fifteenth Annual Convention of the Theosophical Society. In addition to Kōzen and Tokuzawa, Noguchi Fukudō (born as Nukina Zenshirō; 1864–?) also was in attendance at the meeting. Noguchi, a friend of Hirai Kinza, was in Adyar to work out the schedule for Henry Steel Olcott's lecture tour of Japan. Following the meeting, Tokuzawa headed to Benares to continue his study of Sanskrit, while in January 1891 Kōzen made his first trip to Bodh Gayā, traveling with Dharmapāla. Inspired by the experience of Bodh Gayā, Kōzen and

---

107. Noguchi, *Shaku Kōzen*, 13–14. Kōzen detailed the events in a letter to Unshō dated early June, 1890. See Itō, *Unshō/Kōzen iboku shū*, 354–55.

108. SUS 2: 164–65, Letter from Unshō to Kōzen, August 7, 1890.

109. SUS 2: 170–71. The letter from Unshō to Dogi is dated August 7, 1890, less than two months following Kōzen's full ordination.

Dharmapāla resolved to do what they could to wrest control of Bodh Gayā from the Hindus.[110] Attempting to establish a constant Buddhist presence at the site, Kōzen, at the behest of Dharmapāla, remained in the Burmese rest house at Bodh Gayā for six months before returning to Ceylon. According to Japanese accounts, they also resolved to collect one thousand yen from each Buddhist community in Burma, Ceylon, Siam, and Japan to purchase and restore the site as a Buddhist pilgrimage center. Working by post in conjunction with a group of clerics back in Japan that included Unshō and Dogi Hōryū, Kōzen helped solicit the necessary funds from Japanese Buddhists.[111] Kōzen, according to Dharmapāla's account, was distraught about being without monastic companions while at Bodh Gayā, but Japanese sources indicate he remained at the temple for six months, despite Dharmapāla's early departure to recruit a monastic contingent to take up residence in their stead.[112]

Kōzen's interactions with Dharmapāla and the growing number of Japanese in Ceylon set in motion an effort on the part of Shaku Unshō and other Japanese Buddhists to assist Kōzen and Dharmapāla in the attempt to place Bodh Gayā in the hands of world Buddhists. The effort within Japan to assist Dharmapāla and South Asian Buddhists in gaining control of Bodh Gayā was given considerable impetus when Dharmapāla and Henry Steel Olcott toured Japan lecturing on the need for world Buddhist unity and the dire plight of Buddhist sites in India.[113] In the wake of their visit and a series of letters updating Unshō about efforts to secure Bodh Gayā by garrisoning a small

110. See Kemper, *Rescued from the Nation*, 186–87. It appears the Mahabodhi Society was formed a bit later, but Kōzen was present when Dharmapala, visiting Bodh Gayā, decided to embark on a mission to retrieve the site for Buddhists. See Jacob Kinnard, "When Is the Buddha Not the Buddha? The Hindu-Buddhist Battle over Bodh Gayā and Its Buddha Image," *Journal of the American Academy of Religion* 68, no. 4 (1998): 817–39 and Alan Trevithick, "British Archaeologists, Hindu Abbots, and Burmese Buddhists: The Mahabodhi Temple at Bodh Gaya, 1811–1877," *Modern Asian Studies* 33, no. 3 (1999): 635–56. Kōzen is mentioned briefly in Alan Michael Trevithick, "A Jerusalem of the Buddhists in British India: 1874–1949" (PhD diss., Harvard University, 1988), 87.

111. Okuyama Naoji, who teaches at Kōya-san University, transliterates the name as Dogi Hōryū in his English-language articles, although the name frequently is romanized as Toki Hōryū. See Okuyama Naoji, "Correspondence between Kumagusu and Dogi Hōryū: On the Newly Found Letters from Kumagusu to Dogi," *Centre for the Study of Japanese Religions Newsletter*, no. 20–21 (Autumn 2010): 20–23.

112. Noguchi, *Shaku Kōzen*, 14–15. Kemper, using Dharmapāla's diaries and other sources states that Kōzen wanted to leave soon after the beginning of the stay, but it appears he remained in India, most likely at Bodh Gayā, until at least May 1891. Noguchi also mentions that Kōzen returned to Ceylon with Dharmapāla. See Kemper, *Rescued from the Nation*, 188n2; 253–54; 451.

113. See Kemper, *Rescued from the Nation*, chapters 2–3, for a detailed account of the visit by the pair to Japan.

contingent of clerics in the Mahābodhi temple—an effort that failed—Unshō worked with a handful of clerics that included Asahi Shūkō, a Jōdo cleric from Tentokuji in Tokyo, Horiuchi Tōkai, Aoshika Shūei, and three others to form the Indo Busseki Kōfuku Kai. Each member was to donate thirty sen per month with the aim of collecting within a year three thousand yen to support a contingent of three Japanese clerics at Bodh Gayā. Unshō wrote to Dogi Hōryū to inform him of the group's efforts, solicit funds, and ask for a letter of introduction for Tōkai Genkō, who planned to visit Minister Hayashi Tadasu to solicit help ascertaining conditions in India pertinent to the efforts to secure Bodh Gayā.[114]

When Kōzen and Dharmapāla returned to Ceylon briefly in mid-1891, Kōzen was met by a disciple of Unshō's, Atō Yūjō, the incumbent at Aizen'in, who brought one thousand yen gathered in Japan to aid with the Bodh Gayā efforts.[115] The following year, Kōzen and Yūjō returned to India to visit important places associated with Buddhism, but their naive plan to acquire these sites failed miserably.[116] In 1893 Kōzen headed back to Ceylon for another brief stay and finally returned to Japan on September 6.

Kōzen regarded Southern Buddhist monastic practice as the fullest expression of the true Buddhist way of life. He hoped to reinvigorate Japanese Buddhism by establishing true Ceylonese-style practice and ordinations in Japan. Back at his home temple, Sanneji, just outside Yokohama, Kōzen set about transforming the religious artifacts, liturgy, and calendar in accordance with his new understanding of Buddhism. Soon after his return to Japan, Kōzen established the Society for the True Lineage of Śākyamuni (Shakuson Shōfū Kai). In an 1893 broadside announcing the creation of the society, Kōzen wrote that the organization was established to revive the true veneration of the Three Jewels (Sanbō)—Buddha, Dharma (Buddhist teaching), and Sangha (Buddhist monastic order)—in Japan in order to strengthen part of the nation's treasure. The broadside called on all to take refuge in the Three Jewels and receive the Five Precepts. It also spells out that manifestations of the Buddha Jewel, which includes "images of Śākyamuni and his relics as well as the bodhi tree that is his 'body of enjoyment' (juyūshin; S. saṃbhogakāya) and so on, are to be reverently worshipped and venerated." The broadside

114. SUS 2: 158–59.

115. According to a letter from Shaku Unshō to Dogi Hōryū, dated 1890 (no month is specified, but the day given is the fourteenth. This probably is a letter from January 14, 1890, judging from its location among the other letters in the volume), Atō was dispatched from Japan with one thousand yen. SUS 2: 133–34. See also MNB 1: 376.

116. See SUS 1: 126, for information concerning Unshō's efforts to oversee the purchase of Buddhist pilgrimage sites from the British.

also calls for reverencing the Jewel of the Dharma, which "first and foremost included the sutras in the language spoken by the Tathāgatha, that is, Pali." The Jewel of the Sangha, or monastic community, according to the broadside indicated those clerics (*sōryo*) "who preserved the legitimate style and regulations (*shōfū seiki*) of Śākyamuni," in other words, monks who had been ordained in a proper fashion and conducted the *uposatha* confession ceremony (*sange fusatsu katsuma*).[117] These points were clarified further in 1898 when Kōzen, with the approval of Shingon denomination's Great Clerical Chancellor (*daisōjō*) Mikami Kaiun (1836–1905), published the regulations and educational principles for the Sanskrit Special Training Center (Bongo Senmon Dōjō) at Sanneji. At the beginning of the document Kōzen warned those in charge of the various branch temples that Sanneji adhered assiduously to the "true/authentic precepts of Śākyamuni" and that it was mandatory that those at the branch temples, particularly the leaders, do the same.[118] In the actual temple rules, Kōzen announced that Sanneji and its branch temples are Precept-Vinaya temples based on the Tathāgata's Pure Transmission of the Elders (Thera) (*Nyorai junsei Jōza denshō no kairitsu dera*).[119] Written after his visit to Siam, where he practiced for nearly a year, as I will detail below, Kōzen uses the phrase in order to describe more precisely a tradition of practice and precept lineage that embraced both Ceylonese and Siamese Buddhism. In the text, Kōzen defined the Sangha as follows.

> Article 7: The Sangha receives and transmits the precept lineage of the Theravāda, pure in the Tathāgata's moral discipline (*Sōgya wa Nyorai seikyō junsei Jōzabu no kaimyaku o jūden su* 僧伽は如来制教純正上座部の戒脈を受伝す)
>
> Article 8: The Sangha receives and maintains the Sanskrit language of the precept lineage of Theravāda, pure in the Tathāgata's moral discipline (*Sōgya wa Nyorai seikyō junsei Jōzabu no Bongo o juji su* 僧伽は如来制教純正上座部の梵語を受持す)
>
> Article 9: The Sangha preserves the Sangha of the Theravāda, pure in the Tathāgata's moral discipline (*Sōgya wa Nyorai seikyō junsei Jōzabu no sōgya o iji su* 僧伽は如来制教純正上座部の僧伽を維持す)[120]

117. Shaku Kōzen, *Shakuson shōfū o kakuchō suru no shui* (Yokohama: Sanneji, 1893), 1–2.

118. Shaku Kōzen, *Sanneji jihō narabi kyōyō ninka kisoku* (Kanagawa: Sanneji, 1908), 1; see also Itō, *Unshō/Kōzen*, 357, "Kokushi" 告示 (1899). The dates for Minami Kaiun are from the Shingon temple Chishakuin website. See http://www.chisan.or.jp/about/rekidai/, accessed October 17, 2016.

119. *Tathāgata*, literally, "the thus come/gone one," is an honorific epithet of a buddha.

120. Shaku Kōzen, *Sanneji jihō*, 3–6.

In the document from 1908, Kōzen used the term "*Jōzabu*," that is, School of the Elders, namely, Theravāda, to describe the precept and monastic lineages of Ceylon and Siam, rather than as a term indicating the Buddhism practiced across much of South and Southeast Asia. In addition, Kōzen employs the word *Bongo*, usually taken to mean Sanskrit, as a more general term for Indic languages of Buddhism that includes Pali and Sanskrit, as he advocates the use of both languages in many documents he wrote from this period delineating proper Buddhist practice.

According to the same document, Kōzen prescribes that young clerics receive the *sāmaṇera* (S. *śrāmaṇera*; J. *shami*) precepts at Sanneji. From amongst the postulants, a group of no more than five promising clerics, upon reaching the age of twenty, would be chosen to travel to Ceylon to receive the full ordination on the ordination platform at Malwatta Mahavihara, where Kōzen had been ordained by Sumaṅgala. Kōzen's efforts were regarded highly enough for the Nippon Yūsen Kaisha, a major Japanese shipping firm, to offer to pay the ticket cost for up to five clerics to travel to Ceylon for the full ordination. Other expenses associated with their overseas study were to be covered by donations from the Shakuson Shōfū Kai. According to Noguchi, their other travel expenses were paid by Hayashi Tadasu, who, at the time, was serving as minister of foreign affairs (gaimu daijin). Although apparently not wildly popular, the effort to forge contacts with the Ceylonese Buddhist order was supported by both government officials and a major shipping concern.[121]

Kōzen managed to send five disciples to Ceylon for ordination, but only two of them returned to Japan to practice as *bhikkhu*. Traveling in four successive waves were Kojima Kaihō, Toya Nindo (later, he changed his surname to Shaku; d. 1951), Kudō Kyōshin, Mukoyama Ryōun, and Yoshimatsu Kaiyū. Although all five clerics were ordained in Ceylon, only Nindo and Kaiyū continued to practice as *bhikkhu* following their return to Japan. Nindo became the incumbent at the Kanagawa temple, Manzōji, and Kaiyū served as incumbent at the Reikanji in Shimane Prefecture.

According to an account by Ishii Ryōjō, one of Kōzen's disciples, Kōzen instituted a range of changes at Sanneji that reflected his conversion to Ceylonese-style Buddhist practice. For one, Kōzen removed the old object of veneration, a statue of the Maitreya, the future Buddha, from the main altar at Sanneji and replaced it with a statue of a seated Śākyamuni that he

---

121. Noguchi, *Shaku Kōzen to Shakuson Shōfū Kai*, 30; Higashimoto Keikichi, "Shakuson Shōfū Kai no hitobito," *Komazawa Daigaku Bukkyōgakubu kenkyū kiyō* 40 (March 1982): 51–61.

FIGURE 1.4. Main altar case at Sanneji. Courtesy of Sanneji. Photograph by the author.

had acquired in Ceylon. Instead of making Maitreya the central object of veneration, Kōzen believed that Śākyamuni should be the center of veneration. According to Andō Sonjin, who was incumbent at Sanneji in the early 2000s and grand-disciple of Nindo, the statue of Śākyamuni was placed in the main temple hall in the existing Japanese-style lacquered shrine cabinet (*zushi*), constructed according to Kōzen's own plans that is embellished with Bodhi-leaf decorations. (The Bodhi leaf seems to have been a popular symbol with many Meiji Buddhists, who placed it not only on altars, but also used it to ornament the covers of Buddhist books and journals, particularly those works concerned with South and Southeast Asian Buddhism.) (See fig. 1.4.) In addition, Ishii mentions that Kōzen continued wearing the Ceylonese-style yellow *bhikkhu* robes and followed Ceylonese-style Buddhist practices at Sanneji, much to the surprise of parishioners. Kōzen's uncle and teacher, Unshō, was also dismayed by the radical changes in practice at Sanneji and by Kōzen's deportment. As Ishii and Tsunemitsu report, Unshō quarreled with Kōzen, his mentee (Unshō was not his ordination master) and junior, both in biological and ordination age, about Kōzen's new style of practice. As was common in Ceylon, Kōzen now would eat meat, if it was offered to him, and he ceased to recognize the legitimacy of Unshō's claims to seniority and authority. As far as Kōzen was concerned, he, not Unshō, was practicing the

Buddhism of Śākyamuni, as passed to Mahākaśyapa and on to the current day in Ceylon.[122]

Despite attracting some high-level lay support, for example, from Hayashi Tadasu, who continued to donate funds to Kōzen's various endeavors, and a coterie of clerical disciples, Kōzen's foreign style of practice did not catch on widely. Nonetheless, Kōzen's efforts came to the attention of the Siamese minister to Japan, who, in 1907, invited Kōzen and a few of his disciples to spend time practicing in Siam. The invitation came at a time of increased cooperation between Siam and Japan, which were the two uncolonized Asian nations at the dawn of the twentieth century. (For more on Siam-Japan relations, see chapter 4.) Departing Japan in October 1907, with his novice disciple, Wada Keihon, Kōzen met in Singapore Sōbita Toya Nindo and Ānanda Yoshimatsu Kaiyū, who had been ordained as *bhikkhu* in Ceylon. From Singapore, the four Japanese continued to Siam, where they participated in the rainy season retreat that began in January 1908. Returning to Japan in December 1908, Kōzen brought with him more than fifty Śākyamuni statues and numerous Pali canonical texts, including a version of the Tripiṭaka, written in Siamese script.[123] The next year, Kōzen held at Sanneji an exhibition of the Siamese Buddha images, along with reliquaries, relics, and other items collected or received in South and Southeast Asia. In a pamphlet listing the artworks and texts on display, Kōzen encouraged Japanese, clerical and lay, regardless of their sectarian affiliation, to view them. A visit to pay reverence to these tangible remnants of the Buddha would "conduce toward the development of unparalleled happiness and experience of the light of the wisdom of the one hundred acts of merit that created the thirty-two major marks of the Buddha as well as contribute to the great benefits of the flourishing of family fortune, national prosperity, and the happiness of humans and all things (*ninpō*)."[124] In addition, a postcard showing some of the Buddha images brought back to Sanneji by Kōzen was produced. It is unclear if the card was used to adver-

122. Ishii's account is reported in MNB 1: 379–82. Ishii started studying with Kōzen in his twenties and was eighty when he related this account to Tsunemitsu in 1968. In my visits to Sanneji in the early 2000s, I was told by the incumbent that it was a seated image of Śākyamuni received in Siam in 1908 that was placed in the shrine instead of the Maitreya image. Unebe records the same story in his survey of the material objects imported to Sanneji. See Unebe Toshiya, "Taikoku Watto/Rajyashiddaramu jiin hoka shozō shahon ni motozuku zōgai Butten no kenkyū," *Grants-in-Aid for Scientific Research* (Nagoya: Nagoya University, 2012), 41–42.

123. MNB 1: 382.

124. Shaku Kaiyū, and Shaku Kōzen, "Tenjiku Shakamuni Butsuzō oyobi Sanzō shōgyō shōrai no en'yu" (Kanagawa: Shōfū Kai, 1909).

島山三會寺正鳳會參款   天竺請來釋迦如來尊像

FIGURE 1.5. Postcard of Siamese Buddha images on display at Sanneji. Courtesy of Sanneji. The
postcard reads, "Venerable images of Śākyamuni Tathāgata imported from Tenjiku. Possessions of the
Shōfūkai at Toriyama Sanneji."

tise the exhibition of the images or was just for commemorative purposes.
(See fig. 1.5.)

In the wake of his one-year sojourn in Siam, Kōzen made other changes
at Sanneji to increase the focus on Śākyamuni as the center of practice and
veneration. Engaging Itō Chūta (1867–1954), the architectural historian and
architect, Kōzen planned to build a large hall, the Shakuōden, dedicated to
Śākyamuni on a hill overlooking Sanneji. Itō, who had traveled through Asia
in search of the roots of Japanese architecture from 1902 to 1905, drew up
plans in 1912 for two possible buildings, one Japanese-style and the other
reminiscent of Thai temple architecture.[125] (See fig. 1.6.)

In addition to planning the Shakuōden, Kōzen tried to shift to Śākyamuni
the focus of local pilgrimage. Placing Śākyamuni statues in thirty-two branch
temples of the Sanneji in the Yokohama area—one for each of the Buddha's
major distinguishing marks—Kōzen created a pilgrimage route for his parishioners and printed for distribution numerous copies of a broadside detailing the route.[126] In this manner Kōzen attempted to replace the far more com-

125. Itō, *Unshō/Kōzen*, 191; 239, note 241; MNB 1: 382. The plans for the Thai-style building
are still extant. I have not seen the plans for the Japanese-style building, however. For more on
Itō's connections with Buddhist travelers to South Asia, see chapter 5.

126. Itō, *Unshō/Kozen*, 192; 239.

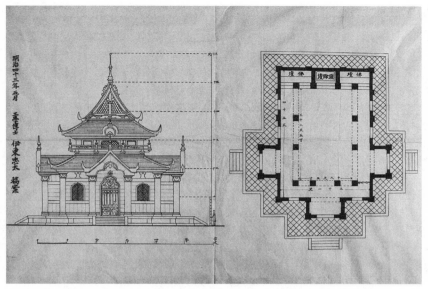

FIGURE 1.6. Itō Chūta's plans for a Siamese-style Buddha Hall at Sanneji, May 1910. Courtesy of the Department of Architecture, University of Tokyo.

mon Kannon- or Kūkai-centered pilgrimage routes with one devoted totally to Śākyamuni Buddha. He also instituted a liturgical calendar at the temple that included the fortnightly observance of the Southern Buddhist confession ceremony (*uposatha*) and, at least as early as 1893, the celebration of Wesak (the South and Southeast Asian Buddhist festival celebrating the birth, awakening, and death of Śākyamuni on the full moon of the fourth lunar month of the year), which, in Sino-Japanese, Unshō called the Beishakyagatsu Mangatsu Kai, that is the "Vesākha Month Full Moon Assembly."[127] Sanneji also became something of a salon for the study of Southern Buddhism. Nanjō Bun'yū, who taught Kōzen Sanskrit before Kōzen's trip to Ceylon; Kawaguchi Ekai, who pioneered the study of Tibetan Buddhism in Japan; and D. T. Suzuki, a disciple of Shaku Sōen's who would soon travel to the United States, all communicated or worked with Kōzen at the temple at the turn of the nineteenth to twentieth century. Along with Kōzen, a number of individuals, each of them having an association with Kōzen, produced polylingual renderings in Japanese, Sanskrit, and Sinhala of the *Verse of Admonishment of the Seven Buddhas* (*Shichibutsu tsūkaige*)—an expression of pan-Asian Buddhist

127. Ōsawa Kōji, *Senjika no Nihon Bukkyō to Nanpō chiiki*, 84–85.

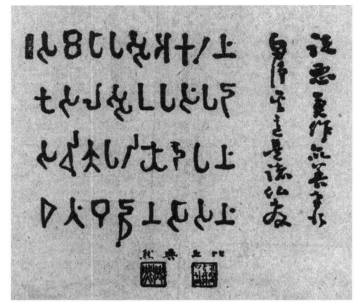

FIGURE 1.7. Shaku Kōzen. *Shichibutsu tsūkaige*, Pali in Brāhmī Script, from *Kaigai Bukkyō jijō* 10, no. 6 (1944).

unity—at the Sanneji and elsewhere.[128] Kōzen wrote at least several versions of the phrase, one in Devanagiri and another in Pali using Brāhmī script (see fig. 1.7). One polylingual calligraphic scroll of the verse by Nanjō Bun'yū, who had studied with Max Müller, was printed in multiple copies, apparently for distribution at Sanneji, where a number of these prints are still extant. (For more on these polylingual calligraphies, see chapter 4.)

In a 1910 pamphlet summarizing the principles of the Shakuson Shōfū Kai and explaining the key practices of the three refuges and the Five Precepts, Kōzen detailed the goal of the society and, one must presume, the purpose of

128. The verse, which is found in the *Dhammapada*, verse 183, as well as numerous other sources, reads, "Refraining from all that is detrimental,/The attainment of what is wholesome,/ The purification of one's mind:/This is the instruction of awakened ones" (*shoaku makusa/ shuzen bugyō/jijō goi/ze shobukkyō*; in Pali the verse reads: *sabbapāpassa akaraṇaṃ/kusalassa upasampadā/sacittapariyodanaṃ/etam buddhāna sāsanaṃ*). See John Ross Carter and Mahinda Palihawadana, *The Dhammapada: A New English Translation with the Pali Text, and for the First English Translation of the Commentary's Explanation of the Verses with Notes* (New York: Oxford University Press, 1987), 44. According to Ketelaar, the *shichibutsu tsūkaige* was emphasized during the mid-Meiji period by Buddhist authors hoping to bridge sectarian differences. See James Edward Ketelaar, *Of Heretics and Martyrs in Meiji Japan* (Princeton, NJ: Princeton University Press, 1990), 185–86.

the various changes that he had instituted at the Sanneji and its branch temples.[129] Like Sōen nearly twenty years earlier, Kōzen lamented the factionalism of Buddhism in Asia, particularly in Japan. In order to create a Buddhism that could flourish in the civilized world, a Buddhism that was unified in belief, practice, and purpose was necessary. Kōzen argued that a return to the teachings of Śākyamuni Buddha was essential for Buddhism to recover its vitality.

> Buddhism is divided into northern and southern lineages and there are hundreds, even thousands, of denominations; however, the original founding teacher for all of them is Śākyamuni Buddha, the teacher to whom we all are greatly indebted. There is no true Buddhism that sets Śākyamuni's teachings aside. Therefore in order truly to illuminate that which makes Buddhism Buddhism, one must, at all costs, return to the living Buddhism of Śākyamuni. We must throw away all of the sectarian teachings and return to the great original Buddhism.[130]

The attempt to overcome the sectarianism of Japanese and even global Buddhism was shared by a number of Japanese Buddhists who experienced Buddhism in South and Southeast Asia firsthand. Sōen, as noted above, sought to rally most Japanese Buddhists around the veneration of Śākyamuni. Oda Tokunō during his two-year journey in Siam likewise found the lack of sectarianism in Siamese Buddhism remarkable. Although the Sangha in Siam was divided into two schools according to their ordination lineage, Oda observed, with regard to Buddhist doctrines, Buddhism in Siam remained unified. Much like Kōzen, Kawaguchi Ekai, as we will see in chapter 2, became convinced by his experience and study of Buddhism in South Asia that sectarianism had vitiated Japanese Buddhism. Revival of the tradition depended on returning to the original teachings of Buddhism, which for Kawaguchi, unlike Kōzen, included much of Mahayana.

In the pamphlet *Shakuson Shōfū*, much as in the 1893 broadside mentioned above, Kōzen details how to take the Three Refuges (P. *tisaraṇa*; J. *sankie*), rendering the Pali verses in katakana and explaining the import of each, concluding that the refuges serve as the "fundamental life of a Buddhist."[131] Expounding on the first refuge, "'*Buddan saranan gacchāmi*' [I take refuge in the Buddha]," Kōzen remarked, "This truly is the wondrous sound of the

---

129. The Three Refuges are taken in the Buddha, the Dharma, and the Sangha. The Five Precepts taken by the laity are not to take life; not to steal; not to commit adultery; not to lie; and not to use intoxicants.

130. Shaku Kōzen, *Shakuson Shōfū* (Toriyama: Sanneji, 1900), 7–8.

131. Shaku Kōzen, *Shakuson Shōfū*, 14.

sweet dew of immortality."[132] While Sōen and Oda had remarked on the unity of worship in Southern Buddhism and Sōen even strategically called for embracing Śākyamuni as the central object of worship for most Buddhists in Japan, Kōzen saw the benefit of worshipping all other buddhas, bodhisattvas, and kami as ultimately flowing from Śākyamuni's virtue. Even the this-worldly benefits granted by Konpira and Inari ultimately derived from the "pure Thusness Dharma Body that is Śākyamuni Buddha" (*shōjō shinnyo hosshin taru Budda Shakuson*). Kōzen elaborated on each of the Five Precepts, once again providing them in Pali, describing them as "the crucial standards for achieving the proper character of a Buddhist."[133] Having set forth the fundamental practices for the Buddhist laity, Kōzen concluded the pamphlet with a summary of how best to revitalize Buddhism in Japan.

> If we talk about why today Buddhism is viewed from the worldly perspective as an encumbrance and has no place in education, it mostly is because of the sins of the [Buddhist] teachers. It is retribution for the clerics not teaching. Throughout the teachings of the Buddha there are the Five Precepts, the Ten Good Precepts, and the universal standard of Gratitude for the Four Obligations. His guidance of us is complete, perfect, and without deficiencies. Lay believers, believe deeply in the Three Refuges, receive the Five Precepts, practice the Ten Good Precepts. It is clearer than looking at a burning flame how lofty a mind of the Way and how perfect a character one will obtain if one's additional energy is used to cultivate the spirit with the two teachings of meditative concentration (*zenjō*) and wisdom (*egaku*).

The pamphlet ends with Kōzen's scathing condemnation of the Buddhism of his day, blaming the current state of affairs on the evil tendencies of a disorderly Mahayana Buddhism. Kōzen wrote, "We will purify the independent streams of a bewildered Buddhism and clear away the tangled brambles. Let us endeavor to single-mindedly return to the fundamentals of Buddhism, proclaiming with a roar and elucidating the fundamental of fundamentals and the essential of essentials that are the true teachings of Śākyamuni."[134]

The pamphlet thus provided an emphasis on Śākyamuni derived from Kōzen's experiences in South Asia and his studies. While echoing, perhaps, the originary emphasis on Pali texts and South Asian Buddhism found in European scholarship, Kōzen did not reject the this-worldly powers of the buddhas, bodhisattvas, and kami. The print technology that made Kōzen's

---

132. Shaku Kōzen, *Shakuson Shōfū*, 14.
133. Shaku Kōzen, *Shakuson Shōfū*, 25.
134. Shaku Kōzen, *Shakuson Shōfū*, 46–47.

pamphlet widely available could disseminate traditional forms of religious praxis as well as disenchanted, Protestant ones.[135]

Kōzen's experiences in Ceylon and India led him to question completely the legitimacy of Japanese Buddhism in its present state. His emphasis on Pali texts as the fundamental written source for Buddhists reflects the prioritization of those materials by Ceylonese clerics and scholars, who had turned to those materials with fervor since the eighteenth century.[136] Like such European Buddhologists as T. W. Rhys Davids, Kōzen was convinced of the primacy of Southern Buddhism and the teachings as they were presented in the Pali version of the Buddhist scriptures. Unlike many European and American orientalists, however, Kōzen did not dismiss contemporaneous Ceylonese Buddhism as a decadent corruption of the pure teachings that were preserved within the Pali canon itself. Rather, Kōzen held that the "living" Buddhist tradition in Ceylon transmitted the essential teachings of Śākyamuni Buddha.[137]

Believing that only the precept lineage of the School of the Elders, that is, the Theravāda school, was valid, Kōzen dismissed all Japanese clerical ordinations as inefficacious and attempted to establish the Ceylonese precept lineage in Japan. Maintaining a self-sustaining Southern Buddhist order in Japan, however, necessitated having at least four other monks ordained in the same lineage in order to have the quorum necessary to conduct full monks' ordinations. Unable to accomplish this goal, Kōzen could not conduct Ceylonese ordinations in Japan. After the death of his disciple Nindo, who became the incumbent at Sanneji following the death of Kōzen's disciple-successor as incumbent of Sanneji, Mukoyama Ryōun, the Ceylonese ordination movement begun by Kōzen in Japan died out. Higashimoto Keikichi (born as Tarō; 1912– 93) reports, based in part on conversations with Nindo, that Kōzen on his death bed said mournfully to Nindo, "My work has accomplished nothing." Consoling his teacher, Nindo replied, "No, Master, have faith in the principle

135. Green, in *Bombay Islam*, 92 ff., also suggests that this was true of technology and enchantment in the case of South Asian Islam.

136. For a detailed analysis of the textual turn in Ceylonese Buddhism in eighteenth-century Ceylon, see Blackburn, *Buddhist Learning*.

137. Rhys Davids wrote, for example, that "it is impossible rightly to understand any one phase of later Buddhism in any country, without starting from the standpoint of the earlier Buddhism of the Pāli Piṭakas. No one can write the history of later Buddhism, say in Thailand or China, without being thoroughly acquainted with the Pāli Suttas. The very interest of the later inquiries lies in the causes that have produced the manifold changes they will disclose." Cited in Guy Richard Welbon, *The Buddhist Nirvāṇa and Its Western Interpreters* (Chicago: University of Chicago Press, 1968), 225.

of cause and effect. What you have done will bear its own fruit. The principle of cause and effect taught by the Tathāgata is not crazy."[138] According to the account of the current incumbent of Sanneji, Andō Sonjin, sometime after Nindo's death the statue of Śākyamuni was removed from the main altar to a reception room for parishioners and replaced with the former image of worship, a statue of Maitreya. The liturgical calendar reverted to the usual Shingon style and the Southern Buddhist period of Kōzen's and Nindo's incumbencies became little more than a historical curiosity. Today Sanneji functions as a typical Shingon temple, with regular performances of the *goma* (esoteric fire ceremony) ritual taking place in the main hall of the temple in front of several large statues of Śākyamuni brought to Sanneji from Siam by Kōzen. Although Kōzen was unable to establish a Theravāda Sangha in Japan as he had hoped, he did raise awareness in Japan of the Buddhism that was thriving in Ceylon, Siam, and across Southeast Asia. Until his death, he also had served as one of the foremost authorities on Pali language, training such individuals as Kawaguchi Ekai and Suzuki Daisetsu in Indic languages at a time when such teaching was not readily available. During the Fifteen Years' War, when the Society for the Study of Overseas Buddhism published a special issue of its Japanese-language journal, *Kaigai Bukkyō jijō*, devoted to Shaku Kōzen that highlighted his pioneering accomplishments.[139]

Stimulated by the translation of such works as Olcott's *A Buddhist Catechism*, Arnold's *Light of Asia*, and Thomas Rhys Davids's *Buddhism* into Japanese, a number of clerics followed Kōzen and Sōen to Ceylon. Some were independent travelers but others were dispatched by the leaders of their denominations of Buddhism to study overseas and forge connections with Buddhists and Buddhist sympathizers in Ceylon, India, and other Buddhist countries in the region. Chief among these denominations were the main branches of Jōdo Shinshū. The regularization of shipping between Japan and India allowed more Japanese Buddhists to travel to South Asia for long-term study of languages, participation in South Asian Buddhist practice, and the strengthening of alliances with Buddhists across the region. The publication of Olcott's *A Buddhist Catechism* in 1886 and the visit of Olcott and Dharmapāla to Japan in 1889 also heightened the interest in South Asia among the Japanese. Akai Toshio has noted the attention that Japanese paid to the *Catechism*, for they quickly arranged its translation into Japanese. Akai observes, "This expressed the great expectation which Japanese Buddhists entertained, and the importance they attached to the advent of the 'white Buddhists.' The pub-

138. Higashimoto Keikichi, "Shakuson Shōfū Kai," 59–60.
139. *Kaigai Bukkyō jijō* 10, no. 3 (1944). For more on the society and its journal see chapter 5.

lication of *The Buddhist Catechism* triggered enormous interest in the Theosophical Society and its activities in British India."[140] Theosophy thus helped stimulate Japanese attention to Buddhists in parts of Asia that prior to the Meiji era had been relatively understudied by the Japanese and Theosophists; for example, Olcott, Dharmapāla, and others, helped facilitate Japanese study in South Asia as well.

Following Kōzen and Sōen to Ceylon and India for extended periods of study were Yoshitsura Hōgen (1865–93); Azuma Onjō (1867–93); Tokuzawa Chiezō (1871–1908); Koizumi Ryōtai (1851–1938); Asakura Ryōshō (1856–1910); and Kawakami Teishin (1864–1922). All of these overseas students were clerics from various sects of Jōdo Shinshū and spent from two to eight years studying abroad, with Kawakami residing in South Asia for eight years, including five years in Calcutta and Darjeeling. By late 1890 all six of these men were studying along with Kōzen at the Vidyodaya Piriveṇa.[141] In keeping with Jōdo Shin's rejection of the home-leaving (*shukke*) style ordination, however, the Jōdo Shin clerics did not undertake either the novice (*sāmaṇera*) or the full *bhikkhu* ordinations in Ceylon. The flows of people, translated works on Buddhism, and new texts between Japan and South Asia catalyzed Japanese Buddhists to reconsider the relationship between Japanese Buddhism and the forms of the tradition found in South and Southeast Asia, to which the Japanese had little direct exposure prior to the late 1880s.

In his essay on the use of the term "Theravāda" as a general rubric for all of Southeast Asian Buddhism, Todd Perreira has highlighted how the interactions between South and Southeast Asian Buddhists and Japanese, starting at the World's Parliament of Religions at the Columbian Exposition in 1893, generated a new sense of Buddhism as a pan-Asian tradition. At the same time, Perreira observes, Buddhists in Asia sought to demarcate what distinguished their own forms of practice and scholarship from that found in other parts of Asia. Like Kōzen, Sōen, and Oda, many Asian Buddhists would divide the Buddhist world into Southern/Southwestern and Northern/Northeastern Buddhism, with partisans from each region arguing for the distinctiveness and superiority of their own tradition. Given the emphasis on originary models of religious development stressing the gradual distortion of traditions over time and the prioritization of Pali sources as the oldest, purest expressions

140. Akai. "Theosophical Accounts in Japanese Buddhist Publications of the Late Nineteenth Century," 188.

141. These names and dates, as well as the length of time spent overseas for each person are found in Okuyama Naoji, "Meiji Indo ryūgakuseitachi ga mita 'Hiei' to 'Kongō' no kōkai," *Tōyō Daigaku Ajia Bunka Kenkyūsho kenkyū nenpō* 43 (2008): 65–81.

of the Buddha's teaching, Japanese Buddhists were presented with the heavy burden of demonstrating the validity, if not the superiority, of Japanese forms of Buddhist practice.[142] Although the Japanese presented their perspective on the topic in English most prominently at the World's Parliament of Religions, as I have shown above, travelers and overseas students like Sōen and Oda had been quick to make those distinctions and stress the superiority of Mahayana Buddhism in Japanese in the late 1880s. Shaku Unshō also stressed that point, which caused a rupture with Kōzen, who returned from Ceylon convinced that only the Pali-based stream of Buddhism was authentic.

There is little doubt that for the English-speaking world, particularly in the United States and Europe, the World's Parliament of Religions provided the first glimpse of the diversity of regional Asian Buddhisms that helped foster the view of Buddhism as a world religion. Particularly remarkable, however, is that most of the Asian Buddhists to appear at the World's Parliament were not strangers to each other, having had numerous exchanges, either in person or by post, before they ever set out to attend the event. Two of the Japanese delegates—Sōen and Noguchi Zenshirō (Fukudō) previously had been to India, Ceylon, and/or Siam, where they had interacted with Olcott, Dharmapāla, Sumaṅgala, and other non-Japanese Buddhists and Buddhist supporters. By the time of the World's Parliament, as Richard Seager noted, Sōen, Dharmapāla, and Sumaṅgala, for whom Dharmapāla served as a proxy, all were members of the Mahābodhi Society.[143] Hirai Kinza (1859–1916), another lay member of the Japanese delegation, founded the Oriental Hall (*Orientaru Hōru*) English-language school in Kyoto and the first Japanese Theosophical Society Lodge. He also played a pivotal role in bringing Olcott to Japan in 1889, by sending Noguchi Zenshirō to the meeting of the Theosophical Society in Adyar to work out details for Olcott's visit.[144] In addition, through Kōzen's cooperation with Dharmapāla and the Japanese Indo Busseki Kōfuku Kai, another member of the Japanese delegation, Dogi Hōryū, was drawn into this network of Asian Buddhists striving to enhance transregional contacts and revive Buddhist sites in South Asia.

The intertwining of themes in the speeches by the Buddhists at the World's Parliament thus should not come as a surprise, given Kōzen and Sōen's on-

142. Perreira, "Whence Theravāda?"

143. Richard Hughes Seager, *The World's Parliament of Religions: The East/West Encounter, Chicago, 1893* (Bloomington: Indiana University Press, 1995), 109.

144. Yoshinaga Shin'ichi, "Hirai Kinza ni okeru Meiji Bukkyō no kokusaika ni kansuru shūkyō shi/bunka shiteki kenkyū" [Hirai Kinza and the Globalization of Japanese Buddhism in the Meiji Era, a Cultural and Religio-Historical Study], Grants-in-Aid for Scientific Research (Category C) (Kyoto, 2007), 9–12.

going contacts with Buddhists in Ceylon and Siam. Sōen's well-received re-marks, which were delivered by Noguchi, presented the principle of cause and effect in Buddhism in his address, "The Law of Cause and Effect, As Taught by the Buddha," stressing the scientific nature of the teaching, much as Olcott had done in *A Buddhist Catechism*.[145] In broad strokes, Sōen described the principle of cause and effect as universal, as well as without beginning or end. Human misery and happiness were not random but "bodily health, mate-rial wealth, wonderful genius, unnatural suffering are infallible expressions of the law of causality which governs every particle of the universe, every portion of human conduct."[146] Without stressing distinctions with regard to how causality was understood by Ceylonese, that is, Hinayana, Buddhists and Mahayanists, as he had done in *Seinan no Bukkyō*, Sōen highlighted pan-Buddhist acceptance of the fundamental principles. "According to the differ-ent sects of Buddhism, more or less different views are entertained in regard to the law of causality, but so far they agree in regarding it as the law of na-ture, independent of the will of Buddha, and still more of the will of human beings."[147] Snodgrass has noted that like Sōen, Dogi Hōryū and Chandradat Chudhadharn of Siam also noted the importance of this principle and the absence of a creator god in Buddhism. As Snodgrass suggests, this attention to cause and effect probably resulted from Buddhist efforts to portray Bud-dhism as consonant with modern science. At the same time, the ongoing in-teractions between Sōen, Dharmapāla, Olcott, Kōzen, Dogi, Noguchi, and others in South Asia and Japan that preceded their appearance in Chicago may also help explain the overlapping topics in their addresses at the World's Parliament.[148]

Following his visit to America to attend the World's Parliament of Re-ligions in 1893, Sōen also arranged for the translation of another English-language presentation of Buddhism. Having met Paul Carus while attending the World's Parliament of Religions in 1893, Sōen worked with his lay disciple, Suzuki Daisetsu (1870–1966), to translate Paul Carus's 1894 *Gospel of the Bud-*

145. Shaku, Soyen (Shaku Sōen), "The Law of Cause and Effect, as Taught by Buddha," in *The World's Parliament of Religions; an Illustrated and Popular Story of the World's First Parliament of Religions, Held in Chicago in Connection with the Columbian Exposition of 1893*, ed. John Henry Barrows (Chicago: Parliament Publishing Company, 1893), 2:829–31.

146. Shaku, Soyen, "The Law of Cause and Effect," 2: 831.

147. Soyen, Shaku, "The Law of Cause and Effect," 2:831.

148. Judith Snodgrass, *Presenting Japanese Buddhism to the West: Orientalism, Occidental-ism, and the Columbian Exposition* (Chapel Hill: University of North Carolina Press, 2003), 211–12. Dogi Hōryū's speech, "Buddhism in Japan," is in Barrows, *The World's Parliament of Religions*, 1:543–49; Chudhadharn's address is found at 1:645–49.

dha into Japanese as *Budda no fukuin*.[149] The Japanese version was introduced by Sōen and carried a biography of Carus by Suzuki. According to Sōen, his intention in publishing a translation of the work, which summarized the teachings of Śākyamuni, was to demonstrate how Buddhism was understood in the United States while using the biography of Śākyamuni to make Buddhism more accessible to the Japanese public, particularly young people.[150]

Soon after the World's Parliament of Religions ended in the early autumn of 1893, Nippon Yūsen Kaisha, with whom Dharmapāla had tried to arrange subsidized pilgrimages to South Asia for Japanese Buddhists, began its first regular shipping service to Bombay. Although the cost of travel remained relatively high, increased traffic between India and Japan helped make passage on steamships to South Asia more accessible to Japanese Buddhists. As the first wave of Japanese Buddhists returning from South Asia, Europe, and the United States began teaching in seminaries, universities, and at their temples, a new generation of Japanese Buddhists was exposed to information about the practice of Buddhism in South Asia and the rapidly evolving understanding of the relationship between early Buddhism and the East Asian tradition. The prioritization of the Buddhist materials in Sanskrit and other Indic languages and the growing accessibility of South Asia to the Japanese spurred pilgrimage and overseas study in South Asia across sectarian lines among Japanese Buddhists. At this very early stage in the emergence of institutions for the study of Indic languages and Southern Buddhism, Shaku Kōzen's Sanskrit Special Training Center at Sanneji introduced some who chose to head to South Asia to Sanskrit, Pali, and the practices of Southern Buddhism. One of the most prominent students to take advantage of Kōzen's learning at the Center was Kawaguchi Ekai, who would study there while preparing for his journey to Tibet at the dawn of the twentieth century.

149. Pōru Kērasu [Paul Carus], *Budda no fukuin*, trans. Suzuki Daisetsu (Tokyo: Satō Shigenobu, 1895).

150. Snodgrass, *Presenting Japanese Buddhism to the West*, 246.

2

Kawaguchi Ekai, Globalization, and the Promotion of Lay Buddhism in Japan

Kawaguchi Ekai (1866–1945), an early traveler to South Asia, is far better known for his exploits outside Japan and his contributions to the development of Tibetan studies in his home country than for his efforts to transform Japanese Buddhism through his scholarship and the founding of several reform-oriented lay Buddhist organizations. Scholars and writers overwhelmingly have pored over the details of Kawaguchi's adventures in Nepal, Tibet, and to a far lesser degree, India. This is understandable in that Kawaguchi, hoping to find Buddhist texts more accurate than those extant in Japan, had made Tibet, first and foremost, and Nepal the destinations for his various journeys to South Asia. Without doubt, Kawaguchi's experiences in those two countries were formative for him, and relationships he formed with Tibetans remained important to him for the rest of his life.

It is surprising, then, to realize that the bulk of the time Kawaguchi spent outside Japan was not in Tibet and Nepal. While Kawaguchi spent approximately eighteen years—in two separate trips—living in South Asia, nearly thirteen and a half years were spent studying and traveling in India and only four and a half years touring and residing in Tibet and Nepal. The journeys into Tibet, particularly the first, covert one, were daring and adventurous, thus deserving the popular and scholarly scrutiny they have received. It was these portions of his travels to which Kawaguchi himself devoted the most attention in writing, in such chronicles as *Chibetto ryokō ki* (translated as, *Three Years in Tibet*), *Nyūzō ki* (Record of Entering Tibet), and *Chibetto nyūkoku ki* (Record of Entering the Country of Tibet), and others. Kawaguchi and those who have written about him have relatively ignored the much longer period in India, during which time Kawaguchi studied Sanskrit and Tibetan with such teachers as Sarat Chandra Das, P. K. Patankar, and others.

Similarly, the thirty-year period—a major chunk of his seventy-nine-year life—that begins with Kawaguchi's return from his travels in 1915 and ends with his death in 1945, particularly Kawaguchi's efforts at reforming Japanese Buddhism, has received less attention than his Himalayan adventures, especially in non-Japanese scholarship. Several Japanese scholars, beginning with Kawaguchi's nephew, Kawaguchi Akira, have helped erase that lacuna to some extent. It was during the last portion of his life, a time punctuated only by a few brief trips to China in 1929, 1933, and 1935 to meet with the Panchen Lama, that Kawaguchi devoted himself to scholarship and teaching concerning Tibetan Buddhism, language, and culture. In the long period following his return from the second South Asian sojourn, Kawaguchi concluded his intensive comparisons of the Tibetan, Sanskrit, and Chinese versions of a variety of Buddhist texts and attempted to actualize his new understanding. His study ultimately led Kawaguchi to reject many aspects of received Japanese Buddhist practice, while promoting a lay Buddhism centered on the veneration of Śākyamuni Buddha and strict adherence to the Five Precepts.

Kawaguchi Ekai came of age during the worst period of Bakumatsu-Meiji anti-Buddhist violence, as did many other Buddhist travelers of the late nineteenth century.[1] The son of a wooden bucket and barrel maker in Sakai, Kawaguchi withdrew from formal schooling at the age of eleven to work in the family business. Although no longer a regular day student, Kawaguchi continued to follow a series of scholarly interests, studying Chinese classics, then English, and even serving for a time as an elementary school teacher. Inspired by his reading of a biography of the Buddha, Kawaguchi, then fifteen, became deeply interested in Buddhism, taking vows of abstinence from drinking alcohol, sexual relations, and meat eating, including fish. Kawaguchi began to study with a local Buddhist cleric, but he refrained from ordination because of resistance from his family. In 1888 he moved to Tokyo, where he began to study at the Tetsugakkan and, in 1890, was ordained by Unno

---

1. A brief biography of Kawaguchi is found in the first chapters of Scott Berry, *A Stranger in Tibet: The Adventures of a Zen Monk* (London: Collins, 1990). The best biography in Japanese is Okuyama, Naoji, *Hyōden Kawaguchi Ekai* (Tokyo: Chūō Kōron Shinsha, 2003). Chronologies of Kawaguchi's life are available in Takayama Ryūzō, *Sekai o kakeru Kawaguchi Ekai* (Uji, Japan: Ōbakushū Seinensō no Kai, 2006), 34–37, and in *Kawaguchi Ekai chosakushū* 16:754–62. (Hereafter KECS.) The most detailed chronology is found in Sakai-shi Hakubutsukan, "<*Shūki tokubetsu ten*> *Kawaguchi Ekai: Bukkyō no genten o motometa hito*," ed. Sakai-shi Hakubutsukan (Sakai: Sakai-shi Hakubutsukan, 1993), 104–11. See also Joseph M. Kitagawa, "Kawaguchi Ekai: A Pious Adventurer and Tibet," in *Reflections on Tibetan Culture: Essays in Memory of Turrell V. Wylie*, ed. Lawrence Epstein and Richard Sherburne (Lewiston, NY: Edwin Mellen Press, 1990), 279–94.

Kizen of the Ōbaku denomination. For most of the rest of his life, Kawaguchi had a complicated relationship with the Ōbaku denomination, bouncing in and out of the order and, eventually, returning to lay life for good in 1926. As with many institutions with which he engaged over the course of his life-time, Kawaguchi maintained a critical stance toward the Ōbaku denomination even while serving as a clerical member. Dissatisfied with the conditions of Ōbaku Zen and the life he was forced to lead as the incumbent of the Gohyakurakan-ji in Tokyo, Kawaguchi stepped down from his position.

Abandoning his clerical rank briefly, Kawaguchi deepened his ascetic practice by following the prohibition against taking meals after noon. He also began the intensive study of the Chinese Buddhist canon that was housed at one of the subtemples of the Ōbaku head temple, Manpukuji. In so doing, Kawaguchi planned to create an accessible Japanese translation of the Chinese Buddhist texts. As he examined the canon intensively from 1891 to 1894, however, he grew doubtful about the orthodoxy of the Japanese Buddhist tradition and the reliability of the texts that had become part of the received canon. Outlining his growing concerns in the introductory pages of his account of his travels to Tibet, *Chibetto ryokō ki*, Kawaguchi comments that, in particular, variant translations of the same texts into Chinese by different translators often were inconsistent.

The key to resolving these issues was finding the Sanskrit versions of the translated texts, which Kawaguchi had been led to believe existed in India, Nepal, and Tibet. In all likelihood, Kawaguchi was aware, through his studies with Nanjō, as well as from translations and journal articles, of the state of European and American scholarship about Buddhism, as he mentions the scholarly claims that although original texts (*gensho*) were no longer extant in India, they were reportedly available in Tibet and Nepal.[2] Furthermore, Kawaguchi contended that according to European scholars, the translations into Tibetan of Mahayana texts were far more accurate than those into Chinese.[3] Retrospectively, in the 1915 serial newspaper article *Nyūzō ki*, Kawaguchi wrote that he found it lamentable that in Buddhist countries the Sanskrit

---

2. Kawaguchi, *Nyūzō ki* in KECS 14:5–6. (The volumes do not provide running pagination. Page numbers start over for each anthologized item.)

3. Max Müller wrote, for example, "The Sacred Books of the Buddhists in Japan are all, or nearly all, Chinese translations of Sanskrit originals. Many of these translations, however, are known to be very imperfect, either because the Chinese translators misapprehended the peculiar Sanskrit of the originals, or because the Indian translators were not able to express themselves correctly in Chinese. Hence the same texts had often to be translated again and again, and of the principal sacred texts used in Japan, the Sukhāvatī-vyūha, 'the Description of the Land of Bliss,' there are no less than twelve Chinese translations." Müller, *Biographical Essays*, 184–85.

texts were not being studied but already in Europe scholars were advancing their command of Sanskrit and Tibetan in order to investigate the nature of the Indic Buddhist materials.[4] It was the purported availability of the Tibetan and Sanskrit texts in the Himalayan region that convinced Kawaguchi to embark on his journey.[5] His decision to head to the Asian subcontinent to pursue his search for original Buddhist materials was made against the growing trend in Japan to look to continental Asia as a site of exploration, a nexus for exchange, and a source of Buddhist renewal.

Along with the concern for other parts of Buddhist Asia, information about "Lamaism" and the Himalayan region also spread in Japan, stimulating an interest with Buddhism in Tibet and Nepal, both of which regions remained relatively inaccessible to Japanese at this time. No doubt the growing prominence of Tibetan Buddhism in China and the machinations of the British, Chinese, and Russians to gain a foothold (or more) in the Tibetan region heightened awareness of Tibet within Japan.[6] In addition, efforts by such scholars as Nanjō Bun'yū and Yang Wenhui (1837–1911), who sought to broaden the range of texts that formed the basis of Buddhist scholarship in East Asia, also helped bring Tibet to the attention of Buddhists in Japan. Max Müller, with whom Nanjō had studied, pushed his Japanese colleague to travel to India and Tibet and acquire texts in Sanskrit and Tibetan, for these, Müller believed, conveyed the earliest and, hence, most authentic Buddhist teachings. Nanjō probably stimulated interest in these early Buddhist texts at institutions with which he was connected, for example, the Tetsugakkan, founded by Inoue Enryō (1858–1919), which was where Kawaguchi studied from 1888 to 1891.[7]

Kawaguchi, who entered Tibet on July 4, 1900, was the first Japanese to arrive in Lhasa, but he soon was joined by Teramoto Enga (1870–1940), a Higashi Honganji cleric, and Narita Yasuteru (1864–1915), who had been sent by the Japanese Foreign Ministry, later in December 1901. Ōtani Kōzui (1876–1948), the head of the Nishi Honganji, initiated a series of contacts with Tibetan Buddhists, including sending a delegation to Wutaishan to visit with the Dalai Lama in 1911. Kōzui also brought a delegation of Tibetans to his

4. Kawaguchi, *Nyūzō ki* in KECS 14: 5–6.

5. Kawaguchi, *Chibetto ryokō ki*. KECS 1:2–3.

6. On the prominence of Tibetan Buddhism in nineteenth-century China, see Gray Tuttle, *Tibetan Buddhists in the Making of Modern China* (New York: Columbia University Press, 2005).

7. Naoji Okuyama, succinctly traces the spread of interest in late nineteenth-century Japan in "The Tibet Fever among Japanese Buddhists of the Meiji Era," trans. Rolf Giebel, in *Images of Tibet in the 19th and 20th Centuries*, ed. Monica Esposito (Paris: École française d'Extrême-Orient, 2008), 210–14.

villa, Nirakusō, in 1911, where they studied Japanese and taught Tibetan to his students and some Japanese military advisers. As part of the exchange, Kōzui dispatched Aoki Bunkyō (1886–1956) and Tada Tōkan (1890–1967) to Tibet in 1913. The latter cleric formally entered the Sera monastery, became a confidant of the Dalai Lama, and returned to Japan in 1924 with a wealth of Tibetan texts and in-depth training in Tibetan Buddhism. For much of the Taishō period, as Okuyama Naoji suggests, the Buddhist world in Japan was in the throes of "Tibet fever" that began with Kawaguchi's adventures.

Kawaguchi spent the better part of twenty-one years getting ready for and engaging in two prolonged periods in India, Nepal, and Tibet. Prior to heading to South Asia, Kawaguchi began the study of Sanskrit and Pali with the best teachers then available in Japan and, judging from his later writings, familiarized himself with the European and American Buddhist scholarship available in Japan. While studying languages with a series of Japanese teachers, Kawaguchi also garnered as much firsthand information as possible about the conditions in South Asia. At the Tetsugakkan, the school that grew into Tōyō University, Kawaguchi studied with Nanjō Bun'yū and, perhaps, Shaku Unshō, who both were lecturing at the school at that time. In 1895, Kawaguchi went to the Mejiro Sōen, an academy founded by Shaku Unshō to institute reforms in precept practice in Japan. In particular, at the academy Unshō emphasized the observance of the Ten Good Precepts (Jūzenkai) by the laity and clergy, founding the popular organization the Jūzenkai to further these efforts more widely. In this effort, Unshō continued the work of the Shingon cleric Jiun Onkō (1718–1805) during the Edo period to popularize the observance of this set of precepts. Aimed at avoiding unwholesome actions of body, speech, and mind, the Ten Good Precepts proscribed killing, stealing, sexual misconduct, lying, malicious speech, verbal abuse, idle gossip, covetousness, ill-will, and wrong views.[8]

After a brief time working with Unshō, Kawaguchi moved to Sanneji to study Sanskrit and Pali with Kōzen, who, in the 1890s, was probably the most erudite scholar of Pali in Japan. Unlike his teacher, Unshō, who emphasized the Jūzenkai, however, Kōzen made central the veneration of Śākyamuni and the practice of the Five Precepts (Gokai) by members of the Shakuson Shōfū Kai.[9] Like Unshō, Kōzen adhered strictly to the Vinaya regulations and the ten novice precepts, although Kōzen used the Theravāda rather than the Dharmaguptaka version. Kōzen urged lay members of his group to follow the Five

8. These translations of the ten unwholesome actions are from PDB, 1086.
9. See chapter 1. Also, Shaku Kōzen, *Shakuson shōfū*, 1–2.

Precepts, which banned killing, stealing, sexual misconduct, lying, and consuming alcoholic drinks. According to Kawaguchi's later accounts, the year of study with Kōzen left a lasting mark on him. In particular, Kōzen's attempt to place veneration of Śākyamuni Buddha at the center of Buddhist practice in Japan became an important element in groups formed by Kawaguchi after his return from Tibet, as did the emphasis on following the Five Precepts. Kawaguchi, however, took issue with Kōzen's rejection of Mahayana Buddhism and embrace of Ceylonese Buddhism as "genuine Buddhism" (*junsei Bukkyō*), claiming that Kōzen's attitudes amounted to little more than narrow parochialism. Kawaguchi hoped to continue studying Pali with Kōzen without having to embrace his other attitudes toward Buddhism, but Kōzen demanded that any cleric practicing in his temple accept the true Buddhism and wear the yellow triple robe of a true Buddhist *bhikkhu*. According to Kawaguchi, Kōzen even suggested that Kawaguchi give up his efforts to head to Tibet in order to practice real Buddhism in Ceylon, but Kawaguchi refused to relinquish his plans and his faith in the truth of Mahayana Buddhism. As a result, in early 1897, Kōzen forced Kawaguchi to leave Sanneji.[10] Kawaguchi left the temple and headed back to Tokyo, where he announced that he would embark on a trip to Tibet.[11]

Later that year, Kawaguchi finally departed for Nepal, stopping first in Darjeeling, where he continued his language study and survey of conditions in Tibet, then Nepal, and, finally, reached Tibet in 1901. In order to prepare for his journey into Tibet, Kawaguchi spent a year in Darjeeling. While in Darjeeling, Kawaguchi had begun studying Tibetan with a lama, Serab Gyatso, but, just as when Kawaguchi argued with Kōzen, with whom he studied Pali, about the relative merits of Ceylonese versus Mahayana Buddhism, Kawaguchi became increasingly discomfited by Serab's insistence on teaching the Japanese cleric about Tibetan interpretations of Buddhist practice and doctrine rather than teaching him the Tibetan language. Serab Gyatso was a paid informant for the British, reporting on suspicious persons who crossed his path. It is an indication of how rife with spies and informants Bengal was that Kawaguchi, dissatisfied with one Tibetan instructor who doubled as a spy, soon found himself lodging with a second mentor, Sarat Chandra Das (1849–1917), who also informed for the British.[12]

10. Kawaguchi, *Chibetto ryokō ki*. KECS 1: 4–6.
11. Kawaguchi's study with Unshō and Kōzen is described in Okuyama, *Hyōden Kawaguchi Ekai*, 118–21.
12. Karl E. Meyer and Shareen Blair Brysac, *Tournament of Shadows: The Great Game and the Race for Empire in Central Asia* (Washington, DC: Counterpoint, 1999), 266.

Sarat Chandra Das was a civil engineering graduate of Presidency College in Calcutta who became the headmaster of a school in Darjeeling. Das had learned Tibetan from Ugyen Gyatso, who became a close associate, and he made a number of other Tibetan friends in the region, while making brief trips into Sikkhim. Das made lasting impressions on the numerous foreigners he met. He reputedly became the model for the character Huree Chunder Mukkherjee—aka, "Babu"—in Rudyard Kipling's novel *Kim*. Similarly, K. Paul Johnson, a scholar of Theosophy, hypothesizes that Das and Ugyen Gyatso, who met Helen Blavatsky and Henry Steel Olcott at Ghoom Monastery near Darjeeling, were two of the historical personages inspiring Blavatsky's disembodied Tibetan Masters.[13] In 1879 and 1881, with the support of the British, Das traveled in the disguise of a religious pilgrim into Tibet, where he gathered intelligence for the British government, while also collecting sources for his own historical, philological, and ethnographic studies.[14] Although some sensitive portions of his work were kept under wraps by the British, Das published an account of his second trip to Tibet in 1902.[15] Das and his Tibetan companion and guide, Ugyen Gyatso, brought camera and surveying equipment on their first journey into Tibet, but in 1881, they considered it too risky to travel with such obvious tools for intelligence gathering. Das's degree in civil engineering at Presidency College in Calcutta probably proved useful, as the two measured the terrain, took photographs, and gathered information, which they subsequently passed on to British intelligence. As Sir Alfred Croft, director of public instruction in Bengal, wrote, "His [Das's] journey has been fruitful of information; the observations of bearings and distances have been carefully taken and recorded, and are of much value for the requirements of mapping."[16] In all likelihood, Das continued spying for the British even while working as a scholar, providing them with details

---

13. See Meyer and Brysac, *Tournament of Shadows*, 263–66. Paul K. Johnson, *The Masters Revealed: Madame Blavatsky and the Myth of the Great White Lodge* (Albany: State University of New York Press, 1994), 6; 191–97. According to Johnson, Das forwarded some of the manuscripts he acquired in Tibet to Blavatsky, although if they were untranslated, it is doubtful they would have been of much use to her.

14. A description of Das's Tibetan missions and career is found in Meyer and Brysac, *Tournament of Shadows*, 212–20.

15. Sarat Chandra Das and William Woodville Rockhill, *Journey to Lhasa and Central Tibet* (London: John Murray, 1904). For biographical information about Das, see Rockhill's preface, pp. v–x.

16. From the *General Report on the Operations of the Survey of India, 1881–1882*, paragraph 196, cited in Sarat Chandra Das, *Autobiography; Narratives of the Incidents of My Early Life* (Calcutta: Indian Studies: Past & Present, 1969) 27 [reprint, 1908–9].

about Kawaguchi, who, like many other Japanese in turn-of-the-century India, the British suspected was a spy.[17]

Following his travels in Tibet, Das published a range of articles and books
concerning Buddhism and Tibetan culture. He was prolific; Hanayama
Shinshō's listings for Das in his bibliography of non-Japanese language studies of Buddhism, runs to 56 relevant titles, most of them published while
Kawaguchi was in India.[18] The list of Das's publications included an edition
of the *Laṅkāvatāra Sūtra*, collections of *jātaka* tales, and other Sanskrit and
Tibetan works, as well as articles on topics ranging from Bön to the Buddhist
doctrine of transmigration. Many of Das's articles appeared in the *Journal
of the Buddhist Text Society of India* and other Indian journals concerning
Asia. Drawing inspiration from both the British Pali Text Society and the
Theosophical Society, Das, along with Rajendralal Mitra (1823/24–91) and
Satis Chandra Vidyabhusan (1870–1920), founded the Buddhist Text Society
in Calcutta in 1892.[19] For the first meeting of the society in 1893, Das invited
Olcott to address the group.[20] Perhaps one of Das's most important scholarly contributions was the 1902 *Tibetan-English Dictionary* that he completed
with considerable assistance from Vidyabhusan.[21] Das clearly was open to
European and American approaches to Buddhism. Writing approvingly of
Paul Carus's work, for example, he said that a "Lama would have seen the
spirit of the founder of the Mahāyāna incarnate, if his *Gospel of Buddha* and
other contributions to Buddhist philosophy were written in Tibetan."[22] Das
thus was an active participant in the rise of indigenous, Buddhist modernist
scholarship in Bengal that had connections to both the scholarly and occultist
strains of modern Buddhism.

Kawaguchi did not write in depth about what he studied while working
with Das, apart from concentrating on learning Tibetan. It does not seem
too wildly speculative, however, to suppose that given Das's active participa-

17. See Berry, *A Stranger in Tibet*, 21–22.

18. Hanayama, *Bibliography on Buddhism* (Tokyo: Hokuseido Press, 1961), 154–58.

19. For details on the formation of the society by Das and Mitra, see Ober, "Reinventing
Buddhism," 82. Ober provides an analysis of Das's work on pp. 97–101.

20. Meyer and Brysac, *Tournament of Shadows*, 266.

21. Sarat Chandra Das, Graham Sandberg, and Augustus William Heyde, *A Tibetan-English
Dictionary, with Sanskrit Synonyms* (Alipore,: Superintendent, Govt. Print., West Bengal Govt.
Press, 1960). Huber mentions Vidyabhusan's role in editing the dictionary, particularly his help
with "the Sanskrit entries together with English glosses." Toni Huber, *The Holy Land Reborn:
Pilgrimage & the Tibetan Reinvention of Buddhist India* (Chicago: University of Chicago Press,
2008), 277.

22. Das, *Autobiography*, 4.

tion in the revival of Buddhist study and practice in Bengal and Kawaguchi's stay in 1902 at the Mahābodhi Society in Calcutta, Kawaguchi's first sojourn in South Asia exposed him to the world of Anglo-Indian, European, and American writing concerning Buddhism. At the same time, Das, in his role as a British agent, may well have told his handlers of Kawaguchi's plans to enter Tibet and reported on Kawaguchi's various travels in South Asia. Their relationship remained cordial, however, with Kawaguchi communicating to Das from Lhasa via letters. Writing about Das's intelligence work, Scott Berry conjectures, "These reports probably spared Kawaguchi British interrogation and detention, as the authorities may have learned enough from Das to make such measures superfluous."[23] When Kawaguchi returned to Japan in 1915 following his second long stay in South Asia, he was accompanied by Das, who was eager to see Japanese Buddhism in its home setting, and Das's son. Das senior, who was in failing health, set off for Japan with Kawaguchi. Unable to return to India, Das died in Japan in 1917.[24]

Prior to heading to Nepal in January 1899, Kawaguchi stopped at Bodh Gayā to visit the site of the Buddha's awakening. There Kawaguchi met Dharmapāla, who had a deep interest in communicating with the Dalai Lama, whom he, perhaps in aspiration, had listed as the lone patron of the Mahābodhi Society on the cover of the organization's magazine. Dharmapāla entrusted Kawaguchi with a silver reliquary that held a relic of the Buddha to transmit to the Dalai Lama, although because his sojourn in Tibet ended abruptly, Kawaguchi ultimately was unable to complete that mission.[25]

On July 4, 1900, after the numerous travails and adventures detailed in his *Chibetto ryokō ki*, Kawaguchi crossed the 5,411-meter high Khung Pass in the Dolpo region of Nepal into Tibet.[26] He thus became the first recorded Japanese to have entered Tibet, albeit in disguise as a Chinese monk. While in Tibet, Kawaguchi moved in relatively elite circles, particularly after his abilities as a practitioner of Chinese medicine (while growing up, Kawaguchi

23. Scott Berry, *Monks, Spies, and a Soldier of Fortune: The Japanese in Tibet* (New York: St. Martin's Press, 1995), 147–48.

24. Berry, *Monks, Spies, and a Soldier of Fortune*, 148.

25. Kawaguchi, *Three Years in Tibet*, KECS 17: 25–26. Huber, *The Holy Land Reborn*, 285.

26. Kawaguchi did not provide details of the course he took into Tibet in his published accounts of the journey, in order to protect anyone who might have aided his entry into that country. His handwritten diary discovered in 2004, however, identifies the location where he crossed the Nepal-Tibet border. See Naoji Okuyama, "Pilgrimage to the Crystal Mountain in Dolpo by the Japanese Monk, Kawaguchi Ekai," in *International Conference on Esoteric Buddhist Studies* ed. International Conference on Esoteric Buddhist Studies Editorial Board (Koyasan University: International Conference on Esoteric Buddhist Studies 2008), 211.

had picked up some knowledge of medicine from his father) became known among the Tibetans, including the Thirteenth Dalai Lama. In Lhasa, Kawaguchi studied at the Sera Monastery and the associated school, entering the monastic training system formally in 1901.

In mid-May 1902, his identity as a Japanese national was discovered by the Tibetans, forcing Kawaguchi to flee Tibet back to India, where, for almost a year while living in Darjeeling, he worked on *Chibetto bunten* (Tibetan Grammar) with the assistance of Das. Kawaguchi then moved to Calcutta, where he briefly stayed at the Mahābodhi Society. In Calcutta, Kawaguchi was at one important hub of the revival of Buddhist studies and Buddhism in India.[27] The building in Calcutta housing the Mahābodhi Society also served as the headquarters for the Buddhist Text Society that Das had helped found in 1892 as well as the Theosophical Society.[28] In Calcutta, Kawaguchi thus stood at the confluence of several imbricated streams of thought and practice contributing to the rise of twentieth-century Asian Buddhism: the reinvigoration of indigenous Indian Buddhist scholarship catalyzed by modern historical and philological methods; the Buddhist revivalism of the international Mahābodhi Society; and the equally global occultism of Theosophy. Along with the Tendai cleric Ōmiya Kōjun (1872–1949), who was in Calcutta studying Sanskrit during the same period, Kawaguchi served as a guide for visiting Japanese Buddhists.[29] For example, Kawaguchi guided a group of important Japanese pilgrims that included Inoue Enryō and Ōtani Kōzui to various important Buddhist sites when they visited India in December 1902.

Kawaguchi returned to Japan in May 1903, but after a short period in Japan occupied with lecturing and exhibiting materials he brought back from Tibet, Kawaguchi embarked again in October 1904 for a much longer period of study and travel in South Asia. Kawaguchi remained based in Calcutta until March 1906, studying Sanskrit at Calcutta University, while living at one of the residences of Rabindranath Tagore (1861–1941). Kawaguchi then traveled once again to Nepal in March 1905, where he presented the Nepalese

27. As both Douglas Ober and Gitanjali Surendran persuasively show, at the time the study of Buddhism was undergoing a major revival in metropolitan centers across India, including Benares, Baroda, Bombay, Calcutta, Chittagong, and Pune. Ober, "Reinventing Buddhism"; Gitanjali Surendran, "'The Indian Discovery of Buddhism': Buddhist Revival in India, C. 1890–1956" (PhD diss., Harvard University, 2013).

28. Kemper, *Rescued from the Nation*, 283.

29. Auerback, *A Storied Sage*, 184, reads the name as Ōmiya Kōnin. I have followed Kawaguchi Ekai, however, who in *Three Years in Tibet*, Romanizes his companion's name Ōmiya Kōjun. See *Three Years in Tibet*, KECS 17: 677. In addition, the National Diet Library entries for his writings give the pronunciation Ōmiya Kōjun.

with a complete set of the Ōbaku edition of the Chinese Buddhist canon that had been printed at Manpukuji.[30] Kawaguchi continued his Sanskrit study and vigorously collected Sanskrit Buddhist manuscripts, returning to India toward the end of 1905. At the suggestion of Tagore, with whom Kawaguchi had frequent contact in Calcutta, Kawaguchi moved to Santiniketan, near Calcutta, to study Sanskrit.

Kawaguchi was not the first Japanese to have gotten to know Tagore, as Okakura Kakuzō had spent eleven months in India, much of them interacting with the poet, beginning in December 1901. In Okakura's wake, a number of other Japanese artists and Buddhists also had visited Tagore in Calcutta, which became one hub of Japanese Buddhist activity in India.[31] Among the visitors following in Okakura's wake was the young Shingon cleric Hori Shitoku (1876–1903), who would die tragically in India from tetanus, just two years after arriving in the country.[32]

Kawaguchi also continued to collect Sanskrit and Tibetan texts, and, during the Panchen Lama's visit to Calcutta in early 1906, promised to exchange a copy of the Chinese Buddhist canon for the Tibetan version. The Panchen Lama, much to the chagrin of the British, who feared the strengthening of ties between Tibet and Japan, engaged with Kawaguchi in a conversation that took place over several days concerning the state of Japanese Buddhism. Both men also participated in the founding of a new organization to help rescue Bodh Gayā for world Buddhists, the Buddhist Shrines Restoration Society. Although achieving little and leaving scarcely a mark in the historical record, this association, according to Huber, did help introduce high-level Tibetan Buddhists to the effervescent world of Buddhist revivalism in India, in which Kawaguchi also was engaged.[33]

Kawaguchi found the level of instruction at Santiniketan unsatisfactory, however. After just one month, in March 1906, Kawaguchi moved to Benares, which was a thriving center for Sanskrit study.[34] As I mentioned in the Introduction, several decades earlier Nanjō Bun'yū had considered continuing his Sanskrit studies in Benares. The head of the Benares Sanskrit College, whom

30. Takayama, *Sekai o kakeru*, 17–19. One of the copies of the canon is still housed in the Royal Library in Nepal.

31. Kemper, *Rescued from the Nation*, 222–31; Stephen N. Hay, *Asian Ideas of East and West; Tagore and His Critics in Japan, China, and India* (Cambridge, MA: Harvard University Press, 1970), 35–44.

32. Ogawara Masamichi and Koyama Satoko, *Ajia taiken to shisō no hen'yō, Kindai Nihon no Bukkyōsha* (Tokyo: Keiō Gijuku Daigaku Shuppankai, 2010), 315–45.

33. Huber, *The Holy Land Reborn*, 278–81.

34. Kawaguchi, *Nyūzō ki* (published 1915) in KECS 14: 242.

Nanjō had met in Oxford, dissuaded him from doing so. At the college in the 1880s, the principal mentioned, only Brahmins could study the Vedas. Working with a tutor as a resident student, which was a common practice, would be a less roundabout way of studying Sanskrit in Benares, but finding suitable and affordable lodgings would be difficult. In addition, few of the pandits in the city knew much Buddhist Sanskrit. Instead, the principal advised Nanjō to work in Pune or Bombay, which by the early twentieth century were becoming regional centers for Pali and Sanskrit Buddhist studies. Kawaguchi, who was not easily deterred, elected to move to Benares, whatever hurdles he may have faced.

Kawagachi's path to Benares perhaps was eased by his contacts with Annie Besant (née Wood, 1847–1943), who was an active presence in the city at the start of the twentieth century. The particulars of how Kawaguchi came into the orbit of Besant are unclear, although, as noted above, Kawaguchi had ties to the Mahābodhi Society and Dharmapāla dating back to 1902 when he stayed in Calcutta toward the tail end of his first period in South Asia. His other close Indian associate and teacher, Sarat Chandra Das, who also knew Olcott and other Theosophists from the Asiatic Society of Bengal, probably also introduced Kawaguchi to Theosophists in India. In Benares, Kawaguchi took up residence in the faculty residence hall at Central Hindu College (later, Benares Hindu University) while studying Sanskrit there as well as at the Government Sanskrit College (a.k.a. Benares Sanskrit College; founded in 1791).[35] Kawaguchi made Benares his base of operations in India for more than seven years, when, in May 1913, he moved to Darjeeling to prepare for his last foray into Tibet.[36]

Perhaps one of the most prominent results of Kawaguchi's proximity to Besant and other Theosophists at the Central Hindu College was his decision to publish an English translation of his Tibetan memoir, *Chibetto ryokō ki*, based on serialized newspaper accounts of Kawaguchi's adventures in South Asia that had been published in Japan in 1904. Although at the urging of several Japanese acquaintances Kawaguchi began preparing an English translation of the book, when accounts from Sven Hedin's British expedition to Tibet were published Kawaguchi abandoned the project, because "I thought my book would not be of any use to the English-reading public."[37] According to

35. Kawaguchi Akira, *Kawaguchi Ekai*, 157–58. The latter school is referred to as Bongo Senmon Gakkō in the book.

36. Kawaguchi, *Nyūzō ki*, KECS 14: 25–26.

37. Kawaguchi. *Three Years in Tibet* in KECS 1: vii. A holograph draft of the preface, which like the published version was written at the Staff Quarters of the Central Hindu College and

Kawaguchi, however, Besant persuaded him to proceed with publishing the translation despite Hedin's imminent publication because "such books would treat of the country from a western point of view, whilst my book would prove interesting to the reader from the point of view of an Asiatic, intimately acquainted with manners, customs, and the inner life of the people." Kawaguchi concludes that without Besant's kind assistance and encouragement "this book would not have seen the light of day."[38]

In moving to Benares, Kawaguchi had placed himself in one of the centers for Sanskrit study in India. By the mid-nineteenth century, prosperous merchants and farmers had subsidized the founding of numerous Sanskrit schools in Benares, making it a leading place for the study of Hindu philosophy and ritual.[39] Unlike Calcutta, Bombay, and other port cities, Benares would have had far fewer resident Japanese, which also might have been an additional attraction to Kawaguchi. As the British attempted to shape education in India, they founded their own schools, for example, Government Sanskrit College, where traditional studies were combined with modern English-style education in language, the sciences, and other subjects. British and British-educated Indian scholars, increasingly strove to incorporate European philology and history into traditional teaching.

The results of the British efforts were uneven, however, with some Indian scholars resisting the wholesale conversion of traditional pandits to European-style Sanskritists, arguing that rather than displacing earlier modes of learning, "Eastern wisdom" should be combined with "Western enlightenment."[40] As Brian Hatcher reminds us, the cultural transformations that occurred in colonial India were mutual, affecting the colonizers and the colonized. "Therefore, to determine how the cultural role and social standing of the pandit may have been transformed as a result of colonial rule requires thinking both about colonial policy and praxis as well as about what role the pandits themselves played as agents in the transformation of their own traditions."[41] Hatcher observed that even at the turn of the nineteenth to the twentieth century, there was among some notable pandits a persistence of a "shastric

dated 1909, is found in KECS 17: 312–284. (The reverse numbering is as found in the Japanese volume.)

38. KECS 1: vii.

39. Vasudha Dalmia, "Sanskrit Scholars and Pandits of the Old School: The Benares Sanskrit College and the Constitution of Authority in the Late Nineteenth Century," *Journal of Indian Philosophy* 24 (1996): 321–23.

40. Dalmia, "Sanskrit Scholars and Pandits of the Old School," 332.

41. Brian A. Hatcher, "What's Become of the Pandit? Rethinking the History of Sanskrit Scholars in Colonial Bengal," *Modern Asian Studies* 39, no. 3 (2005): 689.

imaginary" that continued long-standing pandit practices of reading and argumentation that was rooted in Sanskrit shastra. At the same time, it did not represent a static set of practices, however, as the pandits responded creatively to colonial scholarship and pedagogy, creating scholarship "that reflected a shared attempt to negotiate between existing modes of belief and practice and colonialism's new epistemologies and technologies."[42] According to Hatcher, "through their canny use of Sanskrit sources, their sophisticated understanding of the emerging colonial idioms of reason and historical proof, and their greater facility with print technology, such figures were able to produce work with both immediate and long-term resonances."[43]

Studying Sanskrit in Benares during this transformation would have exposed Kawaguchi to at least vestiges of the older synchronic, embedded view of Sanskrit literature and philosophy as well as efforts on several fronts to revivify Sanskrit education.[44] According to his nephew, Kawaguchi Akira, during the years at Central Hindu College, Kawaguchi worked with Ram Avatar Sharma (1877–1929), P. K. Patankar, and, at the Sanskrit Academy, Rashika Lal Bhattacarya. Sharma, an extremely renowned Sanskritist, lectured on a variety of subjects, including Vedantism, Kālidāsa, the Puranas, and Indian psychology. Bhattacarya lectured on the famed Sanskrit poet Kālidāsa, along with other subjects. This sparked Kawaguchi's interest in the poet, with Kawaguchi translating into Japanese Kālidāsa's drama *Abhijñānaśākuntalam*, which was published in two volumes in 1924.[45] That Kawaguchi's scholarly interests thus were expanded to some degree by his mentors demonstrates how his education in India played a role in shaping his later intellectual interests.

In addition to working with these pandits, Kawaguchi was living at Central Hindu College, where he was presented with another model for Indian

42. Brian A. Hatcher, "Pandits at Work: The Modern Shastric Imaginary in Early Colonial Bengal," in *Trans-Colonial Modernities in South Asia*, ed. Michael S. Dodson and Brian A. Hatcher (New York: Routledge, 2012), 47.

43. Hatcher, "Pandits at Work," 47; 60–61.

44. Nita Kumar, "Sanskrit Pandits and the Modernisation of Sanskrit Education in the Nineteenth to Twentieth Centuries," in *Swami Vivekananda and the Modernization of Hinduism*, ed. William Radice (Delhi and New York: Oxford University Press, 1998), 36–60.

45. Kawaguchi Akira, *Kawaguchi Ekai*, 157–58. The names of the teachers, which are given in *katakana*, are reiterated in Okuyama, *Hyōden Kawaguchi Ekai*, 248, but neither work gives a source for this information. Associate Professor Rasika Lal Bhat Acarya (Rashika-Rāru-Bahatta-Ācharuya) of Sanskrit College is mentioned in the afterword of Kawaguchi's translation of Kālidāsa's Sanskrit play *Abhijñānaśākuntalam*. See *Shakuntarā hime*, KECS 14: 112. Ram Avatar Sharma is listed on the Benares Hindu University website as one of the important early Sanskrit teachers at the university. There is a biography of him in Wikipedia. See https://en.wikipedia .org/wiki/Ram_Avatar_Sharma, accessed June 20, 2016.

education and scholarship. Annie Besant and her Theosophical Society associates founded Central Hindu College in 1898 as part of her broader efforts to build a higher-education system in India that honored Indian traditions. Cultivating the rising tide of nationalism, Besant argued that government-run schools were denigrating Indian language, religion, and literature, turning Indians against their glorious culture. In order to preserve the *sanātana* Dharma (eternal Dharma, which was understood as "orthodox Hinduism"), Besant garnered the support of many wealthy Indians, including the Maharaja of Benares, who augmented the original property holdings with additional land and buildings. At the time of the college's inception, each day began with a Hindu prayer, segregation of students by caste was honored, and religious education in nonsectarian Hinduism as portrayed in the school textbook *Sanātana Dharma*, was emphasized.[46] The founders' concession to modern education was including instruction in science and other subjects that were in tune with the times. As stated in *Sanātana Dharma*, the education was to be "wide, liberal, and un-sectarian in character, while at the same time it shall be definitely and distinctively Hindu."[47]

Over the course of Kawaguchi's seven years in Benares, particularly as Annie Besant became enmeshed in the founding of the Order of the Rising Sun (later Order of the Star in East), which was centered on Jiddu Krishnamurti as the world messiah, Indian supporters sought to wrest control of the college from the Theosophists, fearing that Hindu education was being infused with a Theosophically tinged version of Christianity. By 1911, Madan Mohan Malaviya (1861–1946) and others promoting Hindu education were putting plans in place to forge a university that would "train teachers of religion for the preservation and promotion of the Sanatan Dharma which is inculcated by the *Srutis*, *Smritis* and *Puranas*, and recognised by *Varna-Ashram*." In addition, "the University was to be residential, students were to be admitted directly after the *upanayan* (sacred thread ceremony) and to observe the laws of *Brahmacharya* throughout their student career."[48] At the time of the college's thirteenth anniversary celebrations in December 1911, the Theosophists, including Besant, had lost control of the institution they had begun. Their approach to Hindu education, as expressed in *Sanātana Dharma*, was abandoned for the more orthodox Hinduism of Malaviya and his associates, who

46. Arthur H. Nethercot, *The Last Four Lives of Annie Besant* (Chicago: University of Chicago Press, 1963), 67–68.

47. Central Hindu College, *Sanātana Dharma; An Advanced Textbook of Hindu Religion and Ethics* (Benares: Board of Trustees, Central Hindu College, 1903), i–iii.

48. Parmanand, *Mahāmanā Madan Mohan Malaviya: An Historical Biography*, 2 vols. (Varanasi: Malaviya Adhyayan Sansthan, Banaras Hindu University, 1985), 1:192–94; 216–18.

now controlled the governance of the school.[49] By 1913, as Central Hindu College merged into the new Benares Hindu University, the Theosophists were left with but a nominal role in the institution's governance.[50]

In this tumultuous intellectual environment, Kawaguchi followed a spartan, disciplined regimen that he would continue even after his return to Japan in 1915. Given the push for ever more stringent adherence to rules concerning celibacy and an "orthodox Hindu way of life" at the college, Kawaguchi's celibacy, vegetarianism, and teetotaling would have helped him feel right at home. If he was aware of the struggle between the Theosophists and the conservative Hindus over the college where he was studying, he gives no hint of it in his published writings. Rising each day at 5:30 a.m., Kawaguchi would practice zazen and bathe. Following a thirty-minute teatime, Kawaguchi would then read an English translation of the *Dhammasaṅgaṇi* until 9:30 a.m., when he would turn his attention to practicing Sanskrit reading and grammar for two hours. Following another thirty-minute meal and a break, from 2–5:00 p.m. he would practice orally translating Sanskrit, then review Sanskrit grammar until 6:30 p.m.. Kawaguchi would attend class for an hour from 7:30–8:30 p.m., then continue practicing oral translation until 10:00 p.m., followed by another hour of review![51]

One undated holograph draft of a letter that appears to be from this period reveals the breadth of Kawaguchi's study while he was in India. In the letter, which was apparently addressed to a bookseller, Kawaguchi requested the following books (spelling as in the original letter):

1. A Sanscrit-English Dictionary by Sir Monier-Williams
2. Dharma-Samgraha edited by Kenju Kasahara
3. Buddha Karita, edited of Asvaghosha
4. Vagrakkedica by Max Muller
5. English Sanskrit Dictionary by Apte
6. Asoka by Vincent Smith
7. History of Oratory and Oratories by Henry Hardwick
8. Childers Pali-English Dictionary
9. Pag-sam-jon-zang Part I and Part II published by the Presidency Jail Press, Calcutta.

The list of desired books makes clear that Kawaguchi was keeping up to date on current developments in European Indological and Buddhological schol-

49. Nethercot, *Last Four Lives of Annie Besant*, 162–63.

50. Parmanand. *Mahāmanā Madan Mohan Malaviya*, 218–19.

51. Takagai Shunshi, *Tōzai Bukkyō gakusha den* (Ube: Karinbunko, 1970), 60. Takagai writes this information was taken from Kawaguchi's diary entry for 1907.

arship while studying at the college.[52] He makes no mention of whether his Indian teachers introduced him to these works, but one of them, the "Pag-sam-jon-zang" (dPag bsam ljon bzang), had been edited by his mentor and friend Sarat Chandra Das. Kawaguchi, having been exposed to this wide range of books in India, would continue to draw from a diverse range of international scholarly sources in his work after his return to Japan.

On September 4, 1915, after more than a decade in South Asia, Kawaguchi returned to Japan, bringing with him valuable, large collections of Tibetan, Nepali, and Sanskrit Buddhist texts and ritual objects that he received from his high-ranking Tibetan and Nepali associates or had collected himself. Over the course of his many years in India, Nepal, and Tibet, Kawaguchi had managed to meet and establish cordial relations with a wide range of high-ranking officials, scholars, and clerics, including Tagore, the Dalai Lama, the Panchen Lama, and the prime minister and the king of Nepal. Kawaguchi, along with Kimura Nichiki (see chapters 3 and 5), encouraged Tagore via letter to make a visit to Japan in 1916, although Kawaguchi was highly critical of the overly emotional tenor of Tagore's addresses in Japan and what he perceived to be Tagore's failure to resist vigorously British colonialism in India.[53]

Following his return to Japan in 1915, the promotion of the study of Tibetan language, culture, and religion was one of Kawaguchi's main concerns. For the next thirty years, Kawaguchi taught Tibetan and Tibet studies at a variety of universities, while cataloging, exhibiting, and arranging for the preservation of the vast collection of texts, ritual implements, artwork, as well as flora and fauna specimens, that he had accumulated during his many years of travel in South Asia. At the same time, Kawaguchi began an ambitious program of translation and writing that grew out of his intensive study of Sanskrit and Tibetan and was enabled by the collection of manuscripts and books that he had gathered in South Asia, many of them new or new Indic or Tibetan versions of classic Sino-Japanese Buddhist texts. During the last fifteen years of his life, using texts he had gathered while in South Asia, as well as publications available to him in Japan, Kawaguchi published comparative translations of such important works as the Nyūbosatsugyō (Bodhicaryāvatāra; 1921), Hokekyō (Saddharmapuṇḍarīka-sūtra; 1924), Shō-mangyō (Śrīmālā-sūtra; 1924), Yuimagyō (Vimalakīrti-nirdeśa-sūtra; 1928), the Yuishiki sanjū ju (Triṃśikā-vijñapti-mātratā; 1930), the Muryōjukyō (Sukhāvatīvyūha-sūtra; 1931), the Amidakyō (Amitābha-sūtra; 1931), and the

---

52. The letter is found in KECS 17: 209–8.

53. Okuyama, Hyōden Kawaguchi Ekai, 306. See also Kawaguchi, "Bokokuteki shisōka to shite no Tagōru," in KECS 15: 526–31. The essay originally was published in 1915 in Chūgai nippō.

Dainichikyō (*Mahāvairocana-sūtra*; 1934). In addition, Kawaguchi authored numerous works analyzing Tibetan Buddhism and culture. Based on his investigation of these texts and his experiences of Buddhist practice domestically and in South Asia, Kawaguchi produced a series of tracts advocating the reformation of Buddhist practice in Japan, a number of manuals for lay Buddhist practice, and a vernacular biography of the Buddha for general readers. These works reveal Kawaguchi's impressive linguistic abilities, as well the breadth and depth of his command of the Buddhist textual corpus. Although these tracts and their connection with Kawaguchi's efforts to create a lay Buddhist movement in Japan are one of the most ignored aspects of Kawaguchi's efforts, they represent the culmination of his life's work.

One of the earliest works Kawaguchi published in the 1920s was his translation from the Sanskrit, using the Tibetan translation to gloss difficult passages, of the *Bodhicaryāvatāra*, an exposition of Mahayana practice for bodhisattvas that was written by Śāntideva in India during the late seventh or early eighth century of the Common Era. This text, which exists in both Sanskrit and Tibetan versions, would have been frequently mentioned in elite clerical circles in Tibet, where it was translated into Tibetan at least twice and glossed in a highly regarded Indian commentary (*śāstra*).[54] With thirty extant Sanskrit manuscripts from India, Tibet, and Mongolia, as well as eleven commentaries on the text in the Tengyur, the *Bodhicaryāvatāra* was a revered text in the Indo-Tibet sphere of Buddhism.[55] Although Kawaguchi does not state what precisely initially drew his attention to the text, his studies in India, Nepal, and Tibet would have made him aware of the importance of the text for the Tibetan Buddhist tradition, especially given the growing attention to the *Bodhicaryāvatāra* in Indian and European scholarly circles. Auguste Barth in 1893 claimed that the *Bodhicaryāvatāra* was on a par with some of the finest examples of Christian spiritual literature. As early as 1889, the Russian scholar Ivan Pavlovich Minaev (1840–90) published an edition of the Sanskrit text. In India, one of the leading Sanskrit scholars in Calcutta, Haraprasāda (Haraprasad) Śāstrī released an edited version of the Sanskrit text of the *Bodhicaryāvatāra*, probably based on one of the palm-leaf manuscripts in the Hodgson Collection of the Asiatic Society of Bengal, in the

54. Luis Gómez, "The Way of the Translators: Three Recent Translations of Śāntideva's *Bodhicaryāvatāra*," *Buddhist Literature* 1 (1999): 263.

55. See Yonezawa Yoshiyasu, "Kaisetsu," in KECS 5: 1–2. Prominent scholars and commentators on the text in the Dalai Lama's instructional lineage include Patrul Rinpoche (1808–87) and Kunu Rinpoche (1885–1997). I thank Donald Lopez for his e-mail comments on the importance of the text for the Tibetan Buddhist tradition and his summary of the commentarial tradition in the late nineteenth–early twentieth centuries.

Journal and Text of the Buddhist Society of India.[56] Haraprasad also published a brief article on Śāntideva in 1913. By the beginning of the twentieth century, Louis de la Vallée Poussin also edited and translated Prajñākaramati's commentary the *Bodhicaryāvatāra-pañjikā*, which contained the full text of Śāntideva's work.[57] La Vallée Poussin's edition of the Sanskrit text was published in a series of fascicles in Calcutta by the Asiatic Society of Bengal from 1901 to 1914. In addition, La Vallée Poussin also published a French translation of the *Bodhicaryāvatāra* in Paris in installments between 1905 and 1907. When Kawaguchi turned to translating the text into Japanese around 1919–20, he made use of both Haraprasad's and Minaev's edited texts.

In his introduction to the Japanese translation, Kawaguchi wrote that the *Bodhicaryāvatāra* had the potential to help ameliorate the individual and societal problems that had proliferated in Japan in the 1920s. Following the path set forth by Śāntideva in the seventh century, according to Kawaguchi, would bring an end to individual unhappiness and societal discord. For this reason, Kawaguchi wrote, he undertook translating the text from the Tibetan version found in the Nartan edition of the Tengyur, using several additional Sanskrit editions, including Minaev's, as the basis for correcting, emending, and clarifying the text for the Japanese translation.[58] Kawaguchi also was aware of an abbreviated "translation" of the text into Chinese, the *Putixing jing* (J. *Bodaigyō kyō*), but the text was an awkward and only partial translation, as Kawaguchi showed in his introduction to the *Bodhicaryāvatāra*. Kawaguchi would return to the *Bodhicaryāvatāra* in 1926, just as he was focusing his efforts on creating a purely lay Buddhism. The *Bodhicaryāvatāra* focused on the bodhisattva path for ordained clerics, so Kawaguchi felt the translation could not easily be used by lay Buddhists who wanted to enter the path of the bodhisattva. To assist them in that goal, Kawaguchi wrote *Bosatsudō*, adapting the ideas from Śāntideva's work specifically for "lay bodhisattva" practice.[59]

An account by Yamada Mumon (1900–1988), a spiritually searching student living in Tokyo, provides one glimpse of how Kawaguchi incorporated

56. Śāntideva and Haraprasāda Śāstrī, "*Bodhicaryāvatāram*," *Journal and Text of the Buddhist Text Society of India* 2, nos. 1 & 2 (1894): 2(1):1–16; 2(2):17–32. See Daniel Stender, "Preliminary Survey of Sanskrit Texts of the *Bodhicaryāvatāra*," in *Puṣpikā: Tracing Ancient India through Texts and Traditions: Contributions to Current Research in Indology*, ed. Giovanni Ciotti, Alastair Gornall, and Paolo Visigalli (Oxford and Philadelphia: Oxbow Books, 2014), 150. Haraprasad's name is spelled multiple ways. I have used the common Haraprasad Shastri, without diacritical marks, in the text.

57. Gómez, "The Way of the Translators," 266–67.

58. KECS 5: 1–7.

59. *Bosatsudō*, KECS 5: 1–7. The *Putixing jing* is found at T. 32, no. 1662: 43–562.

his work on the *Bodhicaryāvatāra* into his lectures for one of the lay Buddhist groups he founded. In 1919, Yamada was just beginning the religious search that culminated with his joining the Rinzai denomination in 1922 and becoming one of the most renowned Zen clerics of the twentieth century. Yamada attended Kawaguchi's lectures based on his translation of the *Bodhicaryāvatāra* at the Sessan Shōja (Himalaya Vihāra), the headquarters for the Sessankai that was located in the Hongō section of Tokyo. During one of the talks attended by Yamada, Kawaguchi cited the line from the *Bodhicaryāvatāra*, "Where is there hide to cover the whole world? The wide world can be covered with hide enough for a pair of shoes alone," to explain how the act of giving rise to *bodhicitta*, which is described in the *Bodhicaryāvatāra*, if enacted by each person individually, would end all strife.[60]

Upon hearing the lecture, Yamada decided to become Kawaguchi's disciple, which he did, despite having to overcome his father's objections. Yamada was ordained by Kawaguchi, who became his first teacher. Yamada reminisced in several later articles about the severe practice regimen he endured under his first teacher. Kawaguchi was strictly vegetarian and did not eat after mid-day. Yamada rose each day at 4 a.m. for cleaning the practice place, preparing breakfast, and striking the sounding board for morning practice. After a day of classes at the university, in the evenings he would clean the garden, prepare the bath, and, once a week, help one of his seniors sell vegetables at the market. After a year of practicing with Kawaguchi while attending Tōyō University, Yamada became so ill that he had to return to his home village. Although following recovery from his illness Yamada became a Rinzai Myōshinji-ha cleric instead of returning to practice with Kawaguchi, until the final years of his life Yamada remembered the Sessankai lecture on *bodhicitta* as a major religious turning point.[61]

In February 1921, Kawaguchi, who, almost from the time of his ordination 1890 as an Ōbaku cleric, had taken a critical view of the Ōbaku establishment's approach to Buddhist practice and organization, withdrew his name from the Ōbaku clerical register. Henceforth, he would devote himself to promoting a "pure Buddhism" centered on the veneration of Śākyamuni Buddha. At the same time, a good portion of his prodigious scholarly energy was directed to-

60. As translated in Śāntideva, Kate Crosby, and Andrew Skilton, *The Bodhicaryāvatāra* (Oxford; New York: Oxford University Press, 1996), 35.

61. Takayama Ryūzō, *Tenbō Kawaguchi Ekai ron* (Kyoto: Hōzōkan, 2002), 195–201. Inoue Nobutaka, *Kindai Nihon no shūkyōka 101* (Tokyo: Shinshokan, 2007), 198–99. See also Okuyama, *Hyōden Kawaguchi Ekai*, 326.

wards projects that would provide the intellectual tools necessary for creating a new, non-sectarian lay Buddhist movement in Japan. These works included a set of poems, *Bukkyō wasan*, in which Kawaguchi set forth in accessible language basic Buddhist doctrine and teachings, and a brief liturgical manual, *Bukkyō nikka*, which provided a series of readings to be used at Buddhist services. In the liturgical manual Kawaguchi assembled a set of thirteen texts that reinforced the central practices of the ideal lay Buddhist life. In *Bukkyō nikka*, Kawaguchi began the service with an invocation to Śākyamuni, followed by repentance, taking the Three Refuges and the Five Vows, giving rise to the Mind of Awakening, chanting the Heart Sutra, and, in conclusion, transferring the merit of one's practice to all sentient beings.[62] *Bukkyō nikka* shares some features, for example, repentance, taking the precepts, and giving rise to the mind of awakening, with other texts like the *Shūshōgi*, a manual for the Sōtō laity produced by Ōuchi Seiran for the laity, that were assembled in the late-nineteenth and early twentieth-centuries.

In a group of books about bodhisattva and lay practice written by Kawaguchi around the same time as he was creating his lay groups, Kawaguchi made public his rationale for abandoning Ōbaku Zen and all other existent Buddhist denominations in Japan and renouncing his status as an Ōbaku cleric. The more he wrote, it would seem, the more radical his stance became. By the time of his sixtieth birthday in 1926 he formally returned to lay life, in an effort to demonstrate his conviction that clerical Buddhist practice was no longer viable in the modern age. During the same period, Kawaguchi elaborated in a series of polemical books the reasons for his abandonment of clerical status, rejection of sectarian Buddhism, and founding a lay Buddhist organization. The following titles published during this period were devoted to laying the foundations for this new Buddhism.

1. *Nyū Bosatsugyō* (1921)
2. *Bukkyō wasan* (1921)
3. *Bukkyō nikka* (1922)
4. *Shaka ichidai ki* (1922)
5. *Upāsaka Bukkyō* (1926)[63]
6. *Bosatsudō* (1926)
7. *Shōshin Bukkyō* (1936)

62. Kawaguchi Ekai, *Bukkyō nikka* (Tokyo: Zaike Bukkyō Shugyō Dan, 1940). Orig. ed., 1922, Bukkyō Sen'yō Kai.

63. Kawaguchi specifically attached the *rubi* ウバサカ indicating that was the way to read the characters 在家, more commonly read as *zaike* ザイケ.

Kawaguchi's 1926 work, *Upāsaka Bukkyō*, and the more systematic defense of that work's assertions, *Shōshin Bukkyō*, which was published in 1936 in response to criticisms of *Upāsaka Bukkyō*, amounted to wholesale condemnations of the current state of Japanese Buddhism, as well as advocating Kawaguchi's streamlined style of lay Buddhist practice as the only legitimate form of the tradition for the twentieth century. Genuine (*shōshin*) Buddhism, Kawaguchi asserted, simply refers to the practical Dharma teachings (*jikkōteki kyōhō*) established by Śākyamuni Buddha 2400 years ago to liberate sentient beings. Sadly, however, over time, Buddhism degenerated as non-Buddhist ideas and practices were absorbed by the tradition, distorting the original teachings. Kawaguchi utilized a modified version of Ui Hakuju's tripartite periodization of early Buddhist doctrinal evolution into foundational (*konpon*), primitive (*genshi*), and Hinayana (Shōjō) as the basis for his argument.[64] According to Kawaguchi's interpretation of this tripartite division, foundational Buddhism had accurately reflected Śākyamuni's teachings, the spirit of which also was reflected in the Mahayana sutras. As Buddhism made the transition from its primitive stage to Hinayana, however, Upanisadic doctrines colored the understanding of the Buddha's teachings, leading to grave misinterpretations of cardinal teachings.

Kawaguchi argued in *Shōshin Bukkyō* that many forms of Buddhism after the primitive period, eventually including the various Japanese Buddhist schools, were based on a fundamental distortion of the meaning of the term, "Dharmakāya" (*hosshin*). With catastrophic consequences for practice, many Buddhists and scholars mistakenly viewed the Dharmakāya as a "noumenal Dharmakāya" (*ritai hosshin*). This heterodox understanding was far closer to the Upanishadic notion of an eternal *Brahman-atman* (*Bonga*) and closer to the idea of an eternal Great Self (*daiga*). According to Kawaguchi, the term Dharmakāya properly referred to the virtue body of the precepts (*kairitsu no tokutai hosshin*) and the manifestation by the living Buddha of ideal, virtuous qualities, for example, wisdom, compassion, and skillful instruction.[65] The Japanese understanding of the Dharmakāya as an eternal self baldly contradicted the Buddha's cardinal teachings of impermanence, non-self, the Four Truths, and Twelve-fold Chain of Conditioned Coproduction that were at the

---

64. For current usage of these terms in Japanese Buddhology see IBJ, 286–87; 358–59. Nakamura notes that the term "primitive Buddhism" has been displaced by the more value-neutral term, "early Buddhism" in more recent scholarly literature.

65. A standard contemporary definition of Dharmakāya is that it refers to the "truth body" or "collection of auspicious qualities of the buddha. See PDB, 246.

heart of the Buddha's teaching. Tracing the history of this misinterpretation, Kawaguchi described how, in the Hinayana period, the Sarvāstivāda doctrine of the actual existence of the dharmas in past, present, and future was applied to the concept of the body of all the dharmas. As a result, the Sarvāstivādins came to assert that the body of the dharmas was an actual existent in past, present, and future. This erroneous view, Kawaguchi wrote, became the basis for the notion of the noumenal Dharmakāya in middle and late-Mahayana Buddhism, as well as in all Japanese Buddhist schools.[66]

According to this distorted view, which has infected all of Japanese Buddhism Kawaguchi wrote, the Dharmakāya is widely understood to be the body of the Great Self (*daigatai*) that "is neither produced nor extinguished; absolutely equal; transcendent of good and evil; and beyond the heterodox and orthodox. Realizing this, the ordinary person, just as he is, is the Dharmakāya Buddha. This is called 'seeing one's nature and becoming Buddha' (*kenshō jōbutsu*)."[67] Kawaguchi contended that this distorted idea continues to be perpetuated by many American and European scholars of Indian philosophy who are enamored with the idea of a noumenal Brahman-Ātman in which the individual ātman merges without distinction with Brahman. Modern scholars of Buddhism, including sectarian ones, according to Kawaguchi, based their understanding of Buddhism on this heterodox Hindu doctrine, thus distorting the true meaning of the Dharmakāya. According to these American and European scholars this notion represents the apex of religious thought. In part because of the extreme deference of Japanese scholars for the West, Kawaguchi grumbled, Japanese sectarian scholars as well blindly continue to accept the erroneous interpretations views of the Dharmakāya, regarding it as the true teaching of the Buddha.[68]

In both of these tracts, Kawaguchi offered a scathing assessment of how these distortions had led to the degeneration of Buddhism in Japan, much to the detriment of the broader society. Launching his attack in *Upāsaka Bukkyō*, Kawaguchi opened the work with the following statement about the existing schools of established Buddhism (*kisei Bukkyō*).

> Today is an age in which monks are not monks but rather evil monks as there are no true home-leaving monks. Therefore it is an age without Buddhism that is maintained by home leaving. The dharma teaching today is no more than a dead dharma teaching that is nothing more than a husk [of its former self].

66. KECS 4: 77–80.
67. KECS 4: 4–13.
68. KECS 4: 6–7.

Kawaguchi, in a passage that rivals some of Nichiren's most vitriolic condemnations of other Buddhists in Japan, then described the current state of Buddhism in Japan with ten negations and two affirmations.

1. The world is without a single cleric (*sō*).
2. Therefore the world is without the Buddha or the Dharma.
3. Tendai lacks a basis for its doctrines.
4. Ritsu lacks true practice.
5. Shingon misreads [the sutras], so it lacks the "true word"
6. The alcohol swilling Nichiren [clergy] lack the precepts (*kai*)
7. Rebirth in the Pure Land through chanting *nenbutsu* is not the Buddha's words.
8. Zen, because of forgery, lacks [transmission of] the lamp
9. All of these schools lack proselytization
10. All of these schools lack any efficacy in society
11. Thus these schools harm self and other
12. And they poison the nation state[69]

In a 1926 article on the fundamental revolution in Buddhism, Kawaguchi decried the narrow sectarianism and triumphalist hermeneutical schemes set forth by the numerous Japanese Buddhist denominations. Instead, echoing the One Vehicle Teaching in the Lotus Sutra and the lack of denominational distinctions in such texts as the Āgamas, Kawaguchi wrote that Buddhism was originally of one homogenous flavor and only later came to be divided into Mahayana and Hinayana or the three vehicles.[70]

In addition to advocating the practice of giving rise to the awakening mind, which was one of the central practices described in the *Bodhicaryāvatāra*, in *Upāsaka Bukkyō*, *Bosatsudō*, and *Shōshin Bukkyō*, Kawaguchi described the Three Treasures of Buddha, Dharma, and Sangha in a fashion that marked a radical break with most contemporaneous established Buddhist denominations in Japan. One by one, Kawaguchi sought to return the understanding of each of the Three Treasures to the meaning it held in foundational Buddhism based on etymological analysis and his own rather tendentious periodization of Buddhist canonical materials.

Kawaguchi's view of the nature of the first treasure, the Buddha, was in part shaped by his travels overseas. Here again, as with his direct travel and study experiences in Tibet and India drawing Kawaguchi's attention to the *Bodhicaryāvatāra* and the central importance of bodhisattva practice in Buddhism, Kawaguchi's stay in Tibet and India deepened his con-

---

69. KECS 3: vi. Kawaguchi expands on this point in *Shōshin Bukkyō*, KECS 4: 288–90.
70. "Bukkyō no konponteki kakumei" ō (1926). In KECS 16: 166.

viction that Śākyamuni was the single appropriate object of veneration for Buddhists.

During his long stays in India, Kawaguchi had visited numerous pilgrimage places associated with the life of Śākyamuni and had ample opportunity to witness the practices of other Asian Buddhists at those sites. In his descriptions of Lhasa during his first visit to Tibet, Kawaguchi noted that "in the center of Lhasa is the great temple dedicated to the worship of Shakya Muni Buddha." In his travel record, Kawaguchi describes the temple, noting that it was the most prominent and sacred worship place in the city.[71]

> When I lifted up my thanks before this image of Buddha for my safe arrival in Tibet, I could not help shedding tears over the goodness of Buddha, which enabled me to see His image at this temple as well as at Buddha-gayā in India. I need not say, for the whole story shows it, how great is my faith in Buddha. I do not mean that I do not respect other Buddhist deities; still Buddha claims the greatest worship from me, and I have entirely given myself up to Him and His religion.[72]

In addition to his experiences in Tibet, Kawaguchi, as mentioned above, made a number of trips to various sites in India and Nepal associated with the life of Śākyamuni, often accompanied by other Japanese Buddhists. He reported on the state of these pilgrimage points through letters published in newspapers and magazines in Japan. Touched by his experiences, Kawaguchi noted how more scholars had taken an interest in exploring South Asian Buddhist sites for themselves, while expressing the desire that other Japanese Buddhists would come to feel the necessity to visit the pilgrimage places as well.[73]

These experiences and, no doubt, his reading of scholarly writing on Buddhism produced in Europe, India, and Japan, impressed upon Kawaguchi the central importance of Śākyamuni for Buddhism. Kawaguchi writes at great length in *Upāsaka Bukkyō* and *Shōshin Bukkyō*, and elsewhere about the critical necessity for Japanese Buddhists to recognize Śākyamuni as the only appropriate object of worship (*honzon*). According to Kawaguchi, in our time the only proper object of worship and veneration, that is the "Buddha" of the Three Treasures, was the transformation body (*ōjin*, S. *nirmāṇakāya*) of the Buddha, that is to say, Śākyamuni, who served as the model for all practitioners. In his central declaration of the principles underlying the lay Buddhist

---

71. KECS 1: 336.
72. KECS 17: 288. Diacritical marks as in the original.
73. KECS 15: 511.

movement, *Upāsaka Bukkyō*, Kawaguchi devoted a sizable portion of the
work to demonstrating why the central objects of worship used in Nichiren,
Pure Land, True Pure Land, and Zen temples, among others, should be replaced by the only appropriate image for the age. Only Śākyamuni's transformation body, that is the historical Buddha, Kawaguchi asserted, possessed the
necessary ten virtues necessary for a central object of worship.[74] When one
took refuge in the Buddha, chanting in Pali, *Buddham Saranaṁ gacchāmi*,
according to Kawaguchi, this referred specifically to Śākyamuni Buddha and
no other, although in the chant *Namu Buddaya* (Homage to the Buddha) the
term *Budda* included the numerous buddhas who would follow Śākyamuni
and thus was not a proper noun.[75]

Attempting to return Buddhist practice to its foundations, Kawaguchi
emphasized that although the word "dharma" had multiple meanings, as
the second of the Three Treasures, "Dharma" (*hō*) referred to the teaching
(*kyōhō*) that enabled one to become a buddha and achieve nirvana. Kawaguchi rejected such practices as avoiding calamity and achieving good fortune, rebirth in the Western Pure Land, etcetera, because they were absent
from foundational Buddhism. Instead, Dharma referred to the Eightfold Path
(Hasshōdō) and the Threefold Learning and the Six Perfections (*Sangaku-
Rokudo*). These practical Dharma teachings (*jikkōteki kyōhō*) that aimed at
the achievement of liberation from suffering comprised the essence of True
Buddhism (*Shōshin Bukkyō*) as taught by Śākyamuni "2400 years ago."[76]

Finally, Kawaguchi understood the third of the Three Treasures, "*Sangha*"
in its broad sense to refer to all four segments of the four-fold assembly,
including laymen and laywomen. In *Upāsaka Bukkyō* and *Shōshin Bukkyō*
alike, Kawaguchi rejected the possibility of true home leaving, that is, monastic practice, in the twentieth century. Kawaguchi's first-hand experience
of corruption within monastic Buddhism in Japan and continental Asia,
particularly China and Tibet, reenforced through his study of the Buddhist
textual tradition convinced him that real Buddhist clerics (*bikusō*; S. *bhikṣu/
bhikṣuṇī*) no longer existed.[77] In their place, lay Buddhist clerics (*upāsakasō*),

---

74. In *Upāsaka Bukkyō*, KECS 3: 89–91, Kawaguchi declares that the central image of worship for Buddhism must have ten characteristics. The central image of worship must be: 1) uni-
tary (*yuitsu*); 2) pure beauty (*junmi*); 3) gloriously adorned (*shōgon*); 4) most honored (*saishō*);
5) world saving (*kuse*); 6) tranquil light (*jakkō*); 7) unrestricted (*jizai*); 8) universal (*fuhen*);
9) rational (*gōri*); 10) liberating (*gedatsu*). Only the transformation body of Śākyamuni is replete
with these characteristics, according to Kawaguchi.

75. KECS 108–10.

76. KECS 4: 2.

77. KECS 4: 288–90.

a category invented by Kawaguchi, practiced, preserved, and transmitted Buddhism, forming the Sangha, now renamed the *Upāsaka* Sangha (*upāsaka sōgya*).[78] In place of the distorted forms of Buddhist teaching that had arisen in Japan based on such false notions as the noumenal Dharmakāya, Kawaguchi advocated a lay Buddhism that centered on the veneration of Śākyamuni Buddha, the arousal of the mind of awakening (*bodaishin*) in the practitioner, adherence to the five lay precepts, and the practice of the Eightfold Path, including the Three Learnings and the Six Perfections.

One of the central practices emphasized by Kawaguchi for all *upāsaka* was stringent observance of the Five Precepts of not killing, not stealing, not lying, not committing licentious sexual acts, and not consuming alcoholic beverages. Although the received wisdom in Japan was that adherence to the precepts was not essential, as chanting the *nembutsu* or *daimoku* or seeing into one's own nature (*kenshō*) would enable practitioners to achieve Buddhahood. This was a grave error, Kawaguchi asserted. "Śākyamuni showed directly and indirectly that the precepts and moral regulations (*kairitsu*) were the Dharmakāya (*hosshin*) and the essence of the Buddha (*Buttai*). Therefore, if there is no precept practice (*kaigyō*) there is neither the Dharmakāya nor the essence of the Buddha. Therefore, there also is no Buddhism."[79]

Kawaguchi dismissed the possibility of true monastic practice based on adherence to the Vinaya regulations in current times and rejected the *Bonmōkyō* bodhisattva precepts (*Bosatsukai*) as apocryphal and confused. Despite his own adherence to what resembled an unmarried, monastic lifestyle, Kawaguchi made the five lay precepts and the Ten Good Precepts (*Jūzenkai*) the essential moral code for twentieth-century Buddhism.[80] Kawaguchi's views concerning precept practice undoubtedly were shaped by contemporaneous precept movements in Japan as well as his own experiences with Ōbaku Zen practice and his first-hand encounters with other Buddhists in South Asia and China. In placing emphasis on the Five Precepts and the Ten Good Precepts, Kawaguchi drew upon his exposure to Shaku Unshō and Shaku Kōzen's streams of precept revival in late-nineteenth and early twentieth-century Japan. Although not a long-term acolyte of either man, their emphasis on the Ten Good Precepts and the Five Precepts left a lasting impression on Kawaguchi, even after decades of exposure to Buddhism in Nepal, Tibet, India, and China.

As an ordained Ōbaku cleric, Kawaguchi also would have been exposed

---

78. Kawaguchi uses the variant reading "*upāsaka*" for *ubasoku*.
79. *Shōshin Bukkyō*, KECS 4: 2–3.
80. *Shōshin Bukkyō*, KECS 4: 147–53.

to the Three Platform Ordination (Sandan kaie), the Chinese style of ordi-nation used by the Ōbaku denomination of Zen.[81] In this form of clerical ordination, over an eight-day period, clerics received the ten *shami* (nov-ice Precepts), 250 Shibunritsu (Dharmaguptaka Vinaya Regulations), and the ten major and forty eight minor *Bonmōkyō* (*Fanwang jing*) Bodhisattva precepts. In renouncing the possibility of clerical practice in the twentieth century, Kawaguchi rejected the use of the first two sets of the precepts for lay practice, emphasizing the Five Precepts for the laity instead. Kawagu-chi also questioned the legitimacy of the *Bonmōkyō* precepts, which had been used in Japan in both lay and clerical practice since the time of Saichō (767–822).

Kawaguchi broke with the Ōbaku denomination and other Japanese schools that used the *Bonmōkyō* (C., *Fanwang jing*) precepts as the bodhisat-tva precepts to augment the novice precepts and Vinaya regulations. As early as 1926 in *Upāsaka Bukkyō*, and again in the 1936 *Shōshin Bukkyō*, Kawaguchi called into question the canonical status of the *Fanwang jing* and the under-standing of the precepts contained therein as "Bodhisattva Precepts."[82] In this regard, he was among the earliest of Japanese scholars in the twentieth cen-tury to do so, denying the canonicity of the *Fanwang jing* several years before Mochizuki Shinkō (1869–1948) made similar claims in his 1930 work, *Jōdokyō no kigen oyobi hattatsu*.[83] Kawaguchi had multiple reasons for regarding the *Fanwang jing* as apocryphal, most of them similar to those outlined by Groner in his 1990 essay on the use of the *Fanwang jing* in the Tendai denomination. Based on his reading of the Koguryŏ preface to the sutra that was included in the *Shukusatsu daizōkyō*, Kawaguchi argued that Kumārajīva had not trans-lated from a written text, reciting the text from memory instead. According to Kawaguchi, instead of referring to a process of translation, *yakushutsu*, the preface uses such terms as *juji/ C., songchi* (to recite and keep) or *jushutsu/ C., songchu* (to recite from memory) to refer to how Kumārajīva transmitted the text to his audience. Kawaguchi also wrote that there were neither corre-

81. Helen Baroni, *Obaku Zen: The Emergence of the Third Sect of Zen in Tokugawa Japan* (Honolulu: University of Hawai'i Press, 2000), 95–97. At some point in the twentieth century the Ōbaku school ceased performing the ordination procedures instituted by Baroni. I have been unable to determine whether this occurred during Kawaguchi's lifetime or if Kawaguchi underwent the full eight-day Ōbaku ordination ceremony.

82. *Upāsaka Bukkyō*, KECS 3: 214–16; 4: 147–50.

83. This is based on Paul Groner, "The *Fanwang Jing* and Monastic Discipline in Japanese Tendai: A Study of Annen's *Futsū Jobasatsukai*," in *Chinese Buddhist Apocrypha*, ed. Robert E. Buswell Jr., 281, note 10.

sponding texts in Sanskrit or (wrongly) Tibetan.[84] Kawaguchi also construed the use of the word "abode" (*taku/ C., zhai*) in the rather obscure opening line in the Preface that mentions "All wholesome practices arise from the abode of profound faith" (*mangyō, jinshin no taku ni okoru*) to refer to the mind of Kumārajīva: "the abode of profound faith indicates the mind (*kokoro/xin*) of Kumārajīva."[85] These were clear indications, according to Kawaguchi, that the sutra had been composed in China. Equally problematic were the contents of the text, as the authors had mixed together precepts intended for monastics and those solely for the laity, including together such monastic rules as a ban on sexual relations or rules concerning the eighteen articles used in ascetic practices (*zudagyō*) alongside the lay-centric prohibition against selling alcohol, for example.[86] Kawaguchi concluded that because the text was confused and apocryphal, Saichō's use of the *Fanwang jing* precepts as the Bodhisattva Precepts, attempting to make them the basis for Tendai ordinations, was a grave mistake.[87]

In place of the *Fanwang jing* precepts, Kawaguchi contended that two sets of largely overlapping precepts, the Five Precepts (*Gokai*, S. *Pañcaśīla*) and the Ten Good Precepts together composed the true bodhisattva precepts. According to Kawaguchi, the Ten Good precepts were classified as the true Bodhisattva Precepts and were to be taken as part of the more advanced practice of the Six Perfections. Whether these sets of precepts were considered lay precepts or bodhisattva precepts depended on the practitioner's state of mind and the degree to which both sets of precepts were fully honored. According to Kawaguchi, the meaning of the Five Precepts shifted, depending on whether the recipient continued to cling to the notion of a self or had reached an understanding of the truth of *anātman*. For the former person, the Five Precepts were lay precepts, while for the latter, they became the "Five precepts of the bodhisattva." Kawaguchi wrote, "For example, if one practices the Five precepts with the mind of Mañjuśrī or Samantabhadra, they become the Five precepts of the bodhisattva. If one practices them with the ordinary mind of

84. Groner, "The *Fanwang jing* and Monastic Discipline," 253, notes that this Tibetan version probably is a translation from the Chinese text.

85. *Upāsaka Bukkyō*, KECS 3: 215; *Shōshin* Bukkyō, 4: 150. For a translation of the Preface to the *Bonmōkyō*, see Leo M. Pruden, "Some Notes on the *Fan-Wang-Ching*," *Indogaku Bukkyōgaku kenkyū* 15, no. 2 (1962): 915–25. The original Chinese is "萬行起於深信之宅." CBETA T24n1484_001_0997a04.

86. *Shōshin Bukkyō*, KECS 4: 150.

87. *Upāsaka Bukkyō*, KECS 3: 216.

a *pṛthagjana* (common person), they become like the Five precepts of the everyday layperson."[88]

Although the Five Precepts could thus function as bodhisattva precepts, according to Kawaguchi, precisely speaking, the true Bodhisattva Precepts were the Ten Good Precepts that prohibited the ten unwholesome courses of action (*akugōdō*; S. *akuśala-karmapatha*), that is, not killing; not stealing; not committing adultery; not lying; not speaking harshly; not speaking divisively; not speaking frivolously; not being greedy; not having malice; and not having wrong views.[89] "The true Bodhisattva Precepts are not the Five precepts but the Ten Good Precepts. To receive those, one first must give rise to awakening mind and enter the stage of the bodhisattva, then receive the Ten Good Precepts and engage in the practices of a bodhisattva."[90] Kawaguchi is not given much credit in most Japanese scholarly works for his pioneering research on the precepts, perhaps because he buried these conclusions in polemical tracts that are largely ignored in scholarly circles in Japan. Nonetheless, Kawaguchi's conclusions concerning what he viewed as the true bodhisattva precepts are not too far from those made by Hirakawa Akira more than thirty years later. In his important essay concerning the path of ten good actions (*jūzendō*) in early Mahayana, that is the tradition as presented in the *Prajñā Pāramitā* sutras and the *Daśabhūmika-sūtra*, Hirakawa Akira similarly concluded that ". . . the Mahayana precepts of the early period were the Ten Good Precepts."[91]

As was true of the Five Precepts, however, Kawaguchi noted that the Ten Good Precepts could be either mundane, lay precepts or the supra-mundane precepts of a bodhisattva. For Kawaguchi, a strict teetotalist, the difference revolved around the prohibition against drinking, the one precept contained in the Five Precepts that was not included in the Ten Good Precepts. Because all bodhisattvas began their careers as laypeople, as a matter of course they would begin by receiving the Five Precepts before proceeding to receive the Ten Good Precepts, Kawaguchi argued. "Bodhisattvas originally are laypeople, therefore it is a matter of course that they uphold the Five Precepts. If they do not uphold the Five Precepts and drink alcohol, they are not perfect *upāsaka* and will lack the qualifications of a bodhisattva. Therefore, those who uphold the Ten Good Precepts as bodhisattvas are those who as a matter

88. *Shōshin Bukkyō*, KECS 4: 173–75.

89. PDB, 1086.

90. *Shōshin Bukkyō*, KECS 4: 157.

91. Hirakawa Akira, "Shoki Daijō Bukkyō no kaigaku to shite no Jūzendō," in Hirakawa, *Hirakawa Akira chosakushū* 7: 201–38. (Hereafter HAC.) The quotation is on p. 206.

of course do not drink alcohol, thus comporting with the true nature of the *upāsaka*."[92]

In many of his publications, Kawaguchi tied the welfare of the nation to the strength of Buddhism. He believed that with the extinction of the denomination-riven Buddhism of home-leaving clerics, the lay bodhisattva Buddhism that had been predicted by Śākyamuni and was described in *Upāsaka Bukkyō* would guide the nation.[93] This simple, straightforward form of Buddhism, according to Kawaguchi, was the most vital form of Buddhism for the twentieth century. If the Japanese transformed Buddhist practice in this fundamental way, this would alleviate profound societal problems, thus ensuring that the forces of nihilism (*kyomu shugi*) and Bolshevism did not take root in Japan.[94]

Kawaguchi's identity as a Japanese imperial subject remained central to him throughout much of his career and in his writings he emphasized the necessity of strong Asian nations. Like many well-traveled Japanese of his era, even while traveling in the most remote locations, Kawaguchi would remember Japanese holidays and express his loyalty to Japan. En route to Lhasa through Tibet as 1901 began, Kawaguchi recalled,

> The New Year's Day dawned, but met with nothing special to mark the day, as the Tibetans use the old calendar. Still I got up at three o'clock in the morning and turning east, as I had done every New Year's Day, I began the New Year's reading of the scriptures. For, as Buddhism teaches us, it is our duty to pray for the health of the sovereign, and every Buddhist reads the Scriptures on New Year's Day, in however remote a place he may happen to be, and prays for the welfare of the Imperial Family.[95]

A year later, while in Lhasa as the year 1902 began, Kawaguchi once again performed a ritual "in order to pray for the prosperity of the Imperial Majesties the Emperor and Empress, H. I. H. the Crown Prince, and also for the greater prosperity and glory of the Empire of Japan."[96]

92. *Shōshin Bukkyō*, KECS 4: 212–13.

93. KECS 16: 176–77.

94. For a summary of Kawaguchi's arguments, see "Bukkyō no konponteki kakumei," in KECS 16: 163–77.

95. *Three Years in Tibet*, in KECS Bekkan 1: 260. See also, Kawaguchi Ekai and Okuyama Naoji, *Kawaguchi Ekai Nikki: Himaraya/Chibetto No Tabi* (Tokyo: Kōdansha, 2007), 136. In the *nikki*, Kawaguchi states that he arose at 4:00 AM. Kirihara Kenshin, "Kawaguchi Ekai: Kyūhō no michi no shūchakuten," in *Ajia taiken to shisō no hen'yō, kindai Nihon no Bukkyōsha*, ed. Ogawara Masamichi and Koyama Satoko (Tokyo: Keiō Gijuku Daigaku Shuppankai, 2010), 255–58.

96. *Three Years in Tibet*, in KECS Bekkan 1: 464.

Kawaguchi believed that a healthy nation was necessary for Buddhism's preservation and a vigorous Buddhism would ensure a peaceful, prosperous society. He condemned those, like Tagore, who paid too little heed to the nation. Commenting on the religious perspective expressed in Tagore's book *Jībitasha sādana*, Kawaguchi remarked, "He does not express love for the real India, but instead love for a poetically ideal nation, which is nothing more than fantasy. There is not a hint of a philosophy concerning love of the actual nation. Speaking from this perspective, we can say that Tagore's philosophy is the type that is dangerous for the nation."[97]

The fate of the nations of Asia was of great concern to Kawaguchi, so he was wary of what he perceived as a pan-Asianism that neglected the realities of a strong country. In a lengthy 1905 English-language memorial of advice for the prime minister of Nepal, Chandra Shumsher (1863–1929), who was the de facto ruler, Kawaguchi sought to guide the construction of a robust, independent nation. His aim was that along with Japan and other nations in Asia, "the Asiatic [*sic*] will be combined and act as a body in concert and be a guarantee to the independence of Asia." This would thereby ensure the nurturing of a robust pan-Asian sentiment throughout Asia.[98] To achieve this end, Kawaguchi advised the Nepalese ruler to strengthen the educational system, regularize succession to the reins of power, professionalize the army, develop trade and industry, and foster patriotism. By so doing, the Nepalese would contribute to the peace and prosperity of Asia more generally.[99]

Within years after returning from Tibet, Kawaguchi settled in Tokyo, where he would remain for the remainder of his life, although his residence in the city changed at least three times. In 1918, three years after returning to Japan, Kawaguchi founded a lay group, the Sessankai (The Himalaya Society), and began to style himself Sessan Dōnin, as can be seen on some of his calligraphic works.[100] Kawaguchi gave the group a name that had multiple meanings, as the term "sessan" referred both to the Himalayas and alluded to the story of Sessan Dōji, who was one of Śākyamuni's previous incarnations who had lived as an ascetic in the Himalayas, where he practiced as a bodhi-

97. "Bōkokuteki shisōka to shite no Tagōru," in KECS 15: 531. I believe the Japanese title, *Jībitasha sādana*, which Kawaguchi translates as "The Realization of Life," may refer to *Sādhanā: The Realization of Life*, which was published in English in 1913.

98. "The Memorial: Peace and Glory," in KECS 15: 635–34. The pagination of this English-language memorial, from 643–586, is in reverse order in the volume.

99. KECS 15: 593–87.

100. The term also could be pronounced "Sessen." See Zengaku Daijiten Hensanjo, *Zengaku daijiten* 663a. (Hereafter ZGDJ.)

sattva.[101] In 1920, the name of the group was changed to the Bukkyō Sen'yō Kai (Society for the Promotion of Buddhism). In a document setting forth the basic principles to be followed by members, Kawaguchi listed three aims for the group: (1) teaching the principles of cause and effect; (2) cultivating the independent mind and spirit of perfect honor; and (3) giving people the key for opening the inexhaustible treasure chest that is originally present in each person's nature.

Each weekday morning from 6:30 to 7:30 a.m., Kawaguchi would lecture to the group on such lay-oriented texts as the *Vimalakīrti Sūtra* or his own works *Bosatsudō* and *Upāsaka Bukkyō*. At the weekly Sunday school for children, the group would chant from *Bukkyō nikka* and then Kawaguchi or one of his disciples would tell Buddhist stories. Kawaguchi also would recite poetry to organ music and, on occasion, pass out treats to the children.

As Kawaguchi's ideas concerning Buddhism evolved through his textual analyses and writing, he transformed his lay organizations accordingly. In 1927, one year after publishing *Upāsaka Bukkyō*, Kawaguchi dissolved the Bukkyō Sen'yō Kai, telling the members that the group was not fulfilling the goals he had set for it. In its place, he created the Upāsaka Bukkyō Shugyō Dan (Lay Buddhist Practice Organization). Echoing the prescriptions for proper Buddhist practice set forth in the eponymous tract, Kawaguchi told the members of the new organization that their practice would consist of taking refuge in Śākyamuni Buddha and strictly observing the five lay precepts.[102]

According to accounts of his life after Kawaguchi had moved to his third Tokyo residence with his brother and his family in the Yoda district of Setagaya Ward in 1930, although no longer an Ōbaku cleric and full-throated advocate of lay Buddhism, Kawaguchi, as in Benares, continued to lead an extremely stringent lifestyle. On the second floor of the house, which was Kawaguchi's residence, one room was used as a practice hall. The room contained a number of Buddha images and other objects that Kawaguchi had brought from South Asia, as well as a standing image of Śākyamuni that the famous craftsman of Buddha images Takamura Kōun (1852–1934) carved in 1928 for Kawaguchi from a piece of sandalwood that Kawaguchi brought back from Nepal. According to accounts given by Kawaguchi's niece, Miyata Emi, each day at 5 AM and 9 PM, Kawaguchi would strike a wooden sounding board (*han*) similar to those used in Zen temples, while chanting the verse written on the sounding board reminding practitioners of life's evanescence,

---

101. The story is found in the *Mahāparinirvāṇa Sūtra* (*Dai hatsunehangyō*), SAT Daizōkyō, T. 12.0449b 13–19.

102. Kawaguchi Akira, *Kawaguchi Ekai*, 264–65.

while urging them to work out their liberation with diligence. Kawaguchi ate two simple vegetarian meals each day, strictly following the Buddhist Vinaya practice of forgoing meals after midday. His nephew's family, including Miyata Emi, would have the same spartan pre-midday meals, restricting their consumption of fish and meat to the evening meal, which Kawaguchi did not join. Even so, the fish was cooked outside the home, so that Kawaguchi would not be troubled by the smell of the cooking. Kawaguchi's breakfast consisted of roasted brown-rice flour dumplings, made by mixing miso soup with the flour, and stewed or pickled vegetables. His niece recalls the family members each having one of the dumplings at breakfast, although she found them so distasteful that at times she would hide hers under the kitchen table to avoid having to eat it.[103]

Every Sunday, Kawaguchi would use the fourteen-*tatami* area of the second floor to conduct a meeting of the Bukkyō Sen'yō Kai. Meetings, as they had with the Sessan Kai, consisted of Kawaguchi explicating material that later was contained in several of his works concerning lay Buddhist practice: *Upāsaka Bukkyō* and *Shōshin Bukkyō*. Breaking with Japanese Buddhist practice, instead of celebrating Hana Matsuri on April 8 to honor the birth of Śākyamuni, Kawaguchi conducted a Vesak ceremony on April 15 honoring the birth, awakening, and decease of the Buddha, bringing the holiday in line with the celebration in most other Asian Buddhist countries.[104]

Varying in size from meeting to meeting, according to Miyata Emi, the group was composed of a mixture of Buddhist clerics from various denominations and laypeople, including a variety of accomplished scholars and artists. Although it was never a very large organization, some of its participants were active in various religious and artistic circles, thus giving Kawaguchi's work wider exposure. The following are some of the more prominent members participating in the group's activities.

1. Matsubayashi Keigetsu (1876–1963): Noted Japanese-style painter.
2. Takamura Kōun: sculptor, particularly of Buddhist images.
3. Nakamura Fusetsu (1866–1943): Western-style painter; author.
4. Shiio Benkyō (1876–1971): author; philosopher; religious thinker. Jōdo school Buddhist cleric. Taught at Taishō University, later became the university president.
5. Hashimoto Kōhō: disciple of Ekai's; wrote or translated a number of books on Tibetan and Mongolian Buddhism.

---

103. Miyata Emi, "Oji Kawaguchi Ekai to Sono Omoide," *Setagai* 58 (2006): 42.

104. Kawaguchi Akira, *Kawaguchi Ekai*, 263. Kawahara Hidetoshi, "Setagaya Yoda ni okeru Kawaguchi Ekai," *Setagai* 51 (2000): 53.

6. Hattori Yūtai: disciple of Ekai's; edited a volume on the Tibetan version of the *Dainichikyō* (S. *Mahāvairocanasūtra*).[105]

Kawaguchi's travels and prolonged period of study in India, Nepal, and Tibet shaped his scholarship and Buddhist reform agenda in profound ways. Despite devoting years to the study of Tibetan Buddhism, he was never particularly enamored with much of that culture, writing dismissively about it in *Three Years in Tibet* and other works. Witnessing firsthand in Tibet, China, and Japan what he decided was a tradition corrupted by fornication and other violations of the precepts, Kawaguchi decided that the only practice possible in twentieth-century Japan was lay practice. Kawaguchi's intensive, prolonged engagement with a range of scholars and religious reformers in India gave him the linguistic skills he needed to read the Buddhist Sanskrit sources that he regarded as more trustworthy than the versions surviving in East Asia. While in India, Kawaguchi also directly was exposed to the Indian interpretation of that approach to the study of Indian religion that was represented by Sarat Chandra Das and other members of the Buddhist Text Society in Calcutta, other members of the Bengal Asiatic Society and Tagore, as well as the Euro-American Theosophists' occultist, romanticized pro-Hindu and Buddhist revivalism. No doubt he also was exposed to the latest trends in European and American Indology as well. Thus, for Kawaguchi, as for many other Japanese, South Asia was a central "contact zone," to use Mary Louise Pratt's terminology, where Buddhist texts, ideas, practices, and scholarship, both Asian and European/American, were transformed (Pratt uses the term "transculturated") and disseminated.[106]

Kawaguchi, like other Japanese travelers in South and Southeast Asia, did not move through an inert landscape, absorbing influences. The world of Buddhist archaeology, scholarship, and education was in flux as Kawaguchi moved through it. British efforts like the founding of the Sanskrit College in Benares changed the nature of religious and philosophical instruction in India, bending it toward European standards for historical and philological scholarship. Those pedagogical changes were not accepted without resistance, however, as pandits argued for the utility and veracity of the traditional scholarship that had produced and preserved the Indian classics in the first place. These reaffirmations of Indian culture were tied up with the increasingly vigorous movement for independence, one that was supported by the

105. Kawahara, "Setagaya Yoda ni okeru Kawaguchi Ekai," 52–55.

106. Mary Louise Pratt, *Imperial Eyes: Travel Writing and Transculturation* (New York: Routledge, 1992), 1–11.

Theosophists, who inflected Hindu education in their own distinctive way. In this dynamic environment, Kawaguchi's interactions with all these parties moved him to rethink what Buddhist practice should be and the proper place for Buddhism in building new nation-states across Asia. At the same time Kawaguchi affected those with whom he interacted, for example, adding the prestige of his travel adventures to the Theosophical Publishing Society, putting Japanese-inflected ideas concerning the nation before the Maharaja of Nepal, and passing on the allure of Japan to Das, Tagore, and, probably, many others.

Such works as *Upāsaka Bukkyō*, *Bosatsudō*, and *Shōshin Bukkyō* were a reaction to the global mix of Buddhist scholarship and religious writing that had come into Kawaguchi's possession. Like many other Japanese and, even, some non-Japanese converts to Japanese Buddhism in the Taishō era, for example, the founders of such journals as the *Mahayanist* and the *Eastern Buddhist*, Kawaguchi rose to the defense of Mahayana Buddhism against charges leveled by European and American scholars, for example, Eugène Burnouf, that Mahayana sutras did not reflect the teachings of the historical Buddha.[107] Using the scholarly skills acquired in South Asia, as well as the corpus of Sanskrit and Tibetan texts he had gathered with such vigor, Kawaguchi defended Mahayana as foundational Buddhism and argued that the Mahayana sutras indeed were the words of the Buddha.[108] In the shift from early Buddhism to Hinayana, Kawaguchi believed, heterodox doctrines had been inserted into Buddhism, corrupting the religion. Kawaguchi insisted that the Four Truths of the Noble One and the Twelve-Fold Chain of Codependent Production, that is, the cardinal teachings of Śākyamuni, were the very essence of pure Mahayana Buddhism (*junsei Daijō*), which was isomorphic with foundational Buddhism.[109] Kawaguchi's fundamentalism was a creative attempt return Japanese Buddhist practice to an original Buddhism that included the Mahayana. On this point he was in agreement with the editors of the *Mahayanist* and the *Eastern Buddhist* that Mahayana, rather than Hinayana, reflected the true spirit of the Buddha.[110]

In many respects, Kawaguchi's career as a Japanese Buddhist was highly idiosyncratic. Although for the latter part of his life he was not a member of an established school of Japanese Buddhism, scholars and clerics of the

107. See, for example, Eugène Burnouf, *Introduction to the History of Indian Buddhism*, trans. Katia Buffetrille and Donald S. Lopez Jr. (Chicago: University of Chicago Press, 2010), 160.

108. *Upāsaka Bukkyō*, KECS 3: 155–59.

109. *Shōshin Bukkyō*, KECS 4: 32–35.

110. M. T. Kirby, "The Spirit of the Mahayana," *Mahayanist* 1, no. 3 (1915): 18–19. Kirby was an associate editor of the short-lived journal, which was published in Kyoto from 1915 to 1916.

Ōbaku denomination, at Tōhoku University, where the materials Kawagu-chi brought back from his second Tibet are stored, and at Taishō University, where Kawaguchi taught Tibetan language and culture, have played a role in preserving his legacy. For the most part, it has been Kawaguchi's Tibetan adventures and study of Tibet that has received the most attention from the members of all three institutions. Although Kawaguchi's efforts to radically reform Buddhism have been largely ignored since his death, I believe they tell us a good deal about the transformations that took place in Japanese Bud-dhism during the twentieth century.

Kawaguchi is a particularly interesting figure because his work is repre-sentative in a number of ways of a type of Japanese Buddhist scholarship, which, while informed by nineteenth and early twentieth-century European and American (a.k.a. "Western") Buddhist studies, did not result from the sort of direct training in European Buddhology received by Nanjō Bun'yū and Takakusu Junjirō, for example. Unlike those predecessors, Kawaguchi never traveled to Europe or the United States. Instead, as I have discussed above, Kawaguchi's exposure to modern Buddhology and religious studies came via his brief period of study with Nanjō at the Tetsugakkan in Tokyo and his long tutelage from a series of Indian scholar-pandits that included Sarat Chandra Das, P. K. Patankar, and many others who worked with the au-tochthonous Indian Buddhist Text Society in Calcutta, as well as a multi-year period of study at Annie Besant's Central Hindu College.

Kawaguchi, at least in the published sources, was relatively quiet about his time in India, apart from the descriptions of his schedule and terse mentions scattered in his writings of his Indian, Nepali, and Tibetan mentors. I have been speculative about the level of Kawaguchi's awareness of the intellectual currents surrounding him in India. Perhaps as more archival work is done in South Asia and Japan, particularly at the institutions where Kawaguchi stud-ied, scholars will discover further evidence concerning Kawaguchi's South Asian activities. It is possible, of course, that Kawaguchi was either oblivious to the intellectual life that surrounded him or contemptuous of the pandits who tutored him—we know that he was dismissive of many aspects of Ti-betan Buddhism and culture. Based on the few comments about his studies in South Asia that he makes in his writings, however, I suspect at the very least that his mentors helped shape Kawaguchi's choice of several topics for textual research as well as his distinctive approach to Buddhist studies and practice.

In his scholarship, translating, and writing following his return to Japan from South Asia in 1915, Kawaguchi made ample use of contemporaneous scholarship, particularly textual work, for his own translations. In his effort to create a series of new translations of Buddhist works, for example, his pioneering vernacular translation of the *Bodhicaryāvatāra*, Kawaguchi used modern editions of the Sanskrit text edited by Ivan Pavlovich Minaev (1840–90) and Haraprasad Shastri, while glossing difficult passages with reference to the Tibetan translation. In developing his arguments for the deviation of Hinayana Buddhism from some essential aspects of Buddhist orthodoxy, Kawaguchi created a heavily modified rendition of Ui Hakuju's tripartite periodization of early Buddhist doctrinal evolution into foundational (*konpon*), primitive (*genshi*), and Hinayana (Shōjō).[111]

On the other hand, Kawaguchi marshaled an eclectic set of more traditional Buddhist interpretive strategies culled from Japanese, Indian, and Tibetan Buddhist texts. In his defense of Mahayana as the word of the Buddha, Kawaguchi turned to the Tibetan theory of *gter ma* (*terma*), claiming that the most important Mahayana sutras had been concealed following their revelation, then discovered or re-revealed by later Buddhists.[112] Like some of his Indian teachers who used shastric sources in their attempts to resolve contemporaneous social debates like the one concerning widow marriage, Kawaguchi also tapped classical Buddhist materials in an effort to show how societal problems in Taishō and early Shōwa Japan could be ameliorated through recourse to the proper Buddhist teachings, particularly those concerning ethics.[113] In the context of this project, Kawaguchi formed his views of the Bodhisattva Precepts using classical standards of Buddhist clerical scholarship and canonical consistency, while applying to some degree modern sources, philological methods, and standards of historical proof. Like those Indian pandits who worked within a "shastric imaginary" that blended traditional and imported approaches to scholarship, Kawaguchi's approach to Buddhist doctrine and praxis was rooted in, what I would call, extrapolating from Hatcher, a "dharmic imaginary."

In his focus on South Asia as the source of Buddhist renewal, rejection of monastic and sectarian Buddhism, and emphasis on the importance of the precepts for lay practice, Kawaguchi gave voice to a widely shared vision of how to reform Japanese Buddhism. In creating his lay Buddhism, which drew not just from Sinitic Buddhist sources but also from Tibetan, Indian, and European ones, Kawaguchi attempted to transcend sectarianism in order to recover the true teachings of the Buddha. In this way, Kawaguchi's vision is

111. For current usage of these terms in Japanese Buddhology see IBJ, 286–87; 358–59. Nakamura notes that the term "primitive Buddhism" has been displaced by the more value-neutral term, "early Buddhism" in more recent scholarly literature.

112. *Upāsaka Bukkyō*, in KECS 3: 155–59.

113. Hatcher, "Pandits at Work," 49; *Shōshin Bukkyō*, KECS 4: 5–6.

similar to the sorts of trans-sectarian, global forms of Buddhism that Lopez has called "modern."[114] At the same time, Kawaguchi's continued advocacy of forms of ritual practice, image veneration, and precept practice place him at odds with many of the tendencies that help define Buddhist modernism as described by Lopez.[115]

In his overview of the emergence of Buddhist universities in Japan, Hayashi Makoto argues that although "European-style" Buddhist studies, that is, the study of Sanskrit, Pali, and other non-Sinitic forms of Buddhism, was adopted with fervor in Japan at both imperial universities and Buddhist sectarian ones, that perspective remained largely cordoned off from "the realm of belief."[116] As a result, according to Hayashi, the two forms of Buddhist studies, European-philological and sectarian-doctrinal, emerged as separate streams in Japan. Kawaguchi was an exception to the typology sketched by Hayashi in two important respects: his Sanskrit and Tibetan studies took place in South Asia with pandits, albeit ones informed by colonial education, and Kawaguchi brought his textual scholarship to bear on matters of sectarian belief and practice.

Although the lay groups Kawaguchi founded did not attract a large following, his engaged form of Buddhist scholarship rooted in a dharmic imaginary stood as a possible model for the Japanese Buddhist founders of Buddhist new religions and sectarian scholars alike. Kawaguchi's scathing critique of Japanese Buddhism and his effort to found a lay Buddhist movement centered on Śākyamuni allows us to see the doctrinal and intellectual underpinnings of many of the attacks on established Buddhism in twentieth-century Japan. His claim that the Japanese had lost Buddhism's pure, original Mahayana spirit also foreshadows similar critiques, for example, those from members of the "critical Buddhism movement," claiming the scholarly high ground by using non-Sinitic Buddhist sources to reject the legitimacy of much of the Japanese Buddhist tradition. Although I have not had an opportunity to investigate whether there is a lineal connection between the Japanese proponents of "Critical Buddhism," Hakamaya Noriaki and Matsumoto Shirō, the similarities between Kawaguchi's arguments about the fundamental flaws in Japanese Buddhism being due to acceptance of an Indian, heterodox view of the Dharmakāya and the contention by the Critical Buddhists that almost all Japanese Buddhism was distorted by acceptance of the Brahmanical, monist

114. Lopez, *A Modern Buddhist Bible*, xxxvi–xxxvii.

115. Lopez, *A Modern Buddhist Bible*, vii–xl.

116. Makoto Hayashi, "The Birth of Buddhist Universities," *Japanese Religions* 39, nos. 1 & 2 (2014): 11–29.

doctrine of *dhātuvāda* (locus theory) is striking. In particular, the condemnation of the notion that "there is no essential difference between Śākyamuni's enlightenment and that taught in the Upaniṣads or early Jain philosophy" echoes Kawaguchi's assertion that scholars and many Buddhists, beginning with the Hinayanists, had conflated Upaniṣadic teaching with Buddhism, distorting the latter into heterodoxy.[117]

Kawaguchi was unable to create a group that could continue after his death, but his emphasis on the return to the original teachings and practices of Śākyamuni and rejection of clerical control of the tradition is echoed in many of the Buddhist-based New Religions in Japan today. This has given Kawaguchi's claims concerning the inauthenticity of the central objects of worship in most Japanese Buddhist denominations ongoing salience. The republication of *Upāsaka Bukkyō* and *Shōshin Bukkyō* as part of his selected works in 1998 even triggered a critical analysis of Kawaguchi's attack on the main object of worship (*Gohonzon*) by a member of the Nichiren denomination. In the riposte to Kawaguchi, the author of the article suggested this was not just an academic exercise because of the close resemblance between Kawaguchi's positions and those of some of the New Religious Movements critical of mainstream Nichiren Buddhism.[118]

Although always a true believer in the authenticity of the Mahayana, Kawaguchi attempted to tie Mahayana doctrine to the basic teachings of foundational Buddhism (*konpon Bukkyō*). A similar effort to draw inspiration and claim ties with foundational Buddhism was seen in the turn to the Āgamas by Kiyozawa Manshi (1863–1903), the founder of the "Spiritualist" movement in Higashi Honganji True Pure Land Buddhism.[119] More recently, Kiriyama Seiyū (1921–2016), the founder of the Agonshū, by adopting that name for his organization similarly attempts to claim authenticity by associating his school with foundational Buddhist teachings represented by the Āgamas, however superficial the actual ties with those texts might be. In effect, we can see in all these cases the way in which the emphasis on Buddhist origins in European and American Buddhist scholarship and notions of early

117. See Shirō Matsumoto, "The Doctrine of the *Tathāgata-garbha* Is Not Buddhist," in *Pruning the Bodhi Tree: The Storm over Critical Buddhism*, ed. Jamie Hubbard and Paul L. Swanson (Honolulu: University of Hawai'i Press, 1997), 165–73. On *dhatu-vāda*, see Nobuyoshi Yamabe, "The Idea of *Dhatu-Vāda* in Yogacara and *Tathāgata-garbha* Texts," ibid., 193–204.

118. See Hayasaka Hōjō, "Kawaguchi Ekai no Nichiren kyōgaku hihan ni tsuite," *Gendai shūkyō kenkyū* 31 (1997): 170–81.

119. Mark L. Blum, "Shin Buddhism in the Meiji Period," in *Cultivating Spirituality: A Modern Shin Buddhist Anthology*, ed. Mark L. Blum and Robert F. Rhodes (Albany: State University of New York Press, 2011), 35–36.

Buddhism derived by the Japanese through direct contact with the Buddhism of South and Southeast Asia pushed some Japanese Buddhists to reconceptualize their tradition in light of these new documents and understandings of Buddhist history. In this sense, Kawaguchi was an important pioneer among the emerging generation of Buddhist scholars in Taishō and early Shōwa-era Japan.

Like Shaku Kōzen, Kawaguchi's encounter with other forms of Buddhism in South Asia led him to question the orthodoxy of Buddhism as it existed in Japan at the start of the twentieth century. But Kawaguchi was only one of many cleric-scholars who studied extensively in South Asia prior to entering the ranks of one of the Buddhist sectarian universities. While Kawaguchi was living in Benares, travel to South Asia by Japanese Buddhists for study and pilgrimage became more common. As I will discuss in chapter 4, Kawaguchi and other early twentieth-century Japanese travelers to India played a pioneering role in mapping routes of pilgrimage for the Japanese Buddhists who would travel to India in the wake of World War I. Although these later pilgrims were not stimulated by their South Asian sojourns to radically reform their denominations' practices, like Kawaguchi, their time in South Asia gave them the scholarly tools to defend Japanese Mahayana Buddhism against claims of inauthenticity. Such cleric-scholars as Yamakami Tensen/ Sōgen (1878–1957) and Kimura Ryūkan/Nichiki (1882–1965), began studying Sanskrit and Buddhism in India with native scholars in the early twentieth century. They also became lecturers at Calcutta University before returning to teach in Buddhist sectarian universities. They, too, became part of a stream of Buddhist learning and practice in twentieth-century Japan that looked West through South Asia, rather than Europe and the United States, in their effort to create a Buddhism that could prosper in the new century.

3

Following the Cotton Road: Japanese Corporate Pilgrimage to India, 1926–1927

Between December 4, 1883, when the Jōdo Shin cleric Kitabatake Dōryū and his fellow Japanese traveler Kurosaki Yūji became the first Japanese on record to reach Bodh Gayā, and 1937, with the outbreak of full-fledged hostilities between Japan and China, travel by Japanese Buddhists to South Asia became increasingly common, as did published accounts, often containing maps and photographs, documenting the trips. From the mid-Meiji until the mid-Shōwa period, a number of notable Buddhists, artists, and intellectuals, including Shaku Kōzen, Shaku Sōen, Nanjō Bun'yū, Takakusu Junjirō, Inoue Shūten, Ōtani Kōzui, Hioki Mokusen, Kuruma Takudō, Tani Dōgen, Kanokogi Kazunobu, Hara Giken, Fujita Giryō, Hori Shitoku, Okakura Kakuzō, Murakami Myōsei, among many others, made the journey to visit Buddhist sites in South Asia. In dozens of published travel diaries, these pilgrims documented their impressions and experiences. Just a small sampling of the diaries published between the mid-Meiji and the start of the Shōwa eras is found in table 3.1.[1]

This is not a complete survey of this South Asian pilgrimage literature, but in the course of my research I have uncovered more than twenty diaries of travel in South Asia from 1884 to 1945. No doubt there are more accounts with titles lacking the words "Indo" or "Tenjiku" in the title, particularly by those who traveled to India for reasons other than the study of Buddhism. In addition, countless newspaper and magazine accounts that travelers frequently published in Japan concerning their travels add even more volume to the genre. Authors of these travel accounts frequently used the work of their predecessors, citing the comments by earlier travelers within their own

---

1. Full bibliographic details on these volumes are found in the bibliography.

TABLE 3.1. Japanese South Asian travel diaries and other accounts

Travel date	Publication date	Author	Title
1887	1887	Nanjō Bun'yū 南条文雄	Indo kikō 印度紀行
1898	1903	Inoue Shūten 井上秀天	Indo jijō 印度事情
1900	n.d.	Ōmiya Kōjun 大宮孝	Busseki shihyō 仏跡指標
1907	1913	Seki Rokō 関露香	Ōtani Kōzui Haku: Indo tanken 大谷光瑞伯印度探検
	1910	Ebe Zōen 江部蔵円 (Ebe Ōson 江部鴨村)	Indo seiseki shi 印度聖跡誌
1909–10	1914	Hasebe Ryūtai 長谷部隆諦	Indo shūkyō jikken ki 印度宗教実見記
1910–11	1911	Shaku Daishin 釈大真	Toin nisshi 渡印日誌
1911	1916	Kuruma Takudō 来馬琢道	Mokusen Zenji nangoku junrei ki 默仙禅師南国巡礼記
1912	1962	Tani Dōgen 渓道元	Tani Dōgen Nan'a ryoko ki 渓道元南亜旅行記
1916	1918	Oka Kyōtsui 岡教邃	Indo Busseki shashin chō 印度仏跡写真帖
1918	1920	Kanokogi Kazunobu 鹿子木員信	Busseki junrei kō 仏跡巡礼行
1920	1922	Seki Seisetsu 関清拙	Tenjiku angya 天竺行脚
1921	1927	Fujita Giryō 藤田義亮	Busseki junpai 仏跡巡拝
	1925	Takakusu Junjirō 高楠順次郎 and Ōshio Dokuzan 大塩毒山	Indo Bukkyōshi chizu narabi[ni] sakuin 印度仏教史地図並「二」索引
1922	1931	Amanuma Shun'ichi 天沼俊一	Indo ryokō ki 印度旅行記
1922	1942	Nakatsuji Masanobu 中辻正信	Indo ryokō ki 印度旅行記
1923	1926	Kumagaya Kunizō 熊谷国造	Indo Busseki jissha 印度仏跡実写
1924	1926	Hara Giken 原宜賢	Indo busseki Biruma Shamu shisatsu shashin roku 印度仏跡緬甸暹羅視察真録
1926	1928	Akegarasu Haya 暁烏敏 and Teruoka Yasunori 暉峻康範	Indo Busseki junpai ki 印度仏跡巡拝記
1926	1927	Izawa Heizaemon 伊沢平左衛門	Indo Busseki sanpai nisshi 印度仏跡参拝日誌
1926	1944	Murakami Myōsei 村上妙清	Nyūjiku bikuni 入竺比丘尼

accounts of their travels, building multilayered accounts of the sites they visited as they crossed Asia. We thus see in many accounts frequent citations of such classic accounts of South Asian travel as Xuanzang's *Da Tang xiyu ji* (646) and Faxian's *Foguo ji* (a.k.a. *Faxian zhuan*; fifth c.) alongside the more recent records listed in the table of diaries above. Akegarasu and Teruoka, for example, who wrote one of the main accounts to be analyzed in this chapter, turn to Hara Giken, Takakusu Junjirō, Fujita Giryō, and Kanokogi Kazunobu to compare these predecessors' impressions of various Buddhist sites with their own. In this fashion, each wave of Japanese pilgrims left literary and, albeit rarely, physical markers like the stele Kitabatake Dōryū had erected at Bodh Gayā for their countrymen to follow across South Asia.

In the previous chapter, I mentioned how Kawaguchi Ekai, as a long-term resident in India, served as a guide for a series of Japanese Buddhists who traveled to South Asia in the early twentieth century. Among those travelers hosted by Kawaguchi were Ōtani Kōzui, Hasebe Ryūtai, Inoue Enryō, Tani Dōgen, and Masuda Jiryō. Some of these travelers were visiting India for a short time; others—for example, Hasebe and Masuda—would, like Kawaguchi, remain in India for an extended period. The number of Japanese Buddhist travelers to India increased steadily in the years prior to World War I, then dropped off for a time during the war years. In the wake of World War I, however, Japan underwent a flowering of internationalization that Frederick Dickinson has characterized as a second "national opening" (*kaikoku*) akin to the opening of Japan to foreign influence and overseas travel that occurred in the mid-nineteenth century.[2] As part of this trend, Japanese partook in overseas travel in unprecedented numbers, with approximately sixty thousand travelers to Europe in 1919. In particular, defeated Germany, with an exchange rate highly favorable to the Japanese, attracted large numbers of overseas students, who were able to take advantage of the run-away inflation to purchase "wagon loads" of books.[3] Although travel to India by Japanese never approached the numbers headed to Europe, following the end of World War I, as can be seen in the table of travel diaries above, more Japanese Buddhists than ever before were able to journey to the subcontinent.

By the end of the Taishō era, the numbers of Japanese traveling to India had become large enough to warrant the beginning of organized group tours to India. The earliest of these corporate journeys were run by Nippon Yūsen Kaisha (hereafter, NYK Line), a major Japanese shipping firm founded in 1885 and still in existence. The NYK Line's launching of these corporate pilgrimages through South Asia was a watershed event in Japanese Buddhist travel, as it helped formalize a set route through India for subsequent travelers. The NYK group pilgrimages signaled the standardization of religious travel to South Asia. As we have seen in previous chapters, at Dharmapāla's urging, NYK had entertained the thought of giving discounted passage to pilgrims to India as early as the start of the twentieth century. The company also had offered subsidized passage to monastic students of Shaku Kōzen to travel to Ceylon in the Meiji era. (See chapter 1.) In conjunction with Thomas

2. Frederick Dickinson, *World War I and the Triumph of a New Japan, 1919–1930*, Studies in the Social and Cultural History of Modern Warfare (Cambridge: Cambridge University Press, 2013), 32.

3. Hayami Akira, and Kojima Miyoko, *Taishō demogurafi: rekishi jinkōgaku de mita hazama no jidai* (Tokyo: Bungei Shunjū, 2004), 225; Dickinson, *World War I and the Triumph of a New Japan*, 32, note 85.

Cook and Company, NYK offered its first group trip to India for a group of Japanese passengers in 1923, but I have not found detailed information about that trip.[4] Such previous travelers to South Asia as Kōzen, Sōen, Kawaguchi, Oda, and others were mostly scholar-clerics interested in learning Indic languages, collecting texts, doing archaeological exploration, and undertaking long-term study. The trips sponsored by NYK, by contrast, attracted a more casual sort of Buddhist tourist, although, because of the costs and time involved in such a journey, travel to South Asia would remain the province of the well-heeled, the famous, and the especially devout.

The second group expedition to Buddhist sites in India organized by NYK, which departed from Kobe on December 2, 1926, was chronicled in detail in two published accounts. The first, *Indo Busseki junpai ki* (A Record of Pilgrimage to Indian Buddhist Sites), written by Akegarasu Haya (1877–1954) and Teruoka Yasunori, was published in 1928.[5] Akegarasu, the better known of the coauthors, was an Ōtani-ha Jōdo Shin cleric and leading disciple of Kiyozawa Manshi (1863–1903). Although a sexual scandal forced Akegarasu to return to his home temple in Ishikawa Prefecture, he remained one of the most popular Buddhist preachers in Japan in the first half of the twentieth century.[6] Izawa Heizaemon (1862–1934) wrote the briefer *Indo Busseki sanpai nisshi* (Diary of Pilgrimage to Indian Buddhist Sites), which was published on Buddha's birthday, April 8, 1927, to commemorate his journey. Izawa was a prominent Sendai financier, saké brewer, and politician. A deeply religious layman, Izawa had even contemplated practicing at Eiheiji in his youth. Although he never was ordained, Izawa remained an avid patron of both Buddhist and Shinto institutions in Sendai, giving generously his time and money in their support. Izawa also became a prominent member of the Sendai Bukkyō Rengō Kai (Sendai Pan-Sectarian Buddhist Association), which supported his journey to South Asia.[7]

4. "Japanese Tourist Party to India," *Young East* 26, no. 2 (1926): 251.

5. Akegarasu Haya and Teruoka Yasunori, *Indo Busseki junpai ki* (Ishikawa Prefecture: Kōsōsha, 1928). The diary has a complicated structure, as it was written in part by each of the two authors during and after the actual trip through South Asia. A portion of it was composed while actually on the journey, with Akegarasu dictating his account to Teruoka. I have been unable to determine the life dates for Teruoka.

6. A concise summary of Akegarasu's travels in India and, later, in the Middle East, Europe, and the United States is found in Fukushima Eiju, *"Seishin Shugi" no kyūdōshatachi: Kiyozawa Manshi to Akegarasu Haya*, Kōka Sōsho, Vol. 5 (Kyoto: Kōka Joshi Daigaku, Tanki Daigaku Shinshū Bunka Kenkyūjo, 2003). I thank Jeffrey Schroeder for bringing this book to my attention.

7. For a description of Izawa's religious activities, see Shōji Ichirō, *Izawa Ryōan Ō den* (Sendai: Izawa Ryōan Ō Den Kankōkai, 1935), 58–62; 125–26.

Both travel diaries document the NYK-run trip through India in 1926–27. Together they provide a glimpse of how some prominent members of the Japanese Buddhist world responded to developments in academic Buddhist studies and their encounters with the Buddhist world of South Asia. In this chapter, while providing a detailed summary of the itinerary and encounters that took place during the time in South Asia, I will focus on the wider context for the trip and the importance of India for these pilgrims and their audience in Japan.

For Buddhists the focus on India and South Asian Buddhism more generally was stimulated by the encounter with European and American scholarship concerning Buddhism, much of which placed its emphasis on the historical Buddha and the origins of the tradition. Over the course of the nineteenth century, the British, through the efforts of the Archaeological Survey of India, mapped, unearthed, and restored many of the sites associated with the life of the historical Buddha and the early Buddhist community. Using newly translated versions of the travel records by Faxian and Xuanzang, James Prinsep, Alexander Cunningham, John Marshall, and Vincent Smith literally put such sites as Rājagṛha, Gṛdhrakūtaparvata (Vulture Peak), Nālandā, Sārnāth, Lumbinī, and Kuśinagarī on the map.[8] At the same time, the Mahābodhi Society promoted Buddhist pilgrimage in India to a global audience, beginning tours of important Buddhist monuments and places in India as early as 1904. According to Tony Huber, Dharmapāla and other leaders of the Mahābodhi Society promoted pilgrimage in India in order to unite global Buddhists. As a result of their efforts, as well as a variety of global economic and infrastructural changes, which I will discuss below, "from the 1920s until the outbreak of World War II, a veritable modern Buddhist pilgrimage industry sprang up around the archaeologically recovered and discursively redefined Buddhist holy land."[9]

In addition to the proximate, religious factors that stimulated interest in South Asia, however, there were also a set of larger historical forces driving the growth in Japanese interest in India and, more generally, in South Asia, while facilitating ever-more pilgrimages and journeys by Japanese to that region in the first decades of the twentieth century. Earlier travelers to India from East Asia, for example, Xuanzang, had followed various trade routes that in the nineteenth century became known collectively as the "Silk Road"

---

8. A popular account of this history is found in Charles Allen, *The Search for the Buddha: The Men Who Discovered India's Lost Religion* (New York: Carroll & Graf, 2003).

9. Toni Huber, *The Holy Land Reborn*, 293–95.

to India in their efforts to reach sites associated with Buddhism.[10] Modern Japanese pilgrims to India, like Akegarasu, Teruoka, Izawa, and many others, however, increasingly followed what I would call the new "Cotton Road" that was created by the steam-power revolution at the center of global capitalism. Steam engines made industrial textile production possible, driving the mechanical spindles that were essential for the new cotton factories. At the same time, the growing demand for raw materials and finished cloth was quenched by coal-fired steamships that brought bales of raw cotton from India and other regions to Japan and then distributed the final product to markets around the globe.

The efflorescence in travel to India by Japanese Buddhists coincided with the rapid industrialization of the Japanese economy and period of national opening that occurred following World War I. From the start of the Meiji era through the 1920s, Japan's economy shifted from a primarily agricultural to an industrial one enmeshed in global trade networks.[11] Textile manufacturing, particularly of silk and cotton cloth, was the "gateway" industry for the revolution that occurred in Japanese industry. Production of these goods, particularly cotton cloth, grew at a phenomenal pace. From 1893 to 1902, Japanese raw cotton imports, which primarily came from India and the United States, rose from 125 to 446 million pounds, reaching more than a billion pounds by 1920.[12] This amounted to a significant amount of the raw cotton exported from India, comprising by 1906 38 percent of the total Indian output.[13] By as early as 1902, 62 percent of all Japanese cotton imports came from India.[14]

During the first third of the twentieth century, cotton goods accounted for 26 percent of exports and 15 percent of all industrial production in Japan.[15] The raw cotton imported to Japan from Korea, China, and, predominantly, India, was woven into cloth that was then sold back to markets in China and India, where domestic cloth production was decimated by competition from

10. The term "Silk Road" was not widely used in English until the publication of the English translation of Sven Hedin's book, *Sidenvägen* (Silk Road). According to Green, the German scholar Ferdinand von Richtofen coined the term *Seidenstrasse*, in the late nineteenth century. See Nile Green, "From the Silk Road to the Railroad (and Back): The Means and Meanings of the Iranian Encounter with China," *Iranian Studies* 48, no. 2 (2015): 166–67.

11. Dickinson, *World War I and the Triumph of a New Japan*, 38.

12. Sven Beckert, *Empire of Cotton* (New York: Alfred E. Knopf, 2014), 340–41.

13. Beckert, *Empire of Cotton*, 293.

14. Beckert, *Empire of Cotton*, 341.

15. Brett L. Walker, *A Concise History of Japan*, Cambrdge Concise Histories (Cambridge: Cambridge University Press, 2015), 209.

industrial textile mills in Europe and, increasingly, Japan. During the post–
World War I era, Japanese cotton export business expanded in India, Southeast Asia, and elsewhere in the Pacific region.[16] Using leverage derived from
Japan's position as one of the prime export destinations for raw Indian cotton, Japanese textile merchants forced open the Indian market for their cloth
against the wishes of the British. As a result, the amount of cloth sent from
Japan to the Indian market increased from 7 million yards of cotton piece
goods in 1913–14 to 579 million yards in 1933.[17] By 1936 Japan was the largest
exporter of cotton piece goods in the world, with textile exports of all types,
including wool and silk, accounting for 58 percent of Japan's total exports to
foreign markets.[18] India thus had become of vital and steadily growing economic importance for the Japanese by the beginning of the twentieth century.

The development of the cotton textile industry in Japan connects with our
story of Indian pilgrimage and, in particular, the NYK group trip in several
ways. Of direct relevance for understanding the NYK pilgrimage and the efflorescence of travel by Japanese and, perhaps, East Asian, Buddhists to India,
is the crucially important role that India had come to play in Japan's economy
in the first half of the twentieth century, thanks to the cotton industry, just as
in the last quarter-century US interest in Japan and, subsequently, China has
tracked closely with the economic importance of those two countries for the
United States. In the first half of the twentieth century, the large amount of
import and export business with India from Japan required a concomitantly
sizable infrastructure in Japan, India, and on the seas to facilitate the trade.
By the time the NYK group reached India in 1927, there were a significant
number of Japanese merchants, bankers, military officers, and consular officials staffing the consulates, banks, trading houses, and shipping firms in the
subcontinent, as well as numerous long-term overseas Japanese students. The
Japanese had a presence even in such remote places as the Indian hinterland
of Berar, where much of the cultivable land had been given over to cotton
production. In 1926, the year that the NYK pilgrims headed to India, the cotton concern Tōyō Menka Kaisha had 156 subagencies in place to purchase
and export Indian cotton.[19] In port cities, the Japanese presence was even
more pronounced. Teruoka states in his diary that when the group arrived in
Bombay in February 1927, there were approximately three hundred Japanese

16. Dickinson, *World War I and the Triumph of a New Japan*, 39.

17. Beckert, *Empire of Cotton*, 406.

18. William W. Lockwood, *The Economic Development of Japan: Growth and Structural
Change, 1868–1938* (Princeton, NJ: Princeton University Press, 1954), 65.

19. Beckert, *Empire of Cotton*, 315.

residents working for firms that included, among others, Tōyō Menka, Nihon Menka, Mitsui Bussan, Shōkin Ginkō, Nippon Yūsen, and Ōsaka Shōsen.[20] Representatives of these firms met with and assisted Japanese travelers, including the members of the NYK pilgrimage and at least one earlier traveler, Hara Giken, who details his visit to Nihon Menka in Bombay in his account of his pilgrimage to Buddhist sites in India.[21] Even when traveling in the countryside, pilgrims encountered Japanese commercial outposts. As they headed to the caves at Ajanta in Maharashtra State, an important cotton-growing region, the NYK pilgrims saw branch offices of Tōyō Menka and other concerns in the town of Jalgaon.[22]

As Japanese commercial interests in South Asia began to clash with those of the British, geopolitical arguments supporting Indian independence also were on the rise by the early Taishō years. Ōkawa Shūmei (1886–1957), in particular, gave voice to the notion of a Japanese-led Asian order that was rooted in Tagore and Okakura Tenshin's civilizational pan-Asianism. Although Okakura's ideas were given widespread attention by the English-reading public, it was, according to Cemil Aydin, Ōkawa who successfully incorporated Okakura's ideas into Japanese discourse concerning pan-Asianism, starting on the eve of World War I.[23] In the wake of Tagore's visit to Japan in 1916, a trip that was facilitated by Kawaguchi Ekai and Kimura Ryūkan/Nichiki, Ōkawa published a work expressing sympathy for the Indian independence movement while also advocating the creation of a Japanese-led Asian order that was bound together by shared religious, artistic, and philosophical traditions.[24] By the height of World War I, Ōkawa became an opponent of the Anglo-Japanese Alliance. Ōkawa, who had studied with Anesaki Masaharu at Tokyo Imperial University, was well connected with Japanese government leaders and prominent intellectuals, thus gaining traction for his ideas in important venues for Japanese policy formation. So prominent was his role in shaping Japanese

---

20. Akegarasu, *Indo Busseki junpai ki*, 377.

21. Hara Giken, *Indo busseki Biruma Shamuro shisatsu shashin roku* (Tokyo: Tōkōdō, 1926), 89–91.

22. Akegarasu, *Indo Busseki junpai ki*, 346.

23. Cemil Aydin, *The Politics of Anti-Westernism in Asia: Visions of World Order in Pan-Islamic and Pan-Asian Thought*, Columbia Studies in International and Global History (New York: Columbia University Press, 2007), 113. Aydin provides an insightful, detailed analysis of Ōkawa's thought, including his support for Indian independence, on pp. 111–21.

24. Aydin, *The Politics of Anti-Westernism*, 115–16. Kimura used the name Ryūkan in the early stages of his career, then took the new Buddhist name Nichiki/Nikki. I will refer to him by Nichiki, the name found in several English-language publications, unless the context dictates using Ryūkan or Nikki instead.

policies in Asia that he was held to account "as the chief civilian ideologue of Japanese expansionism" at the Tokyo War Crimes Tribunal.[25] The rising tide of pan-Asianist and Indian pro-independence thought as epitomized in Ōkawa's strategically planned public appearances and publications thus stoked Japanese interest in India in the mid-Taishō and Shōwa years.

In the English-language journal *Young East*, which was launched on June 8, 1925, we see the explicit melding together of the growing commercial and religious ties between India and Japan in the mid-1920s. The founder of the journal, Sakurai Gichō (1868–1926), had been an ordained Nishi-Honganji Jōdo Shin cleric until later in life, when he renounced his clerical status. Sakurai was one of the driving forces behind a number of notable Buddhist publishing ventures. These include the journal of the Buddhist temperance society *Hanseikai zasshi*, which metamorphosed into *Chūō kōron*.[26] Deeply interested in exchange with the wider Buddhist world, Sakurai also was involved in the founding of the Buddhist Propagation Society (Kaigai Senkyō Kai) in Kyoto, along with the publication of the group's two journals, *Kaigai Bukkyō jijō* and its short-lived, English-language counterpart journal, *Bijou of Asia*.[27]

In 1898, en route back to Japan from Europe, Sakurai made his first trip to India. Sakurai became deeply involved with India due to his interest in its Buddhist sites and developing business ventures in the subcontinent. He visited the country several times and forged a number of close personal and business ties with Indians in the process. Sakurai had a reputation for regarding India as his "second home" and was known to proclaim "First, Japan; Second, India."[28] By the 1920s, Sakurai obtained exclusive rights to procure and import the vital industrial compound creosote from Mysore State to Japan. Sakurai was the founder and a trustee (*hyōgiin*) of the Japan-India Society (Nichi-In Kyōkai), which was founded in 1903. In his obituary in the *Young East*, the editors note that "the service he rendered to India, which he loved next to Japan, cannot be overestimated. He was always a very good friend to Indian students studying in our schools and a warm-hearted host to Indian statesmen, writers, businessmen and other leaders traveling to this country. For this reason, Mr, Sakurai was well known among a great many Indians by the name of Sakurai of India."[29]

25. Aydin, *The Politics of Anti-Westernism*, 112.

26. Details of Sakurai's biography are found in MNB 1: 362–70.

27. Nakanishi Naoki, Yoshinaga Shin'ichi, and Kaigai Senkyōkai, *Kaigai Bukkyō jijō: The Bijou of Asia*. Fukkokuban, 3 vols. (Kyoto: Sanjin Sha, 2014–15).

28. MNB 1: 368.

29. "Death of the Editor of the *Young East*," YE 2, no. 3 (1926): 104–5.

The *Young East* was aimed at a global Buddhist audience in an effort "to harmonise and bring to mutual understanding our brothers and sisters of the Asiatic countries, to make them recover their lost vigour and to unite their efforts for the restoration of ancient civilization of the Orient, which gave birth to great religions, deep philosophies and noble arts."[30] On the first page of the inaugural issue of the journal, which launched in 1925, the editors proclaimed irenically,

> We are followers of the Mahayana school of Buddhism. As such we are neither dreamers nor pessimists. We make much of action, and while earnestly thinking of the life beyond, we seriously regard the life we live now. Towards other religions we are tolerant and entertain no enmity whatever against people holding faith different from ours, while in regard to race and other matters, we have no notion whatever that East is East and West is West.[31]

Despite its aim to reach across Asia, in both its content and advertisements the journal reflected a focus on an India-interested audience. Beginning with the second issue in July 1925, Takakusu Junjirō wrote a five-part article "What Japan Owes to India." The journal carried numerous articles by Indian authors, including Tagore, Ganga Charan Lal, and Har Dayal (multiple articles). The advertisements in the magazine, while diverse, also tilted toward those with interests in India. In the February 1927 issue, for example, the journal carried advertisements for such Indian journals as *Modern Review*, *Mohabodhi* [sic, *Mahābodhi*], and *Indian Thinker*. Announcements for books on India—for example, *The Complete Works of Swami Vivekenanda*, *The Life of Ramakrishna*, and *Prabuddha Bharata or Awakened India*—many of them published in India, also appeared.[32]

Sakurai's new publication thus reflected the growing importance of cultural, religious, and economic ties between Japan and India. The editors made explicit reference to the intertwining of Japanese and Indian commercial and religious interests in a brief note in the September 1925 issue. Combining optimism with superciliousness, the passage offered spiritual assistance to Indians while ignoring their history and vital spiritual traditions.

30. "To Our Friends and Readers," *YE* 1, no. 1 (1925): n.p.

31. "To Our Friends and Readers," *YE* 1, no. 1 (June 1925): n.p.

32. See the advertising pages at the back of the magazine in *YE* 2, no. 9 (1927). The focus on India diminished following the death of the founding editor. Amid growing ties with Italy and Germany after 1937, the editors of later issues of the journal, Takakusu Junjirō and Kimura Nichiki, included more articles by such European scholars as Giuseppe Tucci, Bruno Petzold, with articles in German and Italian augmenting the primarily English-language ones.

India is a country of raw materials. Not only is she a country in which concrete materials are richly produced, but is or rather was one which gave to the world spiritual materials in abundance. Japan was one of the countries indebted to her for her priceless gift of Buddhism. Thanks chiefly to it, the Japanese have formed their national spirit and moulded their characteristics, and though in recent years, they have extensively adopted Western civilization, it is its material side only that they have taken. In spirit they are not as yet Westernized, but still retain the thought and idea taught by Buddhism.

This makes us feel that the duty and responsibility of returning Buddhism to India devolves on us Young Buddhists of Japan. Commercial Japan buys 70 to 80 percent of India raw cotton exports abroad and sells to her cloth manufactured by it. Japan imported Buddhism from India more than one thousand years ago and has refined it into a world religion in the form of Mahayana. Buddhism as it exists in Japan is a great living force fit for the needs of the present day and having the prospect of bringing the world under its benign influence. We feel that before giving it to any other countries, we must take it back to the country that gave it to our ancestors.[33]

The editors of *Young East* concluded the piece by offering Buddhism to India without "asking for price for what we desire to give back to India." Noting the rise of the *swadeshi* self-sufficiency movement in India that called for a boycott by Indians of foreign goods in the wake of the partition of Bengal in 1905, the editors stoically distanced themselves from the immediate economic consequences of the movement and hoped it would lead to self-sufficiency in spiritual matters as well.

Our manufacturers and exporters of cotton cloth may perhaps rue the day when the Swadesi movement attains its object and Indians no longer buy products from their factories. But nothing will give us greater pleasure than if Swadesi-made Buddhism rises in India and gathers under its fold her sons and daughters. As we think of undertaking return of Buddhism to India, we cannot help hoping that Indians themselves will first start a Swadesi movement along this line.

As economic ties between Japan and India grew in Japan, particularly in the textile industry, shipping to and from India increased accordingly, with NYK beginning regular service between India and Japan. The shipping company coordinated with the Japan Cotton Spinner's Association to bring raw cotton shipments from India to Japan on beneficial terms for the companies.[34] The first regular NYK service to Bombay came in response to pleas from

33. "What Japan Owes to India." *YE* 1, no. 4 (1925): 129–30.
34. Lockwood, *The Economic Development of Japan*, 29, note 42.

R. D. Tata, who was known as "the cotton king of Bombay," during Tata's visit to Japan in 1891, and from his cousin, J. G. N. Tata, in 1893. Both the Tatas and Japanese textile manufacturers pressed NYK representatives for the opening of regular service between India and Japan in order to bring down the cost of cargo transport between the two regions. Once an agreement concerning guarantees for the amount of cargo to be shipped and the shipping rates, service between Bombay and Japan began on November 7, 1893, with the ship *Hiroshima Maru*, making the journey.[35] By the beginning of the Shōwa period (circa 1926), NYK had expanded regular service to include Calcutta and Madras, in addition to Bombay. Of the six ships assigned to the Yokohama–Bombay line, three were hybrid passenger-cargo ships and the remaining were solely cargo vessels. It was on ships of this line, the *Sado Maru* and the *Tanba Maru*, that Akegarasu, Izawa, Teruoka, and the other NYK pilgrims would travel to and from India.[36] (Akegarasu would continue his Middle East–Europe leg of the journey on another NYK vessel, the *Hakozaki Maru*.) The expanded Japanese infrastructure and shipping to India helps account for the small, but notable uptick in Japanese travels to South and Southeast Asia that can be seen in the table of chronicles of Indian travels above.

According to Akegarasu and Izawa, advertisements were placed in *Chūgai nippō* and *Jiji shinpō* newspapers in September 1926. The brief advertisement in *Chūgai nippō*, which was reproduced in Akegarasu's travel account, read:

> **Inviting Applications for the Second Group Pilgrimage to Indian Buddhist Sites**
>
> Date of Departure: December 2, 1926, Kobe, Sado Maru
>
> Return Date: March 10, 1927, Kobe, Tanba Maru
>
> Approximately 50 days in India, entertainment, steamship, rail, lodging, all First Class. Prospectus [available from] Nippon Yūsen Kaisha Passenger Department in Marunouchi, Tokyo, and the Thomas Cook Company in the Oriental Hotel, Kobe, etc. Apply to the nearest branch office.[37]

35. Nihon Yūsen Kabushiki Kaisha, *Golden Jubilee History of Nippon Yusen Kaisha, 1885–1935* (Tokyo: Nippon Yusen Kaisha, 1935), 18–21.

36. For information on the development of these shipping lines and vessels, see Nippon Yūsen Kabushiki Kaisha. *Shichijūnenshi* (Tokyo: Nippon Yūsen Kabushiki Kaisha, 1956), 40; 105; 216–18.

37. *Akegarasu Haya zenshū* 23: 3. Izawa Heizaemon. *Indo Busseki sanpai nisshi* (Sendai: Izawa Heizaemon, 1927), 1. Izawa writes that the advertisement was in the September 15, 1926, issue of *Jiji shinpō*, but I have been unable to locate it in that issue of the paper. The advertisement as quoted above is found in the version of the Akegarasu-Teruoka diary reproduced in Akegarasu, *Akegarasu Haya zenshū* at 23: 3. (Hereafter AHZ.) According to Nomoto Towa, *Akegarasu Haya den* (Tokyo: Daiwa Shobō), 377, the advertisement was discovered by Akegarasu on September 17, while Akegarasu was traveling in Kyūshū.

Responding to the advertisement, both Akegarasu and Izawa signed up for the trip, along with seven others, including Akegarasu's friend and coauthor of the travel account Teruoka Yasunori.

Six other people, most of them Buddhist clerics or laypeople with strong ties to Buddhist organizations, joined Akegarasu, Teruoka, and Izawa on the second NYK group pilgrimage to Buddhist sites in India. Almost all the participants were temple incumbents or otherwise prominent members of the Buddhist community. A number of them also published tracts on various facets of Buddhism. In addition to Akegarasu and Izawa, the group included the following individuals.

- Teruoka Yasunori: incumbent at the Nishi-Honganji temple Kongōji, in Kagoshima; friend of Akegarasu; and coauthor of *Indo Busseki junpai ki*
- Mamiya Eishū (a.k.a. Mamiya Giyū; 1871–1945): incumbent at the temple Rinsenji in Kyoto. Following the death of his first teacher, Mamiya received permission to teach koan (*inka*) from Shaku Sōen. Mamiya was the author of a number of works on Zen, including a commentaries on the *Hekiganroku* and the *Rinzairoku*. He eventually became the chief incumbent (*kanchō*) of the Rinzai Hōkōji-ha in Shizuoka.
- Hata Kenjō: Jōdo Shinshū Honganji-ha, incumbent of Kyōnenji, in Hyōgo Prefecture
- Hayashi Tan'yu, from Osaka, incumbent of the Jōdo temple, Ganshōji.
- Kobayashi Gidō: from Kobe, Jōdoshū, incumbent of Higashi Gokurakuji and author of *Nyūmō angya ki*.
- Haruyama Takematsu (1885–1962): At the time of the trip, Haruyama was art critic for the *Ōsaka Asahi Shinbun*. He was the author of several books on the history of Japanese painting, wall paintings at Hōryūji, etcetera.
- Shimada Isoko, proprietress of the Tsuki no Ya, a traditional Japanese-style restaurant in Shanghai, and the only female member of the tour.
- Kawahara Eiichi and Nagatomo Ichirō: representatives from NYK who accompanied the tour for much of the journey.
- Mr. Hook(?) (Hokku shi) from the Thomas Cook Travel Agency, which provided in-country assistance to the tour group.[38]

Izawa, Haruyama, Hata, Hayashi, and Kobayashi boarded the *Sado Maru* in Kobe, while Akegarasu, Mamiya, and Teruoka boarded in Moji, where the ship stopped for coal. The last member, Shimada, came on board following a stop by the group in Shanghai. Once underway from Moji, members of the group selected Mamiya to serve as the head (*danchō*) and Kobayashi as steward (*kanji*).[39]

---

38. The members of the group are listed in Izawa, *Indo Busseki sanpai nisshi*, 35.

39. Izawa, *Indo Busseki sanpai nisshi*, 35; Akegarasu, *Indo Busseki junpai ki*, 21.

Travel between Japan and India during the steamship era remained expensive, despite improved efficiencies in shipping. Fujita Giryō, who traveled to India to tour Buddhist sites in 1921, mentions that his journey, in which all transit—ship and train—was in third class, cost ¥2,000/US $960, which is approximately US $12,900 in 2016.[40] According to Akegarasu, the NYK trip cost approximately ¥5000, which today would amount to roughly US $3,100 in 2016.[41] This included the expense of the trip, which was ¥3,050, plus an additional ¥1,950 for books and other purchases.[42]

Given the high cost, it is not surprising that the group had only nine members! That the travelers and their supporters were willing to bear the expense of the travel to India is a good indication of the perceived value of the pilgrimage. For a wealthy individual like Izawa, the trip, although expensive, was affordable. As noted in his biography, between 1916 and 1926 Izawa made a series of donations totaling more than ¥50,000 to support shrine and temple renovations, famine relief, reforestation, school construction, and exhibitions in the Sendai region.[43] Thus, the ¥3,000 for the pilgrimage fee was not an obstacle for him.

On the other hand, Akegarasu and, probably, many of the others on the tour needed to raise the funds by soliciting donations from friends and supporters. In the version of the travel account found in Akegarasu's collected works, he includes a series of brief letters to his wife, Fusako, describing some of the donations he received in amounts ranging from ¥100 to ¥500, while reassuring her that he would be able to gather the necessary funds.[44] To gather funds from supporters, Akegarasu published a request for financial assistance in the November 1926 issue of his journal *Gan'e*, about which he later wrote, "The number of readers are counted over ten thousand, and you will find several hundred of readers in the United States of America and Hawaii."[45]

---

40. Fujita Giryō, *Indo Busseki junrei*, 3.

41. Akegarasu, *Indo Busseki junpai ki*, 8–9. I thank my colleague Simon Partner, a Japan economic historian, for his help making the conversion to today's dollar and yen values. Yen-dollar exchange values were determined using Sōmuchō Tōkeikyoku and Nihon Tōkei Kyōkai, *Nihon chōki tōkei sōran*, 5 vols. (Tokyo: Nihon Tōkei Kyōkai, 1987). The value of dollars today was calculated using the website "Measuring Worth," http://www.measuringworth.com, accessed August 13, 2018. When Mark Twain joined a group tour of the Holy Land and the Mediterranean region in 1867, he mentions in his humorous account *Innocents Abroad*, the journey cost US $1250, the rough equivalent of US $20,900 in 2016.

42. *Akegarasu Haya den*, 377.

43. Shōji Ichirō, *Izawa Rōan Ō den*, 44–45.

44. AHZ 23: 4.

45. Akegarasu, Haya, Shinran, and Manshi Kiyozawa, *Selections from the Nippon Seishin (Japanese Spirit) Library* (Kitayasuda, Ishikawa-ken, Nippon: Kōsōsha, 1936), 7. The request for

Akegarasu clearly had staunch support from the magazine's readers, making this early form of crowd-funding highly effective. Prior to his departure from Moji on December 5, Akegarasu had accumulated more than double of the amount he sought, that is, ¥12,000.[46] Flush with far more money than needed for travel to India, Akegarasu decided to continue his journey from India to Europe. He also used some of the funds to acquire Sanskrit and Pali texts for future Buddhist studies, asking Akanuma Chizen (1884–1937), a specialist in Indian Buddhism who had studied in India, Ceylon, and England, to use the funds for that purpose.[47]

Both published accounts of the NYK's second group journey give every indication that this was not a run-of-the-mill trip. As advertised, the group traveled in first class onboard ship and, whenever possible, on the trains on which they crisscrossed South Asia. Wherever top-notch colonial hotels were available, for example, Queens Hotel in Kandy, the Taj Connemara Hotel in Madras, the Taj Mahal Hotel in Bombay, Hotel Cecil in Delhi, and the Grand Hotel in Calcutta, the group stayed in them. In the evenings, particularly en route to India, the group ate in fine restaurants like Tsuki no Ya in Shanghai, which Akegarasu describes as a splendidly furnished Japanese-style establishment.[48] Upon arrival in Calcutta, at the beginning of 1927, the group was treated to a Japanese banquet at the consulate that included such traditional Japanese New Year's foods as rice cake soup (zōni) and herring roe (kazunoko).

Despite the high price of the trip, the travelers had money to spare for the purchase of artworks, Buddha images, books, textiles, and other souvenirs. Akegarasu, as noted above, had accumulated enough funds for him to purchase books and other items freely while abroad. On several occasions, the accumulated purchases grew voluminous enough for the travelers to have representatives of shipping companies in India pack the items and deliver them to Japan.[49] Although the travel account does not make clear what happened to the numerous souvenirs that were purchased, if these Buddhist pil-

---

funds, which was written on October 16, 1926, and published in the November issue of Gan'e on November 1, is reproduced in AHZ 23: 9–11.

46. The list of donors is found in a letter to Akegarasu's wife, Imagawa Fusako, dated October 11, 1926. See AHZ 23: 4.

47. *Akegarasu Haya den*, 380. The *Shinshū jinmei jiten* gives 1884 as Akanuma's year of birth. The *Nihon Bukkyō jinmei jiten* gives 1885. (Hereafter NBJ.)

48. Akegarasu, *Indo Busseki junpai ki*, 21. Seki Seisetsu in *Tenjiku angya*, 9, mentions that he also had a dinner banquet at Tsuki no Ya in Shanghai while en route to India.

49. For example, see, Akegarasu, *Indo Busseki junpai ki*, 315, which describes the group shipping their purchases from Delhi.

grims were at all like those who preceded them, for example Shaku Kōzen, Kawaguchi Ekai, and Kuruma Takudō, perhaps some of these objects were placed on display at their temples, thus embodying in tangible form their intimate ties to the land of Buddhism's birth.[50] Without doubt, the "religious capital" that accrued to those who successfully toured the sites associated with the life of Śākyamuni and early Buddhism was considerable, and pilgrims took great pride in completion of the journey. For example, after his trip, Izawa and his biographer, Shōji Ichirō, used the title Nyūjiku Koji Rōan Mujin (Rōan Mujin, the Buddhist layman who entered India) for Izawa, thus laying claim to the prestige of a successful Indian pilgrimage.[51]

The NYK group pilgrimage was not an official, government-sponsored one, but in terms of the treatment the group received from Japanese diplomatic officers, military attachés, representatives from Japanese company branch offices all across Asia, and Buddhist clerics managing overseas branch temples, this was not an ordinary private tour either. In terms of cost and scale, the NYK Buddhist pilgrimage closely resembled the ambitious journey undertaken in 1911 by Hioki Mokusen and Kuruma Takudō, who were dispatched from Japan to attend the coronation of King Rama VI (Vajiravudh; 1881–1925) of Siam on November 11, 1911, as representatives of the chief incumbents of all Japanese Buddhist denominations and the Young Buddhists Association, respectively. Like Akegarasu and Mamiya, Hioki and Kuruma visited Japanese communities between Japan and South Asia, lecturing and, in the case of Hioki, overseeing the formal opening ceremony for Saiyūji, the Sōtō temple in Singapore that had been named for Hioki and Kuruma's teacher, Nishiari Bokusan. Following the coronation ceremonies in Siam, Hioki and Kuruma spent six months traveling in South and Southeast Asia, while being greeted by Japanese high officials and business people all along their route.[52]

Both Akegarasu and Izawa described the trip, which, despite the high-class accommodations, was an expensive and rigorous journey, as an opportunity to fulfill their long-standing desires to travel to India. In the dedicatory chapter of the Akegarasu-Teruoka account, which was written by Akegarasu on October 16, 1926, in Kagoshima, Akegarasu expresses his profound gratitude to "the Great Benefactor and Teacher Śākyamuni Buddha," for having

50. On the importance of Buddhist material culture in the construction of Japanese Buddhist pan-Asianism, see chapter 4.

51. Shōji Ichirō, *Izawa Ryōan Ō den*, 58; 88.

52. Their journey is detailed in Kuruma Takudō, "<*Mokusen Zenji*"> *Nangoku junrei ki* (Tokyo: Nangoku Junrei Ki Hensanjo, 1916).

provided the physical and spiritual foundations of his life. Despite the distance of time and place, Akegarasu remarks that he is all the more amazed
that he can feel such intimacy with Śākyamuni and his teachings. Akegarasu
mentions that filial concern for his aging mother and his own failing eyesight
made a long-desired trip to India all but impossible for many years. With the
death of his mother in 1925 and, at last, the possibility of traveling to India in
a group along with his close friend Teruoka, however, he now could undertake the journey. Having long wanted to trod the ground where Śākyamuni
walked and view the sights that Śākyamuni saw, Akegarasu notes how thrilled
he was to be able to participate in the NYK Line's second group trip to India,
thus realizing his long-standing desire.[53]

As was standard for NYK ships on the Japan-India run, the *Sado Maru*
made ports of call where the Japanese had established an infrastructure for
trade and maritime support. After leaving Moji, Japan, the *Sado Maru* visited
Shanghai, Hong Kong, Singapore, Penang, and Colombo, where the NYK
tour group disembarked to tour the area and visit with members of the resident Japanese community. This was an elite group of travelers and they were
treated accordingly. At each stop, the local Japanese overseas communities
provided hospitality and in-country guidance to the group. At many places,
including in India, the contingent was met not only by representatives from
NYK, but also by Japanese consular officials, military officers, representatives
from in-country branches of Japanese firms, and other members of the resident Japanese community. In Shanghai, for example, Akegarasu and the group
were welcomed by a committee of ten people that included the incumbent of
the Ōtani sect Honganji Betsuin, Sasaki E'on. Along with Teruoka, Akegarasu
spent his first night in Shanghai at the Betsuin. In Singapore, the group was
met by representatives from the local Nishi Honganji and Sōtō temples. Later,
Akegarasu and Teruoka visited the home of the vice-president of the East
Asia branch of the League of Nations (Kokusai Renmei Tōyō Shibu) as well as
the home of the Japanese general consul for Singapore, Nakajima Seiichirō,
who, unfortunately, was out by the time they arrived. In Calcutta, one of the
first major cities they visited after arriving in India, Akegarasu dined at the
home of the president of the NYK Calcutta branch office along with the Japanese deputy consul (*ryōji dairi*) for Calcutta, the Japanese military attaché
stationed in Delhi, and Kimura Ryūkan/Nichiki, a long-term Japanese resident of India who was a professor at Calcutta University.[54] The travelers also

---

53. Akegarasu, *Indo Busseki junpai ki*, 3–10.

54. Akegarasu, *Indo Busseki junpai ki*, 134. For more about Kimura Nichiki, see chapters 4,
5, and 6.

participated in a mourning ceremony for the Taishō emperor, conducted at the Japanese consulate in Colombo on December 25 and, toward the very end of their journey in Bombay, which had a sizable Japanese community, on February 7, 1927, the date of the Taishō emperor's public funeral in Japan. At the ceremony, which was held at the Japanese consulate in Bombay, the pilgrims personally were greeted by the Japanese consul and his wife, who then introduced the travelers to some of the other members of the Japanese community.[55] After separating from the rest of the group for his trip to the Middle East and Europe, Akegarasu briefly returned to Ceylon, where he stayed at the Japanese consulate and was guided through the city by a Mr. Nomura from the Tōgō Shōkai, a Japanese trading firm.[56]

En route to South Asia, in cities with sizable numbers of resident Japanese, Akegarasu and Mamiya, who were clearly the most well-known members of the group, gave lectures. The prominence of Akegarasu and Mamiya and the relative dearth of high-level Japanese clerics in the entrepôts of Japanese trade that punctuated the Sado Maru's route rendered the usual sort of sectarian dividing lines irrelevant. Akegarasu, an Ōtani sect cleric, spoke to groups of Japanese at Nishi Honganji branch temples and Mamiya, a Rinzai cleric, did likewise at a Sōtō temple. During the port call at Shanghai, Akegarasu spoke at the Nishi Honganji temple about a section of the *Muryōjukyō* (*Sutra of Infinite Life*) and at the Japan Club later that evening on the nature of Śākyamuni's awakening. Mamiya addressed a group at Tōa Dōbun Shoin, an academy in Shanghai in part supported by the Japanese Foreign Ministry that trained Japanese students in Chinese language and culture.[57] In Singapore, where the large Japanese merchant community had helped establish several Japanese temples, Akegarasu lectured at the Nishi-Honganji branch temple, while Mamiya spoke at the temple Saiyūji, a Sōtō temple eponymously named for its honorary founder, Nishiari Bokusan (1821–1910).[58]

These sorts of visits, lectures, photographing of sites, and fairly regular meetings by members of the NYK tour with Japanese business representatives, consular officials, and military officers stationed in India may well have raised the suspicions of British officials in India and Ceylon that the group was spying on behalf of the Japanese government. The behavior of the tour group

---

55. Akegarasu, *Indo Busseki junpai ki*, 377–78. The two months of the tour overlapped with the death and funeral of Emperor Taishō on December 25, 1926, so several death-related ceremonies were conducted during the tour.

56. Akegarasu, *Indo Busseki junpai ki*, 425–26.

57. Izawa, *Indo Busseki sanpai nisshi*, 7; Akegarasu, *Indo Busseki junpai ki*, 21. On the Tōa Dōbun Shoin, see Hotta, *Pan-Asianism and Japan's War*, 38.

58. Izawa, *Indo Busseki sanpai nisshi*, 7–8.

did little to assuage English fears about Japanese sub-rosa activities while on the subcontinent. Members of the NYK tour group visited pro-independence Indians, for example, Tagore and members of the Theosophical Society, some of whom, like Annie Besant, were outspoken supporters of greater Indian autonomy. Akegarasu also went to see Nyanatiloka, a German convert to Buddhism who was briefly interned in Australia during World War I.

During the World War I era and after, despite the Anglo-Japanese Alliance, the relationship between the British and Japanese grew increasingly fraught. One source of the tension was growing Japanese support for Indian independence. In addition, diplomatic friction on a number of fronts led British officials to doubt the intentions of Japanese toward India, at official and private levels. The Japanese reluctance to hand over Rash Behari Bose, who had fled to Japan in 1915, following an unsuccessful attempt to assassinate the viceroy of India, Lord Hardinge (1858–1944), to the British authorities undermined their trust in their Japanese allies. By 1917, the British, using a series of agents, both Indian and Japanese, discovered the whereabouts of Bose and another pro-independence provocateur, Heramba Lal Gupta, but were unable to get the Japanese to extradite them. The British authorities saw this as a prime indicator of Japanese support for anticolonial subversion. The British grew even more incensed when the two Indians escaped Japanese detention entirely, going into hiding at the atelier behind what would become one of Japan's most venerable curry houses, Nakamuraya, in Shinjuku, Tokyo.[59] The prominence of pro-Indian-independence sentiments in the pan-Asianist works of Ōkawa Shūmei, Uchida Ryōhei (1874–1937), Kanokogi Kazunobu (1884–1949), and others also contributed to the atmosphere of distrust, despite the continuation of the Anglo-Japanese Alliance until 1922. Even the management of NYK was suspected of undermining British interests in order to gain a larger share of shipping to and from India.[60]

59. Toyama Mitsuru (1855–1944) aided Bose and Gupta, who were wanted by the British and Japanese authorities. Much to the frustration of the British, the Indians went into hiding at the atelier owned by Sōma Aizō (1870–1954) and his wife, Kokkō (1876–1955), in Shinjuku, Tokyo, where they remained for a number of years. Bose married one of the Sōma's daughters, Toshiko, and became a Japanese citizen in 1923. Nakamura-ya's famous "Indian Curry" recipe purportedly was transmitted to the Sōma family by Bose. See Nakajima Takeshi, *Nakamura-Ya no Bōsu: Indo dokuritsu undō to kindai Nihon no Ajia shugi* (Tokyo: Hakusuisha, 2005); and Eri Hotta, "Rash Behari Bose and His Japanese Supporters," *Interventions* 8, no. 1 (2006): 119–20. See also Richard J. Popplewell, *Intelligence and Imperial Defence: British Intelligence and the Defence of the Indian Empire, 1904–1924* (London: F. Cass, 1995), 276–89.

60. Antony Best, "India, Pan-Asianism, and the Anglo-Japanese Alliance," in *The Anglo-Japanese Alliance, 1902–1922*, ed. Phillips Payson O'Brien (London: RoutledgeCurzon, 2004), 238–40.

By the time of the NYK pilgrimage, it was well known in Japan that Japanese who contacted pro-independence figures in India would be tailed by British police and even deported. Kōra Tomi (1896–1993), a translator of Tagore's work and frequent traveler in India, observed that in the first half of the twentieth century, British authorities in India were convinced that most Japanese travelers were spies and so regarded them suspiciously.[61] British government reports from the second two decades of the twentieth century, cataloged in detail by Popplewell, list a litany of suspicions concerning the activities of Japanese businessmen, pilgrims, and explorers in South and Southeast Asia. As early as 1913, agents working for the Department of Criminal Investigations, a branch of the British colonial government, reported that Okakura Kakuzō had been meeting with suspected "revolutionaries" in Bengal.[62] In addition, Grant Goodman describes how in that same year, Japanese agents reported in detail on Dharmapāla's activities in Japan, concluding that there must have been an informant in the inner circle of people meeting with the Ceylonese activist during his visit.[63] Japanese Buddhist expeditions also drew the attention of the intelligence authorities. Ōtani Kōzui, given his large-scale, well-funded exploration and mapping activities across Asia also sparked the suspicions of the British. When Ōtani was invited to receive a courtesy reception from the colonial government in 1916, he returned to Japan hastily, claiming health problems. When later that year he emerged in Shanghai, the Intelligence Bureau in China sarcastically reported that he seemingly had made a miraculous turn for the better.[64]

One of the more notorious instances of supposed espionage involved Kanokogi Kazunobu, a Japanese philosopher and well-known mountaineer who had studied extensively in Germany, where he received a doctorate in philosophy. Following his return to Japan in 1912, Kanokogi became involved in right-wing politics. He also began developing a pan-Asianist vision for Asian development, which inspired him to head to India in 1917.[65] While traveling in India to survey Buddhist sites and study Indian philosophy, Kanokogi's itinerary certainly seemed to confirm British questions about his

61. Hashimoto Yorimitsu, "Kanokogi Kazunobu no Indo tsuihō to sono eikyō," *Osaka University Knowledge Archive* (2013): 84. http://hdl.handle.net/11094/27380. I thank Yoshinaga Shin'ichi for the reference to this article.

62. Popplewell, *Intelligence and Imperial Defence*, 281.

63. Grant Kohn Goodman, "Dharmapala in Japan," *Japan Forum* 5, no. 2 (1993): 195–202.

64. Popplewell, *Intelligence and Imperial Defence*, 281–82.

65. Christopher W. A. Szpilman, "Kanokogi Kazunobu: 'Imperial Asia,' 1937," in *Pan-Asianism: A Documentary History*, ed. Sven Saaler and Christopher W. A. Szpilman (Lanham, MD: Rowman & Littlefield, 2011), 149–50.

true mission. Kanokogi attended Annie Besant's lectures, visited with Tagore, and attempted to meet the exiled supporter of Indian independence, Sri Aurobindo, in French-controlled Pondicherry. Further heightening British suspicions, Kanokogi lodged at the Calcutta guest house of the Mitsui Bussan Kaisha, a company long-suspected of commercial espionage and worse in India. British intelligence agents in Japan, described Kanokogi as "an enthusiastic promoter of the Pan-Asiatic movement," which led Department of Criminal Investigation to dispatch an agent—in all likelihood, Kanokogi's traveling companion, Sarat Chandra Das's son—to report on Kanokogi's activities. As a result, Kanokogi was summarily arrested in Calcutta in 1919. His belongings were searched, the police seized his travel records, then deported Kanokogi to Singapore, where he briefly was jailed. Kanokogi, soon after his return to Japan, claimed innocence and outrage about his mistreatment by the British.[66] From the British perspective, however, the documents told a different story. According to Popplewell, the seized materials demonstrated Kanokogi's association with Indian "revolutionaries" and included letters from Bengali "terrorists" that Kanokogi wanted officials at Mitsui Bussan to smuggle to their compatriots in Japan. Officials at the Department of Criminal Investigations concluded that "certain Japanese in India have behaved in a most improper and outrageous manner and that a great deal of suspicion was more than justified." The viceroy of India concluded that "the case of Kanokogi . . . has strikingly confirmed our apprehensions of danger of a powerful section of the Japanese people, with or without their government's sanction, engaging in a campaign of spying and incitement to sedition in India itself."[67]

Following his removal to Japan, Kanokogi would advocate for Indian independence. Although he acknowledged Japan's profound debt to both Indian and Chinese civilizations, Kanokogi, following Okakura Tenshin's line of argumentation, believed that only Japan had successfully blended Indian, Chinese, and Euro-American cultures. As a result, Japan alone deserved to lead other Asians in the effort to ward off European and American colonialism.[68] In his 1937 work *Sumera Ajia*, Kanokogi argued for an Imperial Japan–led pan-Asianism that would synthesize the best of both the Chinese and

---

66. Hashimoto, "Kanokogi Kazunobu no Indo tsuihō to sono eikyō," 84–92. See Kanokogi's own description of the arrest and seizure of his travel diary in Kanokogi Kazunobu, *Busseki junrei kō* (Tokyo: Daitōkaku, 1920), 7–8.

67. British government communications cited in Popplewell, *Intelligence and Imperial Defense*, 281–82.

68. Szpilman, "Kanokogi Kazunobu: 'Imperial Asia,' 1937," 152

Indian spirits and create a "great Asian federal state that is marked by control, order, instruction, and organization."[69]

Another traveler from the same era, Fujita Giryō, also reported suspicions about his mail to Japan being read surreptitiously, the untrustworthiness of Anglo-Indians, and being tailed by an Englishman when traveling to the Himalayas.[70] Kimura Ryūkan, who served as a guide for the NYK group in Calcutta, was a close associate of Tagore's. He also was reputed by some of his Indian associates at Calcutta University to be a spy for the Japanese.[71] Given the ubiquity of these questions concerning most Japanese travelers, it is likely that the NYK pilgrims were watched closely while they traveled in British colonial territory.

Members of the group spent the long hours onboard ship—it took twenty-one days to travel from Moji to Colombo—conversing, meeting on deck, in the dining room, and the smoking lounge, and reading, both individually and communally out loud. The growing body of literature in Japanese concerning Indian Buddhism, the biography of the Buddha, as well as Indian history and culture, shaped their imaginations prior to arrival in South Asia and framed their experiences of the subcontinent. En route to Sri Lanka from Shanghai, for example, members of the tour group took turns reading aloud from the Akanuma Chizen's 1914 Japanese translation of Paul Bigandet's Burmese biography of the Buddha, *Biruma Butsuden*, Seki Seisetsu's *Tenjiku angya*, and *Konnichi no Indo* by Yamakami Tensen (a.k.a. Yamagami Sōgen; 1878–1957). After departing Singapore, they were entertained by a new passenger, Furuta Gi'ichi, reading Hayama Yoshiki's novel *Umi ni ikuru hitobito*.[72] Akegarasu also whiled away the time on ship consuming accounts by himself of Japanese pilgrims who had preceded him to India by a few years, moving through some of the aforementioned works the group was reading aloud as well as Hara Giken's *Indo Busseki Biruma Shamuro shisatsu shashin roku* (Photographic Record of a Tour of Buddhist Sites in India, Burma, and Siam), Ōtani Kōzui's *Hōrō manki* (A Desultory Record of [My] Wanderings), and *Indo zatsuji* (An Indian Miscellany) by Matsumoto Bunzaburō (1869–1944).[73] As a result of these readings, both oral and private, by the time they reached South Asia,

69. From Kanokogi's *Sumera Ajia*, translated in Szpilman, "Kanokogi Kazunobu: 'Imperial Asia,' 1937," 153. *Sumera* is one Japanese reading of the character for imperial/emperor, 皇.

70. See Fujita Giryō, *Busseki junrei*, 242–44.

71. Hay, *Asian Ideas of East and West*, 347, n. 6.

72. Akegarasu, *Indo Busseki junpai ki*, 14–15; 28; 78.

73. Akegarasu, *Indo Busseki junpai ki*, 63. The text gives Yamagami's name as "Yamakawa Tensen" 山川天川, a typographical mistake.

the travelers, even if they only participated in the group oral readings, would have surveyed some of their countrymen's latest impressions of the region.

The NYK travelers traveled with extensive knowledge of India in hand. Since the start of the Meiji era, Japanese-language works covering the life of the historical Buddha and places associated with his life in India had been accumulating. First and foremost were the numerous travel accounts mentioned above. In addition to the travel accounts of such Chinese travelers as Xuanzang, which had served as essential guidebooks for the first generation of Japanese Buddhists who headed to India, Akegarasu and company found a growing body of Japanese and translated European scholarship concerning Indian Buddhism, culture, and geography available to them. In addition to the various works read aloud onboard the ship en route to South Asia, numerous other analyses of Indian Buddhism, life, and religious history were utilized during the journey and for the construction of the published travel account. In the diary Akegarasu and Teruoka include lengthy descriptions of sites they visited from such guides as *Indo Busseki jissha* (Photographs of Indian Buddhist Sites), published in August, 1926.[74] (For more on this work, see chapter 4.)

Commentaries and accounts of previous Japanese travelers, for example Kawaguchi Ekai and Seki Seisetsu (1887–1945), also are woven into the descriptions of the sites the NYK pilgrims visited. Many of the volumes available to them contained maps of varying quality of sites visited by the Japanese authors. Although not directly referred to by Akegarasu, one of the most-detailed maps, compiled by the cartographer Oshio Dokuzan (1890–?), working with Takakusu and several other scholars, was published in 1924 and demonstrated the sophisticated level of knowledge concerning Indian Buddhist sacred geography in Japan.[75] The proximate history of Japanese travel to South Asia and exchanges with other Buddhist nations (for example, Siam's gifting of relics discovered at Priprawaha to Japan [see chapter 4]) served as the backdrop for Akegarasu and Teruoka's understanding of Indian Buddhist archaeological sites at the start of the Shōwa era. Together with the numerous accounts of previous Japanese pilgrims to South Asia, these works provided the group with a fairly standard itinerary of Buddhist and other sites to view while in South Asia. The order in which the sites were visited varied considerably in the various accounts cited above, depending on whether the

74. Takakusu Junjirō, Wada Sanzō, and Kumagaya Kunizō, *Indo Busseki Jissha* (Tokyo: Kōgeisha, 1926).

75. Ōshio Dokuzan, "Indo Bukkyō shi chizu narabi [ni] sakuin" (Tokyo: Daiyukaku Shobō, 1924).

pilgrim disembarked in Calcutta or Bombay. Nonetheless, the authors of almost all the travel accounts listed above visited many of the same landmarks and sightseeing attractions while on the subcontinent. Traveling alone on a much tighter budget in 1921, Fujita Giryō visited almost all the same sites as the NYK tour group, as well as visiting Burma, although Fujita's journey took six months, as opposed to the three months required for the NYK group to cover the same route and more.[76]

Along with time spent reading, the pilgrims spent time in conversation with their fellow passengers, many of whom were not Japanese. This provided Akegarasu an opportunity to test and practice his English, which he had studied as a student in middle school in Kanazawa and at higher school in Kyoto, and to engage non-Japanese in discussions on a variety of subjects.[77] After leaving Shanghai, for example, Akegarasu struck up a conversation with an English banker, Mr. Perry, from Hong Kong, who happened to be Jewish. Much to Akegarasu's delight, he found he could understand the passenger's English and, in the course of the conversation, discovered that of all the figures in the Hebrew Bible, the Englishman admired Moses the most. Akegarasu, presenting his Shin perspective on human weakness, disagreed, arguing that Moses was too strict in his adherence to rules that ultimately one could not follow fully.[78]

Although the accommodations were lavish, the journey must have been rigorous, for, apart from travel days onboard ships or trains, the group does not seem to have taken many days off to rest. Once the group departed from the *Sado Maru* in Colombo on December 25, 1926, the pace of travel was relentless. (See fig. 3.1.) While in Sri Lanka, the NYK group traveled to the Temple of the Tooth in Kandy, as well as visiting Anurādhapura, and Mihintale, before departing via train to Tailamanar and from there by ferry to Dhanshukodi, India. From there the group traveled to Madras, arriving on January 1, 1927. In the space of a little more than five weeks, when on February 12, 1927, all but Akegarasu boarded the *Tanba Maru* in Bombay for the return journey to Japan, the group then managed to traverse much of the Indian subcontinent, including brief trips into Nepal and what is now part of Pakistan. (Akegarasu continued on to the Middle East and Europe after a brief return to Sri Lanka.)

76. Fujita Giryō, *Busseki junpai*.

77. Akegarasu, *Selections from the Nippon Seishin (Japanese Spirit) Library*, 132–34. Akegarasu discusses his struggles with English and sense of national betrayal the emphasis on English in the schools represented.

78. Akegarasu, *Indo Busseki junpai ki*, 30–32.

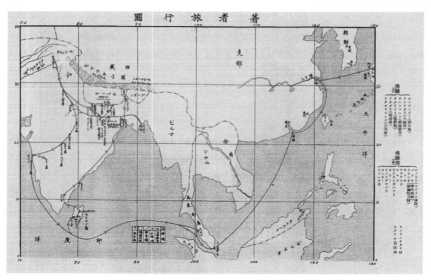

FIGURE 3.1. Route taken by the pilgrims on the NYK India pilgrimage tour, 1926–1927. From Akegarasu and Teruoka, *Indo Busseki junpai ki* (1928).

During that time the tour group used just about every conveyance imaginable, including steamships, ferries, trains, automobiles, horse-drawn carriages, ox carts, camels, and elephants, to reach their destinations. On this count as well the itinerary was comprehensive. The pilgrims were able to visit many of the most important sites in India, including Bodh Gayā, Rājagṛha, Gṛdhrakūṭaparvata (Vulture Peak), Nālandā, Sārnāth, Lumbinī, Kuśinagarī, Kapilavastu, Śrāvastī, Sāñcī, Ellorā, and Aurangābād. En route to these Buddhist landmarks, the tour also visited museums in the major cities and such non-Buddhist but historically significant attractions as the Taj Mahal, Lucknow, Fort of Fatehpur Sikri, caves at Elephanta and Kanheri, and Santiniketan. Continuing on his own, following the return of the group, including Teruoka, to Japan on the *Tanba Maru*, Akegarasu traveled back to Madras, visiting the Theosophical Society headquarters in Adyar, and back to Sri Lanka, to visit Nyanatiloka at the Island Hermitage at Ratgama Lake and the Vidyodaya Piriveṇa, founded by Hikkaḍuvē Sumaṅgala. In Colombo, Akegarasu boarded the *Hakozaki Maru*, bound for Aden on February 24, thus ending the South Asian portion of his trip. On board the *Hakozaki Maru*, Akegarasu helped his fellow Japanese passengers while away the time by relating to them the biography of Śākyamuni, a story that was fresh on his mind.

The extensive network of railways the British colonial government built was another by-product to a large extent of the international cotton trade, whose proponents sought to construct rail lines to bring raw cotton to international shipping ports like Bombay as quickly as possible. In the region of Jalgaon Station was Khamgaon, for example, which the British connected to Bombay by train precisely in order to convey cotton from the Berar region to port. As summarized by Lord Dalhousie (1812–60) in 1853, the main objectives for the railways were to enhance military operation and provide support for commercial import and export.[79] The numerous steam-driven trains traversing India allowed the NYK tour group to crisscross the subcontinent in relative comfort in just a bit more than fifty days. Thus, like other Buddhist travelers on the subcontinent, the Japanese were beneficiaries of the infrastructural improvements and extensive archaeological excavations the colonial government undertook in the late-nineteenth and early twentieth centuries. Tony Huber observed how Tibetan pilgrims to India quickly adapted to rail transportation for their pilgrimages during the same era.[80] This provides another example of the way in which the spread of modern technologies, in this case the steam locomotion and railway networks, rather than being corrosive for traditional religious practices, served only to enhance some of them and render them available to larger numbers of people.

The pilgrims on the NYK trip, like many Japanese of their era, were no strangers to rail travel. What stood out to Teruoka and Akegarasu about Indian trains was the lack of punctuality, with Teruoka commenting when they reached one station, "The train that was scheduled to reach Jalgaon Station at 8:00 AM on the Fourth, in Indian-style, arrived late at 11 AM."[81] On that particular occasion the group's insistence on seeing as much as possible caused consternation among the guides from NYK and the Thomas Cook Company. Despite arriving three hours late at Jalgaon Station, they insisted that they tour the caves at Ajanta as planned. The guides protested, as the group had to make a "seventy-mile" round trip (in actuality, closer to one hundred miles) to the caves, conduct their tour, then get back to Jalgaon Station in time for their evening train to Manmad. Quickly hiring cars to take them to Ajanta and back, the pilgrims managed to tour the caves, then return to the station before 8 p.m., leaving enough time for a quick dinner prior to boarding their next train.[82]

As discussed in chapter 1, Japanese Buddhists needed to come to terms with a growing body of Buddhological scholarship that frequently called into

79. Ravi Ahuja, "'The Bridge Builders': Some Notes on Railways, Pilgrimage and the British 'Civilizing Mission' in Colonial India," in *Colonialism as Civilizing Mission: Cultural Ideology in British India*, ed. Harald Fischer-Tiné and Michael Mann (London: Anthem Press, 2004), 106.

80. Huber, *The Holy Land Reborn*, 308–10.

81. Akegarasu, *Indo Busseki junpai ki*, 346.

82. Akegarasu, *Indo Busseki junpai ki*, 346–58.

question the legitimacy of Mahayana Buddhism. For denominations of Japanese Buddhism which focused on buddhas other than Śākyamuni, for example, Jōdo Shinshū, in which Amitābha was the central buddha, explaining the relationship between the historical Buddha and their central buddha was pressing. In their account, one can see Akegarasu and Teruoka wrestling with these issues, as they describe at length the depths of religious sentiment they experienced as they visited the major Buddhist pilgrimage sites associated with the life of Śākyamuni and the early Buddhist community. Upon reaching Rājagṛha and Vulture Peak (S. Gṛdhrakūṭaparvata; Ryōjusen/Gijakussen), on January 16, 1927, for example, Akegarasu describes movingly the group's visit to the purported site of the first Buddhist council and where many Buddhist sutras, including some of the Nikāya sutras and such important Mahayana sutras as the Lotus Sūtra, were supposedly preached. Led by Teruoka, who held Akegarasu's hand, thus helping his visually impaired companion, the duo, along with the others in the group, arrived at the top of Vulture Peak, where they discovered the ruins of what Akegarasu surmised must have been a memorial stupa. Upon reaching the summit, members of the party each lit incense and spread out their own bowing cloth (*zagu*) and began quietly reciting sutras of their choosing.[83] Similarly, Izawa comments that each pilgrim read a sutra in order to repay the debt to the Buddha.[84]

According to the account given by Akegarasu and Teruoka, having arrived at the place where the Buddha had preached the *Dai muryōjukyō*, the two of them began quietly chanting portions of the sutra. The sutras delivered at Vulture Peak, for example, the Lotus Sūtra, the *Laṅkāvatāra Sūtra*, and the *Dai muryōjukyō*, Akegarasu comments, all conveyed to later generations "Śākyamuni's inner life" (*naiteki seikatsu*).[85] For Akegarasu, who had been born in an "*araṇya* (a monastic residence) where Amitābha was worshipped," it was deeply moving to be present at the site where Śākyamuni preached the *Dai muryōjukyō*, thus revealing Amitābha Buddha to the world. In his reflections at Vulture Peak, Akegarasu addresses the World Honored One, telling him that he came as a representative of numerous Japanese Buddhists who supported his pilgrimage. His worship of Śākyamuni, whom he addresses as the World Honored One, thus represents the obeisance not just of Akegarasu alone, but all his supporters across Japan. In his reflections, Akegarasu mentions his deepening engagement with the *Dai muryōjukyō* over the course of his life, highlighting how at the age of forty, he realized that Amitābha was

---

83. Akegarasu, *Indo Busseki junpai ki*, 174.

84. Izawa, *Indo Busseki sanpai nisshi*, 17.

85. Akegarasu, *Indo Busseki junpai ki*, 175.

てに山崛闍者日六十月一年二和昭

FIGURE 3.2. NYK tour group on Vulture Peak. From Akegarasu and Teruoka, *Indo Busseki junpai ki* (1928).

not separate from the World Honored One, but instead was "within the heart (*kokoro*) of the World Honored One." According to Akegarasu, the "Great Self" who pronounced "I always am present on Vulture Peak" transcended even the ever-present Dharmakāya. Akegarasu writes that in the midst of his contemplation, he was moved to tears as he envisioned the Great Self that was one with the Dharmakāya of limitless life and limitless light, vowing always to remain aware of Vulture Peak and allow the heart of the ever-present Vulture Peak to become manifest.[86] (See fig. 3.2.)

A few days later, on January 18, 1927, the group reached Bodh Gayā, traveling by automobile from the town of Gayā. As at Vulture Peak, Izawa tersely mentions how moving it was to get his first glimpse of the Mahābodhi stupa. For Akegarasu as well, the visit provided him and Teruoka the opportunity to reflect upon the nature of the awakening Śākyamuni had achieved at the site. Akegarasu writes that it is the Buddha's thought at the moment of awakening that is the origin of Buddhism. Śākyamuni, according to Akegarasu's interpretation of that experience, at that juncture abandoned all reliance on external agents and forces, as the origin and end of suffering were not to be found in

86. Akegarasu, *Indo Busseki junpai ki*, 175–78.

the objective, external world. Instead, plumbing the depths of his self (*jiko nai-shin*), Śākyamuni realized that the origin of suffering was internal, not external. Neither gods nor teachers nor mundane things could enable the Buddha to free himself from suffering. Putting a decidedly Jōdo Shin interpretation on the awakening, Akegarasu reflects that through this process of introspection, Śākyamuni was able to proclaim his own fundamental foolishness (*gu*) and, consequently, achieve liberation. According to Akegarasu, the dispelling of ignorance requires that one proclaim that one's life is fundamentally rooted in foolishness, which is how the Buddha achieved his awakening. At the foot of the Diamond Throne, Akegarasu reflects on his own realization, writing,

> For a long time, I mistakenly thought that through my own perspicacity I could understand/perceive the World Honored One's awakening. In addition, I looked reverently upon the World Honored One off in a distant place. However, thirteen years ago, in the spring of my 37th year, at the time I felt the pain of the smashing of my self, internally and externally. When I discovered the great, dark self that was difficult to save, whether it be based on birth, death, the worldly, or the supra-worldly, I was able to apprehend the Way of Awakening from ignorance embodied by the World Honored One beneath the Bodhi tree. Is this not the reason that the World Honored One took for himself the name of Buddha? Here, prostrate before the Diamond Throne, I anew am aware of my own foolishness and together with the World Honored One proclaim this foolishness and must rejoice in the spectacle of the faith (*shinnnen*) refulgent with light.[87]

From a religious perspective, travel to South Asia affording encounters with scholars and native Buddhists was a means for Japanese Buddhists to see their own tradition in a wider perspective and test the orthodoxy of their understanding, but for the most part, Akegarasu found his insights into Buddhism that were arrived at through introspection, the process he emphasized as central to his practice of True Pure Land Buddhism, confirmed by his encounters rather than transformed. Clearly the account demonstrates Akegarasu was deeply moved when he reached some of the most important pilgrimage sites of Buddhism, for example, Vulture Peak, Bodh Gayā, Lumbinī, Kuśinagarī, Nālandā, and Sārnāth. At some of those places, Akegarasu wrote the sorts of emotional, reflective supplications for Śākyamuni like those quoted above. Although Akegarasu valued experiencing the archaeological traces of Buddhism, this reinforced the understanding of Buddhism that he had achieved in Japan. More than being shaken in fundamental ways by the pilgrimage, Akegarasu seems to have gone to report firsthand to the

---

87. Akegarasu, *Indo Busseki junpai ki*, 201.

ever-present Buddha that he too understood the teaching. Inspired by the Mahābodhi Temple and Diamond Throne at Bodh Gayā, Akegarasu described to the ever-present Buddha how self-introspection led to a hard-won awakening to his own frailty and insufficiency, as well as deepened insights into the nature of the path and buddhas. As he describes in the essay "Men above Gods," which was delivered just slightly more than one year prior to the India pilgrimage, the key to Buddhism was introspection.

> To turn to Śākyamuni. In the study of his life we discover that he progressed step by step in light of introspection. The eighty years of his life may be regarded as a progressive evolution from introspection to introspection. Therefore all the gospels reflect the idea of self-examination. Not a single volume is void of the idea. It is especially apparent in the gospels of Daijō-Bukkyō or Mahāyāna Buddhism of which are known to have been preached by Śākyamuni himself.[88]

Akegarasu's pilgrimage also gave him ample opportunities to express his perspective on the relationship between the historical Buddha, Śākyamuni; Amitābha Buddha, who was central buddha for the Jōdo Shin denomination; and the ever-manifesting Dharmakāya. Like other members of the "*seishin shugi*" (spiritual cultivation) movement, for example, Soga Ryōjin (1875–1971), Akegarasu wrestled with the relationship between Amitābha, the central buddha of the Pure Land sutras central to Jōdo Shinshū, and Śākyamuni, who received ever-increasing focus as the historical founder of original Buddhism. Robert Rhodes, analyzing Soga's view of Buddhist history put forth in 1935, makes the following observation.

> Although Soga recognized the importance of these objective studies on Buddhist history, he was not fully satisfied with them, for he understood Buddhist history primarily as the history of the practice and actualization of the Buddhist path. Following Shinran's *Kyōgyōshinshō*, Soga argues that the 2,000-year long history of Buddhism is none other than the history of the religious tradition flowing forth from the *Sutra of Immeasurable Life*. In other words, it is the history of the transmission of nenbutsu and the history of the progress of Amida Buddha's original vow. Hence, Soga is critical of the evolutionary view of the Buddhist history current in his day, which held that Buddhism was founded by Śākyamuni and developed in various ways over time.[89]

88. Akegarasu, *Selections from the Nippon Seishin (Japanese Spirit) Library*, 80. The lecture was delivered in Japanese December 3, 1925, and translated into English by Hata Taigan and Hanaoka Kimi. See also the Japanese text, "Kamigami o koeta ningen," in AHZ 16: 214–15. "Introspection" translates *naisei*.

89. Robert Rhodes, "Soga Ryōjin: Life and Thought," in *Cultivating Spirituality: A Modern Shin Buddhist Anthology*, ed. Mark Laurence Blum and Robert Franklin Rhodes (Albany:

Likewise, Akegarasu's study of Buddhist history and visits to sites associated with the historical Buddha left him well acquainted with the scholarly emphasis on Śākyamuni as the founder of Buddhism and a historical personage. Thus, it was imperative for Akegarasu to explain the origin of texts he most valued, for example, the *Sūtra of Immeasurable Life* (*Bussetsu muryōjukyō/Dai muryōjukyō*), and their connection with the historical Buddha. He also needed to clarify the relationship between Amitābha, the central object of worship for Jōdo Shinshū, and the historical Buddha. While at Vulture Peak, walking the ground supposedly tread by Śākyamuni, Akegarasu pondered these matters in light of his own spiritual evolution.

> When, at the age of forty, I discovered my own life within the *Bussetsu muryōjukyō* that I previously recited habitually, I deliberately deepened further my recollection of the World Honored One. Until then, I continually called the name of Amitābha Buddha seeing him as other than the World Honored One. However, ever since that time, I came to worship Amitābha Buddha within the heart (*kokoro*) of the World Honored One and worshipped the World Honored One within myself. Ever since, with the passing days and months, along with studying the profundities of the self of the *Bussetsu muryōjukyō*, I increasingly integrated my recollections of the thought of the World Honored One.[90]

Reflecting on the meaning of the *Sūtra of the Eternal Buddha* (*Bussetsu muryōjukyō*) and its central importance to Shinran in a lecture given in 1922, Akegarasu commented,

> The one who smoothly passed his life in accordance with the dictation of his inmost original will (*jiko chūshin no yōkyū*), without deception and flattery, was Shinran Shōnin. It was he who declared that the true and real instruction of the Buddha is *the Sūtra of the Eternal Buddha*. He walked through the world which he found as his own in that grand and sublime writings that Sūtra. Shinran Shōnin who said that the other power is that of the "original vow" itself, was the one who took to himself that power by combining it with his own inmost will. And that *Sūtra of the Eternal Buddha* is nothing but the record of the inner life of Śākyamuni Buddha himself (*Shakuson jishin no naiteki seikatsu no rekōdo*). Amitābha Buddha mainly described in that Sūtra is the principal figure of the new work which was devoted to the description of the inner life of Śākyamuni Buddha. In other words, *the Great Sūtra of the Eternal Life* is the work in which the Buddha exhibited his own spiritual life. It faithfully re-

State University of New York Press, 2011), 104–5. Soga writes about the relationship between Śākyamuni and Amitābha in his 1935 lecture "Shinran's View of Buddhist History," in Blum and Rhodes, *Cultivating Spirituality*, 119–38.

90. Akegarasu, *Indo Busseki junpai ki*, 175.

cords his innermost desire for getting absolute freedom; and this was the original will of *Hōzō Bosatsu* [who is described in the *Dai muryōjukyō*]. When one
faithfully appreciates this innermost desire of the Buddha, the [vow (*nengan*)]
directly becomes one's own. When we say we have true faith in this power of
the "original vow" it amounts to finding out the will (*ishi*) of Amitābha Buddha which was represented by the Buddha Śākyamuni. This "original vow" is
natural, and it is at the same time, my (the writer's) own original will.[91]

Akegarasu sought confirmation of his understanding of Buddhism in encounters with some of the scholars and Buddhists he met in South Asia. While
in Calcutta, for example, Akegarasu was introduced by Kimura Ryūkan to
Benidhamab Barua (1888–1948), a specialist in Pali at Calcutta University.[92]
Discussing Buddhism with Barua, Akegarasu was happy to find that the spirit
of Śākyamuni that Akegarasu had discovered through self-introspection was
the same as that Barua had found through his research concerning the early
Pali Buddhist texts.[93] Similarly, describing his discussions of Buddhism with
Nyanatiloka at the Island Hermitage, Akegarasu remarks that he was pleased
to hear Nyanatiloka state that the foundation of Buddhism was the Eightfold
Path of the Noble Ones (Hasshōdō), because this accorded with Akegarasu's
understanding of the tradition.[94] For Akegarasu, it appears, the early Buddhism that was a product of orientalist scholarship, the Ceylonese Buddhist
revival, and convert enthusiasm was the yardstick by which one's understanding of the tradition had to be measured. Reflecting on his journey to South

91. "The Present Mental Tendency and the Belief of Shinran Shōnin," trans. Imadate Tosui.
In Akegarasu, *Selections* from the Nippon Seishin (Japanese Spirit) Library, 108–9. I have modified Imadate's translation slightly based on the original text. The original text is found in "Gendai
shichō to Shinran kyōgi," the published version of a lecture delivered by Akegarasu to the Young
Buddhists Association at the Hiroshima Higher Normal School on October 27, 1922. The passage
above is found in Akegarasu Haya, "Shinran Shōnin No Shinnen" (Kita Yasuda: Kōsōsha, 1925),
15–16. I thank Dr. Nobuo Haneda for sharing a copy of the pamphlet with me. Imadate translates
Bussetsu muryōjukyō as *Great Sūtra of Eternal Life*, whereas Rhodes uses *Sūtra of Immeasurable
Life*. In the Japanese, the second to the last line reads, "When we have true faith in this power of
the "original vow," it is to discover the will of Amitābha that is inscribed within oneself."

92. Akegarasu, *Indo Busseki junpai ki*, 162, mentions that Boruwafu, a professor at Calcutta
University, studied in England with Rhys Davids, along with Ui Hakuju (1882–1963), so I am
guessing this is Benimadhab Barua. Barua in the preface to Beni Madhab Barua, *A History of
Pre-Buddhistic Indian Philosophy* (Delhi: Motilal Banarsidass, 1970), reprint 1921, xi, mentions
that he studied with T. W. Rhys Davids and Caroline Rhys Davids. For details on Barua's role
in the revival of Pali studies in India, see Surendran, "The Invention of Buddhism," 123–39; and
Ober, "Reinventing Buddhism," 174–75; 228. Akegarasu's rendering of Indian names in the diary
is problematic at times, with Nyanatiloka rendered as Niyayachiroka, for example.

93. Akegarasu, *Indo Busseki junpai ki*, 162.

94. Akegarasu, *Indo Busseki junpai ki*, 428.

Asia a decade later, Akegarasu concluded, "I found light and vitality on my faith that is cultivated from Buddhism, by this trip to India."[95]

At times, the sites visited and conversations with non-Japanese encountered along their route prompted both Akegarasu and Teruoka to reflect on the state of Buddhism past and present. After visiting the caves at Ajanta, for example, Teruoka writes that he and Akegarasu discussed how the artwork of the caves, for example, the pillar carvings of naked men and women embracing, was a tangible sign of Indian Buddhism's declining vitality. They concluded that in Japan as well, Buddhism had grown overly aestheticized. "One can think that the aestheticization of religion does not indicate it is flourishing but that it is declining. That visiting Ajanta forced us to think about these matters was another benefit of our pilgrimage to Indian Buddhist sites," Teruoka wrote to sum up their conversation.[96]

On occasion, encounters with non-Japanese Asians during the journey raised questions concerning aspects of Japanese Buddhist custom that had long been second nature for the pilgrims. Teruoka, on board the *Tanba Maru* for the return to Japan, struck up a conversation with an Indian from Punjab who had resided for three years in Kobe for business purposes, in the process becoming rather fluent in Japanese. After discussing foods he had missed while in Japan, the Indian, apparently unaware that Southern Buddhists also ate meat on occasion, critically questioned Teruoka about why, despite living in a Buddhist country, the Japanese ate beef. He then urged Teruoka henceforth to refrain from eating beef in commemoration of his successful pilgrimage to sites associated with Śākyamuni in India. Teruoka, while not committing himself to that prohibition, did confess that he felt more than a little bit moved by the earnest efforts by the Punjabi businessman to get him to do so.[97]

In South Asia, the pilgrims' experience was enriched by the network of Buddhist and Asian intellectuals that had developed in Asia. These international contacts while in India and Ceylon were facilitated by Japanese long-term overseas students in South Asia who served as a bridge between the Japanese pilgrims and native scholars. Kimura Ryūkan, for example, who spent decades studying Sanskrit and Indian Buddhism in Calcutta, met Akegarasu and the rest of the group in Calcutta. In the travel diary, Akegarasu and Teruoka mention that he is a professor at Calcutta University and author of *Upa-*

95. Akegarasu, *Selections from the Nippon Seishin (Japanese Spirit) Library*, 8.

96. Akegarasu, *Indo Busseki junpai ki*, 357–58.

97. Akegarasu, *Indo Busseki junpai ki*, 396–97.

nishaddo monogatari (Tales from the Upaniṣads).[98] While the group was in Calcutta, Kimura served as their guide, taking the group to the Calcutta Museum, lecturing to them on various aspects of Indian Buddhist history, and accompanying them to various religious sites in the city. Kimura introduced Akegarasu to Professor Benidhamab Barua, with whom Akegarasu discussed how Buddhism was presented in Pali texts.

Kimura Ryūkan, during his first extended stay in India from 1908 to 1915, had studied Sanskrit with Bidhushekhar Shastri (1878–1957), who was serving as Santiniketan's librarian during Akegarasu and Teruoka's visit. Along with Kawaguchi Ekai, Kimura had encouraged Tagore to visit Japan in 1916. Tagore wrote to Kimura in February 1915 asking that Kimura help shield him from too many receptions and invitations while he was in Japan. Kimura, who had returned to Japan for 1915–17, before returning to India for another decade, was thus present to help with Tagore's visit. When Tagore addressed attendees at a reception in his honor at Kan'eiji temple in Tokyo on June 13, 1916, Kimura served as his interpreter.[99] Kimura's personal letter of introduction for Akegarasu and Teruoka carried enough weight to get them a personal audience with the well-known poet and scholar. On January 12, 1927, Akegarasu, along with Teruoka, traveled to Santiniketan from Calcutta. During their visit they toured the school and the library, as well as spending time with Tagore in his home, discussing literature, religion, poetry, and philosophy. After describing his two visits to Japan and praising Japanese culture, according to Akegarasu, Tagore characterized Western culture as technologically oriented, narrow, and in decline, apart from Russia, which remained spiritually vital. By contrast, Eastern culture had broad horizons and was spiritually oriented. Judging from Akegarasu's account, there were broad areas of agreement between the three men, as the discussion moved from acknowledging Śākyamuni's greatness as a teacher who, according to Akegarasu, "opened his wisdom eye" (*chigen*), while Tagore, in good Hindu fashion, praised the Buddha as a "manifestation of God" (*kami no gonge*). The discussion then turned to Russian and German literature, with the three men deliberating over the comparative virtues and flaws of Dostoevsky, Tolstoy, Turgenev, Chekhov, Strindberg, with Akegarasu preferring Turgenev and Tagore, Dostoevsky.[100] Tagore had many Japanese friends, some from his visits to Japan and others from their visits to

---

98. Kimura Ryūkan, *Upanishaddo monogatari* (Tokyo: Shinchōsha, 1916). For more on Kimura and his role as a bridge between South Asian and Japanese Buddhists, see chapter 6.

99. Hay, *Asian Ideas of East and West*, 53; 66.

100. Akegarasu, *Indo Busseki junpai ki*, 151–62.

India. They, too, became topics of the conversation, as he inquired about each of them.

Following the return of the other pilgrims to Japan on February 12, 1927, Akegarasu returned to Madras and then Ceylon, where he boarded the *Hakozaki Maru* bound for Aden. From there, Akegarasu continued on to Palestine and Europe. Akegarasu used the time in Madras and Ceylon to visit several other Buddhists and Buddhist sympathizers who, like Tagore, had previous Japan connections. While in Madras, Akegarasu traveled to Adyar to see the Theosophical Society. There he toured the impressive library containing religious texts in English, Pali, Sanskrit, and Tibetan. He also noted in the diary the worldwide reach of the Society, which even had ties in Japan with such individuals as Suzuki Daisetsu (1870–1966).[101]

After returning to Ceylon to board the *Hakozaki Maru* for Aden, Akegarasu also met with the German converts to Buddhism, Nyanatiloka (Ñāṇatiloka, born as Anton Gueth; 1878–1957) and his fellow *bhikkhu* Vappo (born as Ludwig Stoltz; 1873–1960) at the Island Hermitage in Ratgama, Ceylon. Nyanatiloka, who left Ceylon during World War I to avoid British internment, lived in Japan for much of 1920–26. During that time, he taught Pali, German, and lectured on Buddhism at a variety of universities, including Taishō, Komazawa, and Meiji universities. Principal among his Japanese friends were Watanabe Kaigyoku (1872–1933), Tachibana Shundō (1877–1955), Kawaguchi Ekai, and Takakusu Junjirō, all of whom had spent time studying and traveling either in South Asia, Europe, or both places. Following his return to Sri Lanka in 1926, Nyanatiloka met with a number of Japanese scholars and visitors at the Island Hermitage.[102] A Japanese resident overseas student and Tendai cleric, identified only by the surname Furukawa, who was studying Buddhism on the island guided Akegarasu to the Island Hermitage to meet with Nyanatiloka and Vappo. As in his conversations with Barua noted above, Akegarasu once again was pleased to find that his understanding of Buddhism concurred with that of Nyanatiloka, who told Akegarasu that the heart of Buddhism was nothing more than the Eightfold Path. During the visit Nyanatiloka pointed out a Japanese Buddha image that had been sent to Nyanatiloka by Beatrice Lane Suzuki, another tangible sign of the global Buddhist network that developed in the twentieth century. After dining and conversing with the *bhikkhu*, they watched Akegarasu leave the island to return to Colombo. Akegarasu was moved by the encounter with the two Ger-

---

101. Akegarasu, *Indo Busseki junpai ki*, 420–21.

102. Hellmuth Hecker and Bhikkhu Ñāṇatusita, *The Life of Ñāṇatiloka Thera: The Biography of a Western Buddhist Pioneer* (Kandy, Sri Lanka: Buddhist Publication Society, 2008), 82–105.

man converts living a life of utmost simplicity while devoting themselves to the spread of Buddhism through their translation and writing. Looking back at the island from across the river, Akegarasu reflected, "Feeling deeply the love of these men, living in such quiet surroundings, towards others, I was touched. While amidst the noise, people certainly cannot love others. When one separates from others to live quietly alone, for the first time one becomes able to keenly love others. I thought there would be value even in just having come to Ceylon to meet Nyanatiloka and Vappo."[103] Following the visit to the Island Hermitage, Akegarasu also visited the Vidyodaya Piriveṇa, where Furukawa, like Kōzen decades before him, was studying Pali, and Ānanda College, a Buddhist school for educating children until the age of eighteen.

After the two memorable days in Ceylon, Akegarasu boarded the *Hako-zaki Maru* for Aden. Filled with impressions from his two months in South Asia, en route to Aden from Colombo, Akegarasu regaled his fellow Japanese passengers onboard ship with his rendition of the biography of the Buddha, now grounded in his firsthand experience of the pilgrimage sites in South Asia.

The routinization of travel routes across South Asia made possible short-term trips like the NYK pilgrimage taken by Akegarasu, Izawa, Teruoka, and company, allowing devout Buddhists to reaffirm their faith by visiting sites associated with Buddhism's South Asian past. Encountering in South Asia native and Indian specialists in Buddhism, pilgrims like Akegarasu could explore how Japanese understandings of the tradition stood in relationship to Buddhism as it now was understood by scholars and practitioners in South Asia. Those fortunate enough to be able to undertake a pilgrimage to South Asia frequently did so with the support of their Buddhist communities in Japan. The merit they accrued by visiting sites associated with the life of Śākyamuni thus was dedicated to their supporters as well as themselves. Receptions honoring returning pilgrims and the publication of pilgrimage diaries further allowed nonparticipants to share vicariously in the experience.

For other Japanese, like Sakurai Gichō, the deepening connections with South Asia provided an opportunity to thank South Asians for their contributions to Japan by nurturing the growth of Buddhism in its original homeland and exposing South Asians to Japanese Mahayana teachings. Sakurai's call to return living Buddhism to South Asia would be echoed by others, including Fujii Nichidatsu/Nittatsu (1885–1985), the founder of the Nichiren Buddhist order Nipponzan Myōhōji, and such long-term Japanese Buddhist residents in South Asia as Kimura Ryūkan, whose career we will examine

103. Akegarasu, *Indo Busseki junpai ki*, 428–29.

further in chapter 5.[104] These connections bolstered a growing sense of pan-Asianism in Japan and the anticolonial resistance in South Asia. The spirit of pan-Asianism found expression not only in person-to-person contacts and in writing but also in the form of the material cultural exchanges that I will examine in the next chapters.

104. On Fujii's efforts in India in the early 1930s, see Robert Kisala, *Prophets of Peace: Pacifism and Cultural Identity in Japan's New Religions* (Honolulu: University of Hawai'i Press, 1999), 49.

4

Buddhist Material Culture, "Indianism," and the Construction of Pan-Asian Buddhism in Twentieth-Century Japan

As Japanese Buddhists traveled to Buddhist countries in South and Southeast Asia, they returned from overseas to Japan bearing with them not only impressions but material reminders of their journeys and sojourns. Depending on their wealth and status, the travelers returned with varying amounts of manuscripts, published books, art objects, Buddha images, relics, and photographs.[1] Many published accounts of their travels that included maps detailing their routes and photographs of the sites seen and people met along the way. As I showed in the previous chapter, Akegarasu Haya and some of his fellow pilgrims on the NYK-sponsored pilgrimage to India had enough surplus funds to make copious purchases of books, clothing, artwork, and other souvenirs to bring back from India with them. Akegarasu mentions that he set aside ¥2,000 (more than $12,000 today) just for this purpose. This was a prodigious sum, given the prices in India and Ceylon. As documented in their travel account, on several occasions the group of nine pilgrims had Japanese shipping firms pack up the items the travelers had accumulated and send them back to Japan. Kawaguchi Ekai similarly brought back numerous Buddha images, texts, biological specimens, items of clothing, and ritual implements from his two long periods in South Asia. These ended up in several different locations in Japan, including the Tōyō Bunko, the Ōbaku denomina-

1. This chapter draws on my earlier articles, Richard Jaffe, "Shakuson o sagashite: kindai Nihon Bukkyō no tanjō to sekai ryokō," *Shisō*, no. 943 (November 2002): 64–87; "Seeking Śākyamuni: Travel and the Reconstruction of Japanese Buddhism," *Journal of Japanese Studies* 30, no. 1 (2004): 65–96; "Buddhist Material Culture, Indianism, and the Construction of Pan-Asian Buddhism in Pre-War Japan," *Material Religion* 2, no. 3 (November 2006): 266–93; "Senzen Nihon ni okeru Bukkyōteki busshitsu bunka, 'Indo shumi,' oyobi han Ajia Bukkyō no keisei," trans. Kirihara Kenshin and Orion Klautau, *Tōhoku shūkyōgaku* 4 (2008): 157–89.

tion's head temple, Manpukuji in Uji, and Tōhoku University in Sendai, where they now comprise the "Kawaguchi Collection." Even more impressive are the objects, purchased or looted, brought back to Japan by Ōtani Kōzui and other members of his expeditions to Central and South Asia. Although for much of a century those materials sat in storage in Kyoto, they now comprise an important part of the Ryūkoku University Museum in Kyoto, where they are periodically placed on exhibition.[2]

Buddhist visual and material culture was of central importance in the construction and dissemination of new notions of Japanese and pan-Asian Buddhism. Japanese artistic interpretations of their exchanges with Buddhists in other parts of Asia, exhibitions of imported Buddhist art wares, novel displays of pageantry surrounding the arrival of Buddhist images and relics from Asia, and the creation of new forms of Buddhist architecture expressive of the deep ties with the broader Buddhist tradition all impressed upon parishioners, ordinary clerics, and government officials the global context for Buddhist practice. Although disparate and, for the most part, uncoordinated in any overarching way, a wide range of scholarly, archaeological, architectural, and artistic renderings that were brought to or created in Japan during the late nineteenth and early twentieth century helped make Japan's connection with the other regional Buddhisms in Asia visible and tangible. These concrete markers of Japan's Asian Buddhist heritage are an understudied example of how developing notions like "Asia" were given expression in a way that reached a mass audience in Japan. At the opening of these exhibitions, the unveiling of these buildings, and the display of sacred objects brought to Japan from South and Southeast Asia, tens if not hundreds of thousands of Japanese turned out for the events. Such public displays thus brought home to the Japanese public the deepening connection between Japanese and South Asian Buddhists. These buildings, collections, and processions were crucial elements in constructing Buddhism as a pan-Asian and, even, world religion for the larger Japanese populace. Simultaneously, they embodied moder-

2. For examples of some late twentieth-century exhibitions of these kinds of material objects, see Sakai-shi Hakubutsukan, <Shūki tokubetsu ten> Kawaguchi Ekai: Bukkyō no genten o motometa hito (Sakai: Sakai-shi Hakubutsukan, 1993); Ariga Yoshitaka, Haruka naru akogare Chibetto (Sendai: Tōhoku Daigaku Sōgō Gakujutsu Hakubutsukan, 2004); Ōbaku Bunka Kenkyūsho, <Ōbakusan Manpukuji Bunkaden Heisei Jūnendo shūki tokubetsuten> Kawaguchi Ekai Nepāru-Chibetto nyūkoku hyakushūnen kinen: sono sho kōkai shiryo to Ōbakusan no meihō (Uji, Japan: Ōbakusan Bunkaden, 1998); Ryūkoku Daigaku Ryūkoku Myūjiamu, ed., Bukkyō no kita michi: Shiruku Rōdo tanken no tabi (Kyoto: Ryūkoku Daigaku Ryūkoku Myūjiamu, 2013); Ryūkoku Myūjiamu, ed., Nirakusō to Ōtani tankentai: Shirukurōdo kenkyū no genten to taiintachi no omoi: tokubetsuten (Kyoto: Ryūkoku Museum, 2014).

nity for the Japanese precisely because these material forms tied Japan to a broader Asia.

To date much of the scholarly discussion of the emergence of the notion of "world religions" or the development of an understanding of Buddhism as a pan-Asian phenomenon has primarily focused on textual, particularly scholarly, sources.[3] In this chapter I focus on one important way that ordinary clerics, Japanese lay Buddhists, and government officials were exposed to the idea that Buddhism was an Indian, "pan-Asian," or, even, "world religion." For all that has been written in the last few decades about the constructed, artificial nature of the so-called "world religions," little attention has been paid to what impact, if any, this redefinition might have had for nonscholars. Nor has much thought been given to the question of how ordinary worshippers might come in contact with this new conceptual terrain.[4] The Japanese case illustrates the importance of nontextual sources in building these new understandings of Buddhism and disseminating them to a larger audience. Although a great deal of the reconceptualization of Buddhism in Japan took place at the level of scholarship and doctrine in the Buddhist sectarian and imperial universities, changes in Japanese Buddhist visual and material culture helped constitute these changes while also facilitating the spread on the denominational and popular levels of the notion of Buddhism's pan-Asian or even global reach. In this sense, the Japanese case detailed in this chapter demonstrates more than how religious material culture served *to communicate* the transformation in the discourse about Buddhism that was taking place in the scholarly and popular literature. Precisely because the sorts of temples described in this chapter were visible to the Japanese and available to them as spaces for all kinds of activities that touched their lives, they actually created pan-Asian spaces in Japan that recalled Buddhism's past, instantiated its modern present, and evoked its future. As suggested by scholarship concerning visual culture and American religion, Buddhist material culture in Japan not only influenced religious life; material culture, including architecture, played a central role in *constituting* Buddhism as a pan-Asian religion with a global future. Like religious material culture elsewhere in the world, Buddhist architecture in Japan played a variety of functions fundamental to

---

3. See, for example, Almond, *The British Discovery of Buddhism*; Richard King, *Orientalism and Religion: Postcolonial Theory, India and 'the Mystic East'* (London: Routledge, 1999); Tomoko Masuzawa, *The Invention of World Religions, or, How European Universalism Was Preserved in the Language of Pluralism* (Chicago: University of Chicago Press, 2005).

4. The genealogy of the concept of "world religions" is traced in Masuzawa, *The Invention of World Religions.*

religious life.[5] On the one hand, these temples were sites where people could initiate contact with the spirits of the deceased or were places to communicate with buddhas and bodhisattvas. They also served as loci for the creation of networks of Buddhists that included not only Japanese devotees but also Buddhists across Asia, both past and present. In their instantiation of Buddhism's global dimension, these structures function very much like the "translocal" shrine of Our Lady of Charity in Miami described by Tweed, which, despite its modern design, "transported viewers to a collective past."[6]

Japanese travelers to South and Southeast Asia, many of whom were influential members of the Buddhist elite, spread word of their adventures in published accounts. As I have noted in my discussions of Shaku Sōen, Kawaguchi Ekai, and Akegarasu Haya, it was common for travelers to publish a running commentary on their travels via serialized articles in Japanese newspapers. Once the pilgrims returned home, they also published travel diaries. The accounts—for example, Kuruma Takudō's *Nangoku junrei ki* (1916) and *Gaitō no Bukkyō* (1934), Seki Seisetsu's, *Tenjiku angya* (1922), and Murakami Myōsei's *Nyujiku bikuni* (1944)—all had covers decorated with symbols that had become synonymous with South Asia: the Bodhi leaf, an elephant, or scenes from the life of the Buddha. As I note in the discussion of Akegarasu's travels, pilgrims headed for South Asian destinations read these accounts diligently, but I have no evidence of the size of the readership for this literature. Even if sitting unread on a temple reception-room bookshelf, however, the books decorated with South Asian motifs would have served as reminders to people of Japanese Buddhism's South Asian ties.[7]

Most of these travel accounts also were illustrated with maps, drawings, and, as the twentieth century progressed, photographs of increasingly high quality. At first the travelers themselves took photographs of the places they visited in India or included stock images of Buddhist sites in their books. As photographic technology in Japan became less expensive and lone travel gave way to groups, including exploratory expeditions, skilled photographers documented the journey. By the time NYK sponsored the pilgrimage described in the previous chapter, large-format works with carefully produced

5. David Morgan and Sally M. Promey, *The Visual Culture of American Religions* (Berkeley: University of California Press, 2001), 2–17.

6. Thomas A. Tweed, ed., *Retelling U.S. Religious History* (Berkeley: University of California Press, 1997), 112.

7. Japanese temple reception rooms frequently have glass cases displaying books published by the denomination headquarters, past and present incumbents, and significant works associated with the particular denomination, for example, a history of the head temple or writings of the founder of the denomination.

images of Buddhist sites were available to the public. One such example is *Indo Busseki jissha* (1926). The photographer of this work, Kumagaya Kunizō (1887–?), had lived in India and Burma from 1911 to 1925, taking the bulk of the photographs for the book in 1923. Working with advice from such long-term Japanese students in India as Kimura Nichiki, Kumagaya photographed Buddhist sites. He relied on the expertise of Wada Sanzō (1883–1967), a Japanese painter who traveled in India and Burma in 1914–15, in producing the photographs for the book. Takakusu Junjirō, who had visited India in 1912, provided a short biography of Śākyamuni, based on the latest scholarship, as a separate volume accompanying the book of photographs, noting at the end of the biography how the book was being published just as the 2,500-year anniversary of Śākyamuni's birth, which he calculated to be in 1934, approached.[8] In addition, Takakusu wrote the explanatory notes for the photographs, explaining their significance and the history of the sites where they were located. Akegarasu Haya and other members of the NYK tour made use of the work in their journey, but the photographer, Kumagaya Kunizō, had made the images available so that even those who could not make such a journey would get a sense of the land of the Buddha. In the same genre, the massive two-volume collection of reports from the various expeditions of Ōtani Kōzui, *Shin seiiki ki*, which was published in 1937, contained hundreds of photographs taken across South, Central, and East Asia, as well as copious documentation of the archaeological objects gathered by the explorers. These gold-embossed, leather-bound volumes were a testament to Ōtani's ambitious program of Asian exploration and a sourcebook for actual and armchair travelers alike.[9]

In addition to the published accounts, the Buddhist pilgrims also returned to Japan with numerous samples of Buddhist material culture from South, Central, and Southeast Asia. The travel records of many of the pilgrims and overseas students that I have examined in earlier chapters mention Buddhist objects received or collected while overseas. Kuruma Takudō, Ōtani Kōzui, Kawaguchi Ekai, and Akegarasu Haya all mention acquiring Buddhist texts and material objects while traveling in South Asia. On my visits to temples associated with some of the travelers and their relatives, for example, Shaku Kōzen, Shaku Sōen, Kawaguchi Ekai, and Kuruma Takudō, I viewed a multiplicity of Indian and Southeast Asian Buddhist objects brought back by the former incumbents of the temples. Only a handful of these items are mentioned in the pilgrims' travel records and probably only a small portion of

8. Takakusu Junjirō, Wada Sanzō, and Kumagaya Kunizō, *Indo Busseki jissha* (Tokyo: Kōgeisha, 1926), *Kaisetsu*, 21.

9. Uehara Yoshitarō, *Shin seiiki ki: Ōtanike zōban*, 2 vols. (Tokyo: Yūkōsha, 1937).

them are on display at their temples. In addition, many items have ended up in storage at universities or temples where they sit largely unexamined and uncataloged, off limits, at least for now, to most researchers. Now often the personal property of the travelers' descendants, a detailed accounting of these items will require a great deal of legwork, good luck, and the cooperation of those who now possess them. In addition, almost all of these items, including much of the sculpture, has escaped the attention of art historians, inside and outside Japan, so, for the time being, determining the age of the objects and their exact provenance is extremely difficult.

Nonetheless, even the limited number of imported items that I have been able to track down based on travel diaries and temple visits demonstrate clearly that Indian and Southeast Asian Buddhist material objects held great allure for the Japanese. The Buddhist objects brought to Japan by travelers were extremely diverse, including collections of textual materials in Indic languages, paintings, Buddhist ritual implements and clothing, relics, pieces of ruins, soil, and rocks, from pilgrimage sites, coins, flora and fauna, and sculptures, particularly Buddha images. Some of the collections of texts became the object of scholarly inquiry, as a few of the pilgrims, particularly Kawaguchi Ekai, donated many of the treasures acquired overseas to Japanese universities and libraries, including the Tōyō Bunko and Tōhoku University. Nonetheless, many of these foreign religious objects were not placed permanently on display in museums for the general public, as was often the case in Europe and the United States. Rather, the pilgrims kept a large number of these artworks and sculptures in their temples, where they were kept alive or, in the case of Indian materials, brought back to life as objects of veneration or put on display—in a temple context—for the public. On occasion, the owners of these objects launched exhibitions to display a large number of the objects collected at once. As described in chapter 1, along with the palm-leaf manuscripts, paintings, and ritual objects gathered in Siam and Ceylon, Shaku Kōzen placed many of the Buddha images and other objects he had received on public display on several occasions at his temple, Sanneji. In a similar fashion, Kawaguchi Ekai held an exhibition of the items he brought to Japan from India, Nepal, and Tibet at the Tokyo School of Fine Arts (Tōkyō Bijutsu Gakkō) on November 3, 1903, just six months after returning from South Asia. Kawaguchi arranged a similar event after he returned from his lengthier sojourn in India, Nepal, and Tibet. On October 8, 1915, just a bit more than one month after disembarking in Kobe after nearly eleven years overseas, Kawaguchi again held a six-day exhibition, "Exhibition of Objects Brought from Tibet, Nepal, and India" (Chibetto/Nepāru/Indo Shōraihin

Tenrankai), of his acquisitions at the Tokyo School of Fine Arts.[10] In addition, the prominent placement of reliquaries, paintings, photographs, and sculptures marked the resident of the temple as one that had made the pilgrimage to realms associated with the origins of the tradition, thus enhancing his prestige as a well-educated, cosmopolitan Buddhist.

Buddha images, in particular, attracted the attention of Japanese pilgrims traveling in South and Southeast Asia. Buddha images also were a popular gift, as Indian museum managers, scholars, and Southeast Asian rulers alike bestowed them on the Japanese. I have described how Shaku Kōzen and Kawaguchi Ekai made use of some of these images, placing them at the center of their temple or lay group liturgies. Some of the other travelers we have touched on in the previous chapters also collected and enshrined the Buddha images they acquired while in South Asia, although I have been able to gather far less information about the emplacement of the images or the sculptures themselves. The kings of Siam, in particular, gave numerous Buddha images to visiting Japanese Buddhist dignitaries.

As I noted in chapter 1, Shaku Kōzen returned with many Buddha images, large and small. The seated image of Śākyamuni, which is a beautiful cast sculpture, appears to have been received by Kōzen during his year in Siam, as it bears the inscription "a manifestation of the essence of the Dharma in the supreme country of Siam, Rattanakosin Year 127," a date that corresponds to 1908–9.[11] (See fig. 4.1.) As mentioned above in chapter 1, Kōzen for a time made the Śākyamuni image the central image of worship at Sanneji. He also held a public exhibition of the many images he brought back from Siam and used some of them along the Śākyamuni pilgrimage route that he created at Sanneji and its branch temples. Today, some of those images have been placed in a side room connected with the main hall of worship at the temple.

Hioki Mokusen, as well, received multiple images during his visit to Siam for the coronation of Vajiravudh (Rama VI), on November 11, 1911. Following his return to Japan, Hioki held exhibitions of the Buddhist items he had acquired at his temple, Kasuisai in Fukuroi, and at the Nissenji in Nagoya. (For more on both of these temples, see below in this chapter.) In addition, Hioki distributed several of these images to temples in Japan and the greater

---

10. For dates for the exhibitions, see Sakai-shi Hakubutsukan, ed., <Shūki tokubetsu ten> Kawaguchi Ekai, 108–9.

11. The inscription is transcribed and translated into Japanese in Unebe Toshiya, "Tai watto/ Rajyashiddaramu jiin hoka shozō shahon ni motozuku zōgai Butten no kenkyū," in Grants-in-Aid for Scientific Research (Nagoya: Nagoya University, 2012), 41–42.

FIGURE 4.1. Siamese Śākyamuni image at Sanneji. Courtesy of Sanneji. Photograph by the author.

FIGURE 4.2. Siamese Śākyamuni image at Entsūji, Hyōgo Prefecture. Courtesy of Entsūji. Photograph by the author.

empire. One of these Śākyamuni images, a Siamese Śākyamuni sculpture that Hioki received while in Singapore from a "Mr. Ōtsubo" (Ōtsubo-shi) remains on display at Hioki Mokusen's home temple, Entsūji, in Hyōgo Prefecture, while others were given to temples in the Osaka area (see fig. 4.2). According to Kuruma, one "ancient Buddha image" (ko Butsuzō) acquired by Hioki and Kuruma in Siam was enshrined as the main image of worship at the Osaka temple, Chōtokuji. A second stone Buddha image from Bodh Gayā was enshrined as the central image of worship at Buddagayasan in the suburbs of Osaka, while another Buddha image from Siam was enshrined as the central image of worship at a new temple in the Alishan mountain region of Taiwan.[12] A second stone image presented to Hioki and Kuruma by the Mahant of Bodh Gayā was enshrined at the Young Men's Buddhist Association Preaching Hall. In addition to the various images that Kuruma and Hioki had enshrined in temples, they also used the rock and dirt they had collected at a number of Buddhist sacred sites in India to cast a large panel that was then inscribed with Japanese-style Buddha's footprints, creating a Bussokuseki that was housed at the temple Kaizōji in the Komagome district of Tokyo. Revealing the intentions underlying the creation of this unique Buddhist object of veneration, Kuruma wrote that by making clear the relationship between Japan and India, the stone would help all sentient beings deepen the karmic ties that would result in their achieving Buddhahood.[13]

Another striking artistic form produced by Japanese Buddhists who traveled to South and Southeast Asia, particularly those who achieved a level of facility with one of the Buddhist languages used in those regions, was polylingual calligraphy of Buddhist texts like the one done by Kōzen that is described in chapter 1. To my knowledge, no systematic study of this genre of calligraphy has been published in Japanese or English. During the course of my research, I have discovered numerous examples of this type of calligraphy at temples and at exhibitions. Most of the travelers who achieved some facility with one or more of the Buddhist Indic languages and scripts produced these sorts of calligraphies. Here again my sampling of their productions is desultory and I have not been able to review the archives or visit the temples of all the long-term overseas students and travelers mentioned in this book. Using a combination of Sino-Japanese (that is, kanbun), Japanese, and a range

12. Several of these images can be seen in the plates at the beginning of Takashina Rōsen and Kuruma Takudō, Hioki Mokusen Zenji den (Tokyo: Hioki Mokusen Zenji Denki Kankōkai, 1962). (No pagination or numbering of the plates is provided.) The enshrinement of the images at various temples is mentioned in Kuruma, Nangoku junrei ki, 858–59.

13. Kuruma, Nangoku junrei ki, 864.

of scripts for writing Pali or Sanskrit, the travelers produced calligraphed renditions of Buddhist maxims, many of them expressing Buddhist teachings held in common across the Asian region. On occasion I have seen examples hanging in temples associated with the overseas travelers, for example, at Shinpukuji, an Ōbakushū temple associated with Kawaguchi Ekai's family. In all likelihood these calligraphies were similarly displayed at the time of their production, at least on an occasional basis, but, without further evidence, that is just a working hypothesis. Nonetheless, the display of calligraphic scrolls at temples is common, so it is likely that these testaments to the calligraphers' travels and command of multiple Buddhist languages were used to adorn their temples and living quarters. In addition, some of the polylingual calligraphies seem to have been produced in multiple copies that were then distributed to parishioners and other faithful, perhaps as gifts or as a means of raising funds for the temple.

One of the most commonly written Buddhist maxims was the "Verse of Admonishment of the Seven Buddhas" (*Shichibutsu tsūkaige*): "Commit no evil, Do all good acts, Purify your thoughts; This is the teaching of all buddhas."[14] According to William Bodiford, this summary of the Buddha's teachings was long cited and commented upon in Japan, particularly in Chan/Zen texts. Dōgen Kigen (1200–1253), to give one famous example, quotes the whole verse at the beginning of the *Shōbōgenzō* fascicle "Shoaku makusa" (Commit No Evil), which was written in 1240, as well as in several other places in his corpus.[15] During the Meiji era, the phrase became an expression of Buddhist unity, as a summation of the teaching acceptable to Buddhists of all denominations.[16] The efflorescence of citations of the Admonition was in part probably stimulated by the production of books outlining the fundamental teachings of every Buddhist denomination, many of them entitled something along the lines of the various editions of the *Jūnishū kōyō* (Essentials of the Twelve Denominations) that proliferated in the late nineteenth century.

During the nineteenth century in Ceylon, the verse was reinterpreted and

---

14. *Shoaku makusa, shuzen bugyō, jijō goi, zesho Bukkyō*. On a calligraphy hanging in Shinpukuji in Utsunomiya, Kawaguchi Ekai's Japanese rendering from the *kanbun* is, "すべてのあくをなすなかれ、あらゆる善をつとむべし、自らこゝろをきよむるは、これぞ仏のをしえるなる" (*Subete no aku o nasunakare, arayuru zen o tsutomubeshi, mizukara kokoro o kiyomuru wa, kore zo Hotoke no oshieru naru*).

15. William Bodiford, "Treasury of the Eye of the Dharma Book 31: Not Doing Evils (Shoaku Makusa)," Stanford University, https://web.stanford.edu/group/scbs/sztp3/translations/shobogenzo/translations/shoaku_makusa/shoaku_makusa.intro.html. Accessed June 6, 2017.

16. Ketelaar, *Of Heretics and Martyrs in Meiji Japan*, 186.

raised in prominence within the Sangha and among foreign promoters of a Buddhist revival on the island. For much of Ceylonese Buddhist history, the verse had been understood as linked with several proximate verses in the *Dhammapada* as an expression of ideal adherence to the monastic rule (S. *prātimokṣa*; P., *pāṭimokkha*). As Henry Steel Olcott attempted to forge a unified statement of "Buddhistic Principles" acceptable to both Northern and Southern Buddhists, he reinterpreted the Admonition. After a good deal of negotiation with members of the Ceylonese Sangha, Olcott cobbled together an anodyne set of fourteen "principles" to which, he hoped, all Buddhists could assent.[17] Among them was the Admonition, which Olcott described as "the essence of Buddhism, as summed up by the Tathāgata himself."[18] The Admonition, which was found in Verse 183 of the *Dhammapada* as well as in many Sinitic Buddhist texts, thus provided a bridge between Southern and Japanese Buddhism. Having overlapped with Olcott as he developed and sought approval for *A Buddhist Catechism* in Ceylon and across Asia, such students as Shaku Kōzen, Shaku Sōen, and Noguchi Zenshirō would have been exposed to the verse in Ceylon. Sōen quoted at length from the English version of the *Catechism* in his diary (see chapter 1), so it is likely many of the Japanese Buddhists in Ceylon at the end of the nineteenth century witnessed the deployment of the Admonition on the island as well as at home in various pan-sectarian contexts. With the dissemination of Olcott's *Catechism* in Japan in both English and Japanese, attention to the well-known verse seems to have been heightened. Trainor, in his investigation of *Dhammapada* 183, focuses on the use of the verse by members of the Ceylonese Sangha and such foreign Buddhists as Olcott and Charles Webster Leadbeater in his effort to trace the verse's reinterpretation and rise to prominence in the nineteenth and twentieth centuries. It is possible that the circulation of numerous Japanese, Ceylonese, and American Buddhists between Ceylon and Japan may have increased attention to the Admonition, transforming the understanding of it globally.

As Japanese Buddhist travelers and overseas students acquired facility with a range of Buddhist languages and scripts, they calligraphically rendered this particular expression in a variety of script combinations. As we

17. Kemper, *Rescued from the Nation*, 140–44. On the shifting interpretations of *Dhammapada* 183, see, Kevin Trainor, "Buddhism in a Nutshell: The Uses of *Dhammapada* 183," in *Embedded Languages: Studies of Sri Lankan and Buddhist Cultures: Essays in Honor of W. S. Karunatillake*, ed. Carol S. Anderson, Suzanne Mrozik, R. M. W. Rajapakse, and W. M. Wijeratne (Colombo, Sri Lanka: Godage International Publishers, 2009), 109–48.

18. Henry Steel Olcott, *Buddhist Catechism* (Sri Lanka: Ministry of Cultural Affairs, 1908), 131–32.

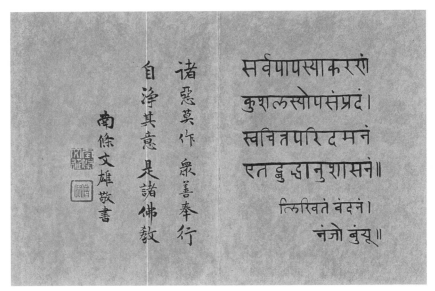

F I G U R E   4 . 3 . Nanjō Bun'yū's calligraphy of the *Shichibutsu tsūkaige*, Sanskrit in Devanagiri script. Courtesy of Sanneji.

have seen, Shaku Kōzen produced an undated calligraphy in Sino-Japanese and Pali, written in Aśokan Brāhmi, that after his death was used on the cover of a special issue of *Kaigai Bukkyō jijō* honoring Kōzen's contribution to the understanding of Southern Buddhism.[19] Another example that I received during a research visit to Sanneji was written by Nanjō Bun'yū in Sanskrit using Devanagari script. Printed in multiple copies and stamped with Nanjō's seal in red, perhaps for distribution, this was also in the possession of Kōzen's temple, Sanneji (see fig. 4.3). Nanjō also wrote a scroll of the *Tsūkaige* in Sanskrit-Devanagari/English/Sino-Japanese in 1919 that was given to or otherwise came into the possession of Shinshōji.[20] Located in Gifu Prefecture, Shinshōji also preserves many pieces of Kawaguchi Ekai's artwork.

As other Japanese mastered various Indic and Southeast Asian languages, they used them to create different scriptural combinations of the Admonition. Shaku Sōen created a large scroll of the saying written in Pali, using Sinhala script, along with the corresponding Sino-Japanese, that remains in his retirement temple, Tōkeiji in Kita-Kamakura. (See fig. 4.4.) Kawaguchi

19. *Kaigai Bukkyō jijō* 10, no. 6 (1944).

20. Ōbaku Bunka Kenkyūsho, *Kawaguchi Ekai Nepāru-Chibetto nyūkoku hyakushūnen kinen*, 15.

was one of the most prolific polylingual calligraphers. Like many of the others who had mastered other Buddhist languages, Kawaguchi reproduced the Admonition of the Seven Buddhas, at times combining the phoneme, *hūṃ*, written in Tibetan, along with the classical Japanese translation of the Admonition. (See fig. 4.5.) The calligraphy now adorns the main worship hall at the temple Shinpukuji in Utsunomiya, where Kawaguchi's younger brother,

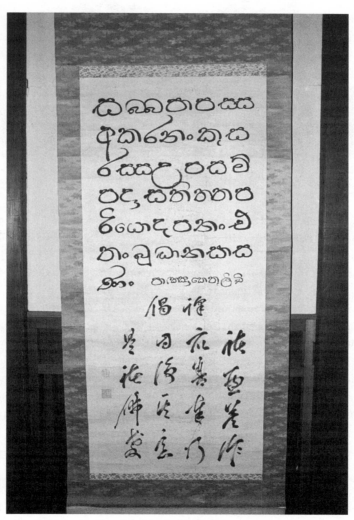

FIGURE 4.4. Shaku Sōen's calligraphy of the *Shichibutsu tsūkaige*, Pali in Sinhala script. Courtesy of Tōkeiji. Photograph by the author.

FIGURE 4.5. Kawaguchi Ekai. The seed syllable *HŪM* in Tibetan script and a Japanese translation of the *Shichibutsu tsūkaige*. 1921. Courtesy of Shinpukuji.

Nishikawa Hōzan, had served as incumbent.[21] Kawaguchi also demonstrated his linguistic mastery by writing the verse in Pali with Sinhala script, Tibetan, and Japanese.[22]

Far more than just Admonition was written in this polylingual mode. Kawaguchi Ekai was particularly prolific in this regard. On one scroll, Kawaguchi inscribed the three sacred phonemes, *OM AḤ HŪM*, above a Buddhist mortuary verse (*kanmon*) that was used in the *Sho ekō shingi* (T. 2578) and the Sōtō denomination's *Gyōji kihan*, among other places. The mortuary verse reads, "Originally there is no East or West,/Where is there North and South?/Deluded [one is imprisoned] in the castle of the Three Realms,/Awakened the ten directions are empty"(*honrai mu tōsai/ga sho u nanboku/mei ko sangai jō/go ko jippō ku*)[23] (see fig. 4.6). Most of the polylingual calligraphies that I have

21. Ōbaku Bunka Kenkyūsho, *Kawaguchi Ekai Nepāru-Chibetto nyūkoku hyakushūnen kinen*, 14.

22. Ōbaku Bunka Kenkyūsho, *Kawaguchi Ekai Nepāru-Chibetto nyūkoku hyakushūnen kinen*, 13.

23. SAT Database, T2578_.81.0660a16. Kawaguchi has transposed the last two lines of the verse as the first two on the scroll. Ōbaku Bunka Kenkyūsho, *Kawaguchi Ekai Nepāru-Chibetto nyūkoku hyakushūnen kinen*, 11. I have followed the Sino-Japanese reading in Sōtōshū

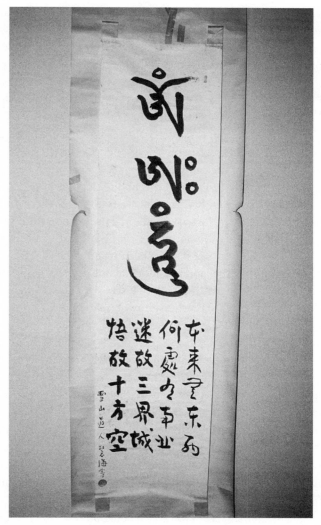

FIGURE 4.6. Kawaguchi Ekai. The seed syllables *OṂ AḤ HŪṂ* in Tibetan script and a Sinographic Buddhist mortuary verse, Courtesy of Shinpukuji.

uncovered were the work of one calligrapher, although, as often was the case in Japan, the verse was inscribed on another person's painting. An example of this is Kawaguchi inscribing painting by Nakamura Fusetsu (1866–1943) of

Shūmuchō, ed., *Standard Observances of the Sōtō School*, trans. T. Griffith Foulk (Tokyo: Sōtōshū Shūmuchō, 2010), 1:620.

Śākyamuni descending a mountain following his ascetic practice, a painting that is inscribed with a verse written in Tibetan and Japanese.[24]

One set of calligraphies, however, was produced collaboratively by individuals with command of different Buddhist languages. These examples I discovered at the Nichirenshū temple, Jōzaiji, where, as I will discuss in the next chapter, Ehara Ryōzui, Victor Pulle, and G. S. Prelis worked together translating Japanese and Chinese texts into English. During the course of their stay at Jōzaiji in 1935–36, the three men also calligraphed a handful of Pali maxims and texts in Sinhala script on scrolls and *shikishi*, the hard card stock frequently used in Japan for calligraphing poetry and other texts, at times working collaboratively to produce scrolls in both Japanese and Pali.

Although many regions in East Asia have a tradition of this style of calligraphy, to my knowledge this sort of calligraphic production for display is not as common among South and Southeast Asian Buddhists. In this particular instance, Pulle and Prelis appear to have been inspired by their environment to produce calligraphy in the Japanese mode. None of these items are on display at Jōzaiji today. Following the death of Ehara Ryōzui, they were inherited by his children, none of whom reside at the temple. Like many of the sculptures described above, they are rarely seen outside the family homes and are in danger of being lost altogether in the future. Although I have not been able to view the original calligraphies, members of the Ehara family and the current incumbent at Jōzaiji have shared photographs of them with me.

Several calligraphies were produced by the Ceylonese at Jōzaiji. On the first, a rectangular *shikishi*, the Ceylonese calligraphed in Pali, using Sinhala script a portion of the protective verse (*paritta*), "May blessings attend you. May all the gods protect you. By the powers of all the Buddhas may happiness always be with you." A second calligraphy, on a round *shikishi*, bears the verse, found in multiple places in the Pali canon, "Who gives light, gives eyes" (*Dīpado hoti cakkhudo*), signed on the back by Victor Pulle, dated "Summer 1935" (see fig. 4.7).[25] One large scroll was a collaborative effort by one of the Ceylonese perhaps, Pulle, and Ehara Ryōzui. The Pali-Sinhala text quotes a text again found in multiple Pali sources, for example, the *Dhammapada*. "The fragrance of the good ones moves against the wind; / All directions a

24. Two examples of Kawaguchi and Nakamura's joint work are in Ōbaku Bunka Kenkyūsho, *Kawaguchi Ekai Nepāru-Chibetto nyūkoku hyakushūnen kinen*, 10.

25. See for example, the *Kindada Sutta* (*Saṃyutta Nikāya* 1.42) in Bodhi, *The Connected Discourses of the Buddha: A New Translation of the Saṃyutta Nikāya; Translated from the Pāli; Original Translation by Bhikkhu Bodhi*, 2 vols. (Somerville, MA: Wisdom Publications, 2000), 1:120–21.

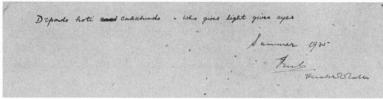

FIGURE 4.7. Victor Pulle (Soma Thera). Pali in Sinhala script. Courtesy of Jōzaiji.

good person pervades."[26] Beneath the Pali, Ehara, using his Buddhist name, Nichikyō, wrote the corresponding lines from the *Bieyi za ahan jing* (the Shorter Chinese *Saṃyuktāgama*).[27] Another large scroll inscribes a Ceylonese verse concerning filial piety in Pali-Sinhala. This truly was a team effort,

26. See *Dhammapada* Verse 54. The late Unebe Toshiya, who translated the Sinhala for me, noted that there is a discrepancy between the verse as written on the scroll and the received Pali text. It is unclear whether this was a mistake by Pulle or because he was working from a variant text. I thank Ehara Ryōzui's son, Ehara Ryōsen, for making these calligraphies available to me. Unebe Toshiya kindly translated and romanized the Pali on the Jōzaiji calligraphies.

27. SAT DB, T0100_.02.0377a02–a03.

as both Pulle and Prelis signed the Sinhala, Ehara Ryōzui translated the text into Japanese, and his daughter, Sachiko, who inherited most of these scrolls, calligraphed the Japanese.[28] Perhaps the contents of the verse inspired Ryōzui and Sachiko—father and daughter—to work together on the Japanese calligraphy. The text, as kindly translated from the Pali by an anonymous scholar at the Buddhist Publication Society in Sri Lanka, reads as follows.

> Filled with compassion,
> The generator who is the father of mine,
> He fed and nourished me,
> I worship that father of mine!
>
> Having made from the blood in her body,
> The milk that is full of love,
> Giving it suck to me, she nourished me well,
> I worship that mother of mine![29]

The flows of Buddhist material culture in Asia were not unidirectional, although I have seen far less about Japanese Buddhist texts and artwork being brought to South and Southeast Asia. As I have noted in passing, Kawaguchi Ekai brought a copy of the Tetsugen edition of the Chinese Buddhist canon from Manpukuji to Nepal, where it remains in the Royal Library to this day.[30] Akegarasu Haya, as well, mentions the presence of a Buddha image given to Nyanatiloka by Beatrice Suzuki.

On occasion Japanese Buddhists marked sacred places of significance by commissioning a stele placed at the site to commemorate their successful pilgrimage. As discussed in chapter 1, Kitabatake Dōryū, the first recorded Japanese to reach Bodh Gayā, left a memorial stone noting the date of his visit. Decades later, the Nichirenshū cleric Oka Kyōtsui (d. 1945), who spent several years studying in India beginning in 1915, similarly commemorated his visit to Vulture Peak, where purportedly the Lotus Sūtra, central to his denomination, had been expounded by the Buddha, making the mountain a crucial landmark for the Nichirenshū. After successfully ascending the mountain in 1917, Oka erected a stele recording the visit in Year 2610 Buddhist Era (Taishō 6.12.2, that is, December 2, 1917), by the Japanese śramaṇa Kyōtsui. On the center of the stele, Kyōtsui wrote "Homage to the Wondrous Lotus Sūtra"

28. Again I thank the late Unebe Toshiya for his help deciphering the calligraphy.

29. I thank Nyanatusita and the staff of the Buddhist Publication Society for their assistance with translating this scroll.

30. Takayama Ryūzō, "Kawaguchi Ekai kenjō no zōkyō o motomete: 1998 nen Nepāru hōkoku," *Ōbaku bunka* 118 (1998–99): 14–27.

(*Namu myōhō renge kyō*) flanked with the remarks that "[here] Śākyamuni Buddha expounded the Lotus Sūtra and others" (*Shakamuni Butsu seppō Hokekyō nado*) and "Eternal Vulture Peak, the Ultimate Foundational Place" (*Jōzai Ryōjusen Konpon Saishō Chi*). When Seki Seisetsu arrived at the peak a year later, he noted in his account the presence of Oka's stele.[31]

Of even greater significance for Buddhist politics and identity building in the early twentieth century was the exchange of Buddha statues between Dharmapāla and Asahi Shūkō, a Jōdo cleric who was the incumbent at Tentokuji in Tokyo. During his first visit to Japan in 1891 Dharmapāla presented Tentokuji with a small Gupta-period Buddha image he had taken from Bodh Gayā. There the image was placed on display. Dharmapāla also suggested to some of his Japanese associates that in return they might contribute a statue to be enshrined at the Mahābodhi Temple. Asahi Shūkō, reciprocating, presented Dharmapāla with a purportedly Kamakura-period Amida image. To the Japanese, as Satō Tetsurō speculates, sending the statue to India was a potent symbol for the return of Japanese Buddhism to the land of its origins. As with Akegarasu and other Pure Land Buddhists, connecting their central Buddha, Amitābha, to Buddhism's homeland and Śākyamuni was a pressing concern in the context of the growing emphasis on Buddhism's origins. For Dharmapāla, on the other hand, the use of the Japanese image at Bodh Gayā represented a deepening Japanese involvement in his movement to return the site of Buddha's awakening to Buddhist control. After returning to Bodh Gayā, Dharmapāla unsuccessfully but dramatically attempted to enshrine the statue at Bodh Gayā, claiming that it was a gift from Japan, rather than from just one denomination of Buddhism. This strategy backfired, however, as the British feared encouraging Japanese meddling in Indian affairs. The British attitude further hardened, as Kemper observes, when Japanese military prestige grew in the wake of victories in the Sino-Japanese and Russo-Japanese wars. After finally losing a protracted court battle in 1910, Dharmapāla was ordered to remove the image, which temporarily had remained in the Burmese rest house at Bodh Gayā, from the site altogether. Subsequently the statue was enshrined at the Mahābodhi Society's Dharmarajika temple at their Calcutta headquarters, where it remains today.[32]

Japanese Buddhist material and artistic contributions to the work of the Mahābodhi Society, continued into the 1930s. Most prominently, the artist Nosu Kōsetsu (1885–1973) painted a series of murals depicting the life of

31. Seki Seisetsu, *Tenjiku angya* (Kyoto: Baiyō Shoin, 1922), 174.

32. The information concerning the image combines the account in Kemper, *Rescued from the Nation*, 194–203, and that in Satō, *Daiajia shisō katsugeki*, 339–40.

Śākyamuni on the walls of the Mahābodhi Society's Mūlagandhakuṭī Vihāra at Sārnāth in 1933. Blending together styles in a manner reminiscent of Yokoyama Taikan's *Ryūtō*, Nosu painted pictures of the major events in the life of Śākyamuni. The Vihāra, which was opened in 1931, was built by the Mahābodhi Society at Sārnāth, at the site where supposedly Śākyamuni gave his first sermon. According to Huber, the members of the Mahābodhi Society, who still did not have control of Bodh Gayā as a Buddhist sacred site, made Sārnāth their ritual center instead, conducting annual celebrations and fund raising activities from the Vihāra.[33] Nosu's contribution to the new Vihāra grew out of the intersection of the Japanese artistic-cultural and spiritual engagement that began with Okakura and Tagore's long collaboration, as well as the Japanese participation in Dharmapāla's activism that aimed for the restoration of Bodh Gayā to Buddhist hegemony.

These Japanese Buddha images and stele encountered by Japanese travelers in Bodh Gayā and at the Island Hermitage in Ceylon provided tangible evidence of ongoing Japanese involvement in international Buddhist politics and Buddhist cultural exchange. As more Japanese studied and traveled in South Asia, the landscape was inscribed with ever more evidence of the connection with Japan that had been left by previous pilgrims.

An even more conspicuous incorporation of "Asian/Indian" elements into Japanese Buddhist material culture—what I would call "Indianism"—was the emergence of an Indian and Southeast Asian-inflected architectural style that was used for Buddhist temples, villas, and monuments. These structures were the product of a growing collaboration between Japanese clerical travelers, who had witnessed overseas Buddhist art and architecture firsthand, denominational leaders, who wanted to find temple forms expressive of modern, expansive, twentieth-century Japanese Buddhism, and Japanese architects striving to move Buddhist architecture in a new direction.[34] One architect in particular, Itō Chūta (1867–1954), worked in conjunction with several of the most influential Japanese Buddhist pilgrims to create a distinctively new form of Indian-inflected Japanese temple architecture. Itō was one of the

---

33. Huber, *The Holy Land Reborn*, 295–96; Satō, *Daiajia shisō katsugeki*, 430–31; Auerback, *A Storied Sage*, 218. Reproductions of Nosu's paintings are published in Nosu Kosetsu and Basil Woodward Crump, *Mulagandhakuti Vihara Wall Paintings* (Sarnath: Benares, 1940); and Nosu Kōsetsu, *Shakuson eden* (Kawasaki: Numata Yehan, 1960).

34. Several Japanese scholars have discussed briefly some of these new forms of South and Southeast Asian-inflected Buddhist architecture in recent years. See Yamada Kyōta, "Kindai Bukkyō kenchiku no Higashi Ajia—Minami Ajia ōkan," in *Bukkyō o meguru Nihon to Tōnan Ajia chiiki*, ed. Ōsawa Kōji (Tokyo: Bensei Shuppan, 2016), 87–105; and Ōtani Ei'ichi, Yoshinaga Shin'ichi, and Kondō Shuntarō, eds., *Kindai Bukkyō sutadīzu* (Kyoto: Hōzōkan, 2016), 248–50.

most influential architects of his day, planning the main shrine building at the Heian Shrine (1895) and Taiwan Shrine (1901), the memorial for victims of the Great Tokyo Earthquake of 1923 (Shinsai Kinendō), and the Honganji Tsukiji Betsuin (1934). In 1943 Itō was awarded the Order of Culture Prize (Bunka Kunshō) for his achievements, the first architect to receive that honor.

Itō had studied architecture at the newly created College of Engineering (Kōbu Daigakkō) at Tokyo Imperial University, becoming the first Japanese to receive a doctorate in architecture, in 1898. There he had worked with some of the first professional architects in Japan, including Tatsuno Kingo (1854–1919), a student of Josiah Conder (1852–1920), the British architect who founded the architecture program at the College of Engineering (later incorporated into Tokyo Imperial University's School of Engineering). Itō also worked closely with Kiko Kiyoyoshi (1845–1907), a master carpenter turned teacher of Japanese architecture at the College of Engineering whom Tatsuno Kingo had tasked with teaching the history of Japanese architecture.[35] Kiko, according to Cherie Wendelken, first made Itō aware of the importance of Japanese architectural history and the importance of shrine and temple design for creating buildings suited to Japan.

Working with Kiko, Itō studied a range of Japanese temples and shrines, conducting field surveys and studying their architecture. In his 1893 doctoral thesis, "Hōryūji kenchiku ron" (An Architectural Study of Hōryūji), Itō continued this research on the sources of Japanese Buddhist architectural style. In this early effort, which was the first doctoral dissertation on architecture written in Japan, Itō contended that Hōryūji was a prototype for Japanese Buddhist temples. Itō based his arguments about the temple in part on the work of James Fergusson, who had dubbed the Buddhist art of Gandhāra in northwest India (today, Pakistan), where Greek, Persian, and Indian cultural forces had met, "Greco-Indian." Itō traced the roots of Hōryūji's design to northwest India, contending that while the design incorporated features imported from the Asian continent, it also preserved elements of the Greco–Indian art that had its efflorescence in Gandhāra during the first centuries of the Common Era. According to Itō, for example, the tapered columns and proportions of Hōryūji's main temple hall bore a resemblance to those found in Greek temples.[36] Toshio Watanabe traces the origins of this theory to what

35. Cherie Wendelken, "The Tectonics of Japanese Style: Architect and Carpenter in the Late Meiji Period," *Art Journal* 55, no. 3 (1996): 32. I have followed the *Biographical Dictionary of Japan* and Benoît Jacquet in romanizing the surname as Kiko. Wendelken and others writing in English have romanized the name Kigo.

36. Wendelken, "The Tectonics of Japanese Style," 32.

he describes as Itō's misunderstanding of the book *A Handbook of Architectural Styles*, which was written by Albert Rosengarten and edited by Thomas Smith. Assuming that Rosengarten's use of the word "Asia" included not just the Near East but also East Asia, Itō concluded that there was a continuous architectural tradition embracing both Greece and all of Asia. As a result of this conflation, "Itō argued that the entasis, the pillars whose diameter was greatest at the midsection, found in Hōryūji came from Greek architecture and had traveled from Greece eastward, crossing the Asian continent and finally reaching Japan. This grand hypothesis is now discredited, though it was believed until very recently."[37] Itō, in describing Hōryūji, placed Japanese architecture in the context of a world architectural history supposedly rooted in an Indo-European tradition but also the product of architectural evolution in Asia. By reviving the Indo-European features in his own buildings, Itō aimed to create what Benoît Jacquet has called a "new Japanese 'Oriental' architecture" (*une nouvelle architecture japonaise 'orientale'*).[38]

From 1902 to 1905 Itō traveled through much of Asia, including China, Southeast Asia, India, Central Asia, and Turkey, searching for the pan-Asian roots of Japanese architecture.[39] In so doing, he hoped to verify his thesis concerning the Indo-European roots of Hōryūji's architecture. By showing that Japanese architecture shared its origins with that of Europe and the United States, Itō tried to place the Japanese architectural tradition on an equal footing with Western architecture. One conclusion catalyzed by his travels was that India had been crucially important for the development of the Japanese architectural tradition. As a result, according to Watanabe, Itō subsequently strove to incorporate Indian elements into his own architectural plans, a number of which were created on behalf of various Buddhist sponsors.[40]

Following his three-year world tour, Itō worked with some of the most prominent Buddhist clerics, including Shaku Kōzen, Ōtani Kōzui, and Hioki Mokusen, all of whom also had traveled to other parts of Asia. For almost a

37. Toshio Watanabe, "Japanese Imperial Architecture: From Thomas Roger Smith to Itō Chūta," in *Challenging Past and Present: The Metamorphosis of Nineteenth-Century Japanese Art*, ed. Ellen P. Conant (Honolulu: University of Hawai'i Press, 2006), 249.

38. Benoît Jacquet, "Itō Chūta et son Étude Architecturale du Hōryūji (1893): Comment et pourquoi Intégrer l'architecture japonaise dans l'histoire mondiale," *Ebisu* 52 (2015): 91; 97; 109; and Wendelken, "The Tectonics of Japanese Style," 32.

39. Wendelken, "The Tectonics of Japanese Style," 28–37; and Cherie Wendelken, "Pan-Asianism and the Pure Japanese Thing: Japanese Identity and Architecture in the Late 1930s," *positions* 8, no. 3 (2000): 819–28.

40. Watanabe, "Japanese Imperial Architecture," 250.

third of a century, Ōtani Kōzui (1876–1948) was one of Itō's most important architectural influences, patrons, and collaborators. The twenty-second head of the Nishi Honganji, Kōzui was an avid explorer of continental Asia, bringing back large quantities of archaeological and textual materials, particularly from Dunhuang. Kōzui, with his strong interests in exploration, world travel, and international proselytization, is one of the personalities that tied together many of the pan-Asian architectural structures examined in this chapter. A man of enormous talent and ambition, Kōzui had free access to the vast resources of the Nishi Honganji, one of the largest, wealthiest, and most actively missionary of the Japanese Buddhist denominations. As a result of his wealth and flamboyance, he was frequently a subject for the popular press, which according to one contemporaneous source, "turns to his latest doings when no subject of more immediately exciting character is at hand to titillate the reader."[41] Kōzui remained an ardent supporter of Japanese expansion on the Asian continent throughout his life. Although removed from his position as head of the Nishi Honganji in 1914 for his fiscal extravagance, he remained influential in sectarian and government circles. In 1919 he founded a society, the Kōjukai. The group, which published the journal *Daijō* in Shanghai, aimed to promote Japanese expansionism throughout Asia. Kōzui also served as "supreme advisor" to Sun Yat-sen's government and, later, as a councilor in the Konoe cabinet and on the Greater East Asia Construction Council (Dai Tōa Kensetsu Shingikai) in 1942. As a result of his support for Japanese imperialism in Asia, the Occupation authorities purged Kōzui from office after Japan's defeat in 1945.

Kōzui and Itō got to know each other through two members of Kōzui's Central Asian expedition, whom Itō had met while traveling in Yangsong (near Yunnan Province), China, in late 1903.[42] In the summer of 1906, one year after his return to Japan, Kōzui, then the head of the denomination, invited Itō to the Nishi Honganji. Itō's field notes from that period record the route taken by Ōtani's expeditions, indicating that the two men were sharing information about their world travels. This marked the start of a long collaboration between the two men, begun with Itō providing a series of plans to the Nishi Honganji for overseas branch temples in a number of major Chinese cities. Although over the decades Itō worked with patrons from a variety of denominations, Kōzui and the Nishi Honganji remained his most frequent collaborators. With greater wealth—despite Kōzui's financial profligacy—than most

41. "The Trouble at the Honganji," *Japan Weekly Chronicle*, October 17, 1929, 414.
42. Shibata Mikio, *Ōtani Kōzui no kenkyū: Ajia kōiki ni okeru sho katsudō* (Tokyo: Bensei Shuppan, 2014), 64, n.19.

denominations and increasingly expansive plans for overseas missions on the Asian continent and in the United States, Nishi Honganji officials collaborated directly with Itō and built upon his and Kōzui's vision to design a series of unprecedented temples.

In 1907, for example, Itō drew up plans for a hybrid-style temple building in Dalian (J., Dairen), in the Guandong Territory (Kantōshū), which became a Japanese leasehold concession in the wake of the Russo-Japanese War. As in his grand-mentor Josiah Conder's Ueno Museum, the plans incorporated Indo-Saracenic features like onion-shaped domes and pointed door archways, blended with a classical European-style structure with polychromatic masonry that combined white stonework and red brick.[43] For reasons of high cost and, perhaps, because of its unusual style, the plans were never utilized, however. Instead, a more traditional branch temple was completed in Dalian in 1915.[44] Over the next several years, Itō also produced plans for increasingly hybrid-style branch temple buildings for Hong Kong and Zhenxi, but as with the plans for the Dalian structure, these were never constructed. Features of the plans, particularly specific Indic and South Asian aspects of the designs, for example the *sōrin* (towers) that topped the stupa-like domes, would find their way into some of Itō's realized buildings. In plans for the unrealized Hong Kong Betsuin (1912), which, like the Nirakusō, was designed primarily by Ukai Chōsaburō with Itō's assistance, clearly Asian steeples are coupled with Euro-American church-like elements, a feature that the Nishi Honganji would use again in the 1930 Kobe Betsuin.[45]

Although most of the overseas temples that Itō helped design never were built, the extant architectural plans reflect the same sort of eclecticism visible in Nishi Honganji domestic and overseas temples that were completed. One such structure was the clearly Indian-influenced Nishi Honganji Shanghai Betsuin, which was designed by Okano Shigehisa and completed in 1931.[46] (See fig. 4.8.)

The Honpa Hongwanji Hawaii Betsuin, constructed in 1918, which was designed by the architectural firm of Emory and Webb under the supervision of the Nishi Honganji missionary Imamura Emyō (1866–1932), provides an-

43. Kurakata Shunsuke, "Itō Chūta no sekkei shisō: yōkai to shite no kenchiku," in *Itō Chūta o shitte imasu ka*, ed. Suzuki Hiroyuki (Tokyo: Ōkoku Sha, 2003), 102.

44. Shibata Mikio, *Ōtani Kōzui no kenkyū*, 36–37.

45. Kurakata, "Itō Chūta no sekkei shisō," 105–6. I thank Suzuki Hiroyuki for allowing me to view Itō's architectural drawings.

46. This information is based on the Shanghai Municipal Government Heritage Architecture sign on the site of the building that formerly was the Shanghai Betsuin. The building is at 455 Zhapulu in Shanghai.

FIGURE 4.8. Nishi Honganji Shanghai Betsuin. Courtesy of Ryūkoku University.

other example of the eclectic style of temple building that had become popular within the Nishi Honganji during the Taishō and early Shōwa periods.[47] (See fig. 4.9.) The Honolulu Betsuin combined Indian and Western styles to create a hybrid temple that reflected Hawaiian Buddhism's Japanese roots and American future. George Tanabe suggests that Imamura believed this sort of hybrid architecture reflected the universality of "true religion," which rose above any individual national culture and was symbolic of the Shin triumphalism and universalism as preached by Imamura and another influential Hawaiian Shin Buddhist, Tsunoda Ryūsaku.[48]

Toward the end of the Meiji period (1868–1912), Itō and Kōzui collaborated on two similar "Indo-Saracen," Mughal-style buildings that were constructed in the Kinki region of Japan. Beginning in 1908 Kōzui and the Nishi Honganji–affiliated architect Ukai Chōsaburō, with Itō serving as an adviser, collaborated on a massive project, the construction of Kōzui's villa (bessō)

47. See "Temple History," Honpa Hongwanji Hawaii Betsuin, http://hawaiibetsuin.org/temple-history/, accessed June 1, 2018.

48. George J. Tanabe, "Grafting Identity: The Hawaiian Branches of the Bodhi Tree," 8–9. Unpublished paper, 2002.

FIGURE 4.9. Honolulu Hongwanji, circa 1918. (Today, Honpa Hongwanji Hawaii Betsuin.) Photograph courtesy of George Tanabe.

in the foothills of the Rokkō Mountains outside Kobe in Hyōgo Prefecture. Although Ukai had studied drafting in the United States, unlike Kōzui and Itō, Ukai had not been to South Asia. The Nishi Honganji administration, however, provided Ukai with the photographic work *Indo satsuei chō* (published by the Nishi Honganji in 1904) to use for planning the construction of Kōzui's new villa. Kōzui, who had been struggling with members of the Nishi Honganji establishment over proposed institutional reforms and, increasingly, his use of funds, envisioned the expansive estate as a future center for the education of young, talented Shin clerics. The sprawling villa complex, which was completed in 1909, had estimated land-purchase and building costs of more than ¥300,000—approximately 72 million dollars today.[49] (See fig 4.10.)

In separate articles published not long after the completion of the main buildings in 1913, Itō and Ukai each characterized the exterior design style for the building as "Indo-Saracen" (*Indosarasen*).[50] According to the Nirakusō exhibition catalog published by the Ashiya Museum of Art, the main building was modeled after Akbar-period (late sixteenth-century) Indian Mughal

49. Ashiya Shiritsu Bijutsu Hakubutsukan, ed., <*Modanisumu saikō*> *Nirakusō to Ōtani tankentai* (Ashiya: Ashiya Shiritsu Bijutsu Hakubutsukan, 1999), 59. The editors of the book estimate that the cost was equivalent to ¥8 billion in 2000.

50. Itō Chūta, "Nirakusō no kenchiku," *Kenchiku kōgei sōshi* 20 (1913): 1; and Ukai Chōsaburō, "Nirakusō kenchiku kōji gaiyō," *Kenchiku kōgei sōshi* 20 (1913): 2–6.

FIGURE 4.10. Ōtani Kōzui's villa near Kobe, Japan. Courtesy of Ryūkoku University Library.

architecture, particularly the onion-shaped domes of the Taj Mahal (seventeenth century).[51] The villa, consisting of three stories, was topped by two red-slate domes. As in other Indo-Saracenic buildings designed by Itō, the building had arched second-story windows and intricate Islamicate-style design work on the building's turrets. The villa was equipped with the latest in technology, including a fire-safety system, lightning rods, heating, telephones, and electric lamps. In addition to such "necessities" as tennis courts, the villa also included facilities for processing the materials brought back to Japan by Kōzui's various Asian expeditions, a meteorological station, and a horticultural laboratory. Inside the main building of the villa, in true Euro-American imperial style, were a variety of rooms decorated in keeping with regional themes, for example: an Arabia room, a China room, an Egypt room, a modern English room, an India room. A cable car, installed solely for the villa, brought visitors up the hillside to the building grounds. When, in 1914, Kōzui was forced out of his position as head of the Nishi Honganji, control of the estate reverted to the latter. In 1932, a disastrous fire destroyed the main buildings of the estate.[52]

51. Ashiya Shiritsu Bijutsu Hakubutsukan, ed., <*Modanisumu saikō*> *Nirakusō to Ōtani tankentai II* (Ashiya: Shiritsu Bijutsu Hakubutsukan, 2003), 39.

52. Ashiya Shiritsu Bijutsu Hakubutsukan, *Nirakusō to Ōtani tankentai II*, 138.

While in existence, however, Nirakusō was a popular attraction for visitors to the region. In November 1912, to mention one very early event, Kōzui opened the newly completed main building of the Nirakusō for an exhibition of the villa, including a number of objects acquired during his Central Asian and Indian expeditions. Articles in the *Ōsaka mainichi shinbun* gave a room-by-room description of the villa, including the exotic contents on display. Photographs in the newspaper show large crowds, which, on the second day of the exhibition, numbered some two thousand people by 8 a.m.. Throngs filled the trains heading to the closest station, forcing people to employ rickshaws to reach the foot of the mountain. Over the course of the two days when Nirakusō was open to the public, reporters for the *Ōsaka mainichi shinbun* estimated that 31,000 people visited the estate.[53]

Several years after completing the Nirakusō, Ukai and Itō brought another project for the Nishi Honganji to completion. This building, again with numerous Indo-Saracenic features, was the headquarters for the Shinshū Parishioners' Insurance Corporation (Shinshū Shinto Seimei Kabushiki Kaisha; today, Tokyo Life). Completed in 1912, it is still extant today near the main gate of the Nishi Honganji's head temple in Kyoto, where, as the Dendōin, it now serves as the headquarters of the Jōdo Shinshū Kyōgaku Kenkyūsho and as a small exhibition hall.[54] The two-story red brick structure was highlighted with white stone detailing, a common feature of many Meiji-era Japanese buildings.[55] But the Shinshū Parishioners' building also features arched windows and tiled, domed roofs that, as in the Nirakusō, allude to Indian Islamicate architectural styles.[56]

In mixing Indo-Saracenic design features with European-style structures for these two buildings, Itō and his collaborators were not breaking entirely new ground. Toshio Watanabe has traced the use of Indo-Saracenic architectural forms from the British architect Thomas Roger Smith (1830–1903) to his pupil, Conder.[57] Josiah Conder had incorporated what he labeled "pseudo-Saracenic" features into one of his most famous Japanese buildings, the Ueno Museum, finished in 1881. In the museum Conder used Islamic architectural

53. Ashiya Shiritsu Bijutsu Hakubutsukan, *Nirakusō to Ōtani tankentai II*, 68.

54. Ōsaka Kurashi no Konjaku Kan, "Tōyō + Seiyō = Itō Chūta: Yomigaeta Nishi Honganji 'Dendōin'" (Osaka: Ōsaka Kurashi no Konjaku Kan, 2012), 2; see also Kamekawa Shōshi, *Honganji omoshiro sanpo* (Kyoto: Honganji Shuppansha, 2000), 111–14. Reprint 1985.

55. On the use of red brick in a variety of Meiji-era buildings, see Alice Y. Tseng, "Styling Japan: The Case of Josiah Conder and the Museum at Ueno, Tokyo," *Journal of the Society of Architectural Historians*, 63, no. 4 (December 2004): 484, 486.

56. Kurakata, "Itō Chūta no sekkei shisō," 105.

57. Watanabe, "Japanese Imperial Architecture," 242–43.

elements that had been incorporated into many public buildings built by the British in India and in England as part of what became known broadly as the "Saracenic" style. By using such features as bulbous roof domes and floriated window arches, Conder attempted to impart an "Eastern" flavor to the building. Well aware that he was using in Japan a style derived from a British architectural interpretation of Indian Saracenic architecture, Conder chose to call this twice-removed style "pseudo-Saracenic." Reflecting on these constructions toward the end of his career, Conder wrote that,

> so far as my studies of the national styles went (and I was an enthusiast in the beauties of Japanese art) there were no decorative or ornamental forms, or forms of outline or contour, which lent themselves constructionally to a ligneous or wooden style, and it became necessary to seek in Indian or Saracenic architecture for forms, which, having a logical treatment in brickwork or stonework, would impart an Eastern character to the building.[58]

Although Itō and Kōzui supposedly were inspired by such monumental structures as the Taj Mahal, much of the "Indo-Saracenic" architecture that Kōzui and Itō would have seen in India did not predate British colonial rule. Beginning in the 1870s, the British colonial architects constructed many public buildings, colleges, and museums in the Raj in this style. Although the term "Indo-Saracenic" referred to pre-British Mughal architecture in India, by the 1870s it also had come to describe a prominent style of British colonial architecture developed specifically for the Raj. In this more recent incarnation, "Indo-Saracenic architecture" described a hybrid form of construction created by such British architects as Major Charles Mant, Robert Chisholm, and William Emerson. In keeping with long-standing architectural practice in much of Europe, proponents of the style attempted to meld the best features of Hindu and Islamic architecture in India with the engineering expertise of European builders.[59] Although not without its critics, who argued for a more distinctively European or British form of construction in the colonies, British colonial architects completed numerous colleges, museums, government buildings, palaces, and villas in the Indo-Saracenic style. In an analysis of Indo-Saracenic architecture in India, Thomas R. Metcalf observes that the style, like much orientalist practice, rode roughshod over nuances of archi-

58. The speech from 1920 and cited in *Kenchiku zasshi* 34 (June 1920): 54–55, is quoted in Alice Yu-Ting Tseng, *The Imperial Museums of Meiji Japan: Architecture and the Art of the Nation* (Seattle: University of Washington Press, 2008), 70–71.

59. Giles H. Tillotson, "Orientalizing the Raj: Indo-Saracenic Fantasies," in *Architecture in Victorian and Edwardian India*, ed. Christopher W. London (Bombay: Marg Publications, 1994), 15–34.

tectural regionality and period. "Unlike the 'pure Hindu' style, the 'mixed' Indo-Saracenic ideally suited the British vision of their colonial role in India. By drawing together and then melding forms distinctly labeled 'Hindu' and 'Saracenic,' the British saw themselves, the self-proclaimed masters of India's culture, as shaping a harmony the Indians alone, communally divided, could not achieve."[60] While utilizing older styles of architecture for decorative purposes, Indo-Saracenic buildings also drew upon the most advanced forms of engineering technology and expertise.

In using Indo-Saracenic elements in the Ueno Museum, Conder aimed to give the building a distinctively Eastern flavor. As Alice Tseng has observed, this was the result of a conflation of "the terms 'Japanese,' 'Indian,' 'Saracenic,' 'Eastern,' and 'Far Eastern,' as equivalent signifiers of Japan." Skimming various forms of "non-Western" architecture for ornamental and decorative elements to apply to his structures, Conder showed that "his interest was not in architecture that was Japanese but in architecture that he believed *represented* Japanese-ness."[61] The result was a pastiche of traditional forms constructed using the latest techniques and materials. In this fashion, the Indo-Saracenic buildings constructed by Kōzui and Itō, while evoking wider Asia, particularly India, also reflected colonial and imperial power as projected through the lens of British discourse.

The intended overall effect of such buildings as the Ueno Museum, Nirakusō, and the Shinshū Parishioners' Insurance Corporation headquarters was similar to that achieved by *Ryūtō*, a painting by Yokoyama Taikan, who, while in India in 1903, had met Rabindranath Tagore and his nephew, the painter Abanindranath Tagore (1871–1931), considered one of the pioneers of modern Indian painting. In *Ryūtō*, Yokoyama combined Euro-American, Indian, and Japanese styles to depict Indian subject matter—in this instance, three women dressed in saris beneath a Bodhi tree at a river's edge. Micah Auerback discusses how both Yokoyama and another of Okakura's students who traveled to India early in the twentieth century to work with painters at the Government School of Art in Calcutta added Indian elements to their Buddhist paintings done in the *Nihonga* style. Although receiving mixed reviews from critics, Auerback notes, the use of observations based on their

60. Thomas R. Metcalf, *An Imperial Vision: Indian Architecture and Britain's Raj* (Berkeley: University of California Press, 1989), 75. Tillotson (p. 33) contends that we should be careful about reading too much orientalism into the Indo-Saracenic style, as the sort of borrowing and homogenizing advocated by its proponents also was common practice in domestic European architecture.

61. Tseng, *The Imperial Museums of Meiji Japan*, 71.

direct experiences of India earned plaudits for the authentically Indian-like figures in their work.[62] Reflecting on *Ryūtō*, Miriam Wattles observes that "in its ambiguity, *Ryūtō* reconciled the perceived dichotomies of East versus West and traditional versus modernity. Through its Indian subject, it asserted a Japanese Asia."[63] The painting, Wattles observed astutely, was created in 1909, just as "India was being popularized as the true source of Buddhism, overshadowing in importance the role traditionally assumed by China. This fresh combination of associations, presented in an apparently realistic manner, reinvented India for Japanese viewers. In *Ryūtō* India becomes Japan's rediscovered past."[64] The Indian-inflected paintings of the Buddha from Okakura's disciples similarly invoked for the Japanese viewer Buddhism's Indian roots. For Kōzui, Itō, and Ukai, the same sentiments inspired their Indo-Saracenic architecture, which served as a synecdoche for Japan's Asian modernity. As India became prominent in the Japanese mind, Itō, working in conjunction with a range of collaborators, strove to reflect a Japanese Asia through this "new Japanese Oriental architecture."[65]

At the same time that Itō was collaborating with Kōzui, he was also experimenting on a number of projects with other clerics who, like Kōzui, had been bitten by the "Asia bug." Although the web of connections is not entirely clear, many of those who commissioned Itō to design Buddhist monuments or temple buildings had, like Kōzui, traveled or resided in South and Southeast Asia for extended periods of time. As I have shown in chapter 1, Shaku Kōzen laid out plans with Itō in 1910 to construct a Siamese-style Shakuōden (Śākyamuni Hall) to house some of the numerous Śākyamuni Buddha images that King Chulalongkorn (Rama V; 1853–1910) of Siam had given to him. Kōzen planned to house two large images he had received from Siam: a seven-foot-tall standing Buddha and a six-foot-long reclining one. Itō drew up plans for a Siamese-style Buddha hall to be placed on a hill overlooking the Sanneji compound in Yokohama and Kōzen began collecting funds for its construction, but Kōzen grew ill and died before the construction could be initiated.[66] (See fig. 1.6.)

62. Auerback, *A Storied Sage*, 212–18.

63. Miriam Wattles, "The 1909 *Ryūtō* and the Aesthetics of Affectivity," *Art Journal* 55, no. 3 (1996): 48.

64. Wattles, "The 1909 *Ryūtō* and the Aesthetics of Affectivity," 49.

65. See Benoît Jacquet, "Itō Chūta et son Étude Architecturale du Hōryūji," 91.

66. Jaffe, "Seeking Śākyamuni," 88–90. Information about the plans for the Shakuōden is found in Higashimoto Keikichi, "Shaku Nindo Wajō no omoide," in *Ryōkan no kokoro*, ed. Ryōkan Kai (Tokyo: Bunka Shobō Hakubunsha, 1981), 241–42.

Concurrent with his Nishi Honganji projects, Itō also worked closely with the important Sōtō cleric Hioki Mokusen (1847–1920), the incumbent of Kasuisai, a large, historically significant Sōtō temple complex in Fukuroi, Shizuoka Prefecture. Hioki, like Kōzui and Kōzen, had traveled to continental Asia on several occasions: in 1907, to tour the northeast Asian battlefields of the Russo-Japanese War (1904–5) in order to pray for the repose of the nearly eighty thousand deceased Japanese soldiers; in 1911, to receive the purported relics of Śākyamuni that had passed from the British to the Siamese to Japanese Buddhists; and, back to Siam again in 1911 where he attended the coronation of Chulalongkorn's successor, Vajiravudh (Rama VI; 1881–1925; reigned 1910–25) and then, along with Kuruma Takudō, toured Buddhist sites in India. In 1906, prior to his trip to Manchuria and Korea, Hioki had begun planning and fund raising for the construction of a memorial stupa (*gokokutō*) to be constructed atop a hillside on the grounds of the Kasuisai, after gaining permission to proceed from the Japanese interior minister. Upon returning to Japan, Hioki assembled a group of 166 donors and supporters, drawn from all over Japan, that included a significant number of members from the military, the Diet, and the bureaucracy, as well as private citizens to fund the construction of a Buddhist memorial for the war dead. The committee in charge of planning the stupa chose Hioki's temple, Kasuisai, in central Honshū as the site for the memorial. They also employed Itō Chūta to design the "*gokokutō*," literally, a "nation-protecting stupa," to house the remains and effects of the Japanese war dead (see fig. 4.11).[67]

The stupa at Kasuisai, which was completed in February 1911, represented one early Buddhist effort to compete with state Shinto for the privilege of honoring the war dead.[68] Unlike the few Buddhist monuments for the war dead that preceded it, for example, the pagoda to house and honor the remains of dead Sino-Japanese War (1894–95) soldiers at the Gokokuji in Tokyo, the Kasuisai monument was what Itō referred to as a "Gandhāra" stupa. In 1908 at a planning meeting for the construction of the stupa at Kasuisai, Itō suggested a style reflecting Indian-Gandharan Buddhist architecture because it was from Gandhāra that Buddhism had spread to China at the start of the Common Era and, later, from China to Japan. In effect, Itō claimed, Gandhāra was the "mother country" (*bokoku*) for Japanese Buddhism. Not only did the Gandharan style reflect the Indian origins of Buddhist architecture. Itō asserted at the planning meeting for the Kasuisai stupa that the Chinese-style pagoda, so prevalent in Japan, did not clearly express Buddhism's Indian

67. Gokokutō Hōsan Kai, ed., *Gokokutō shi* (Fukuroi: Gokokutō Hōsan Kai, n.d.), 1–3.
68. Gokokutō Hōsan Kai, ed., *Gokokutō shi*, 5.

FIGURE 4.11. The Gokokutō at Kasuisai in Fukuroi, Shizuoka Prefecture, Japan. Courtesy of Kasuisai. Photograph by the author.

origins.[69] Hence, the Gandharan-style stupa was more appropriate for the "nation-protecting stupa" at Kasuisai. Like many other Buddhist structures Itō designed, although supposedly Gandharan, the stupa incorporated a mélange of architectural forms harvested from across Asia. The entryway arch of the Gokokutō, Itō wrote, was based on that of Indian "cave temples," while the pillars at the entrance derived from "Persian style that had flourished in Gandhāra." The entasis of the columns on the Gokokutō alluded to Itō's theory about the Grecian origins of the Hōryūji pillars, thus linking the stupa

69. Gokokutō Hōsan Kai, *Gokokutō shi*, 6–7. The meeting took place at Kuruma Takudō's temple in Tokyo, Banryūji, in April 1908. Kuruma was a close confidant of Hioki.

not only to Japan's architectural history but also claiming its supposed Indo-European past. The whole upper portion of the stupa—the decorative lotus petals, base of the crowning tower (*roban*), and tower (*sōrin*)—derived from "Lamaist," that is, Tibetan-style, temples in China.[70]

Itō published one of his most detailed explanations of his Buddhist monument and temple design rationale in an article in the journal *Nihon bijutsu* in 1911. There he elaborated the practical and the symbolic concerns that entered into his plans for the nation-protecting stupa. Exigencies of function and cost played important roles in Itō's choice of the Gandharan style for his structure. Unlike the traditional East Asian stupa, the Gandharan stupa had a square foundation with a much broader and taller base in proportion to the rest of the structure. This would allow it to accommodate the various relics of the war dead collected by Hioki and others.[71] Money was another important practical consideration for the private group that was erecting the stupa. In order to economize, Itō drew up plans to build the dome of the stupa out of reinforced concrete, a relatively new construction material in late Meiji Japan. Thus the base of the stupa was made of stone blocks, while the dome itself was poured reinforced concrete. Itō viewed the combination of old and new materials in a structure and the employment of new materials in traditional temple or shrine architectural forms as important elements in the development of a "hybrid" religious architecture, which he called "the eclecticism of old and new" (*shinkyū setchū*), a sort of architectural bricolage (*yoseatsume*). Itō saw this as a way to move religious, particularly Buddhist, architecture forward in Japan, after hundreds of years of stagnation and repetition.[72] In effect the stupa recapitulated Buddhist architectural history and moved beyond it.

Itō's arguments for the Gandharan stupa reveal an attempt to transcend what he argued was a provincial, limited Sinitic form of Buddhism, symbolized by the three- or five-story pagoda, through the return to a Buddhist architectural model that was far closer to its Indian roots. The return to the Gandharan style had the added advantage, according to Itō, that it was not a form biased toward one particular denomination of Japanese Buddhism. Instead, the Indian form of the stupa was transnational and transectarian in nature.[73] In the memorial stupa at Kasuisai, the similar Shōgyōden (completed 1931), which was intended to house autograph manuscripts by Nichiren, at

70. Itō Chūta, "Gokokutō no kenchiku," *Nihon bijutsu*, no. 148 (June 1911): 3–4.

71. Itō Chūta, "Gokokutō no kenchiku," 1.

72. Itō Chūta, *Itō Chūta kenchiku bunken*, 6 vols. (Tokyo: Ryūginsha, 1936), 1: 336; Itō, "Gokokutō no kenchiku," 2.

73. Itō, "Gokokutō no kenchiku," 1–2.

FIGURE 4.12. The Shōgyōden at Hokekyōji, Ichikawa, Chiba Prefecture, Japan. Photograph by the author.

the Hokekyōji, an important Nichiren temple in Ichikawa, Chiba Prefecture, and at Nissenji, Itō, with functional variations would reproduce this style of memorial stupa. (See fig. 4.12.)

At Kasuisai and Hokekyōji, Itō put into practice the theory concerning the Indo-European roots of Japanese temple architecture that he had expressed in his thesis on Hōryūji's architecture. In agreement with James Fergusson, Itō viewed Gandhāra as the contact zone where Greek and Indian styles met, producing that fusion that was Gandharan Buddhist art.[74] In using this style for modern stupa, Itō explicitly tied twentieth-century Japanese Buddhist architecture to "classic" Greek and, therefore, "Western," that is, Indo-European, culture, as Jacquet and Wendelken have observed, creating a new "Asian" Japanese Buddhist architecture.

Of course privileging the Gandharan-Indian aspects of Buddhist architectural history, while eschewing forms for pagoda that were tied to continental East Asian Buddhism, elided Japan's indebtedness to the Buddhisms of Korea and China. The recuperation of the Indian tradition had the added advantage that in India, unlike in China, Korea, and elsewhere in East Asia, few Buddhists were left to contest the growing Japanese Buddhist triumphalism. Itō's stupa "concretized" the growing number of Japanese assertions that only in

74. Itō, *Itō Chūta kenchiku bunken*, 1:7.

FIGURE 4.13. Pre-Great Hanshin earthquake (1995) exterior of the Honganji Kōbe Betsuin (Modan Dera), Kobe, Japan. Courtesy of Honganji Kōbe Betsuin.

Japan could one find the scholarship, complete collections of texts, and even temple architecture necessary for encompassing all of the pan-Asian Buddhist tradition.

The ongoing, developing interest in developing a pan-Asian or even global style of Buddhist architecture within the ranks of the Nishi Honganji clergy is clearly demonstrated by the reconstruction of Zenpukuji, a specially ranked branch temple of Honganji in Kobe. After the temple was destroyed by fire in 1918, the Honganji and the community undertook rebuilding it, which, in 1960, was officially designated as the Honganji Kōbe Betsuin. During the era of its reconstruction, Ōtani Son'yu (1886–1939), one of Kōzui's younger brothers who had studied religious institutions in Europe, served as incumbent of the temple. Completed in 1930, the "Modan Dera" (Modern Temple), as it was soon called, became a prominent Kobe landmark.[75] (See fig. 4.13.)

According to a lengthy newspaper article published several days after the dedication of the new building, it was the temple manager (*kanji*), Fujii Hōshin, a missionary who had worked in Oregon, who came up with the

---

75. "Shingen sōrei o kiwametaru: Kinseishiki daigaran naru Kōbeshi Honpa Honganji bekkaku betsuin Zenpukuji," *Kōbe shinbun*, November 26, 1930: 8. Some of the history is detailed in Honganji Kōbe Betsuin, *Sanpai no shiori*, Honganji Kobe Betsuin Guide (Kobe: Honganji Kōbe Betsuin Hyōgo Kyōku Kyōka Sentā, n.d.).

original plan for the structure. As with a number of the more experimental temples constructed after the 1923 Tokyo earthquake, the building was constructed of stone-covered, reinforced concrete. Similar in style to Itō and Ukai's plans for the Hong Kong Betsuin, the building was extremely eclectic, with a Euro-American church–like exterior, complete with stained-glass windows in addition to the clearly Southeast Asian–style steeples. The building truly was a mixture of multiple architectural styles. According to a *Kōbe shinbun* article, the designers borrowed features from Grecian temples to Hungarian churches, while the five towers—four at the corners and one in the center—on the roof were styled after Burmese stupas. Iron entry doors, which had been ordered by Ōtani Son'yu, were forged in Glasgow in 1879. On both sides of the entrance to the temple were two bronze bas-reliefs of Amida's attendant bodhisattvas, Kannon (Avalokiteśvara) and Seishi (Mahāsthāmaprāpta).[76] In effect, the temple building, flanked by the two bodhisattvas, took the place of Amida Buddha in the traditional triad consisting of Amida and his attendants.

The altars in the main temple hall of the Modan Dera were equally novel and unique. Combining painting, calligraphy, and sculpture in a fascinating brew, Fujii Hōshin brought together central elements of Shin altar design with decorative elements that evoked Japanese Buddhism's Asian past and hoped-for future (see fig. 4.14). Like many Shin temples, the worship hall at the Modan Dera contains three sub-altars, with the central one dedicated to Amida and the others dedicated to Shinran and, in this instance, the former chief incumbent of the Nishi Honganji at the time of the temple's reconstruction, Ōtani Kōzui. The structure of the altars reiterates the Indian and Southeast Asian influences of the exterior design, with each of the three-altar units crowned with a Southeast Asian-style steeple. The designs of all three of the golden altar units were based upon well-known Burmese temples.[77] The central image of veneration was Amida Buddha, but the artwork conflates Amida and Śākyamuni, India and Japan, through the very creative use of Brāmhī script, the same script that was being revived by other Buddhists who had made the journey to South Asia, for example Shaku Kōzen. At the Modan Dera, the curtains of the altar unit (*kūden*) containing the standing image of Amida are decorated with script copied from the Aśokan pillar at Lumbinī, the birthplace of the historical Buddha (see fig. 4.15).[78] While traveling in Nepal in 1902 members of one of the Ōtani Kōzui expedition teams, Shimizu

---

76. "Shingen sōrei o kiwametaru," 8.

77. "Shingen sōrei o kiwametaru," 8.

78. Shirasu Jōshin, *Ōtani tankentai to sono jidai* (Tokyo: Bensei Shuppan, 2002), 85.

FIGURE 4.14. The main hall of worship at Kobe Nishi Honganji Betsuin. Courtesy of Kobe Nishi Honganji Betsuin. Photograph by the author.

FIGURE 4.15. The main altar enshrining Amida Buddha at Kobe Nishi Honganji Betsuin. Courtesy of Kobe Nishi Honganji Betsuin. Photograph by the author.

Mokuji, Inoue Kōen, and Honda Eryū (1876–1944), reached Lumbinī, where Honda photographed the pillar and the team copied the inscription.[79] On one of the expeditions to Buddha's birthplace, rubbings of the inscription also were taken. These were brought back to Japan, where at least one copy is extant at the Nishi Honganji Jōdo Shin temple, Shinshūji in Nagano. A large photograph of the Lumbinī pillar and of a rubbing of the inscription also were included in *Indo Busseki jissha* by Takakusu Junjirō, published in 1926.[80] As translated by Nikam and McKeon, the inscription reads as follows:

> Twenty years after his coronation, King Priyadarśī, Beloved of the Gods, visited this place in person and worshiped here because the Buddha, the Sage of the Śākyas, was born here.
>
> He ordered a stone wall to be constructed around the place and erected this stone pillar to commemorate his visit.
>
> He declared the village of Luṁminī [now Rummindei] free of taxes and required to pay only one-eighth of its produce [about half the usual amount] as land revenue.[81]

The juxtaposition of the Brāhmī pillar inscription and Amida links the two buddhas intimately at the time of Śākyamuni's birth and physically manifests the deep connection between the Nishi Honganji, as representative of Jōdo Shin Buddhism, and the very origins of the Buddhist tradition at Lumbinī.

The same relationship is symbolized by the "Descent of Amida" (*raigō*) relief sculpture that decorates the transom (*ranma*) at the entrance to the inner altar area (see fig. 4.16). According to the article in the *Kōbe shinbun*, Katayama Chōbe-e, the sculptor, closely followed a famous painting, the twelfth-century *Amida shōju raigō zu*, depicting the descent of Amida and his retinue, which is preserved on Mt. Kōya, Wakayama Prefecture, in the temple Kongōbuji.[82] Notable for its mere presence in a Shin temple, where "Descent of Amida" scenes are rare, the polychrome sculpture depicts the usual scene of Amida descending to accompany a dying aspirant to the Pure Land. Instead of placing an image of Amida at the center of the scene, as is typical of traditional *raigō* paintings, the artist has substituted a Bodhi tree, the sym-

79. See Shimizu Mokuji, *Nepāru tanken nikki shō*, in *Shin seiikiki: Ōtanike zōban*, ed. Uehara, Yoshitarō, 2 vols. (Tokyo: Yūkōsha, 1937), 1:98–99. I have been unable to find life dates for Inoue and Shimizu.

80. Takakusu Junjirō, Wada Sanzō, and Kumagai Kunizō, *Indo Busseki jissha* (Tokyo: Kōgeisha, 1926).

81. Aśoka, Narayanrao Appurao Nikam, and Richard McKeon, *The Edicts of Asoka* [in Aśoka's inscriptions translated from Prakrit.] (Chicago: University of Chicago Press, 1959), 69.

82. "Shingen sōrei o kiwametaru," 8.

FIGURE 4.16. Polychrome transom (*ranma*) in the main hall of worship at Kobe Nishi Honganji Betsuin. Courtesy of Kobe Nishi Honganji Betsuin. Photograph by the author.

bol of Śākyamuni that was common in early Buddhist depictions of Bodh Gayā. The scene thus asserted the connection between Amida—and Japanese Buddhism—and the very origins of the religion as it was increasingly understood in European, American, and Japanese scholarly circles. Just as Akegarasu Haya strove to connect Amitābha with Śākyamuni by asserting that the *Dai muryōjukyō* (Great Sūtra of Eternal Life) was the record of Śākyamuni's inner life (see chapter 3), the artwork in the Modan Dera drew the two buddhas together.

At least two of the major newspaper articles describing the dedication of Zenpukuji emphasize above all else the "modern" features of the building. As noted above, Kobe residents soon dubbed the building Modan Dera, that is, "Modern Temple," thus equating its unprecedented, Asian-inflected, European-hybrid design with modernity itself. The reporter for the local *Kōbe shinbun* also emphasized the modernity of the new temple, commenting, "One must say that this novel style, as one that is appropriate for the new age, will provide an epoch-making impulse to the history of temple architecture."[83] Visible from the heavily used Tōkaidō Railway line, the temple became another symbol of the increasingly cosmopolitan port city of Kobe, which, by 1935, had a South Asian Muslim community sizable enough to have its own mosque.[84] Designed by the Czech expatriate architect Jan Josef Švagar,

83. " Shingen sōrei o kiwametaru," 8.

84. Nile Green, "Anti-Colonial Japanophilia and the Constraints of an Islamic Japanology: Information and Affect in the Indian Encounter with Japan," *South Asian History and Culture* 4, no. 3 (2013): 304.

with an Islamicate Indo-Saracenic design resembling that of Itō's Dendōin and other Buddhist buildings, the mosque and Modan Dera added South Asian spice to the cosmopolitan port city's landscape. In the words of the *Kōbe shinbun* reporter, "Aah, this is the manifestation of a great temple in the modern style (*kindai yōshiki*). Through the reconstruction of Zenpukuji, another beautiful, magnificent hue is added to the modern (*modan*) metropolis of Kobe."[85]

Contemporaneous newspaper accounts agreed that the new Zenpukuji had a variety of features that made it well suited to life in modern Kobe. For one thing, several reporters noted, unlike other recently constructed temples, Modan Dera allowed busy parishioners and visitors to enter the main hall of the temple to pay obeisance to "Oyasama," that is, Amida Buddha, without having to remove their shoes. Like other designers of innovative temples constructed in the wake of the 1923 Kantō earthquake, Fujii and his codesigners built the outer worship area (*gejin*) of the main hall (*hondō*) to allow visitors to worship without sitting on tatami. This brought the temple in line with the leading edge of late Taishō–early Shōwa temple design championed by such individuals as Kuruma Takudō in 1925, for example, a hard-floored, chair-filled main hall.[86] The temple was up to date in other regards as well. Takayama Aya, writing in *Chūgai nippō*, noted that the building also included a classroom for youth religious education and a sizable library. In a rather humorous aside, Takayama exclaimed that the temple is equipped with sanitary flush toilets so modern, "not even Daimaru or Mitsukoshi [Department Stores] have them yet."[87]

A number of these design features were repeated in the reconstructed Honganji Tsukiji Betsuin, which, since 2012, is officially named Tsukiji Honganji. Itō's most famous achievement in Buddhist architecture, Tsukiji Honganji, which was completed in 1934, reflects the same eclecticism visible in Itō's earlier architectural ventures and such Nishi Honganji structures as Modan Dera (see fig. 4.17). Again, perhaps with the relatively recent earthquake in mind, Tsukiji was built with reinforced concrete that was embellished to resemble stone. According to a commemorative volume for the temple, the exterior design was "based on the style employed in ancient central India, adapted as appropriate. In addition, augmented with later Indian styles and in the details, Java's Borobudur and other Indian-derived regional styles

---

85. "Shingen sōrei o kiwametaru," 8.

86. See Kuruma Takudō, "Shōrai no Bukkyō kenchiku" (1925), in *Gaitō no Bukkyō*, 131–33.

87. Takayama Aya, "Zenpukuji shin kenchiku to kindai Kōbe jiin," *Chūgai nippō*, November 23, 1930, 2.

FIGURE 4.17. Honganji Tsukiji Betsuin. (Today, Tsukiji Honganji.) Photograph by the author.

have been applied."[88] The arched entryway, like that of the Gokutō, appears to be derived from the cave temples mentioned by Itō in his article concerning the earlier stupa. The two stupa-shaped drum and bell towers adorning the right and left front corners of the temple recall the form of the Gokutō as well as the numerous stupas at Borobudor. Continuing the trend away from traditional floor seating for ceremonies seen in such other domestic Honganji branch temples as Modan Dera, the main worship hall of Tsukiji Honganji had carpeted floors and rows of theater-style seats, rather than Japanese-style tatami flooring. As in Kobe, parishioners were able to worship at the temple without having to remove their shoes or change into clothing suitable for sitting on the floor.

In the Tsukiji Honganji we see Itō asserting Japanese ties with broader Asian and European architectural traditions, while underplaying the traditional elements in Japanese temple architecture. Cherie Wendelken, in a reflective article about the temple, notes that to Itō, "Japanese culture reflected a developmental progression from India through China to its culmination in Japan, and through India, Japan was linked to the West. Itō believed that Japanese architecture needed to reclaim and express this history in order to achieve what he called the next stage of development. He described this as

88. Honganji Tsukiji Betsuin, ed., *Tsukiji Betsuin shi* (Tokyo: Honganji Tsukiji Betsuin, 1934), 1–2.

'Eastern architecture adjusted to Japanese needs.'"[89] Writing for a volume to commemorate the completion of the temple, Kitao Harumichi, an architectural critic, proclaimed that Itō had transcended the old, traditional forms to create a "splendidly elegant new Buddhist architecture fundamentally expressing pure Mahayana Buddhism."[90]

The Tsukiji Honganji, with its large open plaza that served as a convenient gathering place for crowds, became a symbol of pan-Asianism, Japanese ascendancy, and the global reach of Japanese Buddhism. In 1934, the Second Pan-Pacific Buddhist Young People's Association Meeting (Han Taiheiyō Bukkyō Seinen Kai Taikai) convened in Tokyo. With Ōtani Son'yu, who was involved in building Modan Dera, as the president of the meeting, the Tsukiji Honganji, which had the space to accommodate the more than six hundred attendees from the Pacific region, was chosen as the venue. Pointing to the new temple as a symbol of Japanese Buddhist progress, an announcement of the event in *Young East* proclaimed,

> It is interesting to note that this giant structure differs entirely in every respect from other temple buildings in Japan and has many characteristic features of its own and peculiar to the ancient Indian Buddhist Vihara to which it resembles more than any other style, and is therefore a direct importation from the land of the all enlightened one.
>
> Truly a sublime and imposing cream colored dome standing against the background of the azure sky, at once an apt symbol of earnest faith of thousands of devotees and the untiring labor of those who devoted their entire energy rebuilding from the ashes of the great catastrophe of 1923, and last of all but not least an appropriate form in awakening a deep devotional feeling to those who happen to gaze upon it. Another noteworthy feature of the building is none other than the crystallization of that spirit predominant in this school since its foundation and which is amply testified by History, the pioneering spirit always in the vanguard of civilization and the leader and guide of the current thought.[91]

As the Japanese worked to construct the puppet state of Manchukuo, Sano Toshitaka (1860–1956), a professor at Tokyo Imperial University, pressed for the use of "Asianist" or "Asian-revival" style architecture (*Ajiashugi yōshiki*), particularly within the capital city, Xinjing.[92] In nearby Dalian, which was

89. Wendelken, "Pan-Asianism and the Pure Japanese Thing," 821–22.

90. *Tsukiji Betsuin shi*, 1.

91. "A General View of the New Honganji Building at Tsukiji Tokyo Where the Second Pan-Pacific Y. B. A. Conference Will Take Place," YE 4, no. 11 (July–September, 1934): 7.

92. Hotta, *Pan-Asianism and Japan's War*, 116–17.

FIGURE 4.18. Myōshōji in Dalian, China, then part of the Kwantung Leased Territory. From *Manshū kenchiku zasshi*, 18, no. 2 (1938). Courtesy of Tōhoku University.

part of Japan's Kwantung (Guandong) Leased Territory, reflecting this new architectural style, a temple bearing features resembling both the Kobe and Tsukiji Honganji temples, Myōshōji, was completed by 1938 (see fig. 4.18).[93] Itō and Kōzui's vision of a grand pan-Asianist architectural style for temples thus continued to spread across Japan's growing empire.

One of the most publicly prominent Buddhist monuments built by Itō was the Gandharan-style granite memorial stupa (*hōantō*) that enshrined relics gifted to Japan by King Chulalongkorn of Siam. The reception, public viewing, and enshrinement of the relics in Japan were accompanied by enormous public gatherings in major cities from Osaka to Tokyo, making the events surrounding the relics potent examples of Japanese Buddhism's South and Southeast Asian Buddhist ties. The drama of the late nineteenth-century se-

93. Photographs of Myōshōji are found in *Manshū kenchiku zasshi* 18, no. 2 (1938), but no date of completion for the temple is provided. See also Yamada, "Kindai Bukkyō kenchiku no Higashi Ajia," 99.

ries of relic transfers across Asia began with the discovery of a group of reliquary vases by William Claxton Peppé in January 1898 at Piprāhwā near the
Nepal border, not far from the location of what was believed to be the ruins
of Kapilavastu, where Śākyamuni had lived prior to renouncing the home life.
One of the reliquary vases, which contained carved gems and pieces of bone,
had a lid bearing a Brāhmī inscription that led Peppé as well as the British
archaeologists Bühler and Smith to conclude in their initial publications that
the vase contained relics of Śākyamuni Buddha.[94] Although other archaeologists disputed this translation of the inscription soon after the publication of
information concerning the discovery, members of the British government
in India and Buddhists across Asia accepted this initial determination of authenticity and treated the vessel contents as religious objects of great value.

Peppé transferred the vases and their contents to the British Indian government, which then offered the relics to King Chulalongkorn of Siam, the
"only existing Buddhist monarch with a proviso that he will not object to
offer a portion of the relics to the Buddhists of Burmah and Ceylon."[95] In so
doing, the government of India recognized long-standing networks of Buddhist exchange within the Indian Ocean region along which texts, material
objects, ordination lineages, monastics, royalty, and donations circulated.
With Ceylon and, in 1889, Burma, coming under British colonial dominion,
the Siamese monarch was to both the British and Buddhists of the region, the
only remaining Buddhist ruler, upon whose shoulders sat responsibility for
ensuring the vitality of Buddhist teachings and institutions—the *sāsana*.[96] Although the Japanese overseas clerics and students had a noticeable presence
in the region, as we have seen, the community that included Cambodian,
Ceylonese, Laotian, and Siamese Buddhists remained tightly bound by traditions and doctrines not held in common with the Japanese. For this reason,
perhaps, Japan was not included in the government of British India's initial
plan for the distribution of the Piprāhwā relics.

Inagaki Manjirō (1861–1908), who served as the first Japanese deputy min-

---

94. Allen, *The Search for the Buddha*, 272–77; Georg Bühler, "Preliminary Note on a Recently
Discovered Śākya Inscription," *Journal of the Royal Asiatic Society of Great Britain and Ireland*
(1898): 387–89; William. Claxton Peppé, and Vincent Arthur Smith, "The Piprāhwā Stūpa, Containing Relies of Buddha," *Journal of the Royal Asiatic Society of Great Britain and Ireland* (1898):
573–88. The dispute concerning the interpretation of the inscription is discussed in Edward J.
Thomas, *The Life of the Buddha as Legend and History* (London: Routledge & Kegan Paul, 1927),
160–63.

95. "The Recent Discovery of Buddha Relics: Presentation to the King of Siam," *Manchester
Guardian*, December 19 1898, 5.

96. Blackburn, *Locations of Buddhism*, 18; 143–96.

ister resident to Siam, was on hand to witness the transference of the relics and subsequently requested a share for Japan as well. Inagaki had studied at Cambridge under John Robert Seeley. He was concerned with Japan's changing role in Asia, particularly in the context of the Anglo-Russian struggle for power in Eastern Asia and the Pacific region. Inagaki published his study of these issues in English, *Japan and the Pacific and A Japanese View of the Eastern Question*, in 1890 and, the next year, in Japanese.[97] After returning to Japan he entered the diplomatic corps, subsequently heading to Siam in 1897 to serve in the Japanese legation.[98]

As did the many Japanese who had lived in India, Ceylon, and Burma, Inagaki arrived to a country that was in the throes of rapid political, cultural, and religious transformation. Spurred on by the looming threat of colonization and disgraces imposed upon Siam by the European and American powers, the Siamese, much like the Japanese, were in the process of transforming their society. As part of this process, Chulalongkorn had undertaken the academicization of Buddhist study in ways informed by Euro-American orientalist scholarship. He also continued the efforts by King Mongkut (Rama IV; 1804–68) to use modern printing technology to print a version of the Tipiṭaka using a script to transliterate the Pali texts that would be more readily understandable and convenient than the traditional Khmer-script, palm-leaf volumes. Chulalongkorn, as part of his reform efforts in 1893, published a version of the Tipiṭaka in thirty-nine volumes using a modified Thai script that was called the Kan-yut system.[99] According to the editors of the new canon, the texts were produced in the one place, Siam, where Buddhism "stands inviolate." This was a fitting time, they continued, "to look into the scriptures, to purge them, and multiply copies for circulation."[100] Using the Siamese edition of the Tipiṭaka from 1781 as the base text, the editors edited the texts while comparing them to cognate Burmese, Sinhala, and, notably, Pali Text Society versions. Robert Chalmers, describing the significance of the new Tipiṭaka, noted that although the editors had referred to the aforementioned streams of textual variation in footnotes, they did not deviate from the earlier Siamese edition. In effect, according to Chalmers, they were "restoring the national

97. Inagaki Manjiro, *Japan and the Pacific and a Japanese View of the Eastern Question* (London: T. Fisher Unwin, 1890).

98. Nishino Junjirō, *Nichi-Tai yonhyakunen shi* (Tokyo: Jiji Tsūshinsha, 1978), 49.

99. Anil Sakya, "King Mongkut's Invention of a Universal Pali Script," in *How Theravāda Is Theravāda?* 410.

100. The preface is translated from the Siamese in Robert Chalmers, "The King of Siam's Edition of the Pāli Tipiṭaka," *Journal of the Royal Asiatic Society of Great Britain and Ireland* 9 (1898): 3.

redaction."[101] Although continuing a Buddhist royal tradition of purifying the canon of errors, to Chalmers, this also marked the creation of a national scholarly product. The king distributed sets of the Tipiṭaka widely, sending copies to other Buddhist communities and European universities. Intent on modernizing other Siamese institutions, Chulalongkorn instituted changes in most aspects of Siamese life, from education to the military, much as had been undertaken by the Japanese state in the wake of challenges to its sovereignty from Europe and the United States.

In January 1900, soon after the relics were apportioned to the Buddhist communities of Burma and Ceylon, Inagaki wrote to Prince Devawongse Varopakar (1858–1923), the foreign minister of Siam, requesting a portion of the relics for his nation in which there were "more than 30 million Buddhist parishioners and more than 70 thousand clerics."[102] The Siamese responded favorably, setting in rapid motion planning in Japan to send a mission of high-ranking Buddhist clerics to receive the relics from the Siamese king. The Japanese request for the relics and its favorable reception by the Siamese took place in the context of shifting strategic concerns in Asia. As both the Siamese and the Japanese attempted to renegotiate the unequal treaties with which both nations had been saddled by the Europeans and Americans, they had more than religious comity to gain from enhanced diplomatic relations. For both nations this meant balancing their relationship with the colonial powers with the forging of new alliances with other Asian nations, as they sought their own territorial expansion. To cite just one example, although probably not precisely a quid pro quo arrangement, just a few years following the exchange of the relics in Siam, Inagaki sent a telegram to the Foreign Ministry in Tokyo informing them that the Siamese sought Japan's help in strengthening the Siamese navy. Sent in the midst of the Russo-Japanese War, in which Japan displayed to the world its naval prowess, the August 4, 1904, telegram informed Minister Komura that the Commander-in-Chief of the Siamese Legation would soon be ordering "men-of-war and torpedo-boats, which will be built annually." In addition, he wanted to know whether Siam could place ten students in the Japanese Naval College and, if so, whether the

---

101. Chalmers, "The King of Siam's Edition of the Pāli Tipiṭaka," 8–9. For a slightly different interpretation of these events that emphasizes Chulalongkorn's embrace of "Orientalist's empirical stand," see Maurizio Peleggi, *Lords of Things: The Fashioning of the Siamese Monarchy's Modern Image* (Honolulu: University of Hawai'i Press, 2002), 37–39. Anne Blackburn, in *Locations of Buddhism*, however, provides a useful corrective to Peleggi's lack of attention to the precolonial intellectual trajectories Buddhist communities in the Indian Ocean region.

102. Letter dated January 27, 1900, in Terasawa Genshū, *Shakuson goigyō denraishi— Kakuōzan Nittaiji hōantō no yurai* (Nagoya: Kakuōzan Nittaiji, 1981), 36–37.

Japanese navy would oversee their training once they had learned Japanese. Finally, the Siamese minister was "desirous to know whether it would be possible to engage Japanese Naval Officers and Engineers either before or after the present war is over; if so it is the intention of Commander-in-Chief to disallow renewal of contracts of the European Officers now in the service of Siamese Navy, as their terms expire."[103] As was often the case in the history of Buddhism in Asia, Buddha's relics had not only spiritual meaning but were capable of bestowing apotropaic power in the temporal realm as well.

In a letter informing the Japanese Buddhist leadership that the relics would be transferred to Japan, Inagaki stressed that the event would enable Buddhism, which was one of the three great world religions, to further expand and strengthen, at the very least by bringing together all of Japan's denominations and, perhaps, even by uniting "Northern" and "Southern" Buddhists through the reception of the relics of the historical Buddha. Inagaki compared the potential power of the relics to the nails from the crucifix that were housed in Moscow at the Cathedral of the Dormition (Uspenski Sobor), which drew countless devout worshipers to pay their respects. Inagaki went on to emphasize that the relics were a gift from Siam to all Japanese Buddhists, rather than to just one denomination.[104] Inagaki also sent a letter to the Japanese foreign minister, Aoki Shūzō (1844–1914), again stressing that the relics were being provided to all of the denominations of Japanese Buddhism, not just to one or some subset of them. In other words, Inagaki emphasized to Aoki, probably to prevent sectarian contention among the Buddhists and to enlist the support of the government, for all intents and purposes, these relics were being gifted from Siam to Japan.[105]

At the order of the Meiji government, the Japanese Buddhist community assembled a mission of leading Buddhist clerics to go to Siam to receive the relics from Chulalongkorn in June 1900. The four "welcoming representatives" (hōgeishi), selected by the Buddhist community at a meeting of representatives from all denominations, were Ōtani Kōen (Jōdo Shinshū, Ōtani sect), Fujishima Ryōon (Jōdo Shinshū, Honganji sect), Maeda Jōsetsu (Rinzai, Myōshinji sect), and Hioki Mokusen (Sōtō). In addition, a fourteen-person contingent of assistants that included the Japanese translator from the Siamese embassy in Japan, Nanjō Bun'yū and Nukariya Kaiten, as well as a

103. Gaikō Shiryōkan, Document #3-10-5-4-1, "Kakukuni yori honpō e no ryūgakusei kankei zakken, Shamukoku no bu."

104. Komuro Shigehiro, ed., <Shakuson goigyō> Denraishi (Nagoya: Okabe Toyokichi, 1903), 50–52.

105. Katō Tatsuaki, Hohoemi no hakutō: Shakuson shinkotsu hōan hyakushūnen (Nagoya: Chūnichi Shinbunsha Shuppan Kaihatsu Kyoku, 2000), 30–31.

FIGURE 4.19. Siamese Buddha image that serves as the main image of worship at Nittaiji (formerly Nissenji). Courtesy of Nittaiji. Photograph by the author.

Japanese medical doctor. The group thus included members who could speak French, English, and Siamese, ensuring smooth communication in Siam. On June 15, 1900, the Siamese presented the Japanese mission members with the relics and the group dined at the palace with the king and numerous ministers present. In addition to the relics, the Siamese court also presented the group with a Buddha image to be enshrined as the main image worship where the relics were housed. The statue was a thousand-year-old, large, cast-metal Śākyamuni image in the *bhumi-sparsa* (earth-witnessing) pose (see fig. 4.19). The image had been made north of Chiang Mai but had been moved first to Chiang Mai and then to Bangkok. In addition, the Japanese were given an abbreviated version of the Tipiṭaka that had been written on palm leaves and luxuriously bound using gilt thread and silk.[106] A few days following the ceremonies, the Japanese contingent headed home with the valuable relics, departing from Siam on June 19.

The reception festivities for the relics and the other Buddhist objects from Siam garnered worldwide attention. Foreign missionaries, diplomats, and journalists all published articles concerning the elaborate reception that greeted the relics as they were moved across Japan, prior to being temporarily enshrined in Kyoto. Arriving in Japan on July 11, 1900, the relics were

106. Komuro, *Denrai shi*, 69–72.

FIGURE 4.20. Cloth-covered parade route from Higashi Honganji to the Myōhōin in Kyoto, Japan. From *Overland Monthly* 37 (1901).

temporarily displayed in Nagasaki. Members of the mission then brought them to Osaka, where, once again, they were shown to eager crowds of clerics and parishioners at the temple Shitennōji. On July 19 the relics were taken to Shichijō Station in Kyoto. According to Katō's account, upon the arrival of the relics, temples throughout Kyoto began ringing their large bells and fireworks were lit, as the relics were carried to the nearby Higashi Honganji. From that temple, a group of approximately thirty thousand clerics, Buddhist students, dignitaries, and musicians in formal dress assembled to form the procession that would take the relics to their temporary resting place, the important Tendai temple, Myōhōin, some two kilometers away in the Higashiyama section of Kyoto. The parade moved beneath a tent of cotton cloth that was erected to shield the relics and those accompanying them from the summer sun. An estimated crowd of two hundred thousand onlookers—many in town for the famous Gion Festival as well—lined the route of the procession, hoping to catch a glimpse of the relics (see fig. 4.20).[107]

Although Katō's unsourced numbers for the participants and onlookers

107. Katō, *Hohoemi no hakutō*, 99–100. See also Terasawa, *Shakuson goigyō denraishi*, 76–80.

in Kyoto may be inflated, other contemporaneous accounts, including from non-Japanese observers, confirm that the event took place on a massive scale. Members of the foreign community in Japan, particularly Christian missionaries, were stunned or, perhaps, even dismayed by the sudden outpouring of Buddhist fervor and unity. C. K. Harrington in the *Baptist Missionary Magazine* reported on the events surrounding the reception of the relics in Kyoto:

> According to the *Fukuin shinpō* the enthusiasm of the Buddhists of Kyoto on the arrival of the relics from Siam was something extraordinary. The whole of the road from the Higashi Hongwanji to the Myōhōin was covered in cotton cloth, 1,200 pieces being needed, representing a sum of 3,200 yen ($1,600). After this material had been used for this sacred purpose for one day, so great was the eagerness of the people to possess even a small portion of the cloth that it sold at one yen a foot; and so, after allowing for waste the sum of 68,140 yen ($34,070) was realized by the sale. The fortunate possessors of these new sacred relics purpose handing them down as heirlooms to distant generations. Let no one say that superstition is dying out in Japan.[108]

Similarly, according to Harrington, when a portion of the relics was brought to Tokyo, it too was greeted by a mass of hundreds of clerics in formal dress and thousands of laypeople at Shinbashi Station. The magnitude of the relic-related events led Harrington, a missionary who would go on to work on revising the authorized Japanese translation of the Bible, to conclude, "Buddhism is firmly entrenched yet in Japan and Christianity has her work before her."[109]

David Brainerd Spooner (1879–1925), was another American living in Japan when the relics arrived from Siam. Educated at Stanford, Harvard, and Frederick William University, at the time Spooner was the English tutor to the Siamese legation in Japan. Spooner accompanied one of the main invitees, the minister from the Siamese legation, Phraya Ritthirong-ronachet, to join the relic-welcoming ceremonies in Kyoto. Spooner, although decidedly skeptical about the religious significance of the "holy bones," describes in some detail the scenes he and the minister encountered traveling from Tokyo to Kyoto. Traveling to Kyoto by train, they were met by a contingent of clerics in Nagoya. At each station along the way, the "stations were picturesque with little knots of reverend gentlemen." As they reached Kyoto, they saw that the platform was "packed, jammed with priests." After hours at Higashi Honganji, where the American was treated to "a priestly tiffin of inedible vegetables," Spooner continues,

108. Cited in C. K. Harrington, "Those Relics of the Buddha," *Baptist Missionary Magazine*, June 1904, 206.

109. Harrington, "Those Relics of the Buddha," 206.

the Holy Relics, which had been placed in an ornate golden shrine newly-made, took their place in the procession which had started hours before, and we were off again. First came the shrine, then Lord Ohtani, and two other high-priests returned from Bangkok, then a man in stiff white, with a peaked black cap, bearing aloft a Siamese flag whose elephant was fearfully and wonderfully made, with claws like a Bengal tiger's. In the shadow of this marvelous creature walked the Siamese Minister, with me at his shoulder; then his official interpreter, who long since rescued me, and from there on an endless line of priests.

Like all summer days in Kyoto, it was hot. We had waited four hours, had had practically no tiffin, and to walk through those miles of sweltering people was a test of one's faith; and I alone of all that multitude had none to test. But fortunately they had spent something like seven thousand yen on a covering of white cloth which extended from the Hongwanji clear to the Myohoin, and save for which we had surely given out.[110]

Despite his humorous skepticism in Kyoto, the Priprāhwā relics seemed to have worked some of their magic on Spooner. After his time in Japan, Spooner, a perpetual student, went on to enroll at the Government Sanskrit College and Hindu College in Benares, where he may have met Kawaguchi, who also was a student in Benares at the time. Spooner then worked for the British Archaeological Survey, eventually receiving the Order of the British Empire for his service.[111] While working in India, Spooner himself managed to unearth some "holy bones." In 1908–9, Spooner, who was conducting a dig with the British, discovered the site of the stupa of King Kaniṣka. There, according to Spooner's 1910 account, he unearthed the relic chamber of the buried stupa containing shards that, according to Spooner, King Kaṇiska believed to be relics of Śākyamuni.[112]

Although the relics arrived at their temporary resting place in Kyoto in the summer of 1900, it took years for representatives of the various Japanese Buddhist denominations to agree upon a permanent site for enshrining them. On this point, the missionary Harrington, with some glee, reported the dissension between members of the committee, which found itself split into a Kyoto

110. D[avid] Brainerd Spooner, "Welcoming the Buddha's Most Holy Bones," *Overland Monthly* 37, no. 1 (1901): 585–90.

111. A graduate of Stanford University and Harvard University, Spooner was the first foreigner to graduate with a Lit.D. degree from Tokyo Imperial University. See C. E. A. W. Oldham, "David Brainerd Spooner," *Journal of the Royal Asiatic Society of Great Britain and Ireland*, no. 2 (April 1925): 375–76.

112. David Brainerd Spooner, "Discovery of the Lost Stūpa of Kaṇiska and the Relics of Gautama Buddha," *American Journal of Archaeology* 14, no. 1 (1910): 81–83.

faction and a Nagoya faction, each of which coveted the honor of having the relics permanently housed in their city. According to Harrington, each side, wishing to reap the rewards from the religious tourism that they imagined the relics would generate, competed bitterly for the honor. By 1904, Nagoya, a region that had been favored by Hioki Mokusen, who headed the committee, was chosen by the committee as the home for the relics—the Kakuōden (Palace of the Awakened King)—although the costs associated with creating the temple and moving the items to the city left the Nagoya contingent with some winners' remorse, if Harrington is to be believed.[113] Constructing the large temple complex in Nagoya took several years, but in November 1904, the relics were moved to the site of what would become Kakuōzan Nissenji, that is, the Awakened King Mountain Japan-Siam Temple. (In 1939 when Siam became Thailand, the name of Nissenji was changed to its current name, Nittaiji, Japan-Thai Temple.) At the main hall of the temple, the Japanese enshrined as the principal image the gilt Buddha that had been presented to the Japanese by King Chulalongkorn in 1900.

The new temple was a novel one for modern Japan, in that it was pansectarian, not belonging to any particular denomination. The incumbency of the temple rotated among distinguished clerics from many Buddhist denominations, with the terms of service varying in length. Early incumbents came from the Tendai, Sōtō, Shinshū Ōtani Sect, Sōtō, and Rinzai, denominations. Two of them, Hioki Mokusen (Sōtōshū) and Nanjō Bun'yū (Jōdo Shinshū Ōtani Sect), had been on the mission to Siam that received the relics.[114] Hioki served from 1907 to 1916, when he became the head cleric of the Sōtō denomination. Soon after the founding of Nissenji, Hioki dispatched a number of Sōtō clerics from Kasuisai to Nagoya to help with the construction of the temporary main hall of Nissenji.[115] During his tenure Hioki created a Sōtō branch training hall of the Kasuisai Senmon Sōdō, Nissenji Senmon Sōdō (today, Nittaiji Senmon Sōdō), to ensure that a sufficient number of clerics would be available to care for the temple's liturgical and mundane chores, although Nissenji itself remained nondenominational.

It was not until 1914 that ground breaking for the construction of the final memorial stupa to house the relics was begun. Commissioned to build the stupa at Nissenji, Itō Chūta, as he had done at the Kasuisai, designed an

113. Harrington, "Those Relics of the Buddha," 206.

114. "Jūshoku zainin chō," ed. Nittaiji (Nagoya: Nittaiji, n. d.). I thank the staff of Nittaiji for sharing this document with me.

115. Katō, Hohoemi no hakutō, 143. See also, "Nittaiji Senmon Sōdō" website, http://www .nittaiji.jp/sodo/senmon/index.html, accessed July 24, 2016.

FIGURE 4.21. Memorial stupa for the relics of Śākyamuni Buddha at Nittaiji, designed by Itō Chūta.
Courtesy of Nittaiji. Photograph by the author.

approximately sixteen-meter-tall, Gandharan-style memorial stupa (*hōantō*) that was completed in 1918, thus honoring the Indian origins of the remains for which the temple complex had been constructed. The white granite for the stupa was quarried in the Midono area of Nagano Prefecture (see fig. 4.21).[116] An earthen-wall enclosure was constructed around the stupa compound and, at the front, a worship gate (*raihaiden*) built from cypress wood with a

116. Katō, *Hohoemi no hakutō*, 148.

cypress-bark roof was constructed. Through the *raihaiden* only a portion of the stupa is visible, so, as with the inner sanctum at many Japanese shrines, the *hōantō* only is entirely visible to ordinary worshipers on special occasions, for example, on Vesak.

The Nissenji soon became an important landmark and tourist destination in Nagoya that drew large crowds for special ceremonies, enshrinements, and other occasions. As a symbol of amity between the Siamese and the Japanese people, government officials at all levels and Buddhist leaders gave full support to major events at the temple, particularly when they involved visits by members of the Siamese royal family. Judging from the poster by Hamashima Jitsujirō advertising the temple that was published on April 8, 1921—Buddha's birthday in Japan—it is clear that promoters of Nissenji placed the temple alongside the Nagoya castle as one of the important tourist attractions in the growing Nagoya region. More significantly, events celebrating the relationship between Siam and Japan drew large numbers of the general public, reinforcing the image of Japan as part of a broader Buddhist Asia (see fig. 4.22).

The temple also remained an important nexus for Siamese-Japanese interactions, as landmark events in Siam and visits by Siamese dignitaries

FIGURE 4.22. *Nagoya Higashiyama Kakuōzan Nissenji sannai no zu.* Courtesy of the Aichi Prefectural Library. Photograph by the author.

frequently involved Nissenji's leading clerics. When Vajiravudh (Rama VI; 1881–1925) ascended to the throne, following the death of Chulalongkorn in 1910, Hioki Mokusen, accompanied by the head of the Young Men's Buddhist Association, Kuruma Takudō, traveled to Siam to attend the coronation ceremony on November 11, 1911. At the time, Hioki was serving as incumbent of Nissenji, so he and his contingent went representing all the Buddhists of Japan, rather than their own denominations. The Buddhist delegation, however, journeyed in a semi-private capacity, as an official Japanese state mission headed by Prince Fushimi Hiroyasu (1875–1946), and took part as well. In a display of Japan's growing naval might, the prince, an officer in the Japanese navy, arrived on the new battle cruiser Ibuki (commissioned 1907). With the earlier communication concerning Siam-Japan naval exchanges in the background, perhaps this also was a sign of the growing military cooperation between the two nations.[117] The Buddhist delegation was an integral part of the proceedings, despite its nongovernmental status. Following their return to Japan, Vajiravudh sent a solid-gold incense burner to the chief incumbents of every Buddhist denomination in Japan, as a token of his gratitude for the Buddhist delegation's attendance at the coronation. These were presented to the clerics in a ceremony conducted by the Siamese ambassador at Nissenji on January 17, 1913.[118]

Another event was the reception in 1927 of a new gold Buddha image that King Rama VII (a.k.a. Prajadhipok, 1893–1941) donated to Nissenji. As with other instances of public displays associated with these pan-Asian Buddhist sites, the celebrations surrounding the arrival of the Buddha image clearly demonstrate how the exhibition of Buddhism's pan-Asian reach touched the lives of the broader Japanese public. When the train bearing the statue from Siam arrived at Nagoya Station on November 6, a sizable crowd was on hand to greet the Buddha image. The statue was placed in a portable shrine (*mikoshi*) that was drawn by oxen from Nagoya Station to Nissenji. In addition to a group of twelve thousand clerics and parishioners from the various denominations of Japanese Buddhism, a contingent of approximately eleven thousand singers, students, confraternity members, and high-ranking clerical leaders were on hand at the station to take part in the procession for the one-kilometer journey to Nissenji. The event was extraordinarily popular, as an estimated crowd of one hundred thousand people lined the one-kilometer route to Nissenji on that fine, sunny autumn Sunday. People continued to

117. Kuruma, *Nangoku junrei ki*, 166–77.
118. Kuruma, *Nangoku junrei ki*, 859.

flock to Nissenji to see the statue, which was on display for several weeks after the event, and to attend the three-day ceremony welcoming the image to the temple.[119]

Between the middle of the Meiji era through the start of the Pacific War in Asia in 1937, Buddhist material culture, particularly Buddhist architecture, played a significant role in displaying and disseminating the view of Buddhism as a pan-Asian tradition with a global future. In its attention to the wider Asian sphere, Japanese temple architecture mirrored the inexorable expansion of Japan into Asia through the outright colonization of Taiwan and Korea and the ever more ambitious incursions in China. Although not ignoring past Sinitic architectural influence completely, the new temple architecture of the twentieth century embraced a South Asian Buddhist architectural past that for centuries had been relatively unknown in Japan and a Southeast Asian Buddhist present that was increasingly important to the Japanese. The absorption of European and American architectural elements, particularly in such buildings as Modan Dera, Tsukiji Honganji, and the Shinshū Parishioner's Life structure, also demonstrated the missionary aspirations of Japanese Buddhists, many of whom desired to make Buddhism more than just a "world religion" in name. These novel buildings, although mostly ignored today as architectural idiosyncrasies, drew a good deal of attention from newspaper reporters and the public at the time of their opening. In the much sparser urban landscapes of Kobe, Kyoto, Nagoya, and Tokyo during the first third of the twentieth century, these large-scale temples would have been all the more remarkable. When Japanese Buddhists returned home with sacred images and relics, large throngs of Japanese—if contemporaneous reports are to be believed, the crowds numbered in the hundreds of thousands at times—gathered to pay reverence to the Buddhist objects from South and Southeast Asia. These events and buildings thus made clear to the larger Japanese public the connections between Japanese Buddhism and its past in South Asia. Well-attended public events to welcome relics and images from Southeast Asia also strengthened the sense of pan-Asian Buddhist solidarity among the Japanese public.

As we can see in the architectural examples detailed above, Japanese Buddhist leaders were exceedingly resourceful in their adaptation of the latest archaeological and scholarly studies—not just European and American ones, but increasingly their own—to the various liturgical, doctrinal, and scholarly demands of their own religious organizations. By displaying the latest

119. Katō, *Hohoemi no hakutō*, 155–57.

archaeological finds within the frame of their own specific liturgical practices, Japanese Buddhist leaders were able to imply a connection between
current practices and a venerable Indian–South Asian past that was the focus
of much European and American orientalist scholarship. In drawing upon
Asian architectural examples, some of which, for example, the Indo-Saracen,
were themselves the product of the European colonial vision, the Japanese
were able to embrace Asia as the source of their civilization while downplay-
ing the long-standing connection between Japanese Buddhist temple architecture and Sinitic architectural models. Finally, through the very process of
picking and choosing from a palette of Asian architectural motifs, Japanese
temple builders asserted the supremacy and power of Japan, while expressing solidarity with the rest of Asia. The motivations driving the construction
of a pan-Asianism were clearly conflicted. Temples such as Nissenji, which
trumpeted the common ground between Japanese Buddhists and the rest of
Asia, grew out of the sentiment that, as Rebecca Karl noted, was "rooted in
non-state-centered practices and in non-national-chauvinist culturalism."[120]
As I will elaborate in chapter 5, that attitude reflected the growing spirit of
internationalism in Taishō Japan, particularly in the wake of World War I.
At the same time, however, the construction of Buddhist pan-Asian architecture, particularly in the Indian-inflected style that characterized many of
the overseas missions and important branch temples of the Nishi Honganji,
is an example of how, as Prasenjit Duara described, nationalism, while deeply
rooted in the idea of a universal civilization, in this case a Buddhist one, ap-
propriated those same ideas for "expansionist purposes."[121]

   These examples also demonstrate the need for us to move beyond simple
models of bipolar exchange and Euro-American influences in the creation of
Japanese modernity. The construction of the "modern" in Japan—a project in
which Buddhists had an important, if overlooked role—involved not only the
importation and transculturation of practices encountered in the "far West,"
that is, Europe and the United States. In a significant way, as we have seen,
the formation of the Buddhist modern in Japan also involved a turning to
the "South West," namely, South and Southeast Asia. For the Japanese the
"*modan*" was signified not only by clearly European-style buildings like Tokyo Station or the Akasaka Detached Palace (Akasaka Rikyū). The modern

120. Rebecca E. Karl, "Creating Asia: China in the World at the Beginning of the Twentieth
Century," *American Historical Review* 103, no. 4 (1998): 1,097.
   121. Prasenjit Duara, "The Discourse of Civilization and Pan-Asianism," *Journal of World
History* 12, no. 1 (2001): 100.

could also be found in the eclectic Zenpukuji/Modan Dera, with its Burmese-style roofline. There, weary visitors to the cosmopolitan port of Kobe could find both spiritual relief in the presence of Amida Buddha without even removing their shoes and with the ability to relieve themselves using the very latest in sanitary plumbing.

5

Global Waves on Ōmura Bay: The English Translation
of the *Gedatsu dōron* (*The Path of Freedom*)

In July 1935, two Ceylonese *bhikkhu*, Kheminda Thera (born as G. S. Prelis, dates unknown) and Soma Thera (born as Victor Emmanuel Perera Pulle, 1898–1960), arrived for what would become more than a year's sojourn at Jōzaiji, a Nichiren denomination temple that overlooks the mouth of the Kawatana River (Kawatanagawa) on Ōmura Bay across from the city of Nagasaki.[1] Although at first glance Jōzaiji and the town of Kawatana seem about as isolated as possible from the currents of exchange that I have described in earlier chapters, the two Ceylonese were but one of a series of global waves that reached the shores of Kawatana. The story of Jōzaiji and the translation of the *Gedatsu dōron* into English make clear, as Sanjay Subrahmanayam suggests, that "for the historian who is willing to scratch below the surface of his sources, nothing turns out to be quite what it seems to be in terms of fixity and local rootedness."[2] From the time of its founding, Jōzaiji and its residents were touched by global flows of people and ideas, ranging from Christianity in the seventeenth century to the US military in the final years of the Fifteen Years' War.

The rather convoluted story of how the two Ceylonese Buddhists arrived at Jōzaiji is sketched in the English translation of what has best become known

---

1. The date of July 1935 is based on the record in Jōzaiji's history (*Yuraiki*) that was kindly shared with me by the current incumbent of the temple, Aikawa Tenshin, and his son, Aikawa Yasumichi. I thank them and the rest of their families for their hospitality and generosity.

2. Sanjay Subrahmanyam, "Connected Histories: Notes Towards a Reconfiguration of Early Modern Eurasia," *Modern Asian Studies* 31, no. 3 (1997): 745. No extant Indic version of the *Gedatsu dōron* exists, so the Pali and Sanskrit titles for the work are speculative. Unattested Sanskrit and Pali titles for works not extant in an Indic language are noted with an asterisk at the start of the title.

as the *Vimuttimagga (The Path of Freedom)*, that is, the *Gedatsu dōron* (C. *Ji-etuo daolun*), based on the title of the translation of the work that the two Ceylonese would help produce in Japan.[3] First published in 1961, the translation contains a brief biography by one of the translators, Kheminda Thera, of his late, dear friend, Soma Thera.[4] As part of the biography, Kheminda described in a somewhat extended fashion the travels, from 1934 to 1937, undertaken by him and Soma, from Ceylon, across Burma, Siam, Malaysia, China, Japan, India, and back to Burma, where they were ordained as *bhikkhu*, before returning home to Ceylon. Particularly remarkable from the perspective of this book is Kheminda's account of their time in Japan, which lasted from sometime in late 1934/early 1935 until they departed for Burma from Nagasaki in October 1936. During their sojourn in Japan, Kheminda and Soma studied Mahayana Buddhism, attending English-language lectures by Kimura Nichiki (1892–1965) on the subject at the Nichiren denomination's sectarian university, Risshō Daigaku, in Tokyo.[5] Through Kimura's introduction, Kheminda and Soma spent more than a year residing in Kawatana at Jōzaiji, the home temple of another Nichiren denomination cleric, Ehara Ryōzui (1902–55). While in residence at Jōzaiji from summer 1935 until October 1936, the two Ceylonese novices helped translate into English the *Gedatsu dōron* and a small collection of Nichiren's tracts and letters. Following the completion of their work on the *Vimuttimagga*, Kheminda and Soma returned to Burma, where they received the *upasampadā* ordination under Pāṇḍava Mahā Thera in Moulmein, Burma. They also paid a visit to U Nārada (a.k.a. Mingun Jeta-vana Sayādaw; 1870–1955), from whose disciple—perhaps Mahasi Sayādaw (1904–82)—they had learned his method for performing Satipaṭṭhāna meditation.[6] From Burma, they finally returned to Sri Lanka, via India, bring-

3. No extant Indic version of the text exists, so the Pali and Sanskrit titles for the work are speculative. Unattested Sanskrit and Pali titles for works not extant in an Indic language are noted with an asterisk at the start of the title.

4. Upatissa, *The Path of Freedom (Vimuttimagga)*, trans. N. R. M. Ehara, Soma Thera, and Kheminda Thera (Kandy, Sri Lanka: Buddhist Publication Society, 1995). The Chinese text is found at T. 32, no. 1648. I have been unable to determine the life dates for Kheminda Thera.

5. Kimura went by Ryūkan until the 1930s, when he took the name Nichiki/Nikki. In his English-language publications he romanized his name inconsistently, but in the English translation of the *Gedatsu dōron*, the translators refer to him as Nichiki. I have used Nichiki, except for publications in which Kimura chose to romanize his name as Nikki. I mention Kimura in chapter 3, as he served as guide to members of the NYK pilgrimage group in Calcutta in 1927, while he was a lecturer at Calcutta University.

6. For a brief summary of Mingun's teachings, see Erik Braun, *The Birth of Insight: Meditation, Modern Buddhism, and the Burmese Monk Ledi Sayadaw* (Chicago: University of Chicago Press, 2013), 160–61.

ing a copy of the complete draft translation of the *Gedatsu dōron* with them. The tale of the *Gedatsu dōron*'s translation demonstrates in a very tangible fashion how the concatenation of happenstance, global flows, and individual determination helped transform twentieth-century Asian Buddhism. A half-century after Kōzen's sojourn in Ceylon, the numerous connections forged between the Japanese and South Asians provided a path for these two aspiring *bhikkhu* all the way from Ceylon to the rather remote town of Kawatana to work together with, of all people, a Nichiren cleric, translating a text about which they probably had little knowledge prior to coming to Japan.

A web of Buddhist travelers and teachers from across Asia with interests in Buddhist practice in Ceylon helped bring Kheminda and Soma to Jōzaiji. According to Kheminda, Wong Mou-lam (a.k.a. Wong Mow-lam; Huang Maolin; 1886–1933), who journeyed to Sri Lanka in 1931, initially made him and Soma aware of the opportunity to study in China. According to Justin Ritzinger, Wong, a native of Hong Kong, had studied Hinayana Buddhism with an Englishman as a young man, before encountering the famous Buddhist reformer Taixu (1889–1947).[7] Wong, who became a lay disciple of Taixu, moved to Shanghai, where, among other things, he began the early English-language journal *The Chinese Buddhist* in 1930.[8] In addition, he translated the *Sūtra of Hui-Neng*, that is, the Platform Sūtra (*Liuzu tan jing*), in 1930, which in 1932 was included in Dwight Goddard's *Buddhist Bible*.[9] Wong also translated the smaller *Sukhāvatīvyūha Sūtra* (*Amituo jing*) and the *Cheng weishi lun* (**Vijñaptimātratāsiddhi*).[10] According to Dwight Goddard's preface to Wong's translation of the Platform Sūtra, Wong was a translator of Chinese texts based in Shanghai who had traveled to "Ceylon, to better fit himself for translation work."[11] Wong lived in Ceylon from 1931 to 1933, where at Taixu's behest he studied Pali and Sanskrit. He died from tubercu-

---

7. Justin R. Ritzinger, "Original Buddhism and Its Discontents: The Chinese Buddhist Exchange Monks and the Search for the Pure Dharma in Ceylon," *Journal of Chinese Religions* 44, no. 2 (2016): 153–54. I thank Brooks Jessup for identifying the characters and Mandarin pronunciation of Wong's name and death date.

8. Francesca Tarocco, *The Cultural Practices of Modern Chinese Buddhism: Attuning the Dharma* (New York: Routledge, 2007), 78.

9. The translation of the Platform Sūtra is found in Dwight Goddard, *A Buddhist Bible, the Favorite Scriptures of the Zen Sect; History of Early Zen Buddhism, Self-Realisation of Noble Wisdom, the Diamond Sutra, the Prajna Paramita Sutra, the Sutra of the Sixth Patriarch* (Thetford, VT: Dwight Goddard, 1938).

10. *Zhongguo fojiao renmin da cidian* (Shanghai: Shanghai Cishu Chubanshe, 1999), 625–26; BB, 820.

11. Goddard, *A Buddhist Bible*, 217.

losis on the island in 1933.[12] Although Kheminda mentions that he and Soma met Wong in Sri Lanka in the late 1920s, his account was written in 1960, decades after the event, so in all likelihood the version given by Ritzinger, which is based on Chinese sources, is correct. While in Ceylon, Wong encouraged the Buddhists there to travel to China, in order to help further the Buddhist exchange program and the study of Pali as planned by Taixu.[13] According to Kheminda's account, Wong gave the initial impetus to Soma and Kheminda by alerting them to the possibility of "spreading the *Theravāda* in his country and that there was much that could be translated from the *Mahāyāna* literature of the China."[14] Spurred by Wong, the pair of laymen—they were not ordained as *bhikkhu* until their return journey from Japan—headed to China in 1934, preceded by the more famous Ceylonese *bhikkhu* Nārada, who also had been encouraged by Wong to make that journey. Traveling through Burma, Siam, Penang, Singapore, and Hong Kong, Kheminda and Soma reached Shanghai in late 1934 or 1935. When they arrived, however, they found "there no facilities for study," so they moved on to Tokyo.[15]

Kheminda does not detail how he and Soma made their way to Tokyo, but once there, they met Kimura Nichiki, who, it appears, invited them to attend his lectures on Mahayana Buddhism at Risshō University, a university associated with the Nichiren denomination, where Kimura served as a faculty member. The two Ceylonese may have been directed to Kimura, because he, like Nanjō Bun'yū and Takakusu Junjirō, was conversant in English and knowledgeable about Pali, Sanskrit, and Indian Buddhism. Kimura was one of a growing number of Japanese Buddhist clerics who spent considerable time studying in South Asia and then returned home to join the faculty ranks at one of Japan's Buddhist sectarian universities. This cadre of long-term overseas Japanese Buddhist students in India, much like Nanjō and Takakusu, became prime candidates to host South Asian Buddhists and scholars when they visited Japan.

Kimura introduced Kheminda and Soma to his former junior colleague, Ehara Ryōzui, another Nichiren cleric who, following his graduation from Risshō with a specialization in Indian thought, had spent some time as a visiting graduate student in the Department of Indian Philosophy at Tokyo

12. Ritzinger, "Original Buddhism and Its Discontents," 154.

13. Ritzinger, "Original Buddhism and Its Discontents," 154.

14. The "In Memoriam" piece was written by Kheminda in 1960 when the term "Theravāda" was beginning to be used to refer to the Buddhist tradition practiced in Southeast Asia and Ceylon. As Perreira suggests in "Whence Theravāda," prior to the late 1950s that term was not widely used.

15. Upatissa, *The Path of Freedom*, xiii.

FIGURE 5.1. Photograph of Ehara Ryōzui and his family at Jōzaiji. Ryōzui is seated at the center of the photograph. Courtesy of Ehara Ryōsen, Ehara's son, who is standing in shorts on Ryōzui's right.

Imperial University (see fig. 5.1). In addition to apparently having some fa-cility with English, Ehara had training in Indian thought and languages that made him a suitable host for the two Ceylonese. In 1928, while serv-ing as a lecturer at Risshō, Ehara became incumbent of the temple Jōzaiji in Kawatana. Ehara continued teaching at Risshō until he returned to Jōzaiji in 1933, taking a leave from his university post. Although I am uncertain about the courses Ehara taught while at Risshō, the handful of publications he pub-lished in Nichiren denominational journals give us a glimpse of his research interests and growing expertise in Indian religious thought. In 1926, Ehara published a Japanese translation of the first two chapters of R. E. Hume's work *Thirteen Principal Upanishads* and, in 1928, an article in which he ex-amined the philosophy of the Upaniṣads from the perspective of the notion of transmigration.[16] Ehara also edited a Sanskrit–Japanese glossary of terms that were used by Nichiren in some of his key works; this was also published in Risshō University's journal *Ōsaki gakuhō*.[17] During the Fifteen Years'

16. Ehara Ryōzui, "Upanishatto tetsugaku," *Ōsaki gakuhō* 67 (1926): 139–47; 69 (1926), 109–22; Ehara Ryōzui, "<Rinne shisō o chūshin to shite mitaru> Upanishatto tetsugaku," *Ōsaki gakuhō* 75–76 (1928): 236–307.

17. Ehara Ryōzui, "Nichiren Shōnin goibun Kanbon jii," *Ōsaki gakuhō* 79 (Special Issue: Nichiren Shōnin roppyaku gojū onki kinen tokuson gō) (December 1931): 1–30 (L–R).

War, there is evidence that Ehara served in some capacity in French Indo-china, perhaps because of his knowledge of South and Southeast Asian Buddhism, as well as his language skills. A business card with the name Ehara Akio has been discovered at the Jōdo Shin temple Shōtokuji in Takatsuki. The incumbent at the temple during the 1940s, Utsuki Nishū (1893–1951), worked in French Indochina during the war. On the business card, someone, perhaps Utsuki, has written next to the printed name "Ehara Ryōzui" and "Nagasaki-ken, Kawatana, Jōzaiji," that is, Ehara's address. The card also indicates that Ehara was a member of the "Ichimaru Corps dispatched to French Indochina" (Futsuin haken Ichimaru Butai).[18] The biographical records at Jōzaiji do not record Ehara's service in French Indochina, however. In any case, Ehara would continue as the incumbent of Jōzaiji during and after the war, until 1953, when he became incumbent at the regional head temple, Honkyōji in the nearby town of Ōmura, in 1953. He died at the young age of fifty-three, in 1955.[19]

Ehara was a special sort of temple cleric. Not only did he agree to host two Ceylonese Buddhists for more than a year. He was extremely well educated, had some facility with English, and was quite intellectually curious. When, in 1939, for example, schoolchildren stumbled upon a long-lost Christian grave from 1622 on the hillside near the Jōzaiji graveyard, Ehara took time to investigate it thoroughly, writing a rather lengthy pamphlet about the grave's origins that same year, although it was not published, in cyclostyled form, until 1951.[20] Another story about Ehara is indicative of his generosity and compassion. Toward the end of the Fifteen Years' War, when a US plane shot down by Japanese defense forces crashed on a hillside in the neighboring village, killing the pilot, Ehara, after discussion with the squad leader of the garrison that recovered the corpse, agreed to erect a grave for the deceased in the temple graveyard. According to a later account of the event, the rather "religiously minded" squad leader was dressed down by his superior officer for being too softhearted and the grave was moved to a more remote site on the temple grounds.[21] After the war, however, US occupation forces praised the respectful treatment given to the remains of the dead US pilot. Writing of

18. I thank Ōsawa Kōji for sharing with me the business card that he discovered. See Ōsawa Kōji, "Senjiki Furansuryō Indoshina ni okeru shūkyō kōsaku: Utsuki Nishū to Kuno Hōryū no genchi chōsa," *Tōyō bunka kenkyū* 15 (2013): 109.

19. Biographical details are based on the entry, most of which was written by Ehara, in the Jōzaiji *Yuraiki*, an unpublished manuscript in possession of Jōzaiji. The move to Honkyōji and the death date are written, of course, by another individual.

20. Ehara Ryōzui, *Kirishitan haka engi* (Nagasaki Prefecture: Masuda Sanae, 1951).

21. *Kawatana kyōdo shi*, undated article in the Jōzaiji archive.

Ehara in 1960, Kheminda recalled, "The head of that temple, the Rev. N. R. M. Ehara, had been a lecturer at Risshō for sometime. He was the perfect host—a most understanding, patient, pleasant, witty character with abundant laughter, and he was young."[22] (At the time of Soma and Kheminda's visit, Ehara was thirty-three.)

Not long after returning to Jōzaiji, Ehara undertook the reconstruction of the living quarters and offices of the temple, a task that was underway, as Kheminda notes, when he and Soma arrived at Jōzaiji, having been introduced to Ehara by Kimura Nichiki. Ehara, writing in 1936, noted in the temple necrology (*kakochō*) that the pair arrived at Jōzaiji in the summer of 1935 and departed on October 16, 1936, bound for India. In the necrology entry, Ehara also makes the claim that these were the first two true *bhikkhu* to study abroad in Japan, but I cannot verify that this is true.[23]

Soon after Kheminda and Soma arrived at Jōzaiji, construction of a large, traditional reception room was completed. Although today known at the temple as the "*Shoin*" because of its traditional style of architecture, according to Kheminda's account, Ehara allowed the two visitors to stay in the newly constructed room, informally calling it the "Lion Hall," because the guests who resided there haled from the "Lion Isle." After Kheminda and Soma's arrival in July 1935, according to Ehara's records, the three men set to work reading, discussing, and translating into English portions of Nichiren's writings. These translations were compiled into a cyclostyled pamphlet by Ehara, Kheminda, and Soma. In the introduction Ehara wrote of their collaborative effort, "Accidentally, Mr. V. E. P. Pulle and Mr. G. S. Prélis visited my temple this summer. We talked about Nichiren every day and read together many of his letters. The nobility and beauty of Nichiren's sentiments and his burning zeal for Truth inspired my friends and the few letters translated here are the result of our joint labours. I hope that this collection will give to those who do not know the language of Nichiren a glimpse of the radiance of the sun-lotus which blossomed in the Land of the Gods."[24] Exactly how Kheminda and Soma felt about Nichiren's version of Buddhism is unclear, but Kheminda did note that they had helped Ehara work on translations of Nichiren's writings. From 1936 to 1937, Ehara published selections of the letters in three parts, a brief biography of Nichiren, and a translation of Nichiren's important treatise *Risshō ankokuron* (On the Establishment of Righteousness and the

---

22. Upatissa, *Path of Freedom*, xiii.

23. "Jōzaiji kakochō, 1928–1942," entry for 1936 (Shōwa 11). In the *kakochō*, it is recorded that the entries for this year were made in July 1951. The *kakochō* is in possession of Jōzaiji.

24. N. R. M. Ehara, "Nichiren," Jōzaiji. Kawatana, Japan, 1935, 8.

Security of the Country).[25] The translations were published in the *Young East*, the Japanese, primarily English-language, journal aimed at disseminating Japanese Buddhist teachings throughout the Buddhist world. In addition, at some point the team completed a translation of Nichiren's work, *Kaimokushō*, which was published by the International Buddhist Society in 1941.[26]

According to Kheminda's *In Memoriam* piece for Soma that is contained in *The Path of Freedom*, sometime later in 1936 Ehara also told Kheminda and Soma about the existence of the *Gedatsu dōron*, showing them an edition of the Chinese work in the Jōzaiji library.[27] The text today perhaps is best known by the English title *The Path of Freedom (Vimuttimagga)*, which was given to the revised translation by Ehara, Soma, and Kheminda published in 1961 by the Buddhist Publication Society.[28] Kheminda gave the following account of how they came to work on the translation.

> Some days after we went into residence in the Lion Hall, our friend showed us around his new library. Pointing to three thin volumes he said that that was the Chinese translation of the *Vimuttimagga*, and that originally it was supposed to have been written in Pali in Ceylon by a Sinhalese Thera. With one voice both of us exclaimed that we were ready to begin translating it that very instant—of course, with his help. And our friend, with his great big ringing laughter, readily agreed.[29]

Awareness of the *Gedatsu dōron* had been stimulated by 1919 articles in Japanese and in English by the Japanese Jōdo Shin, Takada-ha, scholar Nagai Makoto (1881–1970), who had studied in the Department of Indian Philosophy at Tokyo Imperial University with Takakusu Junjirō, with whom he later would work on the editing of the Japanese translation of the Pali canon, the *Nanden daizōkyō*.[30] His attention to this text was part of a small flurry of

25. See N. R. M. Ehara, V. E. P. Pulle, and G. S. Prelis, "Selections from Nichiren's Writings: Epistle from Sado (Sado Gosho)," *Young East* 6, no. 1 (1936): 19–25; N. R. M. Ehara, V. E. P. Pulle, and G. S. Prelis, "Selections from Nichiren's Writings: On the Establishment of Righteousness and the Security of the Country (Risshō Ankoku Ron)," *Young East* 6, no. 2 (1936): 16–27; and Ehara Ryozui, "A Brief Sketch of Nichiren's Life," *Young East* 6, no. 3 (1936): 34–40.

26. Nichiren. *The Awakening to the Truth or "Kaimokushō,"* trans. N. R. M. Ehara and assisted by: Bhikkhu Soma and Bhikkhu Kheminda (Tokyo: International Buddhist Society, 1941).

27. Upatissa, *The Path of Freedom*, xiv.

28. Upatissa, *The Path of Freedom*.

29. Upatissa, *The Path of Freedom*, xiv.

30. The articles are Nagai Makoto, "The Vimutti-Magga the 'Way to Deliverance': The Chinese Counterpart of the Pali Visuddhi-Magga," *Journal of the Pali Text Society* 7 (1919): 69–80, and "*Gedatsu dōron* ni tsuite," *Tetsugaku zasshi* (July 1919). Nagai also published a comparative study of the *Gedatsu dōron* and the *Visuddhimagga* in 1922. See Nagai Makoto, "Gedatsu Dōron

activity surrounding the search for surviving Buddhist texts in Chinese that were translations from Pali works. Takakusu Junjirō (1866–1945), who studied in Europe, primarily with Max Müller, from 1890 to 1897, first drew attention to this phenomenon when he announced the existence of a Chinese text, the *Shanjianlü piposha* (J. *Zenkenritsu bibasha*) that he asserted was a translation of the Pali *Samantapāsādikā*, a detailed commentary on the Vinaya. (Although some recent scholarship has called into question the attribution to Buddhagoṣa and even that the Pali *Samantapāsādikā* is the root text of the *Shanjianlu piposha*, which was the received wisdom for much of the twentieth century.)[31] In an effort that lasted several decades, Takakusu, Nagai, and, toward the end of the project, Mizuno Kōgen, edited a romanized version of the Pali *Samantapāsādikā* in seven volumes, published 1924–47.[32]

Extending his mentor's research into vestiges of Pali texts in the Chinese Buddhist canon, Nagai turned his attention to the *Gedatsu dōron*, concluding in several articles that it, like the *Shanjianlu piopsha*, in all probability also was a Chinese translation from a Pali original. Unlike the *Shanjianlu piopsha*, however, the Pali text of the *Gedatsu dōron* was no longer extant. Nagai contended that the *Gedatsu dōron*, which had been translated into Chinese by Sōgyabara (*Saṃghabhara; 460–?), was written by Upatissa prior to the composition of Buddhaghosa's *Visuddhimagga* and had served as a model for the latter text.[33] After first publishing his findings in Japanese, at Takakusu's suggestion, Nagai then translated the article for publication in English in the *Journal of the Pali Text Society*. According to Kheminda, Nyanatiloka (Ñāṇatiloka), who arrived in Japan in 1920, where he would teach Pali at

---

to Visuddhimagga to no taishō kenkyū," in *Konpon Butten no kenkyū*, ed. Nagai Makoto (Tokyo: Tenchi Shobō, 1922), 237–50. Along with Takakusu and several other scholars, Nagai was one of the editors of the Japanese translation of the Pali canon and extracanonical materials, the *Nanden daizōkyō*. See Takakusu Junjirō, Ui Hakuju, Nagai Makoto, Tsuji Naoshirō, and Mizuno Kōgen, *Nanden Daizōkyō* (Tokyo: Daizō Shuppan, 1935).

31. Takakusu announced his discovery of the text in Takakusu Junjirō. "Pali Elements in Chinese Buddhism: A Translation of Buddhaghosa's Samanta-Pasadika, a Commentary on the Vinaya, Found in the Chinese Tripitaka." *Journal of the Royal Asiatic Society* (July 1896). On the authorship of the text, see Ann Heirman, "The Chinese 'Samantapāsādikā' and Its School Affiliation," *Zeitschrift der Deutschen Morgenländischen Gesellschaft* 154, no. 2 (2004): 381.

32. Buddhaghosa, Junjiro Takakusu, Makoto Nagai, and Kogen Mizuno, *Samantapasadika: Buddhaghosa's Commentary on the Vinaya Pitaka* [in Pali]. [Texts in romanized Pali—Pali Text Society] (London: Pali Text Society, 1924–47).

33. Nagai, "The Vimutti-Magga the 'Way to Deliverance,'" 79–80. For a summary of current scholarship on the *Gedatsu dōron*, see Heirman, "The Chinese 'Samantapāsādikā' and Its School Affiliation," 373–76; Naniwa Senmyō, ed., *Gedatsu Dōron*, Shin Kokuyaku Daizōkyō, Vol. 19, Ronshūbu 5 (Tokyo: Kōei Bunka Sha, 2001, 7–28).

Taishō University, hearing about the existence of the *Gedatsu dōron*, urged that the text be translated from the Chinese, although that effort was unsuccessful.[34] Nagai's studies of the *Gedatsu dōron/*Vimuttimagga* were prominent enough in the world of Buddhist studies that by 1932 the *Gedatsu dōron* had come to the attention of P. V. Bapat, a student of Dharmanand Kosambi in Baroda State. Bapat, on Kosambi's urging, went to Harvard University, where he completed a PhD thesis comparing the *Gedatsu dōron* with the *Visuddhimagga*.[35] According to Bapat, following the publication of Nagai's article, the **Vimuttimagga* was soon mentioned in Pe Maung Tin's English (1923) and Nyanatiloka's German (1931) translations of the *Visuddhimagga*.[36] Ehara, as a graduate student of Indian philosophy at Tokyo Imperial University in the 1920s when both Nagai and Nyanatiloka were present, was in all likelihood aware of research concerning the *Gedatsu dōron*, as well as the interest in the text among South Asian Buddhists. In addition, by 1933 Higata Ryūshō had published a Japanese translation of the *Jietuo daolun* as part of the *Kokuyaku issaikyō* collection.[37] It would not be surprising, therefore, if Ehara told his two Ceylonese guests about the text and, in return for their help with the Nichiren translations, offered to work on a full English translation of the text while Kheminda and Soma were at Jōzaiji (see fig. 5.2).

However the text became a subject of conversation, the three men worked intensively on translating the text in the late spring of 1936. Beginning prior to Hanamatsuri (Buddha's birthday festival) on May 28, 1936, they worked as much as twenty hours per day, completing a draft translation by September 30, 1936. The last four months of their stay at Jōzaiji—one quarter of their time at the temple—thus was occupied with full-time work on the translation of the *Gedatsu dōron*. They then mailed copies of the cyclostyled draft translation to a group of fifty scholars. In the acknowledgments to the translation draft, the team thanks such noted scholars and clerics as C. A. F. Rhys

34. Upatissa, *The Path of Freedom*, xiv.

35. Kosambi, *Dharmanand Kosambi*, 23, n. 48; Purushottam Vishvanath Bapat, "Vimuttimagga and Visuddhimagga: A Comparative Study" (PhD diss., Harvard University, 1932), subsequently published in 1937 as P. V. Bapat, *Vimuttimagga and Visuddhimagga a Comparative Study* (Kandy: Buddhist Publication Society, 2009). Bapat mentions Nagai's essay on the *Gedatsu dōron* in his introduction, xv.

36. See Bapat, *Vimuttimagga and Visuddhimagga*, xv, n. 1.

37. Upatissa, *The Path of Freedom*, xxvii. Nyanatusita, who has a new English translation of the *Jietuo daolun* forthcoming, mentioned via email communication (August 14, 2018) that some sections of the text were elided by Ehara, Pulle, and Prelis and there are some errors in the translation. In addition to using Higata's Japanese translation they were extremely literal in their translation of the text. Higata's translation of the *Jietuo daolun* is found in *Gedatsu dōron*, translated by Higata Ryūshō, in Iwano Shin'yū, *Kokuyaku issaikyō [Indo senjutsubu]* Ronshūbu 7.

FIGURE 5.2. Ehara Ryōzui, G. S. Prelis (both seated), and Victor Pulle at work at Jōzaiji probably during the winter of 1935–36. Courtesy of the Buddhist Publication Society, Kandy, Sri Lanka.

Davids, Wilhelm Geiger, Nyanatiloka, Nārada Thera, Ogiwara Unrai, Kimura Nichiki, Nagai Makoto, and Akanuma Chizen, among others, so it is likely those individuals received copies of the translation. In a prefatory note, the three men expressed their gratitude to Higata Ryūshō for his Japanese translation of the text, from which they "derived much help."[38] Kheminda wrote

38. The acknowledgments in the draft translation are dated August 29, 1936, and are reproduced without changes in Upatissa, *The Path of Freedom*, xxix. The translators thank Higata in the "Prefatory Note to the Original Draft Translation," dated May 28, 1936, which is reproduced on p. xxvii.

in the *In Memoriam* chapter that he and Soma were excited by the content of the text, so, anxious to put the various cultivations described into practice, they wasted no time in heading back toward Ceylon via Burma, where they intended to receive the full *bhikkhu* ordination before returning home. On October 16, 1936, accompanied to Nagasaki by Ehara and a few other Japanese friends, Kheminda and Soma boarded a ship bound for Rangoon. In November, they both received the full ordination in Burma from Pāṇḍava Mahā Thera.

Their stay at Jōzaiji had been an extremely productive one. In the course of their visit they had assisted Ehara in translating a number of Nichiren's letters and they had completed a full translation of the *Gedatsu dōron*. Their joint translations of Nichiren's writings soon made their way into the pages of the *Young East*. The group also produced the series of polylingual calligraphies that I have discussed in chapter 4. Although the translation of the *Gedatsu dōron* translation was not published until 1961, copies of the draft circulated in the South Asian Buddhist world. Kheminda mentions mailing a copy of the cyclostyled draft to Nyanatiloka in Sri Lanka. By 1937, a partial copy of the draft translation also was passed to P. V. Bapat by Ānanda Kasalyāyana when Bapat visited the Mūlagandhakuṭi Vihāra of the Mahābodhi Society in Sārnāth.[39] At that time, Bapat was completing work on his own book, *Vimuttimagga and Visuddhimagga: A Comparative Study*, which was a revised version of his 1932 PhD thesis. Having been brought to the attention of English-speaking Buddhists in Ceylon in the 1930s, the translation by Ehara, Prelis, and Pulle has continued to circulate. Since its publication it has served as a resource for practitioners of Vipassanā-style meditation. Pariyatti, an organization with a publishing arm aimed at supporting Vipassanā meditation, still sells the 1960 edition of the **Vimuttimagga*. In addition, insight meditation teachers, particularly those exploring concentrative meditation, use the Ehara-Prelis-Pulle translation of the **Vimuttimagga* as an authoritative reference, and therapists using insight-style meditation therapeutically also cite the descriptions of the meditative path that are found in the text.[40]

The tale of the *Gedatsu dōron*'s translation into English reveals a number of important features of Buddhist Asia during the 1930s. The complicated

39. Bapat, *Vimuttimagga and Visuddhimagga*, v.

40. For example, see Leigh Brasington, "Practical Jhānas: Right Concentration and the Suttas," in *Secular Buddhism* (Barre, MA: Barre Center for Buddhist Studies, 2013), 77; Andrea Grabovac, "The Stages of Insight: Clinical Relevance for Mindfulness-Based Interventions," *Mindfulness* 6, no. 3 (June 1, 2015): 590, 594; Anne Murphy, "Mindfulness-Based Therapy in Modern Psychology: Convergence and Divergence from Early Buddhist Thought," *Contemporary Buddhism* 17, no. 2: 298.

route taken by Kheminda and Soma en route to Japan makes clear that a number of Asian entrepôts across Asia had become hotbeds of exchange for Buddhist ideas and interpersonal contacts. Among those mentioned in Kheminda's accounts of his travels are Rangoon, Moulmein (Mawlamyine), Shanghai, and Tokyo. Travels by Buddhists through the region enlarged the net of contacts, for example, as when Wong Mou-lam headed from Shanghai to Sri Lanka, catalyzing further travel by Buddhists. The story told by Kheminda and Soma also reveals that in the 1930s Burma continued to hold great attraction as a center for learning such new or revived methods of Buddhist cultivation as *Satipaṭṭhāna*. Although by the 1930s the increasingly chaotic situation in China made it difficult for foreigners to engage in the serious study of Buddhism, places with large numbers of overseas Japanese temples, for example Shanghai, may have served as an important contact zone for Asian and Japanese Buddhists. From there, Asian Buddhists could enter Japan, where facilities for the sort of study and translation Kheminda and Soma were seeking were plentiful. With Japan as a center for the study of Buddhism in Asia, Koreans, Chinese, and, as in the case in this chapter, South and Southeast Asians would have brought what they discovered in Japan, including such texts as the *Gedatsu dōron* that previously were unknown outside of the Sinitic linguistic world, back with them to South Asia, where the texts were given a new, different life. The translation of the *Gedatsu dōron* translation highlights how Japan functioned as a locus for the dissemination of Buddhist scholarship and new texts in Asia.

The story of the *Gedatsu dōron*'s translation also demonstrates how Japan functioned as a Buddhist metropole in the 1930s. On the one hand, Japanese Buddhists helped create translations and studies of texts that helped change perceptions of the tradition in the wider Buddhist world. For the first four decades of the twentieth century, Japanese contacts with South and Southeast Asian Buddhists and native scholars provided opportunities for the Japanese to expand their participation in global Buddhist scholarship through English-language publications. At the same time, Buddhists from across Asia, particularly those areas within the Anglophone sphere, contributed to Japanese Buddhist efforts to disseminate Japanese teachings to a non-Japanese-speaking or -reading audience and expand Japanese Buddhist scholarship concerning such languages as Pali, Sanskrit, and Tibetan. The temple of Watanabe Kaigyoku (1872–1933), Saikōji in Shinagawa, for example, was frequented by such important expatriates as Nyanatiloka, the Chinese cleric Milin, and Rash Behari Bose.[41] Japanese English-language jour-

---

41. Okuyama, *Hyōden Kawaguchi Ekai*, 343.

nals, for example, the *Young East*, also served as a venue for the exchange of Buddhist ideas across Asia, drawing together Japanese scholars with a wide range of South and Southeast Asian Buddhist authors. The *Young East* and other Buddhist-studies English-language publications published in Japan served as a venue for the construction of a shared transnational Buddhist culture in Asia. By necessity, English became the common language for discussing Buddhism in a pan-Asian setting.

The biographies of many of the actors involved in this story also underline the importance of India and Southeast Asia as a training ground for Japanese Buddhists and Buddhist scholars. A growing number of Japanese Buddhist overseas students returned home where they served not only as university teachers but also as liaisons between Japan and visitors from across Asia. India, in particular, also served as an important outlet for Japanese Buddhist scholarship in English. Kimura Nichiki, who hosted Soma and Kheminda at Risshō and guided them to Ehara's temple, is an important representative of this group of Japanese Buddhists who studied abroad in South Asia before joining the ranks of the Japanese Buddhist academic world, so it is worth taking a closer look at his career. Born in 1882 in Fukui Prefecture, Kimura Shōzaburō was ordained as a Nichiren cleric in 1896 and went by the name Ryūkan until 1931, when he changed his name to Nichiki.[42] Kimura studied at several sectarian academies and an English-language school prior to entering Tōyō University in 1906. In 1908, having completed the preparatory course and one year of university study at Tōyō, Kimura headed to India as a Nichirenshū overseas student. Kimura first studied at a Sanskrit academy in Chittagong, a city that by the nineteenth century was one of the few in India with a significant number of Buddhists. As Kimura recalled, "I went to India as a resident student to study Buddhism in that country and stayed in Chittagong—the only centre of the Southern Buddhism (Hīnayāna) that remained in India."[43] In the mid-nineteenth century, Chittagong became a center of Buddhist revival activity in India when the Arakanese *bhikkhu* Saramitra Mahasthavir established the Sangharāja Nikāya in 1855.[44] Graduating from that school in 1911, Kimura then moved to Calcutta, where until 1914

---

42. Biographical information is based on the chronology in Kimura Nikki, "Hokekyō Kōwa: Nichiren Shōnin to Hokekyō" (Tokyo: Kimura Nikki, 1966), 97–99, and NBJ, 162.

43. Nikki Kimura, "My Memory about the Late Rash Behari Bose," in *Rash Behari Basu, His Struggle for India's Independence*, ed. Rash Behari Bose, Radhanath Rath, and Sābitri Prasanna Chatterjee (Calcutta: Biplabi Mahanayak Rash Behari Basu Smarak Samity, 1963), 38.

44. On the revival of Buddhism in Chittagong, which produced a number of important Indian Buddhist scholars and *bhikkhu*, see Surendran, "'The Indian Discovery of Buddhism,'" 125–26; and Ober, "Reinventing Buddhism," 120–28.

he studied with Santiniketan's librarian, Bidhushekhar Shastri (1878–1957). Kimura also studied at the Asian Studies Department of the Sanskrit College. After graduating in 1914, Kimura then studied Buddhist Sanskrit and ancient Indian epigraphy with Haraprasad Shastri. In addition to learning Sanskrit, Kimura became proficient in Bengali as well as other Indic languages and, in 1915, he received the honorific title of Vidya Ratna from the Eastern Bengal Sanskrit Society as well as a gold-medal prize from the Literary Association of Bengal for his monograph on the philosophy of the Madhyamaka School.

While in Bengal, Kimura, like Okakura Kakuzō, who had resided in the region in 1901–2, was drawn into the orbit of Rabindranath Tagore. When Tagore began planning a trip to Japan in 1915, he wrote to Kimura, who was still at Calcutta University, asking him to head back to Japan to lay the groundwork for his visit. Tagore wrote,

> Instead of starting for Japan immediately my intention is to wait a few months longer. Meanwhile sending you there to make necessary preparations. I want to know Japan in the outward manifestation of its modern life and in the spirit of its traditional past. I also want to follow the traces of ancient India in your civilization and have some idea of your literature if possible. I doubt not that you will be able to protect me, while I am there, from pressure of invitations and receptions and formal meetings. I want to live very simply and quietly."[45]

Tagore's trip to Japan roused some suspicion among the British authorities, probably in part because in 1915 the revolutionary Rash Behari Bose had fled to Japan disguised as a member of Tagore's family. In addition, the ship that took Tagore to Japan, the *Tosa Maru*, had previously been used by a group of Bengali revolutionaries in an effort to smuggle arms into India.[46] Like other Japanese company officials and travelers who were suspected of working against British interests in India (see chapter 3), Kimura was considered by some, including his Indian colleagues, to be a Japanese spy.[47]

At Tagore's request, Kimura returned to Japan in 1915 to help prepare for the poet's visit, which took place as a stopover while Tagore was en route to the United States. At a formal reception for Tagore on June 13, 1916, Kimura

45. Letter cited in Hay, *Asian Ideas of East and West*, 53.
46. Hay, *Asian Ideas of East and West*, 56.
47. Hay bases this assertion on a 1960 interview with a former staff member of Calcutta University. The individual mentioned that Kimura had been reputed to be a spy while he resided in Calcutta. Hay, *Asian Ideas of East and West*, 347.

translated Tagore's remarks from Bengali into Japanese for the crowd of approximately 250 clerics, government officials, and others who gathered at the temple Kan'eiji. During the two-year Japan interlude, Kimura published a book concerning the philosophy of the Upaniṣads, *Upanishaddo monogatari*, and was promoted to the rank of *gonsōzu* (lower-ranked bishop) in the Nichiren denomination.[48] He also met for the first time Rash Behari Bose, who was in hiding in Tokyo at that time. Kimura was impressed with Bose, recalling that after meeting Bose in Tokyo, "I paid my highest respect to his sincerity and knew the high value of his true heart. After the interview, I became his intimate friend."[49]

By 1917, with the permission of his denomination, Kimura was back in India, where he began studying Indian Buddhist history under Haraprasad Shastri. The next year, he began lecturing at the postgraduate level in the Department of Arts at Calcutta University. Kimura received the enthusiastic support of the vice-chancellor and president of the Post-Graduate Council of University of Calcutta, Ashutosh Mookerjee (1864–1924). Mookerjee was vice-chancellor of the university from 1906 to 1914 and again from 1921 to 1923, while simultaneously serving as president of the Mahābodhi Society from 1911 to 1924.[50] Inspired by the activities of the Bengal Buddhist Association and close to its founder, Kripasaran Mahathera, Mookerjee assembled a coterie of scholars studying Pali and Buddhism. An adroit judge of scholarly talent and commitment to Buddhism, over the course of the early twentieth century Mookerjee hired such notable Buddhist scholars as Beni Madhab Barua and Dharmanand Kosambi. Under Mookerjee's tenure, the University of Calcutta also established the first department for Pali in India. In addition, Mookerjee arranged for the university to employ a series of overseas Japanese Buddhist students in India as lecturers on Buddhism. These included Yamakami Sōgen/Tensen (1878–1957), Masuda Jiryō (1887–1930), and, from 1918 to 1931, Kimura.[51] Kimura was given the title of lecturer in Indian Buddhist History and Mahayana Philosophy. At the university he taught "Buddhist philosophy and Buddhist history." In 1924, the University of Calcutta administration even sent Kimura back to Japan to establish ties with every

---

48. Kimura Ryūkan, *Upanishaddo monogatari* (Tokyo: Shinchōsha, 1916).

49. Kimura, "My Memory about the Late Rash Behari Bose," 40.

50. Ober, "Reinventing Buddhism," 174. Although according to Ober Mookerjee was not serving as president in 1915–21, Kimura refers to him as "President Asutosh Mookerjee" in the preface to a 1920 book, thanking Mookerjee for his support. See Ryukan Kimura, *The Original and Developed Doctrines of Indian Buddhism in Charts* (Calcutta: University of Calcutta, 1920), v.

51. See below for more about Yamakami and Masuda.

Japanese university. Kimura also presented the major Japanese universities with the University of Calcutta's various publications.[52]

During his time teaching at Calcutta University, Kimura produced a series of articles and books in Japanese and English concerning South Asian Buddhism. The Japanese publications published prior to his return to Japan were mostly articles in sectarian journals that reported on Indian Buddhism.[53] As noted above, he also published a book concerning the Upaniṣads in 1916. The English publications Kimura produced were more substantial works based on his lectures and published by the University of Calcutta. In the prefatory material in several of those publications, Kimura thanked Ashutosh Mookerjee for his supportive leadership and Indian colleagues such as B. M. Barua and Sailendranath Mitra, while also acknowledging the assistance of his students, particularly those at the graduate level.[54] The books published by Kimura included *The Original and Developed Doctrines of Indian Buddhism in Charts* (1920); *Introduction to the History of Early Buddhist Schools* (1925); and *A Historical Study of the Terms Hinayāna and Mahāyāna and the Origins of Mahāyāna Buddhism* (1927). Kimura made it a point to distribute at least one of the books, *Introduction to the History of Early Buddhist Schools*, to multiple libraries, where signed copies of the book remain to this day.[55]

Kimura saw these publications as a unified effort to present in a systematic way the relationship between various schools of Indian Buddhism and their doctrines, while clarifying the use of the terms Hinayana and Mahayana. Since the late nineteenth-century penetration of European Buddhological scholarship into Japan, Japanese had wrestled with the perception that East Asian Buddhism—the so-called "Northern Buddhism"—was a deviation from the Buddha's original teachings that reflected superstitious interpolations into the tradition. According to Perreira, Japanese Buddhists like Shaku Sōen contributed to the global discussion of the relationship between the streams of Buddhism based on the Pali-language textual tradition and those that took Sinitic or Tibetan materials as foundational. Perreira writes,

52. Kimura, "My Memory about the Late Rash Behari Bose," 40.

53. For example, Kimura Ryūkan, "Indo kenbun dan," *Hokke* 2, no. 5 (May 1915); and "Nichiren shugi o shiru mae ni Hokekyō o shirubeshi, Nichiren Shōnin o shiru mae ni Budda o shirubeshi," *Hokke* 7, no. 3 (March 1920).

54. See for example, Ryukan Kimura, *A Historical Study of the Terms Hinayāna and Mahāyāna and the Origin of Mahāyāna Buddhism* (Patna: Indological Book Corp., 1978), originally published 1927, xi–xii.

55. Separate signed, dedicated copies of the book are found in the Komazawa University Library in Tokyo and the Center for Research Libraries in Chicago, Illinois.

As a consequence of, and in direct response to, the implication of the above findings [dividing Buddhism into "Southern" and "Northern" schools], beginning in the 1870s there emerged in Meiji-era Japan a new historical consciousness concerning Buddhism that profoundly transformed not only the way the Japanese approached the study of Buddhism but, in turn, led to a new conceptualization of Japanese Buddhism itself that was, by the turn of the century, hugely influential and directly responsible for redefining the very terms by which the study and conceptualization of Buddhism was carried out in Asia and the West from this period forward.[56]

Perreira notes the importance of the Japanese delegation's presentations at the World's Parliament of Religion and of subsequent English-language publications of Shaku Sōen and D. T. Suzuki, for example, in his groundbreaking work *Outlines of Mahayana Buddhism* (1907), as contributing to the dissemination of these ideas about Hinayana and Mahayana from Japan to Europe and the United States. In addition, Buddhist English-language journals published in Japan, in particular the *Mahayanist* and the *Eastern Buddhist*, attempted to disseminate a more favorable view of the Japanese Mahayana tradition. Kimura's work, along with that of Yamakami Sōgen and Masuda Jiryō, all of which were published in India, can be seen as part of the same effort to spread the Japanese perspective on Buddhist history to an Anglophone audience. In the process, Kimura was able to provide through lectures the Japanese Mahayana perspective to a rising generation of Indian Buddhist scholars while also addressing Buddhist scholars outside Japan through his English-language writings published in India. Along with publications by Japanese scholars in the *Journal of the Pali Text Society* and other journals, Indian academic publishing became an important venue for addressing a wider audience outside Japan.

Kimura's *A Historical Study of the Terms Hinayāna and Mahāyāna and the Origins of Mahāyāna Buddhism* drew the attention of several prominent British scholars who expressed reservations about the work. In one review, William Stede criticized Kimura for not having sufficient grasp of Pali Buddhism, which Stede wrote was the essential foundation for truly understanding the nature of Mahayana Buddhism. Urging Kimura to take "up the study of Pali more thoroughly," Stede admitted that some "promising work in this respect is getting done by the 'middle generation' of Japanese Buddhist scholars, and I wish we had a few more Indian and European ones to join them."[57] Kimura's

---

56. Perreira, "Whence Theravāda?" 458.
57. W. Stede, "Review of a Historical Study of the Terms Hinayāna and Mahāyāna and the

effort to describe the filiation of Buddhism into Hinayana and Mahayana
from the latter perspective by characterizing Mahayana as the expression of
"ontological" teachings implicit in Buddha's post-awakening understanding
sparked criticism from C. A. F. Rhys Davids. Although praising Kimura's detailed genealogy of the terms Hinayana and Mahayana, the reviewer objected
that

> he, teaching, among other things, Pali in India, comes to take up the lower
> lying strata of Indian Buddhology. And he approaches it from the Mahāyānist
> standpoint. Or at least from his own standpoint, but under the *dominating*
> influence of Mahāyānist tradition. Now this is, for pure disinterested histori-
> cal criticism of the inception of Buddhology in India, something approaching
> what the world of sport calls "disqualification."[58]

Like Stede, however, Caroline Rhys Davids saw value in Kimura's efforts, despite disagreeing with some of the author's assertions. "But the substance of
this thesis and its historical value lies in a detailed inquiry into how the terms
Hīnayāna and Mahāyāna arose. Readers who have to meet with the terms
full blown have here an opportunity of learning how much and how little
is known as to that, and will have reason to be grateful for the painstaking
research put before them."[59]

In 1929, Kimura returned to Japan and assumed a position as professor
at Risshō University. He did not formally give up his position at Calcutta
University, however, until 1931, by which time he had become head of the Vo-
cational Studies Division (Senmonbu Buchō) at Risshō and achieved the rank
of higher-ranked bishop (*daisōzu*) in the Nichiren denomination.[60] Kimura
continued to produce a small number of publications in English, but with
his return to Japan, the bulk of his work was in Japanese. In those works,
Kimura focused on providing what he believed was the foundational knowledge required for understanding Nichiren Buddhism as well as a number of
works concerning Indian thought.[61] According to information for the years

---

Origin of Mahāyāna Buddhism by Ryukan Kimura." *Journal of the Royal Asiatic Society of Great Britain and Ireland* 4 (1928): 952.

58. C. A. F. Rhys Davids, "Review of a *Historical Study of the Terms Hinayāna and Mahāyāna and the Origin of Mahāyāna Buddhism* by Ryukan Kimura," *Bulletin of the School of Oriental Studies (London)* 4, no. 4 (1928): 856–57. Diacritics as in the original.

59. Rhys Davids, "Review of a Historical Study," 857.

60. Kimura, *Hokekyō kōwa*, 98.

61. For example, Kimura Ryūkan, "Indo no saishi girei ni tsuite," *Ōsaki gakuhō* 30 (November 1930): 74–80; Kimura Ryūkan, "Konpon Bukkyō yori Hokekyō made," *Ōsaki gakuhō*, Nichiren Shōnin roppyaku gojyū onki kinen tokushū gō (December 1931): 229–302; Kimura Nikki,

1938–41, at Risshō University Kimura taught courses on advanced Sanskrit, Indian philosophy, history and philosophy of Indian Buddhism, and the Lotus Sūtra.[62] As noted above, it was while teaching these sorts of courses that Kimura met Pulle and Prelis at Risshō University in 1934 or 1935. Although I have not seen a record of their meeting, it is clear that the two Ceylonese were involved in Risshō University activities by 1935, as Pulle published a cursory article on Ceylonese Buddhism in English in a Risshō academic journal in that year.[63] At the conclusion of the article, Pulle, as did many of the Japanese who worked in India and Ceylon, points to the importance of Buddhism for Asia's future. "Also, the study of Ceylon's history and people and its great archaeological remains is essential to the proper understanding of the religion of the future, Buddism [*sic*], which has made our Asia great, noble and strong in the past and which will make it greater, nobler and stronger in the future."[64]

In addition to teaching at Risshō following his return to Japan, Kimura became a permanent trustee (*jōnin riji*) of the Kokusai Bukkyō Kyōkai (International Buddhist Society), which had begun in in 1933.[65] Founded in order to promote the international dissemination of Buddhism, the society published a Japanese journal, *Kaigai Bukkyō jijō*, and two English-language serials aimed at an international audience, the *Young East* and *Studies on Buddhism in Japan*. In order to promote the society's mission, members would gather information about overseas Buddhism, do translation work, and support students studying overseas Buddhism. In 1937, as full-scale war in China broke out, Kimura became the third head representative of the permanent trustees (*daihyō jōnin riji*) of the society. While Kimura held that position, a Bengali Buddhist *bhikkhu*, Rastrapala Sandilyāyana, studied at Risshō with Kimura and published an article in the *Young East* and the pamphlet *A Short History of Japanese Buddhism* with the Society.[66] Given the international mission of the society, it is possible that it was in his capacity as an officer of the Society for International Buddhism that Kimura brought Kheminda, Soma, and Sandilyāyana to Risshō.

"Daijō Shōjō to iu meimeigi no rekishiteki kenkyū," *Ōsaki gakuhō* 81 (1932): 76–114; "Aiku Ō no kyōhō," *Ōsaki gakuhō* 83 (1933): 113–40; and *Indo gendai shichō* (Tokyo: Iwanami Shoten, 1935).

62. Courses on Buddhism taught in Japanese universities are listed in International Buddhist Society, "Studies on Buddhism in Japan," 4 vols. (Tokyo: International Buddhist Society, 1939–42).

63. V. E. P. Pulle, "Buddhism in Ceylon," *Ōsaki gakuhō* 87 (December 1935): 2–6 (Left-Right).

64. Pulle, "Buddhism in Ceylon," 6.

65. Ōsawa, *Senjika no Nihon Bukkyō to Nanpō chiiki*, 60–64. For more on Kimura's activities in the Fifteen Years' War period, see chapter 6.

66. Rastrapala Sandilyayana, *A Short History of Japanese Buddhism* (Tokyo: International Buddhist Society, 1940).

In addition to Kimura, a small but significant number of Japanese Buddhists studied long-term in India before assuming teaching positions in Japan, primarily at sectarian academies and universities. For many of these Buddhists, their return coincided with the rapid expansion of Japanese higher education during the Taishō and early Shōwa eras.[67] Several of them, like Kimura, were employed as lecturers at the University of Calcutta as Asuthosh Mookerjee attempted to build the Buddhist-studies program. Prior to Kimura's embarking for South Asia, the Sōtō cleric Yamakami Sōgen had been sent on a similar mission by the Sōtōshū.[68] Following his graduation from the Sōtōshū University (Sōtōshū Daigaku, later Komazawa University) in 1906, Yamakami headed to India as an overseas student. Yamakami first studied Sanskrit in Colombo with Hikkaḍuvē Sumaṅgala for a year, before moving to the University of Calcutta. There, Yamakami worked with Harinath De, who, like Ashutosh Mookerjee, was interested in supporting Pali studies in India. De had been a professor of English at Presidency College in Calcutta before moving to the University of Calcutta, where he became one of the founding members of the Linguistics Department. De progressed in his study of Pali under the tutelage of the Indian *bhikkhu* and pioneering scholar of Buddhism Dharmanand Kosambi.[69] Over the course of his career, De edited and translated a variety of Buddhist texts, including an edition of the text of the *Laṅkāvatārasūtra* and a translation published serially of Tāranātha's history of Indian Buddhism (*Rgya gar chos 'byung*). In addition, Yamakami assisted De with the translation of a series of selections from Nāgārjuna's *Mūlamadhyamakakārika* (Verses on the Middle Way) and Āryadeva's commentarial treatises on the former text.[70] Given that some of Āryadeva's treatises are extant only in Chinese and are accompanied by a rich commentarial tradition in East Asia, Yamakami probably was a valuable aid to De in his work on those texts.

At the University of Calcutta, Yamakami studied English, Sanskrit, Indian philosophy, and literature. In 1910, he was appointed a reader of Buddhism by Mookerjee, teaching courses on the development of Buddhist doctrine. Yamakami published his lectures through the University of Calcutta for use as a textbook in the course. In the preface to the monograph *Systems of Buddhis-*

---

67. Dickinson, *World War I and the Triumph of a New Japan*, 48–49.

68. His surname also is rendered Yamagami, but I have followed the spelling used in his English-language monograph, *Systems of Buddhistic Thought* and ZGDJ, 1238, where it is Yamakami.

69. Kosambi, *Dharmanand Kosambi*, 187–89.

70. Sunil Bandyopadhyay, *Harinath De, Philanthropist and Linguist* (New Delhi: National Book Trust, India), 1988, 54–56.

tic Thought, Yamakami thanked De and Mookerjee while commenting that "his [De's] linguistic gifts would have proved of invaluable service in what I consider to be the most important task which lies before Indian scholarship, namely, the rediscovery of ancient Buddhistic Works, lost in the original Sanskrit and now to be found in Chinese and Tibetan [*sic*] versions."[71] Yamakami taught at the University of Calcutta until 1913, when he returned to Japan. In 1914, he became a professor at Sōtōshū University, where he taught Sanskrit, Indian religions, and Buddhist studies. Like many other Buddhists returned from extended periods of study in South Asia, in addition to writing works on Buddhism, Yamakami wrote on conditions in India, for example, publishing in 1915 *Konnichi no Indo* (India Today), a work that surveyed Indian social life, politics, military affairs, and religious life.[72] Yamakami rose through the ranks of Sōtōshū higher education, becoming president of Komazawa University from 1943 to 1945, while continuing to publish works on Zen and in support of the war effort.[73]

In addition to Yamakami and Kimura, the University of Calcutta employed one other long-term Japanese Buddhist overseas student as a lecturer, the Shingi Shingonshū cleric Masuda Jiryō (1887–1930). Sent as an overseas student by Buzan University (Buzan Daigaku), which was affiliated with the Shingonshū, Masuda toured Buddhist sites in India and Nepal in the company of Kawaguchi Ekai and Takakusu Junjirō in the winter of 1912.[74] Masuda studied in Baroda and Pune, where the Maharaja of Baroda State, Sayajirao Gaikwad III (1863–1939), was a keen patron of Buddhist scholarship and Sanskrit studies.[75] Masuda's time in Pune and Baroda (today, Vadodara) occurred when such great scholars of Buddhist languages as R. G. Bhandarkar (1837–1925) and Dharmanand Kosambi, whom the Maharaja had lured from his post at the University of Calcutta to Baroda State, were promoting the study of Sanskrit and Pali. During the six years Masuda was in Baroda and Pune, Kosambi was teaching Pali at Fergusson College in Pune and Bhan-

71. Sōgen Yamakami, *Systems of Buddhistic Thought* (Calcutta: University of Calcutta, 1912), v. Spelling and capitalization as in the original.

72. Yamakami Sōgen, *Konnichi no Indo* (Tokyo: Genkōsha, 1915).

73. Biographical information is found in Yamagami Tadashi, ed., *Suirō zuiha* (Tokyo: Kanagawa Shinbun Sha, 1957), 217–21. During the Fifteen Years' War, Yamakami published at least one work to bolster loyalty and the spirit of sacrifice in Japan. See Yamakami Sōgen, *Hagakure bushi no seishin* (Tokyo: San'yū Sha), 1942.

74. These biographical details are drawn from the scattered mentions of Masuda in Okuyama, *Hyōden Kawaguchi Ekai*, 238; 270, ff.

75. Some details of Masuda's time in India are provided in Izumi Hōkei, "Meiji jidai ni okeru toin no Bukkyōto," *Gendai Bukkyō* 105 (1933): 168.

darkar, as vice-chancellor of Bombay University, had introduced Pali into the curriculum. In addition, the Deccan Education Society was offering four scholarships for students of Pali at Fergusson College.[76] Ober mentions that in 1913 the Maharaja installed with fanfare a Japanese Buddha image that had been presented to him by a "Japanese visitor."[77] Although Ober does not provide a name for the visitor, the event occurred while Masuda was studying in Pune and Baroda, so, perhaps, he had given the image to the Maharaja. In any case, Masuda's residence in Pune and Baroda overlapped with the efflorescence of Buddhist studies in that region. As we have seen in the cases of a number of Japanese Buddhists studying in South Asia, what at first glance appears to be a rather random set of destinations—Baroda, Chittagong, Pune—along with major urban areas like Benares, Bombay, and Calcutta turns out to be a list of centers where the renaissance in Indian Buddhist studies that was being led by Das, De, Kosambi, and other Indian pandits was underway.

In 1918, Masuda moved to Calcutta, where he became lecturer for ancient Indian history and culture in the postgraduate department of the university at the same time Kimura Nichiki was lecturing there. While at the University of Calcutta, Masuda published an English translation of the *Yibuzonglun lun*; (J. *Ibushūrin ron*; S. *Samayabhedoparacanacakra*) by Vasumitra (C. Shiyou; J. Seu), a valuable work preserved in Chinese that details the fissiparous history of the early Buddhist Sangha that resulted in the formation of a number of separate *nikāya* (schools). Masuda's early work on the text was published in the University of Calcutta's *Journal of the Department of Letters*, but his father-in-law's death in Japan forced him to leave India in 1921 before completing the translation. According to Ishigami Zen'nō, who wrote an afterword for a posthumous volume of Masuda's essays, "the ten years of overseas study in India had a great effect on Professor Masuda. Probably more than anything, this was being able to touch the soil of India, directly experience the customs of India's diverse people (*minzoku*), and learn the complexity of society in living India. It is no exaggeration to state that unlike a one or two-year period of overseas study, he came to know completely the outside and inside of things."[78]

During his subsequent overseas study in Heidelberg, Germany, which

76. On the activities of the Maharaja in Baroda, see Ober, "Reinventing Buddhism," 78–79, 284–85. On Kosambi's activities to promote Pali in Baroda, see Kosambi, *Dharmanand Kosambi*, 6–7, 22–23, 199–205.

77. Ober, "Reinventing Buddhism," 284, n. 16.

78. In Ōkubo Ryōjun, ed., *Studies in Indian Buddhist History by Jiryo Masuda* (Tokyo: Taisho University, 1986), 235.

lasted from late 1921 to 1925, Masuda worked with Max Walleser. In Germany, Masuda completed the English translation and published it in *Asia Major*.[79] In addition, Masuda published one work in German concerning Yogācāra Buddhism. In 1927, Max Walleser published his own German translation of the *Yibuzonglun lun*, thus making the important work more widely available in Europe.[80] In 1925, Masuda returned to Japan, where he assumed a post as professor at Taishō University, which recently had been founded. At Taishō, Masuda also served in the Sanskrit Studies Research Office (Bonbungaku Kenkyūshitsu) with Ogiwara Unrai. Better known for his work published overseas than within Japan, Masuda died suddenly in 1930, after just five years teaching at Taishō.[81]

Yamakami, Kimura, and Masuda are just three examples of how Japanese Buddhist overseas students in India returned to Japan to take on academic positions in higher education, primarily in the Buddhist sectarian universities that were formed in the 1920s, when Ōtani (1922), Ryūkoku (1922), Risshō (1924), Komazawa (1925), Taishō (1926), and Kōyasan (1926) universities were established.[82] In chapter 2, I noted that Kawaguchi Ekai similarly taught about Tibet and Tibetan language at a number of Japanese institutions, including Taishō University. There were a number of other long-term students in India, Ceylon, and elsewhere in South and Southeast Asia who returned to teach in Japan, thus helping to shape Buddhist studies in the twentieth century. In addition to those mentioned in this and earlier chapters—Kawaguchi Ekai, Kimura Nichiki, Yamakami Sōgen, and Masuda Jiryō—the list of those Japanese Buddhists who went on to teach at Japanese universities after studying for extended periods in South Asia includes such notable figures as Akanuma Chizen (1885–1937); Aoki Bunkyō (1886–1956); Hasebe Ryūtai (1879–1928); Ōmiya Kōjun; Tada Tōkan (1890–1967); and Teramoto Enga (1872–1940). The short-lived serial *Studies on Buddhism in Japan* listed courses taught on

79. Jiryō Masuda, "Early Indian Buddhist Schools," *Journal of the Department of Letters, University of Calcutta* 1 (1920): 1–11; and "Origin and Doctrines of Early Indian Buddhist Schools: A Translation of Hsüan-Chwang's Version of Vasumitra's Treatise," *Asia Major* 2 (1925): 1–78.

80. Max Walleser, *Die Sekten Des Alten Buddhismus*. His: Die Buddhistische Philosophie in Ihrer Geschichtlichen Entwicklung (Heidelberg: C Winter, 1927).

81. Ōkubo, *Studies in Indian Buddhist History*, 235–37.

82. For the creation of the Buddhist sectarian university system and the role of India and South Asia studies in the formation of twentieth-century Buddhist studies in Japan, see Hayashi, "The Birth of Buddhist Universities," 11–29; and Makoto Hayashi, "Religious Studies and Religiously Affiliated Universities," in *Modern Buddhism in Japan*, ed. Makoto Hayashi, Eiichi Ōtani, and Paul L. Swanson (Nagoya: Nanzan Institute for Religion and Culture, 2014), 163–93.

Buddhism at major Japanese universities for the period 1938–41.[83] Those listings reveal that the aforementioned individuals taught a variety of courses including Sanskrit and Tibetan language, Indian Buddhist doctrine, Indian philosophy, and a variety of courses centered on specific Sanskrit and other Indic-language Buddhist texts. Long-term study in South Asia by Japanese Buddhists clearly left a significant imprint upon Buddhist education in Japan during the twentieth century.

Of course, there also was a coterie of Japanese Buddhists whose main overseas work took place in Europe, for example, Nanjō Bun'yū, Ogiwara Unrai (1869–1937), Takakusu Junjirō, and Anesaki Masaharu (1873–1949), to name a few. Although their impact on the development of Buddhist studies and the practice of Buddhism—many of them remained involved in Buddhist sectarian affairs—in Japan was enormous, we should bear in mind that South Asia, particularly India, served as an important conduit for the spread of expertise concerning South Asian Buddhism to Japan as well. In this regard, we need to nuance the view that portrays the spread of Sanskrit and Pali studies in Japanese universities solely as resulting from the spread from Europe of "European-style Buddhology."[84] At the very least, many scholars of the emerging fields in Japan that became known as "Indian philosophy" (Indo Tetsugaku) and "Indian Studies" (Indogaku) studied in India and elsewhere in South-Southeast Asia, where they imbibed indigenous perspectives on classical Indic language learning and the colonial experience.

Although I have not delved in great detail concerning the biographies of all the Japanese Buddhists who followed this trajectory, my research has uncovered a significant coterie of such individuals, a group large enough to suggest that this is an important but overlooked aspect of the development of Buddhist studies in Japan. Apart from Okuyama Naoji's insightful work concerning Kawaguchi Ekai and several related articles, few scholars have thus far examined this phenomenon. Nonetheless, it is striking how much the development of expertise in Indic languages, texts, and doctrinal studies depended upon study in South Asia. At the same time, teaching at Indian universities, particularly the University of Calcutta, and writing for Indian publications were outlets for Japanese Buddhist scholars to the Anglophone academy. Of equal significance, Japanese who lectured to Indian students about Buddhism helped shape a rising generation of Buddhist scholars in

83. International Buddhist Society, *Studies on Buddhism in Japan*. 4 vols. (Tokyo: International Buddhist Society, 1939–42): 1 (1939): 207–15; 2 (1940): 186–96; 3 (1941): 155–64; 4 (1942): 139–55. (Hereafter SBJ.)

84. Hayashi, "The Birth of Buddhist Universities," 16 ff.

South Asia, providing them with a Japanese Mahayana perspective on Indian Buddhist doctrine and history.

The process by which Japanese Buddhists produced and disseminated English translations of Indic texts only extant in Chinese is a vivid illustration of the circular, global nature of Buddhist-studies scholarship in the twentieth century. Masuda, for example, acquired at least some facility with various Indic Buddhist languages in India, working with Indian scholars, some of whom, like Dharmanand Kosambi, may also have studied in Europe and the United States. The University of Calcutta's journal then served as a venue for the Japanese scholar's work to reach an Anglophone audience in India and globally. Traveling to Germany, having spent years studying and teaching in India, Masuda then worked with and, probably, influenced Max Walleser. Similarly, Japanese Buddhists like Akanuma Chizen and Tachibana Shundō trained in South Asia for substantial periods before studying in Europe, thus enhancing their scholarly expertise and exposing them to two different approaches to Indic language study. At the same time, these scholars also shaped Buddhological knowledge in Europe by enhancing the understanding of Sinitic Buddhist texts and their relationship to Indic sources from a Japanese Mahayana perspective. The globalization of Buddhist studies had far-ranging effects that touched Europe, Calcutta, and Colombo. Its ripples even reached Kawatana, on the northern shore of Ōmura Bay.

6

Deploying South Asian Buddhism

By the time Kheminda and Soma arrived in Japan in 1934–35, the interconnections between South and Southeast Asian and Japanese Buddhists were numerous and well established. The imperial universities and the relatively newly established sectarian ones employed specialists in Indian philosophy, Indian studies, Indian Buddhism, Indic languages, and, in several schools, even Tibetan. Indian and Southeast Asian Buddhist-influenced temples were found from Kobe to Tokyo, with similarly styled temples built in areas of Japanese imperial domination on the continent in such cities as Dalian and Shanghai. Temples and museums displayed a range of Buddhist images and objects from the continent and in a number of temples, calligraphies that mixed Sino-Japanese and Indic inscriptions of Buddhist verses decorated the halls. As Japanese scholars and clerics compiled the *Taishō shinshū daizōkyō*, the new edition of the Chinese Buddhist canon that to this day remains the worldwide reference work for the study of Sinitic Buddhism, South Asian, Tibetan, European, and Chinese Buddhists passed through Watanabe Kaikyoku's temple, Saikōji, where, perhaps, they contributed to the massive project. The two Ceylonese visitors availed themselves of the well-worn paths that had been established along the railways and shipping routes that now tied Japan with South and Southeast Asia, economically, religiously, culturally, and, increasingly, militarily.

From the very start of the modern Japanese exchange with South and Southeast Asia, when Kitabatake Dōryū arrived, mosquito-bitten, at Bodh Gayā, there had been ambiguity in Japanese attitudes toward South and Southeast Asia, particularly those portions of it that had been colonized by the Europeans. In the attitudes of the Japanese travelers one can see the intertwining of the "Teaist" and "Meishuron" types of pan-Asianism delineated by

Hotta. The tension between the two can be glimpsed in the woodblock print depicting Kitabatake at Bodh Gayā, sharing Buddhism with the half-naked, benighted natives (see fig. 1.2). On the one hand, for Japanese Buddhists India, above all else, was a place of pilgrimage and source of Buddhism. The spiritual values that Okakura Tenshin and many others viewed as the source of superiority over a materialistic Europe and the United States were shared with South Asians.

On the other hand, South Asia stood as an object lesson of the ignominy that came with colonization. After witnessing the conditions in the subcontinent firsthand, Japanese pilgrims like Kanokogi Kazunobu and Kimura Nichiki became vocal critics of British colonialism and advocates for Indian independence. While expressing a sense of comity with South Asians, Japanese Buddhists like Yamakami Sōgen and Sakurai Gichō also sought to reinstill an understanding of Buddhism among their Indian friends. The sense of a shared Asian heritage sat uneasily alongside the increasingly fervent belief that Japan alone could lead other Asians in the reclamation of their shared spiritual legacy.

From the Meiji era onward, Japanese encountered European and American orientalist scholarship that emphasized the primacy of Southern Buddhism, particularly as transmitted in Pali, and denigrated Mahayana Buddhism as anything from a distorted presentation of early Buddhism to a superstitious betrayal of Śākyamuni's teachings. The emphasis on the South Asian origins of the tradition in European and American scholarship worked synergistically with the long-standing desire among some Japanese Buddhists to find the most legitimate transmission of the precepts and authentic texts, thus igniting interest in travel to South Asia to collect texts, go on pilgrimage to Buddhist sites across South Asia, and study languages that would unlock the secrets of what had been largely inaccessible, remote textual sources for Buddhism in Japan. New European scholarship on Buddhism flowed into Japan just as travel by Japanese Buddhists not only became feasible but was encouraged by government officials, denominational leaders, and, even, their lay temple supporters. The result was an efflorescence in exchange between Japanese Buddhists and South Asians that helped transform the understanding of Buddhism globally. By 1941, Japanese Buddhist travel to India was all but impossible, but the circulation of pilgrims, students, texts, and material objects played a crucial role in forging ties to Buddhism in South and Southeast Asia that even would survive the destruction of imperial Japan.

Just as Nanjō bemoaned his failure to get to India during his first long sojourn overseas, the Japanese Buddhist turn to Europe for the acquisition of Indic language skills and philological training was not an end in itself but a means to make what were understood to be the origins of Buddhism accessible. Although the dominance of European and American orientalist scholarship was inescapable, the road to reconceptualizing Japanese Buddhism for the twentieth century—a development that some Japanese came to call *modan* (modern)—for many Japanese Buddhists ran through Colombo, Madras, Benares, Calcutta, and Bombay as much as it did through Oxford, Cambridge, Paris, and Heidelberg. Scholars have long emphasized the importance of Japanese Buddhist study with Max Müller, Sylvain Lévi, Ernst Leumann, and Max Walleser in centers of learning in Europe. We largely have been guilty of the "genesis amnesia" common to much orientalist scholarship, however, with regard to the South and Southeast Asian pandits and clerics who aided Japanese Buddhists in their efforts to understand Southern Buddhism and its relationship, real and imagined, to their tradition.[1] This study has shown that in writing the history of Buddhism in modern Japan, we need to uncover the contributions of Hikkaḍuvē Sumaṅgala, Haraprasad Shastri, Ram Avatar Sharma, Dharmanand Kosambi, Harinath De, Sarat Chandra Das, and numerous other South Asian teachers. While endeavoring to revive South Asian Buddhism, these individuals trained numerous Japanese Buddhists in Indic languages, introduced them to European orientalist scholarship, and provided access to texts, all of which allowed the Japanese to see Buddhism in a new light. The access to South Asian Buddhism in the form of texts, artworks, material objects, and people resulted in a turning toward Japanese Buddhism's South Asian legacy in much the same way that Europeans from the time of the Renaissance had turned to the classical world.

There is no gainsaying that European and American standards of authenticity, historical proof, and critical editions influenced Buddhist self-understanding across Asia. The scholarship that contained those practices and standards, however, was reconceptualized and transculturated as it was embraced by Indian, Ceylonese, and Japanese Buddhists, many of whom, I must note, had tutored some of the European and American scholars whose very scholarship they subsequently reinterpreted. As Japanese Buddhists mastered Indic languages and gained firsthand access to Sanskrit, Pali, and other Indic Buddhist texts, their writings, particularly when published in English, contributed to the shifting understanding of the relationship between the diverse strands of the Buddhist tradition. As Perreira and Snodgrass demonstrate, Japanese presentations at the World's Parliament of Religions claiming the

---

1. The term "genesis amnesia" is used with regard to scholarship concerning Iran and Persianate texts in Mohamad Tavakoli-Targhi, "Orientalism's Genesis Amnesia," *Comparative Studies of South Asia, Africa and the Middle East* 16 (1996): 1–14.

superiority of Northern, that is, Mahayana, Buddhism over Southern, that is, Hinayana, Buddhism were of seminal importance for early twentieth-century understandings of the tradition.[2] More than a decade prior to heading to Chicago for the Parliament, Sōen used that classification, writing about the superiority of Mahayana in *Seinan no Bukkyō*, while experiencing Ceylonese Buddhism firsthand. Oda Tokunō as well, following his return from Siam similarly equated Southern Buddhism with Hinayana and Northern Buddhism with Mahayana in his 1891 work *Shamu Bukkyō jijō*.

The Japanese understanding of the relationship between Hinayana and Mahayana reflected in Sōen and Oda's works was not only disseminated in Europe and the United States: the Japanese, while studying classical and vernacular Indic languages in India and Ceylon, imbibed European and American scholarship from local scholars. In their lectures and writings they transmuted that knowledge in light of their own distinctive understanding of Buddhism, providing Japanese interpretations of Buddhism to Indian students in the classroom and an Anglophone readership around the world. As I have shown, from as early as 1912, Yamakami Sōgen was lecturing about Buddhism at the University of Calcutta. There he promulgated a Japanese perspective on "systems of Buddhistic thought" that describes "Ceylon, Burma, and Siam" as "the Lands of the Lesser Vehicle" while demonstrating the superiority of Japanese Mahayana Buddhism.[3] In the early 1920s, Yamakami's Japanese Buddhist successors Masuda Jiryō and Kimura Ryūkan continued to provide a Japanese Mahayana perspective on Buddhism both in Indian classrooms and in their publications. Even while back in Japan, Kimura continued to educate such South Asian Buddhists as Rastrapala Sandilyāyana, Soma Thera, and Kheminda Thera, who then published works in English that in turn were disseminated globally, thus further shaping Buddhist practice and scholarship outside Japan.

The complicated interchanges that have been described in this book are probably best understood as examples of what historians in the last decade have begun to describe variously as "entangled," "circulatory," or "inter-crossing histories" (*histoire croisée*). Rather than analyzing historical events in a linear fashion or as a back-and-forth exchange between at most a handful of regions, the concepts of entangled, circulatory, or inter-crossing history describe multilevel global interactions like those between Japanese and South Asian Buddhists not just "in relation to one another, but also *through*

2. Perreira. "Whence Theravāda? The Modern Genealogy of an Ancient Term," 512–29; Snodgrass, *Presenting Japanese Buddhism to the West*.

3. Yamakami, *Systems of Buddhistic Thought*.

one another, in terms of relationships, interactions, and circulation."[4] Markovits and his co-editors of *Circulation and Society*, who chose the concept of circulation to capture the complexity of these historical interactions, write, "Circulation is different from simple mobility, inasmuch as it implies a double movement of going forth and coming back, which can be repeated indefinitely. In circulating, things, men, and notions often transform themselves. Circulation is therefore a value-loaded term which implies an incremental aspect and not the simple reproduction across space of already formed structures and notions."[5]

One important feature of this approach is the emphasis on dynamic processes in which historical actors in the process of transformation interact with others who are similarly active agents, for example, Kawaguchi Ekai studying with Sarat Chandra Das, P. K. Patankar, and Ram Avatar Sharma; Kimura Nichiki with Haraprasad Shastri; and Masuda Jiryō with his Indian teachers in Baroda State. Every party involved in the interactions was responding to historical imperatives specific to their personal history as well as their current circumstances. All emerged from the interactions transformed in some fashion, having been exposed to new perspectives on the nation, Buddhism, languages, etcetera. Again, as encapsulated by Werner and Zimmerman, "the entities, persons, practices, or objects that are intertwined with, or affected by, the crossing process do not necessarily remain intact or identical in form. Their transformations are tied to the active as well as the interactive nature of their coming in contact."[6] Brian Hatcher's observations concerning the interactions of such pandits as Haraprasad Shastri with British authorities and British scholars in nineteenth-century India also are germane in this regard.

> The local intellectual did not simply redirect colonial agendas but also actively shaped and was shaped by other existing or emerging vectors of practice and ideology. This is important to note because the difference between "redirecting" and "shaping" (or being shaped) is something like the difference between a bumper redirecting the course of a pool ball and a chemical reagent changing the properties of another chemical. In an organic chemical reaction the properties of the chemical itself, along with other environmental conditions

---

4. Michael Werner, and Bénédicte Zimmerman, "Beyond Comparison: *Histoire Croisée* and the Challenge of Reflexivity." *History and Theory* 45, no. 1 (February 2006): 38.

5. Markovits, Claude, Jacques Pouchepadass, and Sanjay Subrahmanyam, *Society and Circulation: Mobile People and Itinerant Cultures in South Asia, 1750–1950* (Delhi Bangalore: Permanent Black, 2003); Prasenjit Duara, *The Crisis of Global Modernity: Asian Traditions and a Sustainable Future* (Cambridge: Cambridge University Press, 2015), 53–90.

6. Werner and Zimmerman, "Beyond Comparison," 38.

(heat, pressure, etc.) will have specific consequences for the changes that take place in the substrate.[7]

As I have shown in the preceding discussions, even the model of the chemical reaction described by Hatcher falls short of capturing the complexity of Japanese Buddhist exchanges with their South Asian hosts. Rather than having a situation in which two relatively stable reagents are interacting, we have multiple reagents, each of which already is in the process of change when they meet. Hikkaduvē Sumaṅgala, for example, was engaged with British colonial authorities in Ceylon, American Buddhist converts like Olcott, and disputes within the Ceylonese Sangha, even as he taught Kōzen and other Japanese Buddhists arriving in Ceylon at the end of the nineteenth century. The Japanese departed their country as Buddhism was undergoing fundamental changes in the wake of the Meiji Restoration. Complicating the situation even further were the ongoing interventions in their relationships from many additional parties—for example, Shaku Unshō, Dogi Hōryū, Inagaki Manjirō, E. R. Gooneratne, and European scholars of Buddhism. Each of the actors emerged from this web of exchanges transformed in distinctive ways that shaped twentieth-century Buddhism across Asia. In this book I primarily have focused on the Japanese side of these interactions. Given the high profile of many of the Japanese residents in South and Southeast Asia, I would be surprised if various traces of their time in the region did not remain. Unfortunately, time and circumstances have not allowed me to search the archives in India, Sri Lanka, Myanmar, and Thailand. To understand the Indian, Ceylonese, and Siamese sides of the exchanges I have documented in this book, however, will require more research in the future by those with the linguistic abilities—Sanskrit, Pali, Sinhala, Bengali, Hindi, and Thai—plus the archival access required to do scholarly research in those countries.

Over the fifty years since Kitabatake arrived at Bodh Gayā, Japan's geopolitical circumstances changed radically. No longer subjected to unequal treaties and lagging militarily or industrially, Japan had become a colonial power with growing aspirations for Asian hegemony that was at times cloaked in the rhetoric of ending European colonial domination and forging a united, prosperous Asia. Japanese Buddhists helped create a greater understanding of South and Southeast Asia in Japan and promoted a vision of a region bound by a Buddhist-influenced past and a renewed Buddhist future. The British and Indians who had encountered the Japanese Buddhists crisscrossing Asia had long suspected that they traveled not only at the behest of their religious de-

7. Hatcher, "Pandits at Work," 46–47.

nominations but also in service to the Japanese state. At the official level as well, it was always murky whether such ministers as Inagaki Manjirō and Hayashi Tadasu supported Japanese Buddhist exchanges in India and Siam in order to further Japanese geopolitical strategy or to promote their Buddhist faith.

In the period between the end of the First World War and the start of the Fifteen Years' War, officials in the Japanese government turned to Japanese Buddhists with long-term experience in India, Ceylon, Burma, Siam, and elsewhere in South-Southeast Asia for their expertise. Many patriotic Japanese Buddhists, wanting to enhance their individual and denominational reputations, eagerly embraced the opportunity to work closely with the government to further Japanese strategic goals in Asia. Seeking to take advantage of Japan's rising industrial, military, and cultural might, Indians, Burmese, Siamese, and others reciprocated by hosting Japanese Buddhists in their own countries and visiting the nodes of pan-Asian cooperation that had been established in Japan.

As Japanese Buddhists returned from extended periods in India, Ceylon, Siam, Tibet, and elsewhere, they found linguistic and cultural facilities in demand beyond religious and academic settings. Along with command of one or more Indic languages, many of these Buddhists also became at least functionally fluent in English or another European language as well. In the course of the book, I have noted how the skills acquired by such overseas students as Nanjō Bun'yū, Takakusu Junjirō, Shaku Kōzen, Shaku Sōen, and Kimura Nichiki, as well as many others, made them frequent participants in gatherings with Buddhists from South and Southeast Asia in Japan and abroad. Some of them served as hosts and interpreters for Olcott, Dharmapāla, Tagore, and other dignitaries from South and Southeast Asia. Again, as I have shown above, those Buddhists with Indic- and English-language skills were called upon to serve as part of official or semi-official delegations, although in those instances preference seems to have gone to those who trained in Europe, not South Asia, at least during the mid- to late Meiji years, when only a handful of Japanese Buddhists had the requisite experience. For example, when the relics of Śākyamuni were gifted to Japan by the Siamese court, Nanjō was among those dispatched as part of the Japanese Buddhist delegation and, later, he served as incumbent at Nisshenji, where the relics were enshrined. Along with Takakusu and Fujishima Ryōon (1852–1918), who had studied in France with Sylvain Lévi, Nanjō also served as a representative of Japanese Buddhists at the first World Congress of Orientalists that was convened in 1902 in Hanoi as part of the Premier Congrès International des Etudes D'extrême Orient.[8]

8. MNB 1: 252. Brian Bocking, "Flagging up Buddhism: Charles Pfoundes (Omoie Tetzu-nostzuke) among the International Congresses and Expositions, 1893–1905," in *A Buddhist*

When clerics with long-term experience in South Asia returned to Japan in the first third of the twentieth century, they, too, were in demand to serve in official or semi-official capacity. Teramoto Enga, the Higashi-Honganji Jōdo Shin cleric who spent a total of seven years in Tibet, served in Manchuria at the behest of the Manchurian government, and Aoki Bunkyō, who spent fourteen years in Tibet, was commissioned by the Japanese Ministry of Foreign Affairs (Gaimushō) to conduct a survey in Tibet in 1941.[9]

In the early 1930s, as tensions with the United States and European nations grew following the Manchurian Incident and Japan's withdrawal from the League of Nations, the Japanese looked to other Asians for support. Siam, the only power in the League to abstain from condemning Japan, seized upon the opportunity to strengthen diplomatic, military, and economic ties between the two countries. In 1934, the Japanese sent military and trade missions to Siam.[10] The Siamese reciprocated by sending their own trade delegation to Japan. In Nagoya, where the Siamese would establish a consulate in 1935, the mayor, Ōiwa Isao (1867–1955), greeted the Siamese legation with a speech that stressed their common Buddhist ties. Ōiwa highlighted Nagoya's robust economy and pointed to growing commercial ties between Nagoya and Siam. In that context he stressed the importance of the Siamese and Japanese people's shared Buddhist heritage as symbolized by the relics enshrined at Nissenji in Kakuōzan, Nagoya.

> The total amount of the annual industry in this city and all the other towns and villages in Aichi Prefecture [is] over ¥801,000,000, of which the cotton and woolen textile industry as well as the manufacture of the earthenware, and porcelain enamelling, may be specially mentioned, as they reach the highest level accessible to those industries in our country. Accordingly, we feel honoured to accept more and more orders of various goods from your country, the yearly sum of the export and import trade between Siam and Nagoya having amounted in 1933 to nearly ¥3,000,000, which corresponds to 1.6% of the total sum of the foreign trade of this city. Furthermore, of late at the International Conference held at Geneva the year before last, that great goodwill which you had exhibited towards our isolated country could not but excite our people with boundless joy, so that the repeated reminiscences of the history, ancient and modern, are quite enough to engrave on our memory the long and close relationship between the two countries.

Crossroads: Pioneer Western Buddhists and Asian Networks 1860–1960, ed. Brian Bocking, Phibul Choompolpaisal, Laurence Cox, and Alicia Marie Turner (London: Routledge, 2015), 25.

9. NBJ 1; 548.

10. Stefan Matthias Hell, "Siam and the League of Nations: Modernization, Sovereignty, and Multilateral Diplomacy, 1920–1940," (PhD diss., Leiden University, 2007), 241.

Above all it is the greatest glory of our citizens that we have the Nissenji Temple at Kakwozan in the north-eastern part of the city, which is famous for that part of the sacred ashes of Buddha, presented several years ago from your country, and to see many devout followers of Buddhism visiting the temple every day reminds us of the mystic brotherliness of the two nations worshipping as one. We hope you may all understand that great joy and sense of gratitude with which we all meet you here at this sacred city, where the Soul of Buddha reposes.[11]

In 1937, on the cusp of the outbreak of unbridled war with China, Ōiwa oversaw the aspirationally titled Nagoya Pan-Pacific Peace Exposition (Nagoya Han Taiheiyō Heiwa Hakurankai), at which the Siamese sponsored an exhibition hall. Further stressing Asia's pan-Asian Buddhist unity, the organizers housed an off-site Buddhism exposition at Kakuōzan. With an eye toward Buddhism's origins in India, at the entrance the organizers erected a replica of one of the gates of the Sāñcī stupa and in the "Śākyamuni Hall" created a mock-up of the Mahābodhi Temple.[12]

Japanese government officials traveling in Asia for special events also sought to bolster ties with other Asians by stressing their shared Buddhist past, echoing the strategy employed by their predecessors, Inagaki Manjirō, Hayashi Tadasu, and others. One such example is the appearance of the Japanese consul general (sōryōji) to India, Yonezawa Kikuji (1894–1983), at the foundation stone-laying ceremony for the Buddha Vihāra temple in New Delhi on October 31, 1936. Occurring toward the end of Yonezawa's four-year tenure as consul general in India, the event was important enough to prompt him to make the trip from Calcutta to New Delhi to deliver his address. The main Indian donor for the temple's construction was Seth Jugal Kishore Birla (1883–1967), who had made a fortune trading cotton and opium, as well as importing Japanese cotton cloth. In his superb PhD dissertation, Douglas Ober speculates that Jugal Kishore Birla, who, like others in his family was a devout Hindu, may have been initially stimulated to provide strong support for the Buddhist revival because of his business ventures with Japanese merchants.[13] Birla, who moved from Calcutta to New Delhi, provided the funds for the Buddha Vihāra, which was designed by Sri Chandra Chatterjee. At the

---

11. "Address of Welcome to the Part of Official Visitors from Siam to Nippon." Presented June 28, 1934, by the Mayor of the City of Nagoya, J. Ōiwa Isao. Gaikō Shiryōkan Document I-2-1-0-4, Bukkyō kankei taikai zakken. Original in English and Japanese.

12. Katō, Hohoemi no hakutō, 162–63.

13. Ober, "Reinventing Buddhism," 210–14, especially note 52. Ober details the complex strategizing that lay beneath the sponsorship of Buddhist institutions by devoutly militant Hindus like the Birlas.

foundation stone-laying ceremony, Yonezawa delivered a dedication speech that pulled together many of the threads running through the story of Japan's "Western" turn. Here again, we see the linking of Asian economic networks with Buddhism. At the ceremony, Yonezawa was welcomed by members of the All India Mahāsabhā, the conservative Hindu organization in which Jugath Kishore Birla was actively involved. In the welcoming address given to Yonezawa, a representative of the Mahāsabhā stressed the underlying unity of all followers of the "Great Arya Dharma," which included Hindus, "Santanists, Sikhs, Jains, Buddhists, and Ary Samajists." Noting that Yonezawa was "a devoted follower" of the "Bauddha Dharma," the speaker, summarizing the importance of Buddhist teachings for followers of the Arya Dharma, continued, stating that

> it is needless to say that the Bauddha Dharma of which you are a devoted follower, is a branch of the Great Arya Dharma; and considered, even from the point of view of population, it is the most important; for in Asiatic countries such as Japan, China, Tibet, Siam, Burma, Ceylon, etc, [sic] Buddhists number 450 millions. It is really a matter of great pride for all of us who are the followers of Arya Dharma to see that among Buddhist countries, nay, of all countries in Asia, Japan stands foremost and is the Rising Sun of the East.[14]

The speaker, after summarizing basic Buddhist doctrine, including the Four Truths of the Noble Ones, then extended the wish that the Dharma would unite all Asians, and he hoped, "that you will be pleased to convey our feelings of brotherliness to our Buddhist brethren of Japan. It is needless to add that good feelings amongst 700 million Arya Dharmists, called Hindus and Buddhists, can, to a great extent, bring about peace and happiness of the whole world."[15]

Yonezawa, in his remarks at the dedication for the laying of the foundation stone, responded with words that were equally idealistic, stressing the shared religious heritage of all Asians. Echoing his host's remarks about their shared Buddhist legacy, he extended greetings to his Indian audience from "41 million Japanese Buddhists, who are thankful to you for your giving them their religion, their philosophy, and their Buddha," and who, according to Yonezawa, were grateful to see the construction of a new Vihāra in New Delhi.

---

14. The welcome to Yonezawa is included in "Speech Delivered by Mr. K. Yonezawa, Consul-General for Japan at the Ceremony of Laying the Foundation-Stone of a Buddhist Temple in New Delhi," Gaikō Shiryōkan Document I–2–2–0–1: "Gaikoku shinshi oyobi jiin kankei zakken," 140–36 (reverse-paginated).

15. "Welcome to Yonezawa."

With the Japanese already embroiled in the Fifteen Years' War (1931–45), Yonezawa stressed how Buddhism had shaped Asia, while issuing the hope— soon to be dashed completely—for peace, unity, and prosperity. In the final portion of his speech he states,

> In the last 14 centuries since Buddhism was first introduced into Japan the influence which this religion exercised over our culture and people has been universal and great. Buddhism with its broad philanthropy has had an evangelical influence on our people and gave rise to a spirit of mutual help among its adherents. Its philosophical literature stimulated the thought and imagination of our people, while its fine arts have left many masterpieces enriching the cultural life of our people. Its fatalism cultivated a habit of dauntless composure among the Samurai class and a habit of non-chalance among our common people against such mishaps as death, and loss of property caused by floods, earthquakes, typhoons, etc. In fact Buddhism has been the most powerful foreign influence that has become part and parcel of Japanese life. Buddhism with its roughly 71 thousand temples and 41 million adherents is the most powerful among religions in Japan.
>
> Buddhism is essentially an Asiatic religion. It originally started in India and propagated itself throughout Asia and is largely responsible for the moulding of culture and outlook on life of the Asiatic people. Some people say that fatalistic teaching of Buddha has had a retarding effect on the material progress of Asiatic people, who professed Buddhism. But in view of the present unsettling conditions of the world where the so-called civilized peoples are feverishly arming themselves to destroy one another, I cannot but feel that Buddhism, with its emphasis upon spiritualism and protest against selfish materialism which is one of the main causes of strife and war, has a great mission to perform not only in Asia but also in the whole world. Present day world [*sic*] is entangled in a cobweb of bewilderment and so it need [*sic*] most careful nursing. Let the Law of Piety, the very essence of Buddhism, once more govern mankind for eradicating the evils that corrode humanity.
>
> It is, therefore, highly gratifying that we are now going to witness the foundation stone being laid for a Buddhist temple as a mighty signal for the revival of the religion in its mother country.
>
> May this glorious temple in the capital of India become the birthplace of highest toleration for other religions and real contentment for which Lord Buddha worked so incessantly during his lifetime. May this important Buddhist edifice, the construction of which is going to begin shortly, prove to be the fountainhead of the best of all ideas for which Buddhism stands.
>
> Let me sincerely hope that this temple will revive the teaching of Lord Buddha in the country of its birth and this institution will create genuine and sincere love for all humanity in the people of India.
>
> Let me for a moment invoke my inner soul for heavenly lead [*sic*] and help

and let you bestow your soul force on me so that I may gather a combined strength to make the foundation stone a formidable one that can withstand the cold hands of Time.

So armed I will proceed to lay the foundation stone of the new Vihara in the heart of this historic metropolis of the land of Lord Buddha.

Before I conclude, I wish to offer my heartfelt thanks to Seth Jugal Kishore Birla for his unparalleled munificence for the cause of religion and for his untiring efforts to bring about perfect understanding among the followers of Arya Dharma living in various parts of Asia.[16]

It is tempting to interpret these 1930s efforts at Buddhist pan-Asian outreach as rather transparent pretexts for Japan's eventual aggressive incursions into Asia that followed the Marco Polo Bridge Incident of 1937 and the attack on Malaya in 1941.[17] However, taking a hint from Dickinson's warnings against reading this history in overly teleological manner, I believe they may be the last vestiges of the internationalism that characterized Japan's foreign diplomacy in the Taishō and early Shōwa years.[18] As Dickinson suggests, we get a more accurate contemporaneous picture of events by looking forward from World War I, as Ōiwa and Yonezawa, without our hindsight, would have done. This perspective enables us to give due weight to the massive changes in Japanese society in the 1920s. These include the Japanese embrace of multilateralism, party politics, a culture of peace, and a new role "as a world power, with political and economic interests reaching far beyond Asia, across both the Pacific and Indian Oceans."[19] Although Japan did not give up on the idea of empire, Dickinson remarks, "the leap from an Asian empire to world power reflected the evolution from nineteenth-century regionalism to twentieth-century global integration."[20] During the period covered in this study, Japan was transformed from a regional agricultural economy to an industrial one. Japanese Meiji-era aspirations to be "a European-style empire on the edge of Asia" was displaced by a vision of a nation whose reach extended into the Pacific region and, further, globally. Only after a series of assassination attempts and failed coups did the Japanese fully succumb to the authoritarianism and aggressive continental expansionism we associate with Japan in the latter half

16. "Speech Delivered by Mr. K. Yonezawa, Consul-General for Japan at the Ceremony of Laying the Foundation-Stone of a Buddhist Temple in New Delhi."

17. On the debate over terminology for Japan's wartime years that ended with surrender in 1945, including the "Fifteen Years' War," see Hotta, *Pan-Asianism and Japan's War*, 2–6.

18. Dickinson, *World War I and the Triumph of a New Japan*, especially chapters 6 , "World Power," and 7, "Culture of Peace."

19. Dickinson, *World War I and the Triumph of a New Japan*, 194.

20. Dickinson, *World War I and the Triumph of a New Japan*, 191–96.

of the Fifteen Years' War era.[21] Looking forward from the 1920s, which in Japan was a period of internationalism, representative government, and "peace culture," perhaps the optimistic statements made by Ōiwa in Nagoya and Yonezawa in New Delhi are better understood as the last gasps of that earlier, more hopeful era than disingenuous attempts to camouflage the aggressions in Asia soon to come.[22] It did not take much, however, for the more irenic attitudes to be put into the service of Japanese imperialism.

One can see a shift in attitude in Yonezawa's advocacy concerning the importance of India during the height of the Fifteen Years' War, when Yonezawa, then serving as the resident diplomatic minister in Portugal, delivered a speech on March 24, 1942, in Tokyo at the Army Hall (Gunjin Kaikan). In that address, Yonezawa continued to stress, as he had in Delhi eight years earlier, India's importance to Japan. With Japan now fully enmeshed in war with the Allied powers, however, Yonezawa no longer expressed his hopes for peace, as he had in New Delhi. Instead, Yonezawa emphasized India's twofold strategic importance for the Greater Asia Co-Prosperity Sphere (Dai Tōa Kyōei Ken). By fomenting anticolonial rebellion in India, the Japanese would weaken the British. In addition, incorporating India into the Co-Prosperity Sphere would make India's indispensable resources, particularly cotton and jute, available for the war effort.[23]

Kimura Nichiki's career following his return to Japan in 1929 is a prime example of the ways that some Buddhists who trained for long periods in India and elsewhere in South-Southeast Asia became involved in quasi-governmental and governmental work. Kimura served actively with the Kokusai Bukkyō Kyōkai (International Buddhist Society) from the time of its formation. Although not directly associated with the Japanese government, the society increasingly worked to collect statistical and cultural information about Buddhist communities across South and Southeast Asia, while also striving to strengthen a sense of comity among Buddhists across Asia. The target audience and subject of the society ostensibly was Buddhists throughout Asia—the principles of the society mention the Tōa Bukkyō Ken, that is, the East Asian Buddhist Sphere. In its international outreach activities and its Japanese-language journal, however, the members were far more concerned with South and Southeast Asia. During the time of its publication, special

21. Dickinson, *World War I and the Triumph of a New Japan*, 136, 143, 190.

22. On the peace culture of the 1920s in Japan, see Dickinson, *World War I and the Triumph of a New Japan*, 144–66.

23. Yonezawa Kikuji, *Dai Tōa sensō to Indo no chii* (Tokyo: Kokubō Keizai Kyōkai, 1942).

issues of the journal *Kaigai Bukkyō jijō* from 1940 to 1942 were devoted to Buddhism in Burma, Thailand, French Indochina, the South Seas, Tibet, and Ceylon.[24] Kimura became the third permanent representative trustee of the group in 1935 and he was on the editorial board of one of its English publications, *Studies on Buddhism in Japan*, which was published from 1939 to 1942. He also became one of the editors of the *Young East* when that journal's management was taken over by the society. The society's leadership rolls reveal a number of figures that have been discussed in this work serving as board members or in other official capacities. The officer list for 1934, the founding year of the society, includes, in addition to Kimura Nichiki, Takakusu Junjirō, Kawaguchi Ekai, Tachibana Shundō, Ogiwara Unrai, and Nagai Makoto, among those with South-Southeast Asian Buddhist expertise. The roster also bears some other important and familiar names, for example, Rash Behari Bose, Beatrice Suzuki, and D. T. Suzuki, all of whom, perhaps, contributed more to the English-language outreach operations.[25]

Throughout the Fifteen Years' War era, Buddhists used their linguistic skills and pan-Asian Buddhist ties to strengthening alliances with other Asian nations and anti-European independence movements, while also gathering intelligence for the military. Like many other Buddhists with South Asian experience, as the Fifteen Years' War exploded into a confrontation with the Allied powers across the Pacific region, Kimura became even more deeply involved in the military effort. In his memorial reflections for Rash Behari Bose, Kimura makes clear his support for the Japanese war effort in Asia, as well as for Indian independence from the British. Writing without any signs of remorse for the war, Kimura recalls,

> *1941.* Since the outbreak of the 1st Pacific War, the Japanese army advanced to Singapore and Malaya with irresistible force. At that time His Excellency Hideki Tojo was the Prime Minister and Secretary of War. He had an intention to lead India and all countries in South-East Asia to bring about revolutions to realize independence, and assist them to organize and co-operate amongst themselves.
>
> He appointed me to act as an adviser to the Japanese Army General Staff Office, and requested me to render every assistance to realize Indian Independence. In order to do it, the General Staff Office desired to call out all Indians outside India but residing in Asian countries to form a Volunteer Corps by Indian war prisoners in South-East Asia; and to co-operate with the Japanese army.

24. Ōsawa, *Senjika no Nihon Bukkyō to Nanpō chiiki*, 60–80.
25. Ōsawa, *Senjika no Nihon Bukkyō to Nanpō chiiki*, 64.

In view of the above, I was requested by the General Staff Office to recommend a suitable person to be the leader of such Volunteer Corps, for instance, Mr. Subhas Chandra Bose who was at that time a refugee in Germany. . . .

. . . However, I had another plan and proposed that for the time being, it would be better to appoint Mr. Rashbehari Bose as the leader of the Volunteer Corps, who was at that time a refugee in Tokyo, living here for many years. I opined that Mr. Subhas Bose might probably be called on later on, but for a while it would be the best to appoint Mr. Rash Beharibose as their leader. The General Staff Office took my advice and decided to implement it; and requested me to negotiate this matter with Mr. Rashbehari Bose as soon as possible.[26]

In 1942, Rash Behari Bose traveled to Singapore to recruit members from the interned Indian war prisoners for the India Volunteer Army. When Rash Behari's health deteriorated, however, the Japanese military's General Staff decided to recruit Subhas Chandra Bose to take his place. Following Subhas's arrival in Japan, Kimura accompanied Rash Behari to discussions with Subhas about leading the Volunteer Army, which Subhas agreed to do. Kimura recalls that under Subhas's leadership,

the dignified Volunteer Corps advanced up to Imphal under the gallant formation of [sic] Combat Unit. This military operation to Imphal ended in failure. Japan was defeated by atomic bombs dropped by the U.S. Army.

It is to be greatly regretted that Mr. Subhas Chandra Bose died in the aeroplane accident while Mr. Rashbehari Bose died of disease. However, the brilliant and distinguished services rendered by Mr. Rashbehari Bose to his mother country will remain for ever in the histories of Japan and India.[27]

By 1940, the British, French, and Dutch were preoccupied with the war against the Axis powers in Europe. The rhetoric of Japanese pan-Asianists like Ōkawa Shūmei also became bolder, while Japanese expansionists saw Southeast Asian colonies and Thailand (Siam took that name in 1939), as either potential conquests or allies. In addition, British intelligence officials, who for decades had been cautious about Japanese spying in the colonies, grew ever more suspicious of Japanese activities.[28] By the time the Japanese conquered Singapore in early 1942, Ceylon was now in the official war zone and even *bhikkhu* like the German-born Nyanatiloka were interned for the duration of the war in India at Dehra Dun prison camp.[29] Travel to South

---

26. Kimura, "My Memory about the Late Rash Behari Bose," 41–42.
27. Kimura, "My Memory about the Late Rash Behari Bose," 43–44.
28. Best, *British Intelligence and the Japanese Challenge in Asia*, 160–61.
29. Hecker and Nyanatusita, *The Life of Ñāṇatiloka Thera*, 128–29.

Asia thus became off limits, although as parts of Southeast Asia either allied with the Japanese or fell under their control, Japanese Buddhists once again journeyed to those regions, dispatched by the government or military to aid with the war effort.

On the home front as well, the cultural and linguistic fluency acquired by Japanese Buddhists in South and Southeast Asia was employed in an effort to win the cooperation of the Buddhists living throughout the Co-Prosperity Sphere. In 1941, members of the International Buddhist Society, many of whom, like Kimura Nichiki, had command of vernacular and classical Indic languages or had worked with anti-British independence movements, founded the Pali Culture Academy (Pari Bunka Gakuin) to prepare younger clerics for missions in Buddhist Southeast Asia.[30] The following year, on January 31, 1942, society members created the subsidiary organization Nanpō Bukkyō Gakkai (Society for Studying Southern Buddhism) in Tokyo to help further the establishment of the Greater East Asia Co-Prosperity Sphere. The goals of the Society for Studying Southern Buddhism included studying Pali, Sanskrit, and "spoken languages in southern Buddhist countries"; dispatching Japanese to those areas; and establishing research centers in those regions.[31] In August 1942 the Society for Studying Southern Buddhism also convened the twenty-six-day-long "Summer School for introducing the Present Situation of Buddhism in Southern Countries." Courses included Kimura Nichiki teaching "Buddhism in India"; Higashimoto Tarō, Pali; and Rastrapala Sandilyāyana lecturing about a pilgrimage to Tibet and Hindustani.[32]

Rastrapala Sandilyāyana produced at least two publications while in Japan.[33] His 1940 pamphlet, *A Short History of Early Japanese Buddhism*, published by the International Buddhist Society reveals the manner in which Japanese Buddhism was portrayed to the society's English-speaking audience. In the pamphlet the author continues the defense of Japanese Mahayana Buddhism begun in English by Yamakami and Kimura in India. In the midst of the Fifteen Years' War, however, Sandilyāyana is even more emphatic about the unique role that Japanese Buddhism played in the history of Asian civilizations. Like his mentor, Kimura, Sandilyāyana highlighted how the active nature of Japanese Mahayana Buddhism made it uniquely suitable

30. Ōsawa Kōji, "Pari Bunka Gakuin no taigai katsudō: senjiki ni okeru shūkyō senbu kōsaku no ichirei to shite," *Kindai Bukkyō* 14 (2007): 51–81.

31. SBJ 4 (1942): 156.

32. SBJ 4 (1942): 157.

33. Rastrapala Sandilyāyana, "Buddhism and Its Influence on Japanese Culture," *Young East* 8, no. 2 (1939): 22–29; *A Short History of Japanese Buddhism* (Tokyo: International Buddhist Society, 1940).

to the modern world: "The Japanese accepted Mahayana, or Greater-Vehicle Buddhism, rejecting the so-called pessimism of the Hinayana or Lesser-Vehicle Buddhism, which has been chiefly studied by Western scholars who have neglected to investigate the creative power of Japanese Mahayana principles."

According to Sandilyāyana, Japanese Buddhists discarded both the overwhelming emphasis on "spirituality" that one sees in India and the Chinese Buddhist penchant to get entrapped in argument for its own sake. In Japanese Buddhism, these impractical attitudes were replaced by a "utilitarianism" that "has adjusted itself to the spirit of materialistic activity." Sandilyāyana contrasts the Japanese Buddhist penchant for activity and individual judgment that rather than culminating in extreme individualism gave rise to "a freedom to consider the good of the group in light of their ever-revealing creative activity," which was a capacity that was "the natural, spontaneous attitude of the Japanese mind."[34] At first glance, it seems somewhat odd that an expatriate Indian *bhikkhu* in Japan, rather than Takakusu, Kimura, or another Japanese specialist, was selected by the society's members to write several basic, cursory texts on early Japanese Buddhism for the series of pamphlets. The selection of Sandilyāyana, however, helped make the society's presentation of Japanese Buddhism more pan-Asian, perhaps allowing it to appeal to a wider audience, especially in India. In Sandilyāyana's brief history, we see how the Japanese Buddhist view of Mahayana promulgated by lecturers like Kimura and Yamakami in India came to be disseminated by an Indian overseas student in Japan for Anglophone Asian consumption as the Japanese tried to forge an anti-Allies alliance across Asia.

In the final throes of the Fifteen Years' War, even the legacy of Shaku Kōzen's efforts to spread Ceylonese Buddhist practices in Japan, with the help of members of the International Buddhist Society, was turned toward the war effort. During the war years, beginning in 1941, members of the Association for Overseas Buddhism adapted Shaku Kōzen's practice of celebrating Wesak, renaming his Beishakyagatsu Mangatsu Kai the "Southern Buddha Festival" (Nanpō Budda Matsuri). As reported by Higashimoto Keikichi based on Shaku Nindo's account, the first Nanpō Budda Matsuri took place on July 5, 1941, in Hibiya Park. Although it was expected that Sōbita Shaku Nindo would serve as the chief officiant, he precipitously was replaced by the visiting Bengali Buddhist novice, and Society for Studying Southern Buddhism member, Rastrapala Sandilyāyana. Higashimoto reports that although disappointed, Shaku Nindo assented to the decision to have Sandilyāyana lead the

34. Sandilyāyana, *A Short History of Early Buddhism*, 2–4.

ceremony.[35] The ceremony was broadcast live on radio and a newsreel film of the ceremony for distribution to Southern Buddhist countries was produced. The Nanpō Budda Matsuri was conducted throughout the war. Ōsawa Kōji reports that at the fourth occasion, a lecture was given by the staunch proponent of pan-Asianism Ōkawa Shūmei, with such Buddhist luminaries as Nagai Makoto and Ui Hakuju in attendance.[36] By the time of the fifth gathering for Wesak, Hibiya Park could no longer be used because of Allied bombing of Tokyo, which on the day of the ceremony, May 26, 1945, destroyed the Tokyo headquarters of the Association for Overseas Buddhism. Instead, the ceremony was conducted at Nindo's temple, Sanneji, in Yokohama. At this last wartime iteration of Wesak in Japan, Shaku Nindo served as the chief officiant and Kimura Nichiki gave the welcoming remarks. The printed program for the ceremony stressed the importance of the ceremony for the members of the Co-Prosperity Sphere.

For those of us who aim to build the Greater East Asia Co-Prosperity Sphere, spiritual unity with the various peoples of South-Southeast Asia is a vital foundational task. We think that the reality for the many Buddhists who reside among the peoples of the Co-Prosperity Sphere is that they are awaiting a Buddhism that can successfully fulfill this role.

However, within Buddhism there are the Southern and Northern streams. The Buddhists of the Northern stream, which includes Japan, and the Southern Buddhists of Ceylon, Burma, Thailand, Cambodia, and Laos, although both revering Śākyamuni as founding teacher, have considerable differences. Without deep mutual understanding, true cooperation cannot be achieved. At present, we cannot neglect a single day in our endeavor to understand Southern Buddhism.

The Nanpō Budda Matsuri, which Southern Buddhists call Vesākha Pūjā, is the great festival in which Buddha's birth, awakening, and *parinirvāṇa* are celebrated together. We conducted the first festival in 1941, until this year, with the Fifth Nanpō Budda Matsuri being celebrated at the same time as by Southern Buddhists on the day of the full moon residing in the Vesākha constellation.

... Together with the Southern Buddhists who believe that the three auspicious events delimiting the Buddha's life—his birth at Lumbinī, awakening beneath the Bodhi tree, and nirvana amidst the śāla trees—occurred on the same month and day, we praise the virtue of the Great Sage and World-Honored One and hope to forge unbreakable bonds binding our spirits together.[37]

35. Higashimoto, "Shaku Nindo Wajō no omoide," 243–44.

36. Ōsawa, *Senjika no Nihon Bukkyō*, 83–86.

37. Kokusai Bukkyō Kyōkai, *Dai Go Kai Nanpō Budda Matsuri* (Tokyo: Kokusai Bukkyō Kyōkai, 1945).

The celebration of Wesak at Sanneji and its dissemination via radio across Japan and by newsreel to South and Southeast Asia was but one more novel way Japanese Buddhists deployed the understanding of Buddhism in South and Southeast Asia they had accrued through pilgrimage, overseas study, and appropriation in the more than sixty years since Kitabatake first set foot at Bodh Gayā. During those six decades, coming to terms with "Southern Buddhism" had been a crucial component for forging the new Japanese Buddhism that was appropriate for the twentieth century.

Although more aggressive outreach as symbolized by the transformation of the Wesak ceremony at Sanneji may have disrupted the spirit of internationalism that preceded the descent into what the Japanese have called the "dark valley" (*kurai tanima*) of the Fifteen Years' War period, the foundations of exchange that were laid by Japanese, South Asians, and Southeast Asians were not destroyed by Japan's defeat in 1945.[38] In the postwar years, as Japan recovered economically and politically, Japanese renewed the prewar networks of exchange with South and Southeast Asia. In 1958, Kimura Nichiki, who served as an important intermediary for such prewar visitors as Tagore and Rash Behari Bose, became the first president of the newly formed Japan Vedanta Society, whose members noted Kimura's long residency in India and fluency in Bengali.[39] Japanese Buddhist groups also established a series of temples, which often doubled as guest houses for pilgrims, across South Asia. Following the celebration of the 2,500th Jayanthi celebration of Wesak in South Asia, in 1963 Japanese representatives from various denominations formed the Kokusai Bukkyō Kōryū Kyōkai (International Buddhist Brotherhood Association) to oversee the construction of a nonsectarian temple, Indosan Nihonji at Bodh Gayā, which was completed in 1970. The temple houses a kindergarten and a health clinic and sponsors conferences concerning pan-Asian Buddhist exchange, holding, for example, "Buddhism and Buddhist[s] of East and Southeast Asia under Colonialism" in 2012.[40] Other organizations, for example, the Nichiren temple, Tashōzan Isshinji, and the Nishi Honganji have constructed temple guesthouse complexes in Bodh Gayā and Kathmandu (2006), respectively.[41] With the economic boom

38. For an analysis of how the changes in Japan during the Fifteen Years' War served as the foundations for the post-war recovery see, John W. Dower, "The Useful War," *Daedelus* 119, no. 3 (1990): 49–70.

39. Vedanta Society of Japan, "History of the Vedanta Society of Japan." https://www .vedantajp-en.com/society-s-history/.

40. Kokusai Bukkyō Kōryū Kyōkai, "About Us," http://www.ibba.jp/協会について/about-us.

41. Tashōzan Isshinji, "Indo bun'in ni tsuite." http://tashozan-isshinji.org/indiabunin.html; Katomanzu Honganji, "Katomanzu Honganji," http://www.kathmanduhongwanji.org.

that made Japan one of the largest economies in the world, overseas travel also grew. A panoply of organizations, including Buddhist sectarian universities and large temples, now sponsor one to two-week pilgrimages to Buddhist sites in Nepal and India that are reminiscent of, but not as ambitious as, the NYK journey undertaken by Akegarasu, Izawa, and company.[42] As China's might grows globally, the governments of India and Japan have moved to strengthen bilateral ties as a counterweight to Chinese influence. In recent years, the countries have sponsored a series of conferences that commemorate and investigate the sorts of Indo-Japan cooperation and exchange that I have described in this book. Most recently, the conference "Buddhism in Indo-Japanese Relations" was held in March 2017 and another call for papers for "Rethinking Cultural Heritage: Indo-Japanese Dialog in a Globalising World," a conference organized by Himashu Prabha Ray, to be held at the India International Centre in New Delhi, has been issued.[43] Far from bringing Buddhist exchanges between the Japanese and South Asians to an end, the Fifteen Years' War and its aftermath were no more than a temporary interruption in the patterns of exchange described in this book.

In *Seeking Śākyamuni*, I have demonstrated how South Asia became an important nexus for the formation of modern Japanese Buddhist practice and scholarship. Numerous factors made this imperative. In that sense the "Western turn" to South Asia was overdetermined. From the rise of cotton manufacturing in Japan to the emphasis on religious origins in orientalist scholarship, Japanese Buddhists who had long looked to India—imagined or otherwise—as a source of renewal were given further impetus to engage with South Asian Buddhism. In the process, Japanese Buddhism was globalized, not just by engagement with what we have come to call the "West," but with Buddhists across what the Japanese called the "Southern regions."

42. See, for example, Chūō Bukkyō Gakuin, "Busseki junpai ryokō," Chūō Bukkyō Gakuin, http://www.chubutsu.jp/student/travelling.html; Tsukiji Honganji, "Katomanzu Honganji to Nepāru/Indo Busseki junpai: Shakuson shichidai seichi no tabi," Tsukiji Honganji, http://tsukijihongwanji.jp/news/「カトマンズ本願寺とネパール・インド仏跡巡拝; Bīesu Kankō Tōkyō, "Komazawa Daigaku Meiyo Kyōju Minagawa Hiroyoshi Sensei to iku, Dai 27 Kai Indo Busseki junrei no tabi—Shakuson shichidai seichi o tazunete—kokonokakan," Bīesu Kankō Tōkyō, http://tokyo.bs-group.jp/駒澤大学名誉教授%E3%80%80皆川廣義先生といく、第２７回イ/.

43. See, for example, H-Net, "Buddhism in Indo-Japanese Relations," accessed March 20, 2018. https://networks.h-net.org/node/73374/announcements/153398/international-buddhist-conference-buddhism-indo-japanese.

Glossary

Aikawa Tenshin 合川天心
Aikawa Yasumichi 合川泰通
Aizen'in 愛染院
ajari 阿闍梨
Ajia 亜細亜/アジア
Ajia shugi アジア主義
Ajiashugi yōshiki アジア主義様式
Akamatsu Renjō 赤松連城
Akanuma Chizen 赤沼智善
Akasaka Rikyū 赤坂離宮
Akegarasu Haya 暁烏敏
akugōdō 悪業道
Alishan 阿里山
Amanuma Shun'ichi 天沼俊一
Amida shōju raigō zu 阿弥陀聖衆来迎図
Amidakyō 阿弥陀経
Amituo jing 阿弥陀経
Ānanda Yoshimatsu Kaiyū アーナンダ吉松快祐
Andō Sonjin 安藤尊仁
Anesaki Masaharu 姉崎正治
Aoki Bunkyō 青木文教
Aoki Shūzō 青木周蔵
Aoshika Shūei 青鹿秀栄
Arisugawa Taruhito 有栖川熾仁
Asahi Shūkō 朝日秀宏
Asakura Ryōshō 朝倉了昌

Atō Yūjō 阿刀宥乗

Azuma Onjō 東温讓

Banryūji 万隆寺

Beishakyagatsu Mangatsu Kai 吠舎佉月満月会

bessō 別荘

Bieyi za ahan jing 別訳雑阿含経

bikusō 比丘僧

Biruma 緬甸

Biruma Butsuden 緬甸仏伝

Bodaigyō kyō 菩提行経

Bodaisenna 菩提僊那

bodaishin 菩提心

bokoku 母国

Bonbungaku Kenkyūshitsu 梵文学研究室

Bonga 梵我

Bongaku shinryō 梵学津梁

Bongo Senmon Dōjō 梵語専門道場

Bongo Senmon Gakkō 梵語専門学校

Bonmōkyō 梵網経

bonnō 煩悩

Boruwafu ボルワフ

Bosatsudō 菩薩道

Bosatsukai 菩薩戒

Buddagayasan 仏陀伽耶山

Buddan saranan gacchāmi ブッダンサラナンガッチャーミ

Bukkyō mondō 仏教問答

Bukkyō nikka 仏教日課

Bukkyō no taii 仏教の大意

Bukkyō Sen'yō Kai 仏教宣揚会

Bukkyō wasan 仏教和讃

Bunka Kunshō 文化勲章

Busseki shihyō 仏跡指標

Bussetsu muryōjukyō 仏説無量寿経

Bussokuseki 仏足石

Buttai 仏体

Buzan Daigaku 豊山大学

Cheng weishi lun 成唯識論

Chibetto bunten 西藏文典

Chibetto/Nepāru/Indo Shōraihin Tenrankai チベット・ネパール・インド将来品展覧会

Chibetto nyūkoku ki 西蔵入国記
Chibetto ryokō ki 西蔵旅行記
chigen 智眼
chihō 智峯
Chion'in 知恩院
Chishakuin 智積院
Chōtokuji 長徳寺
Chūgai nippō 中外日報
Chūō kōron 中央公論
Dai Ajia shugi 大アジア主義
daiga 大我
daigatai 大我体
Dai hatsunehangyō 大般涅槃経
daihyō jōnin riji 代表常任理事
Daijō 大乗
Daijō Bukkyō 大乗仏教
Dai muryōjukyō 大無量寿経
Dainichikyō 大日経
Dairen 大連
daisōjō 大僧正
daisōzu 大僧都
Dai Tōa Kensetsu Shingikai 大東亜建設審議会
Dai Tōa Kyōei Ken 大東亜共栄圏
Dalian 大連
Damoduoluo chan jing 達磨多羅禅経
danchō 団長
Darumatara zenkyō settsū kōsho 達磨多羅禅経説通考疏
Da Tang xiyu ji 大唐西域記
Dendōin 伝道院
Dogi Hōryū 土宜法竜
Ebe Ōson 江部鴨村
Ebe Zōen 江部蔵円
egaku 慧学
Ehara Akio 江原亮夫
Ehara Ryōsen 江原亮宣
Ehara Ryōzui 江原亮瑞
Enbudai 閻浮提
Engakujō no nehan 縁覚乗ノ涅槃
Entsū 円通
Entsūji 円通寺

Faxian zhuan 法顯伝
Foguo ji 仏国記
fuhen 普遍
Fujii Hōshin 藤井芳信
Fujii Nichidatsu/Nittatsu 藤井日達
Fujishima Ryōon 藤島了穏
Fujita Giryō 藤田義亮
Fukuin shinpō 福音新報
Fukuzawa Yukichi 福沢諭吉
funbo 墳墓
Furukawa 古川
Furuta Gi'ichi 古田義一
Fusako ふさ子
Fushimi Hiroyasu 伏見博恭
Futsuin haken Ichimaru Butai 仏印派遣一丸部隊
Gaimu Daijin 外務大臣
Gaimushō 外務省
Gan'e 願慧
Ganshōji 願生寺
gedatsu 解脱
Gedatsu dōron 解脱道論
gejin 外陣
genshi 原始
gensho 原書
Gijakussen 耆闍崛山
Gohonzon 御本尊
Gohyakurakan-ji 五百羅漢寺
Gokai 五戒
Gokajō no Goseimon 五か条の御誓文
Gokokuji 護国寺
gokokutō 護国塔
goma 護摩
gonsōzu 権僧都
gōri 合理
gu 愚
Gunjin Kaikan 軍人会館
gūzō raihai 偶像礼拝
Gyōji kihan 行持軌範
Hachi Daitō 八大塔
Hakozaki Maru 箱崎丸

Hamashima Jitsujirō 浜嶋実次郎

han Ajia shugi 汎アジア主義

Hanamatsuri 花祭り

Hanseikai zasshi 反省会雑誌

Han Taiheiyō Bukkyō Seinen Kai Taikai 汎太平洋仏教青年会大会

Hara Giken 原宜賢

Haruyama Takematsu 春山武松

Hasebe Ryūtai 長谷部隆諦

Hashimoto Kōhō 橋本光宝

Hasshōdō 八正道

Hata Kenjō 秦謙讓

Hattori Yūtai 服部融泰

Hayama Yoshiki 葉山嘉樹

Hayashi Tadasu 林董

Hayashi Tan'yu 林湛由

Hekiganroku 碧巌録

Higashi Gokurakuji 東極楽寺

Higata Ryūshō 干潟竜祥

Hioki Mokusen 日置黙仙

Hirai Kinza 平井金三

Hiroshima Maru 広島丸

hō 法

hōantō 奉安塔

hōgeishi 奉迎使

Hokekyō 法華経

Hokekyōji 法華経寺

Hokku shi ホック氏

Hokubu 北部

Hokuhō Bukkyō 北方仏教

Hokuhō Daijōsha 北方大乗者

Honda Eryū 本田恵隆

hondō 本堂

Honganji Betsuin 本願寺別院

Honganji Kōbe Betsuin 本願寺神戸別院

Honganji Tsukiji Betsuin 本願寺築地別院

honji suijaku 本地垂跡

Honkyōji 本経寺

honrai mu tōsai/ga sho u nanboku/mei ko sangai jō/go ko jippō ku 本来無
　東西／何処有南北／迷故三界城／悟故十方空

honzon 本尊

Hoppō 北方
Hori Shitoku 堀至徳
Horiuchi Tōkai 堀内東海
Hōrō manki 放浪漫記
Hōryūji 法隆寺
Hōryūji kenchiku ron 法隆寺建築論
hosshin 法身
hosshu 法主
Hōtan 鳳潭
Hōzō Bosatsu 法蔵菩薩
Huang Maolin 黄茂林
Huayan 華厳
hyōgiin 評議員
Ibuki 伊吹
Ibushūrin ron 異部宗輪論
Imagawa Fusako 今川総子
Imamura Emyō 今村恵猛
Inagaki Manjirō 稲垣満次郎
Indo Bukkyōshi chizu narabi [ni] sakuin 印度仏教史地図並「ニ」索引
Indo Busseki Biruma Shamuro shisatsu shashin roku 印度仏跡緬甸暹羅視
　察写真録
Indo Busseki jissha 印度仏跡実写
Indo Busseki junpai ki 印度仏跡巡拝記
Indo Busseki Kōfuku Kai 印度仏跡興復会
Indo Busseki sanpai nisshi 印度仏跡参拝日誌
Indo Busseki shashin chō 印度仏跡写真帖
Indogaku 印度学
Indo jijō 印度事情
Indo kikō 印度紀行
Indo ryokō ki 印度旅行記
Indosan Nihonji 印度山日本寺
Indosarasen 印度サラセン
Indo satsuei chō 印度撮影帖
Indo seiseki shi 印度聖跡誌
Indo Tetsugaku 印度哲学
Indo zatsuji 印度雑事
Inga 因果
inka 印可
Inoue Enryō 井上円了
Inoue Kōen 井上宏円

Inoue Shūten 井上秀天

ishi 意志

Ishigami Zen'nō 石上善応

Ishii Ryōjō 石井亮定

Ishikawa Shuntai 石川舜台

Itagaki Iyo 坂垣イヨ

Itō Chūta 伊東忠太

Itō Hirobumi 伊藤博文

Itō Naozō 伊東直三

Iwayadera 岩屋寺

Izawa Heizaemon 伊沢平左衛門

jakkō 寂光

Jietuo daolun 解脱道論

Jiji shinpō 時事新報

jikkōteki kyōhō 実行的教法

jiko chūshin no yōkyū 自己衷心の要求

jiko naishin 自己内心

jiri ni tomarite keta ni oyobazu 自利ニ止リテ化他ニ及バズ

jishō meigo no ichinen 自性迷悟ノ一念

Jiun Onkō 慈雲飲光

jizai 自在

Jōdokyō no kigen oyobi hattatsu 浄土教の起原及発達

Jōdo Shinshū Kyōgaku Kenkyūsho 浄土真宗教学研究所

jōjū fuhen 常住不変

jōnin riji 常任理事

Jōza 上座

Jōzabu 上座部

Jōzaiji 常在寺

Jōzai Ryōjusen Konpon Saishō Chi 常在霊鷲山根本最勝地

juji 誦持

junmi 純美

junsei Bukkyō 純正仏教

junsei Daijō 純正大乗

jushutsu 誦出

juyūshin 受用身

jūzendō 十善道

Jūzenkai (Ten Good Precepts Society)十善会

Jūzenkai (Ten Good Precepts) 十善戒

jyūni innen 十二因縁

Jyūnishū kōyō 十二宗綱要

Kaen Kaidan 花園戒壇

Ka-I 華夷

kai 戒

Kaigai Bukkyō jijō 海外仏教事情

Kaigai Senkyō Kai 海外宣教会

kaigen 開眼

kaigyō 戒行

kaikoku 開国

Kaikyūroku 懐旧録

Kaimokushō 開目鈔

kairitsu 戒律

kairitsu no tokutai hosshin 戒律の徳体法身

kaishi 戒師

Kaizōji 海蔵寺

kakochō 過去帳

Kakuōden 覚王殿

Kakuōzan Nissenji 覚王山日暹寺

"Kamigami o koeta ningen" 神々を超えた人間

kami no gonge 神の権化

kanchō 管長

Kan'eiji 寛永寺

kanji (steward) 幹事

kanji (manager) 監事

kanmon 棺文

Kannon 観音

Kanokogi Kazunobu 鹿子木員信

kanshi 漢詩

Kantōshū 関東州

Kasahara Kenju 笠原研寿

Kasuga Ryūjin 春日竜神

Kasuisai 可睡斎

Kasuisai Senmon Sōdō 可睡斎専門僧堂

Katayama Chōbe-e 片山長兵衛

Kawaguchi Ekai 河口慧海

Kawahara Eiichi 河原英一

Kawakami Teishin 川上貞信

Kawatana kyōdo shi 川棚郷土誌

Kawatanagawa 川棚川

kazunoko 数の子

Kegongyō 華厳経

Keiō Gijuku 慶應義塾

kenshō 見性

kenshō jōbutsu 見性成仏

Kiko Kiyoyoshi 木子清敬

Kimura Nikki/Nichiki 木村日紀

Kimura Ryūkan 木村竜寛

Kimura Shōzaburō 木村庄三郎

kindai yōshiki 近代様式

Kinō made sora takaku nomi mishi yama mo kyō wa kumo fumu Kiso no kakehashi 昨日マデ空高クノミ見シ山モ今日ハ雲蹈ム木曽ノ棧橋

Kiriyama Seiyū 桐山靖雄

Kitazawa Masanari 北沢正誠

kisei Bukkyō 既成仏教

Kitabatake Dōryū 北畠道竜

Kitabatake Dōryū Shi Indo kikō 北畠道竜師印度紀行

Kitao Harumichi 北尾春道

Kiyozawa Manshi 清沢満之

Kobayashi Gidō 小林義道

Kōbu Daigakkō 工部大学校

ko Butsuzō 古仏像

Kōgaku Sōen 洪岳宗演

Koizumi Ryōtai 小泉了諦

Kojima Kaihō 小島戒宝

Kōjukai 光寿会

Kokkō 黒光

kokoro 心

kokudo 黒奴

Kokusai Bukkyō Kōryū Kyōkai 国際仏教興隆協会

Kokusai Bukkyō Kyōkai 国際仏教協会

Kokusai Renmei Tōyō Shibu 国際連盟東洋支部

Kongōbuji 金剛峯寺

Kongōji 金剛寺

Konnichi no Indo 今日の印度

Konnichi shinbun 今日新聞

konpon 根本

konpon Bukkyō 根本仏教

Konponsetsu Issaiubu binaya 根本説一切有部毘奈耶

Kōra Tomi 高良とみ

kōtei 高弟

kūden 宮殿

Kudō Kyōshin 工藤敬慎
Kumagaya Kunizō 熊谷国造
kurai tanima 暗い谷間
kuronbo 黒ん坊
Kurosaki Yūji 黒崎雄二
Kuruma Takudō 来馬琢道
kuse 救世
Kyōbushō 教部省
Kyōdōshoku 教導職
kyōhō 教法
kyōhōka 教法家
kyomu shugi 虚無主義
Kyōnenji 教念寺
Liuzu tan jing 六祖壇経
Luoyue 羅越
Maeda Jōsetsu 前田誠節
Mamiya Eishū 間宮英宗
Mamiya Giyū 間宮義雄
Mangyō jinshin no taku ni okoru 万行深信の宅に起る
Manpukuji 万福寺
Manzōji 万蔵寺
Masuda Jiryō 増田慈良
Matsubayashi Keigetsu 松林桂月
Matsumoto Bunzaburō 松本文三郎
Meikyō shinshi 明教新誌
Meishuron 盟主論
Mejiro Sōen 目白僧園
Mikami Kaiun 三神快運
mikoshi 神輿
Milin 密林
minzoku 民族
Mitsuda Tamenari 三田為成
Mitsui Bussan Kaisha 三井物産会社
Miyata Emi 宮田恵美
Mizutani Jinkai 水谷仁海
Mochizuki Shinkō 望月信亨
modan モダン
Modan Dera モダン寺
muga 無我
Mukoyama Ryōun 向山亮雲

Murakami Myōsei 村上妙清
Muryōjukyō 無量寿経
Myōe Kōben 明慧高弁
Myōhōin 妙法院
Myōshōji 明照寺
Nagai Makoto 長井真琴
Nagatomo Ichirō 長友一郎
Nagoya Han Taiheiyō Heiwa Hakurankai 名古屋汎太平洋平和博覧会
naiteki seikatsu 内的生活
Nakajima Seiichirō 中島清一郎
Nakamura Fusetsu 中村不折
Nakatsuji Masanobu 中辻正信
Namu Buddaya 南無仏陀耶
Namu myōhō renge kyō 南無妙法蓮華経
Nanbu 南部
Nan'enbudai 南閻浮提
Nanhai jigui neifa zhuan 南海寄帰内法伝
Nanjō Bun'yū 南条文雄
Nanpō Budda Matsuri 南方仏陀祭
Nanpō Bukkyō 南方仏教
Nanpō Bukkyō Gakkai 南方仏教学会
Nanpō Shōjōsha 南方小乗者
Nanpō sōshō no kairitsu 南方相承の戒律
Narita Yasuteru 成田安輝
nenbutsu 念仏
nengan 念願
Nichi-In Kyōkai 日印協会
Nichikyō 日教
Nihon bijutsu 日本美術
Nihon Menka 日本綿花
ninpō 人法
Nippon Yūsen Kaisha 日本郵船会社
Nipponzan Myōhōji 日本山妙法寺
Nirakusō 二楽荘
Nishiari Bokusan 西有穆山
Nissenji 日暹寺
Nissenji Senmon Sōdō 日暹寺専門僧堂
Nittaiji 日泰寺
Niyayachiroka ニヤヤチロカ
Noguchi Fukudō 野口復堂

Noguchi Zenshirō 野口善四郎
Nosu Kōsetsu 野生司香雪
Nukariya Kaiten 忽滑谷快天
Nukina Zenshirō 貫名善四郎
Nyorai junsei Jōza denshō 如来純正上座伝承
Nyorai junsei Jōza denshō no kairitsu dera 如来純正上座伝承の戒律寺
Nyū Bosatsugyō 入菩薩行
Nyūjiku bikuni 入竺比丘尼
Nyūjiku Koji Ryōan Mujin 入竺居士亮庵無尽
Nyūmō angya ki 入蒙行脚記
Nyūzō ki 入蔵記
Ōbakushū 黄檗宗
Oda Tokunō 織田得能
Ogiwara Unrai 荻原雲来
Ōiwa Isao 大岩勇夫
ōjin 応身
Okakura Kakuzō 岡倉覚三
Okakura Tenshin 岡倉天心
Oka Kyōtsui 岡教邃
Okano Shigehisa 岡野重久
Ōkawa Shūmei 大川周明
Ōkuma Shigenobu 大隈重信
Ōmiya Kōjun/Kōnin 大宮孝潤
Orientaru Hōru オリエンタルホール
Ōsaka Asahi shinbun 大阪朝日新聞
Ōsaka mainichi shinbun 大阪毎日新聞
Ōsaka Shōsen 大阪商船
Ōshio Dokuzan 大塩毒山
Ōtani Kōei 大谷光瑩
Ōtani Kōen 大谷光演
Ōtani Kōson 大谷光尊
Ōtani Kōzui 大谷光瑞
Ōtani Son'yu 大谷尊由
Ōtsubo-shi 大坪氏
Ōuchi Seiran 大内青巒
Pannyakētsu パンニャケーツ
Pari Bunka Gakuin 巴利文化学院
Putixing jīng 菩提行経
Ra'etsu 羅越
raigō 来迎

raihaiden 礼拝殿
Rainbu Channeru Baneruzē ラインブ・チャンネル・バネルゼー
ranma 欄間
Rashika-Rāru-Bahatta-Ācharuya ラシカ・ラール・バハッタ・アーチャ
ルヤ
Reikanji 霊感寺
Rinsenji 臨川寺
Rinzai Myōshinji-ha 臨済妙心寺派
Rinzairoku 臨済録
Risshō ankokuron 立正安国論
Risshō Daigaku 立正大学
ritai hosshin 理体法身
roban 露盤
ryōji dairi 領事代理
Ryōjusen 霊鷲山
Ryūtō 流灯
Sachiko 佐智子
Sado Maru 佐渡丸
Saichō 最澄
Saiiki 西域
Saikōji 西光寺
saishō 最勝
Saiyūji 西有寺
Saiyū nikki 西遊日記
Sakurai Gichō 桜井着肇
Sanbō 三宝
Sanbukyō 三部経
Sandan kaie 三檀戒会
sangaku 三学
Sangaku-Rokudo 三学六度
sange fusatsu katsuma 懺悔布薩羯磨
Sangoku 三国
sanjin shichi rokudo mangyō muryō no hōmon 三身四智六度万行無量ノ
　法門
sankie 三帰依
Sanneji 三会寺
Sasaki E'on 佐々木慧音
Seinan 西南
Seinan no Bukkyō 西南之仏教
Seinan no Bukkyōsha 西南の仏教者

Seiron 錫蘭

Seishi 勢至

seishin shugi 精神主義

sekihi 石碑

Seki Rokō 関露香

Seki Seisetsu 関清拙

Sendai Bukkyō Rengō Kai 仙台仏教各宗聯合会

Senmonbu buchō 専門部部長

Sessan Dōji 雪山童子

Sessan Dōnin 雪山道人

Sessankai 雪山会

Sessan Shōja 雪山精舎

Seu 世友

Shaka ichidai ki 釈迦一代記

Shakamuni Butsu seppō Hokekyō nado 釈迦牟尼仏説法華経等

Shakashi no funbo 釈迦師の墳墓

Shaku 釈

Shaku Daishin 釈大真

Shaku Kaiyū 釈快祐

Shaku Kōzen 釈興然

Shaku Nindo 釈仁度

Shakuntarā hime シャクンタラー姫

Shakuōden 釈王殿

Shaku Sōen 釈宗演

Shakuson jishin no naiteki seikatsu no rekōdo 釈尊自身の内的生活のレコード

Shakuson no bosho 釈尊の墓所

Shakuson no kinkan 釈尊の金棺

Shakuson Shōfū Kai 釈尊正風会

Shaku Unshō 釈雲照

shami 沙弥

Shamu シャム

Shamu/Shamuro 暹羅

Shamu Bukkyō jijō 暹羅仏教事情

Shanjianlü piposha 善見律毘婆沙

Shibunritsu 四分律

Shichibutsu tsūkaige 七仏通戒偈

shido kegyō 四度加行

Shiio Benkyō 椎尾弁匡

shikishi 色紙

Shimada Isoko 島田イソ子
Shimaji Mokurai 島地黙雷
Shimizu Mokuji 清水黙爾
shin 心
Shingi Shingonshū 新義眞言宗
shinkyū setchū 新旧折衷
shinnen 信念
Shinnyo 真如
Shinpukuji 新福寺
Shinsai Kinendō 震災記念堂
shinshiki 心識
Shinshōji 真聖寺
Shinshūji 真宗寺
Shinshū Shinto Seimei Kabushiki Kaisha 真宗信徒生命株式会社
Shitennōji 四天王寺
Shiyou 世友
Shoaku makusa 諸惡莫作
Shoaku makusa, shuzen bugyō, jijō goi, zesho Bukkyō 諸惡莫作、衆善奉
　行、自浄其意、是諸仏教
Shōbōgenzō 正法眼蔵
Sho ekō shingi 諸回向清規
shōfū seiki 正風正規
sho gedō no nehan 諸外道ノ涅槃
shōgon 荘厳
Shōgyōden 聖教殿
Shoin 書院
Shōjō 小乗
Shōjō Bukkyō 小乗仏教
shōjō shinnyo hosshin taru Budda Shakuson 清浄真如法身たる仏陀釈尊
Shōkin Ginkō 賞金銀行
Shōmangyō 勝鬘経
Shōmu 聖武
shōshin 正真
Shōshin Bukkyō 正真仏教
Shōtokuji 正徳寺
Shukusatsu daizōkyō 縮刷大藏教
Shūshōgi 修証義
sō 僧
Sōbita Toya Nindo ソービタ鳥屋仁度
Soga Ryōjin 曽我量深

Sōgyabara 僧伽婆羅
Sōma Aizō 相馬愛蔵
Sōma Kokkō 相馬黒光
Sōma Toshiko 相馬俊子
songchi 誦持
songchu 誦出
sōrin 相輪
sōru ソール
sōryo 僧侶
sōryōji 総領事
Sōtōshū 曹洞宗
Sōtōshū Daigaku 曹洞宗大学
Sumera Ajia すめらアジア
Suzuki Daisetsu 鈴木大拙
Tachibana Shundō 立花俊道
Tada Tōkan 多田等観
taitei Shina no Jurei o saiyō shitaru mono 大抵支那ノ儒禮ヲ採用シタル者
Taixu 太虚
Takada-ha 高田派
Takakusu Junjirō 高楠順次郎
Takamura Kōun 高村光雲
Takaoka Shinnō 高岳親王
Takayama Aya 高山文
taku 宅
Tanba Maru 丹波丸
Tani Dōgen 渓道元
Tarō 太郎
Tashōzan Isshinji 太生山一心寺
Tatsuno Kingo 辰野金吾
tendoku 転読
Tenjiku 天竺
Tentokuji 天徳寺
Teramoto Enga 寺本婉雅
Teruoka Yasunori 暉峻康範
Tetsugakkan 哲学館
Tōa Bukkyō Ken 東亜仏教圏
Tōa Dōbun Shoin 東亜同文書院
Tōbu 東部
Tōgō Shōkai 東郷商会
Tōhoku no Bukkyōsha 東北の仏教者

Toin nisshi 渡印日誌

Tōkai Genkō 東海玄虎

Tōkeiji 東慶寺

Toki Hōryū 土宜法竜

Tokuzawa Chiezō 徳沢知恵蔵

Tōkyō Bijutsu Gakkō 東京美術学校

Tōnan nibu no Bukkyō o taishō sen 東南二部ノ仏教ヲ対照セン

Tōrei Enji 東嶺円慈

Torio Koyata 鳥尾小弥太

Torio Tokuan 鳥尾得庵

Toshiko 俊子

Toya Nindo 鳥屋仁度

Toyama Mitsuru 頭山満

Tōyō 東洋

Tōyō Bunko 東洋文庫

Tōyō Menka Kaisha 東洋綿花会社

Tsukiji Honganji 築地本願寺

Tsuki no Ya 月廼家

Uchida Ryōhei 内田良平

Ui Hakuju 宇井伯寿

Ukai Chōsaburō 鵜飼長三郎

Umegami Takuyū 梅上沢融

Umi ni ikuru hitobito 海に生くる人々

Unno Kizen 海野希禅

Upanishaddo monogatari ウパニシャッド物語

Upāsaka Bukkyō 在家仏教

Upāsaka (Zaike) Bukkyō Shugyō Dan 在家仏教修行団

upāsakasō 優婆基/在家僧

upāsaka sōgya 優婆基僧伽

Utsuki Nishū 宇津木二秀

Vesākha Pūjā ヴェーサーカ・プージャー

Wada Keihon 和田慶本

Wada Sanzō 和田三造

Watanabe Iyo 渡辺イヨ

Watanabe Kaigyoku 渡辺海旭

Watanabe Senmyō 渡辺宣明

Wong Mou-lam (Wong Mow-lam) 黄茂林

Wutai-shan 五台山

xin 心

yakushutsu 訳出

Yamada Mumon 山田無文
Yamagata Aritomo 山県有朋
Yamakami Sōgen 山上曹源
Yamakami Tensen 山上天川
Yangsong 楊松
Yang Wenhui 楊文会
Yibuzonglun lun 異部宗輪論
Yijing 義淨
Yokoyama Taikan 横山大観
Yonezawa Kikuji 米沢菊二
Yonezawa Yoshiyasu 米沢嘉康
yoseatsume 寄せ集め
yōshi 養子
Yoshimatsu Kaiyū 吉松快祐
Yoshitsura Hōgen 善連法彦
Yuimagyō 維摩経
Yuishiki sanjū ju 唯識三十頌
yuitsu 唯一
Yuraiki 由来記
zagu 坐具
Zaike Bukkyō 在家仏教
Zeami 世阿弥
zenjō 禅定
Zenkenritsu bibasha 善見律毘婆沙
Zenpukuji 善福寺
zhai 宅
Zhapulu 乍浦路
zōni 雑煮
zudagyō 頭陀行
zushi 厨子

Bibliography

Reference Works and Collected Works

Akegarasu Haya 暁烏敏. *Akegarasu Haya zenshū* 暁烏敏全集. 28 vols. Ishikawa-ken Matsutō-shi: Ryōfū Gakusha, 1975–78. [AHZ]

Buswell, Robert E., and Donald S. Lopez. *The Princeton Dictionary of Buddhism*. Princeton, NJ: Princeton University Press, 2014. [PDB]

Hanayama, Shinshō. *Bibliography on Buddhism*. Tokyo: Hokuseido Press, 1961. [BB]

Hirakawa Akira 平川彰. *Hirakawa Akira chosakushū* 平川彰著作集. 17 vols. Tokyo: Shunjūsha, 1988. [HAC]

Ishida Mitsuyuki 石田充之, and Chiba Jōryū 千葉乗隆. *Shinshū shiryō shūsei* 眞宗史料集成. Saihan. ed. 13 vols. Kyoto: Dōhōsha Media Puran, 2003. [SSS]

Iwano Shin'yū 岩野真雄. *Kokuyaku Issaikyō. [Indo Senjutsubu]* 国訳一切経. [印度撰述部]. 158 vols. Tokyo: Daitō Shuppansha, 1929.

Iwao, Seiichi. *Biographical Dictionary of Japanese History*. 1st ed. Tokyo: International Society for Educational Information, 1978.

Kashiwahara Yūsen 柏原祐泉, Sonoda Kōyū 薗田香融, Hiramatsu Reizō 平松令三, eds., *Shinshū jinmei jiten* 真宗人名辞典. Kyoto: Hōzōkan, 1999.

Kawaguchi Ekai 河口慧海. *Kawaguchi Ekai chosakushū* 河口慧海著作集. 17 vols. Niigata-ken Santō-gun Izumo-machi: Ushio Shoten, 1998. [KECS]

Kusanagi Zengi 草繋全宜, ed., *Shaku Unshō* 釈雲照. 3 vols. Tokyo: Tokukyōkai, 1913–14. [SUS]

Nakamura, Hajime 中村元 et al. *Iwanami Bukkyō jiten* 岩波仏教辞典. 2nd ed. Tokyo: Iwanami Shoten, 2002. [IBJ]

Nanjio Bun'yū 南条文雄, Sasaki Kyōgo 佐々木教悟, Nagasaki Hyōjun 長崎法潤, and Kimura Senshō 木村宣彰, eds. *Nanjō Bun'yū chosaku senshū* 南条文雄著作選集. 10 vols. Niigata-ken Santō-gun: Ushio Shoten, 2001-3. [NBCS]

Nihon Bukkyō Jinmei Jiten Hensan Iinkai 日本仏教人名辞典編纂委員会, ed. *Nihon Bukkyō jinmei jiten* 日本仏教人名辞典. Tokyo: Hōzōkan, 1992. [NBJ]

Oda Tokunō 織田得能, and and Haga Ya'ichi 芳賀矢一 et al. *Bukkyō daijiten* 仏教大辞典. Tokyo: Meicho Fukyūkai, 1981. Orig. ed., 1917. [OBDJ]

Sōmuchō Tōkeikyoku 総務庁統計局 and Nihon Tōkei Kyōkai 日本統計協会. *Nihon chōki tōkei sōran*日本長期統計総覧. 5 vols. Tokyo: Nihon Tōkei Kyōkai, 1987.

Takakusu Junjirō 高楠順次郎 and Watanabe Kaigyoku 渡辺海旭. *Taishō shinshū daizōkyō* 大正新脩大藏経. Tokyo: Taishō Shinshū Daizōkyō Kankō Kai. [T]

Takakusu Junjirō 高楠順次郎, Ui Hakuju 宇井伯壽, Nagai Makoto 長井真琴, Tsuji Naoshirō 辻直四郎, and Mizuno Kōgen 水野弘元. *Nanden daizokyō* 南傳大藏經. Tokyo: Daizō Shuppan, 1935.

Tsunemitsu Kōnen 常光活然. *Meiji no Bukkyōsha* 明治の仏教者. 2 vols. Tokyo: Shunjūsha, 1968. [MNB]

Zengaku Daijiten Hensanjo 禅学大辞典編纂所, ed. 1985. *Zengaku daijiten* 禅学大辞典. 2nd ed. Tokyo: Taishūkan Shoten. [ZGDJ]

Zhongguo fojiao renmin da cidian 中国仏教人民大辞典. 1999. Shanghai: Shanghai Cishu Chubanshe.

Newspapers and Journals

Chūgai nippō 中外日報

International Buddhist Society. *Studies on Buddhism in Japan*. 4 vols. Tokyo: International Buddhist Society, 1939–42. [SBJ]

Kaigai Bukkyō jijō 海外仏教事情

Kawatana kyōdo shi 川棚郷土誌

Manshū kenchiku zasshi 満州建築雑誌.

Meikyō shinshi 明教新誌.

Young East Association. *Young East*. Tokyo: Pitaka, 1925–24. [YE]

Archival Documents and Unpublished Sources

"Address of Welcome to the Part of Official Visitors from Siam to Nippon." Presented June 28, 1934 by the Mayor of the City of Nagoya, J. Ōiwa Isao. Gaikō Shiryōkan Document I–2–1-0–4, Bukkyō kankei taikai zakken 仏教関係大会雑件.

Ehara, Ryōzui. "Nichiren." Kawatana, Japan: Jōzaiji, 1935. Unpublished manuscript.

"Jōzaiji kakochō, 1928–1942" 常在寺過去帳—自昭和参年至全拾七年. Kawatana, Nagasaki.

"Jūshoku zainin chō" 住職在任調, ed. Nittaiji日泰寺. Nagoya: Nittaiji, n. d.

"Kakukuni yori honpō e no ryūgakusei kankei zakken, Shamukoku no bu" 各国ヨリ本邦ヘノ留学生関係雑件、暹国ノ部. Gaikō Shiryōkan Document #3-10-5-4-1.

Nittaiji日泰寺. "Jūshoku zainin chō" 住職在任調. Nagoya: Nittaiji, n. d.

"Speech Delivered by Mr. K. Yonezawa, Consul-General for Japan at the Ceremony of Laying the Foundation-Stone of a Buddhist Temple in New Delhi," Gaikō Shiryōkan Document I-2-2-0-1, "Gaikoku shinshi oyobi jiin kankei zakken" 外国神祠及寺院関係雑件, 140–36.

Yuraiki 由来記. Jōzaiji. Kawatana, Nagasaki.

Primary and Secondary Sources

1898. "The Recent Discovery of Buddha Relics: Presentation to the King of Siam." *Manchester Guardian*, December 19, 5.

1925. "To Our Friends and Readers." *Young East* 1, no. 1: 33.

1925. "What Japan Owes to India." *Young East* 1, no. 4: 129–30.

1926. "Japanese Tourist Party to India." *Young East* 2, no. 2: 251.

1926. "Death of the Editor of the Young East." *Young East* 2, no. 3:103–5.

1929. "The Trouble at the Honganji." *Japan Weekly Chronicle*, October 17, 414.

1930. "Shingen sōrei o kiwametaru: Kinseishiki daigaran naru Kōbeshi Honpa Honganji bek-kaku betsuin Zenpukuji" 森厳壮麗を極めたる―近世式大伽藍成る―神戸市本派本願寺別格別院善福寺. *Kōbe shinbun* 神戸新聞. November 26, 8.

1934. "A General View of the New Honganji Building at Tsukiji Tokyo Where the Second Pan-Pacific Y. B. A. Conference Will Take Place," *Young East* 4, no. 11 (July–September): 7.

Ahuja, Ravi. "'The Bridge Builders': Some Notes on Railways, Pilgrimage and the British 'Civilizing Mission' in Colonial India." In *Colonialism as Civilizing Mission: Cultural Ideology in British India*, edited by Harald Fischer-Tiné and Michael Mann, 95–116. London: Anthem Press, 2004.

Akai, Toshio. "The Theosophical Accounts in Japanese Buddhist Publications Issued in the Late Nineteenth Century, a Select Bibliography." In "Hirai Kinza and the Globalization of Japanese Buddhism in the Meiji Era, a Cultural and Religio-Historical Study," edited by Yoshinaga Shin'ichi 吉永進一, 55–79. Grants-in-Aid for Scientific Research (Category C), Kyoto, 2007.

———. "Theosophical Accounts in Japanese Buddhist Publications of the Late Nineteenth Century: An Introduction and Select Bibliography." *Japanese Religions* 34, no. 2 (2009): 187–208.

Akegarasu Haya 暁烏敏. "Gendai shichō to Shinran kyōgi" 現代思潮と親鸞教義. In *Shinran Shōnin no shinnen* 親鸞聖人の信念, edited by Akegarasu Haya, 1–18. Kita Yasuda: Kōsōsha, 1925.

Akegarasu Haya 暁烏敏 and Teruoka Yasunori 暉峻康範. *Indo Busseki junpai ki* 印度仏跡巡拝記. Ishikawa Prefecture: Kōsōsha, 1928.

Akegarasu, Haya, Shinran, and Manshi Kiyozawa. *Selections from the Nippon seishin (Japanese Spirit Library)*. Kitayasuda, Ishikawaken, Nippon: Kōsōsha, 1936.

Akiyama Tokusaburō 秋山徳三郎. *Sekai shūyū tabi nikki: ichimei Shakamuni Butsu funbo no yurai* 世界周遊旅日記―一名釈迦牟尼仏墳墓の由来. Tokyo: Kyūshunsha, 1884.

Allen, Charles. *The Search for the Buddha: The Men Who Discovered India's Lost Religion*. New York: Carroll & Graf Publishers, 2003.

Almond, Philip C. *The British Discovery of Buddhism*. Cambridge: Cambridge University Press, 1988.

Amanuma Shun'ichi 天沼俊一. *Indo ryokō ki* 印度旅行記. Nara: Asukaen, 1931.

———. *<Teisei zōho> Indo Buttō junrei ki* <訂正増補>印度仏塔巡礼記. 2 vols. Osaka: Akitaya, 1944.

Ariga Yoshitaka 有賀祥隆. *Haruka naru akogare Chibetto* はるかなる憧憬チベット. Sendai, Japan: Tōhoku Daigaku Sōgō Gakujutsu Hakubutsukan, 2004.

Ashiya Shiritsu Bijutsu Hakubutsukan 芦屋市立美術博物館, ed. *<Modanizumu saikō> Nirakusō to Ōtani tankentai* <モダニズム再考>二楽荘と大谷探検隊. Ashiya: Ashiya Shiritsu Bijutsu Hakubutsukan, 1999.

———. *<Modanizumu saikō> Nirakusō to Ōtani tankentai II* <モダニズム再考>二楽荘と大谷探検隊II. Ashiya: Ashiya Shiritsu Bijutsu Hakubutsukan, 2003.

Aśoka, Narayanrao Appurao Nikam, and Richard McKeon. *The Edicts of Asoka*. Midway Reprint. Chicago: University of Chicago Press, 1959.

Auerback, Micah L. *A Storied Sage: Canon and Creation in the Making of a Japanese Buddha*. Buddhism and Modernity. Chicago: University of Chicago Press, 2016.

Aydin, Cemil. *The Politics of Anti-Westernism in Asia: Visions of World Order in Pan-Islamic and Pan-Asian Thought*. Columbia Studies in International and Global History. New York: Columbia University Press, 2007.

Bandyopadhyay, Sunil. *Harinath De, Philanthropist and Linguist*. National Biography. New Delhi: National Book Trust, India, 1988.

Bapat, Purushottam Vishvanath. "Vimuttimagga and Visuddhimagga: A Comparative Study." PhD diss., Harvard University, 1932.

Bapat, P. V. *Vimuttimagga and Visuddhimagga: A Comparative Study*. Poona: P. V. Bapat, 1937.

———. *Vimuttimagga and Visuddhimagga: A Comparative Study*. Kandy: Buddhist Publication Society, 2009. Orig. ed., 1937.

Baroni, Helen. *Obaku Zen: The Emergence of the Third Sect of Zen in Tokugawa Japan*. Honolulu: University of Hawai'i Press, 2000.

Barrows, John Henry. *The World's Parliament of Religions: An Illustrated and Popular Story of the World's First Parliament of Religions, Held in Chicago in Connection with the Columbian Exposition of 1893*. Chicago: Parliament Publishing Company, 1893.

Barua, Beni Madhab. *A History of Pre-Buddhistic Indian Philosophy*. Calcutta: University of Calcutta, 1921.

Barua, Dipak Kumar. *Buddha Gaya Temple: Its History*. 1975. 2nd rev. enl. ed. Buddha Gaya: Buddha Gaya Temple Management Committee, 1981.

Beckert, Sven. *Empire of Cotton: A Global History*. New York: Vintage, 2014.

Benesch, Oleg. *Inventing the Way of the Samurai: Nationalism, Internationalism, and Bushidō in Modern Japan*. Past & Present Book Series. Oxford: Oxford University Press, 2014.

Berry, Scott. *A Stranger in Tibet: The Adventures of a Zen Monk*. London: Flamingo, 1991.

———. *Monks, Spies, and a Soldier of Fortune: The Japanese in Tibet*. New York: St. Martin's Press, 1995.

Best, Antony. *British Intelligence and the Japanese Challenge in Asia, 1914–1941*. Studies in Military and Strategic History. Basingstoke: Palgrave Macmillan, 2002.

———. "India, Pan-Asianism, and the Anglo-Japanese Alliance." In *The Anglo-Japanese Alliance, 1902–1922*, edited by Phillips Payson O'Brien, 236–48. London: RoutledgeCurzon, 2004.

Bīesu Kankō Tōkyō ビーエス観光東京. 2018. "Komazawa Daigaku meiyo kyōju Minagawa Hiroyoshi sensei to iku, Dai 27 kai Indo Busseki junrei no tabi—Shakuson shichidai seichi o tazunete—kokonokakan" 駒澤大学名誉教授　皆川廣義先生といく、第27回インド仏蹟巡礼の旅―釈尊七大聖地を訪ねて～　９日間." Bīesu Kankō Tōkyō. Accessed February 9, 2018. http://tokyo.bs-group.jp/駒澤大学名誉教授%E3%80%80皆川廣義先生といく、第27回イ/.

Blackburn, Anne M. *Buddhist Learning and Textual Practice in Eighteenth-Century Lankan Monastic Culture*. Princeton, NJ: Princeton University Press, 2001.

———. *Locations of Buddhism: Colonialism and Modernity in Sri Lanka*. Buddhism and Modernity. Chicago: University of Chicago Press, 2010.

Blum, Mark L. 2011. "Shin Buddhism in the Meiji Period." In *Cultivating Spirituality: A Modern Shin Buddhist Anthology*, edited by Mark L. Blum and Robert F. Rhodes, 1–52. Albany: State University of New York Press, 2011.

Bocking, Brian. "Flagging Up Buddhism: Charles Pfoundes (Omoie Tetzunostzuke) among the International Congresses and Expositions, 1893–1905." In *A Buddhist Crossroads: Pioneer Western Buddhists and Asian Networks 1860–1960*, edited by Brian Bocking, Phibul Choompolpaisal, Laurence Cox, and Alicia Marie Turner, 16–36. London: Routledge, 2015.

Bodiford, William, trans. 2017. "Dōgen's Treasury of the Eye of the Dharma Book 31: Not Doing Evils (Shoaku makusa)." Stanford University, Stanford, California. Accessed June 6, 2017. https://web.stanford.edu/group/scbs/sztp3/translations/shobogenzo/translations/shoaku_makusa/shoaku_makusa.intro.html.

Bond, George Doherty. *The Buddhist Revival in Sri Lanka: Religious Tradition, Reinterpretation, and Response*. Columbia: University of South Carolina Press, 1988.

Bose, Rash Behari, Radhanath Rath, and Sābitri Prasanna Chatterjee. *Rash Behari Basu, His Struggle for India's Independence*. 1st ed. Calcutta: Biplabi Mahanayak Rash Behari Basu Smarak Samity, 1963.

Bowring, Richard John. *In Search of the Way: Thought and Religion in Early-Modern Japan, 1582–1860*. New York: Oxford University Press, 2017.

Brasington, Leigh. "Practical Jhānas: Right Concentration and the Suttas." Presented at Secular Buddhism Conference, Barre, MA, March 26, 2013.

Braun, Erik. *The Birth of Insight: Meditation, Modern Buddhism, and the Burmese Monk Ledi Sayadaw*. Buddhism and Modernity. Chicago: University of Chicago Press, 2013.

Buddhaghosa, Junjirō Takakusu, and Makoto Nagai. *Samantapāsādikā, Buddhagosa's Commentary on the Vinaya Piṭaka*. London: Pub. for the Pali Text Society by the Oxford University Press, 1924.

Bühler, Georg. "Preliminary Note on a Recently Discovered Śākya Inscription." *Journal of the Royal Asiatic Society of Great Britain and Ireland* (1898): 387–89.

Burnouf, Eugène. *Introduction to the History of Indian Buddhism*. Translated by Katia Buffetrille and Donald S. Lopez Jr. Buddhism and Modernity. Chicago: University of Chicago Press, 2010.

Central Hindu College. *Sanâtana Dharma: An Advanced Text Book of Hindu Religion and Ethics*. Benares: Board of Trustees, Central Hindu College, 1903.

Chalmers, Robert. "The King of Siam's Edition of the Pāli Tipiṭaka." *Journal of the Royal Asiatic Society of Great Britain and Ireland* 9 (1898): 1–10.

Childers, Robert Cæsar. *A Dictionary of the Pāli Language*. London: Trübner & Co., 1875.

Chūō Bukkyō Gakuin 中央仏教学院. "Busseki junpai ryokō" 仏跡巡拝旅行. Chūō Bukkyō Gakuin. Accessed February 9, 2018. http://www.chubutsu.jp/student/travelling.html.

Clarke, Shayne. "Miscellaneous Musings on Mūlasarvāstivāda Monks: The *Mūlasarvāstivāda Vinaya* Revival in Tokugawa Japan." *Japanese Journal of Religious Studies* 33, no. 1 (2006): 1–49.

Clifford, James. *Routes: Travel and Translation in the Late Twentieth Century*. Cambridge, MA: Harvard University Press, 1997.

Connected Discourses of the Buddha, The: A New Translation of the Saṃyutta Nikāya. Translated by Bhikkhu Bodhi. 2 vols. Somerville, MA: Wisdom Publications, 2000.

Conrad, Sebastian. *What Is Global History?* Princeton, NJ: Princeton University Press, 2016. Kindle.

Dalmia, Vasudha. "Sanskrit Scholars and Pandits of the Old School: The Benares Sanskrit College and the Constitution of Authority in the Late-Nineteenth Century." *Journal of Indian Philosophy* 24 (1996): 321–37.

Das, Sarat Chandra. *Autobiography; Narratives of the Incidents of My Early Life, 1908–1909*. Reprint. Indian Studies. Calcutta: Past & Present, 1969.

Das, Sarat Chandra, and William Woodville Rockhill. *Journey to Lhasa and Central Tibet*. New ed. London: John Murray, 1904.

Das, Sarat Chandra, Graham Sandberg, and Augustus William Heyde. *A Tibetan-English Dictionary, with Sanskrit Synonyms*. Alipore: West Bengal Government Press, 1960.

Davis, Winston. *Japanese Religion and Society: Paradigms of Structure and Change*. Albany: State University of New York Press, 1992.

Department of Finance, ed. *Returns of the Foreign Trade of the Empire of Japan for the Thirty Two Years from 1868 to 1899 Inclusive*. Tokyo: Department of Finance, 1901.

Dhammapada, The: A New English Translation with the Pali Text, and for the First English Translation of the Commentary's Explanation of the Verses with Notes. Trans. John Ross Carter and Mahinda Palihawadana. New York: Oxford University Press, 1987.

Dickinson, Frederick R. *World War I and the Triumph of a New Japan, 1919–1930*. Studies in the Social and Cultural History of Modern Warfare. Cambridge: Cambridge University Press, 2013.

Dodson, Michael S., and Brian A. Hatcher, eds. *Trans-Colonial Modernities in South Asia*. Routledge Studies in the Modern History of Asia 74. Abingdon, Oxon: Routledge, 2012. Kindle.

Dower, John W. "The Useful War." *Daedelus* 119, no. 3 (1990): 49–70.

Duara, Prasenjit. "The Discourse of Civilization and Pan-Asianism." *Journal of World History* 12, no. 1 (2001): 99–130.

———. *The Crisis of Global Modernity: Asian Traditions and a Sustainable Future*. Asian Connections. Cambridge: Cambridge University Press, 2015.

Ebe Zōen 江部蔵円. *Indo seiseki shi* 印度聖跡誌. Tokyo: Naigai Shuppan Kyōkai, 1910.

Ehara Ryōzui 江原亮瑞. "Upanishatto tetsugaku" ウパニシャット哲学. *Ōsaki gakuhō* 67 (1926): 139–47; 69 (1926): 109–22.

———. "<Rinne shisō o chūshin to shite mitaru> Upanishatto tetsugaku" <輪廻思想を中心として見たる>ウパニシャット哲学. *Ōsaki gakuhō* 75–76 (1928): 236–307.

———. "Nichiren Shōnin goibun Kanbon jii" 日蓮上人御遺文漢梵辞彙. *Ōsaki gakuhō* 79 (1931; Special Issue: Nichiren Shōnin roppyaku gojū onki kinen tokuson gō 日蓮聖人六百五十遠忌記念特輯号): 1–30 (L–R).

———. *Kirishitan haka engi* 切支丹墓縁起. Nagasaki Prefecture: Masuda Sanae 増田早苗, 1951.

Ehara, N. R. M., V. E. P. Pulle, and G. S. Prelis. "Selections from Nichiren's Writings: Epistle from Sado (Sado Gosho)." *Young East* no. 6, no. 1 (1936): 19–25.

———. "Selections from Nichiren's Writings: On the Establishment of Righteousness and the Security of the Country (Risshō Ankoku Ron)." *Young East* 6, no. 2 (1936): 16–27.

———. "Selections from Nichiren's Letters." *Young East* 7, no. 2 (1937): 26–36.

Ehara, Ryozui. "A Brief Sketch of Nichiren's Life." *Young East* 6, no. 3 (1936): 34–40.

Emoto Ryūzō 江本隆三. *Kitabatake Dōryū shi Indo kikō* 北畠道竜師印度紀行. Tokyo: Emoto Ryūzō, 1884.

Eskildsen, R. "Of Civilization and Savages: The Mimetic Imperialism of Japan's 1874 Expedition to Taiwan." *American Historical Review* 107, no. 2 (2002): 388–418.

Frost, M. "'Wider Opportunities': Religious Revival, Nationalist Awakening and the Global Dimension in Colombo, 1870–1920." *Modern Asian Studies* 36, no. 4 (2002): 937–68.

Fujita Giryō 藤田義亮. *Busseki junpai* 仏跡巡拝. Kyoto: Naigai Shuppan, 1927.

Fukushima Eiju 福島栄寿. *"Seishin shugi" no kyūdōshatachi: Kiyozawa Manshi to Akegarasu Haya* 「精神主義」の求道者たち：清沢満之と暁烏敏. Kōka Sōsho 5. Kyoto: Kōka Joshi Daigaku, Tanki Daigaku Shinshū Bunka Kenkyūjo, 2003.

Goddard, Dwight. *A Buddhist Bible, The Favorite Scriptures of the Zen Sect; History of Early Zen Buddhism, Self-realisation of Noble Wisdom, the Diamond Sutra, the Prajna Paramita Sutra, the Sutra of the Sixth Patriarch*. 2nd ed. Thetford, VT.: Dwight Goddard, 1938.

Gokokutō Hōsan Kai 護国塔奉賛会, ed. *Gokokutō shi* 護国塔誌. Fukuroi: Gokokutō Hōsan Kai, n.d.

Gombrich, Richard Francis, and Gananath Obeyesekere. *Buddhism Transformed: Religious Change in Sri Lanka*. Princeton, NJ: Princeton University Press, 1988.

Gómez, Luis. "The Way of the Translators: Three Recent Translations of Śāntideva's *Bodhicaryāvatāra*." *Buddhist Literature* 1 (1999): 262–354.

Goodman, Grant Kohn. "Dharmapala in Japan." *Japan Forum* 5, no. 2 (1993):195–202.

Goonetilleke, Janaka, ed. *Atapattu Walawwa: Residence of the Gooneratne and Dias Abeyesinghe Families of Galle.* Galle, Sri Lanka: Atapattu Walawwa, 2012.

Gordon, Andrew. *A Modern History of Japan: From Tokugawa Times to the Present.* 3rd ed. Oxford: Oxford University Press, 2014.

Grabovac, Andrea. "The Stages of Insight: Clinical Relevance for Mindfulness-Based Interventions." *Mindfulness* 6, no. 3 (2015): 589–600.

Green, Nile. *Bombay Islam: The Religious Economy of the West Indian Ocean, 1840–1915.* New York: Cambridge University Press, 2011. Kindle.

———. "Anti-Colonial Japanophilia and the Constraints of an Islamic Japanology: Information and Affect in the Indian Encounter with Japan." *South Asian History and Culture* 4, no. 3 (2013): 291–313.

———. "From the Silk Road to the Railroad (and Back): The Means and Meanings of the Iranian Encounter with China." *Iranian Studies* 48, no. 2 (2015):165–92.

Hallisey, Charles. "Roads Taken and Not Taken in the Study of Theravāda Buddhism." In *Curators of the Buddha: The Study of Buddhism under Colonialism,* ed. Donald S. Lopez Jr., 31–61. Chicago: University of Chicago Press, 1995.

Hamashima Jitsujirō 浜嶋実次郎. *Nagoya Higashiyama Kakuōzan Nissenji sannai no zu* 名古屋東山覚王山日暹寺山内之図. Nagoya: Hamashima Jitsujirō, 1921.

Hara Giken 原宜賢. *Indo Busseki Biruma Shamu shisatsu shashin roku* 印度仏跡緬甸暹羅視察写真録. Tokyo: Tōkōdō, 1926.

Haraprasāda Śāstrī. *"Bodhicaryāvatāram."* *Journal and Text of the Buddhist Text Society of India* 2, nos. 1 & 2 (1894): 2, no. 1: 1–16; 2, no. 2: 17–32.

Harrington, C. K. "Those Relics of the Buddha." *Baptist Missionary Magazine* (June 1904): 206.

Hashimoto Yorimitsu 橋本順光. "Kanokogi Kazonobu no Indo tsuihō to sono eikyō" 鹿子木員信のインド追放とその影響. *Osaka University Knowledge Archive* (2013): 84–92.

Hatcher, Brian A. "What's Become of the Pandit? Rethinking the History of Sanskrit Scholars in Colonial Bengal." *Modern Asian Studies* 39, no. 3 (2005): 683–723.

———. "Pandits at Work: The Modern Shastric Imaginary in Early Colonial Bengal." In *Trans-Colonial Modernities in South Asia,* edited by Michael S. Dodson and Brian A. Hatcher, 45–67. New York: Routledge, 2012. Kindle.

Hay, Stephen N. *Asian Ideas of East and West; Tagore and His Critics in Japan, China, and India.* Harvard East Asian Series. Cambridge, MA: Harvard University Press, 1970.

Hayami Akira 速水融, and Kojima Miyoko 小嶋美代子. *Taishō demogurafi: rekishi jinkōgaku de mita hazama no jidai* 大正デモグラフィ：歴史人口学で見た狭の時代. Bunshun Shinsho. Tokyo: Bungei Shunjū, 2004.

Hayasaka Hōjō 早坂鳳城. "Kawaguchi Ekai no Nichiren kyōgaku hihan ni tsuite" 河口慧海の日蓮教学批判について. *Gendai shūkyō kenkyū* 31 (1997): 170–81.

Hayashi, Makoto. "The Birth of Buddhist Universities." *Japanese Religions* 39, nos. 1 & 2 (2014): 11–29.

———. "Religious Studies and Religiously Affiliated Universities." In *Modern Buddhism in Japan,* edited by Makoto Haysahi, Eiichi Ōtani, and Paul L. Swanson, 163–93. Nagoya: Nanzan Institute for Religion and Culture, 2014.

Hayashi Tadasu 林董. "Nochi wa mukashi no ki" 後は昔の記. In Yuii Masaomi, ed. 由井正臣. Tokyo: Heibonsha, 1994. Accessed September 11, 2016. http://view.japanknowledge .com.proxy.lib.duke.edu/toyodviewer/html/viewer.html?id＝0173000061054&key＝d8de7a7d7af16311d25f8e355b54798a81014b01.

Hecker, Hellmuth, and Bhikkhu Ñāṇatusita, eds. *The Life of Ñāṇatiloka Thera: The Biography of a Western Buddhist Pioneer*. Kandy, Sri Lanka: Buddhist Publication Society, 2008.

Heirman, Ann. "The Chinese 'Samantapāsādikā' and Its School Affiliation." *Zeitschrift der Deutschen Morgenländischen Gesellschaft* 154, no. 2 (2004): 371–96.

Hell, Stefan Matthias. "Siam and the League of Nations: Modernization, Sovereignty, and Multilateral Diplomacy, 1920–1940." PhD diss., Leiden University, 2007.

Higashimoto Keikichi 東本慶喜. "Shaku Nindo Wajō no omoide" 釈仁度和上のおもいで. In *Ryōkan no kokoro* 良寛のこころ, edited by Ryōkan Kai, 230–46. Tokyo: Bunka Shobō Hakubunsha, 1981.

———. "Shakuson Shōfū Kai no hitobito" 釈尊正風会のひとびと. *Komazawa Daigaku Bukkyōgakubu kenkyū kiyō* 40 (March 1982): 51–61.

Higashimoto Tarō 東本多郎. "Gunaratana Shaku Kōzen Wajō den" グナラタナ釈興然和上伝. *Kaigai Bukkyō jijō* 10, no. 3 (1944): 3–47.

Hirakawa Akira, "Shoki Daijō Bukkyō no kaigaku to shite no Jūzendō" 初期大乗仏教の戒学としての十善道, in *Hirakawa Akira chosakushū* 7: 201–38.

Honganji Kōbe Betsuin 本願寺神戸別院. *Sanpai no shiori* 参拝のしおり. Honganji Kobe Betsuin Guide. Kobe: Honganji Kōbe Betsuin Hyōgo Kyōku Kyōka Sentā, n.d.

Honganji Tsukiji Betsuin 本願寺築地別院, ed. *Tsukiji Betsuin shi* 築地別院史. Tokyo: Honganji Tsukiji Betsuin, 1934.

Honpa Hongwanji Hawaii Betsuin. "Temple History." http://hawaiibetsuin.org/temple-history/. Accessed June 1, 2018.

Horiguchi Ryōichi. "Léon de Rosny et les premières missions bouddhiques japonaises en Occident." *Cipango* 4 (1995): 121–39.

Hotta, Eri. "Rash Behari Bose and His Japanese Supporters." *Interventions* 8, no. 1 (2006): 116–32.

———. *Pan-Asianism and Japan's War 1931–1945*. Palgrave Macmillan Series in Transnational History. New York: Palgrave Macmillan, 2007.

Huber, Toni. *The Holy Land Reborn: Pilgrimage and the Tibetan Reinvention of Buddhist India*. Buddhism and Modernity. Chicago: University of Chicago Press, 2008.

Inagaki, Manjiro. *Japan and the Pacific and a Japanese View of the Eastern Question*. London: T. Fisher Unwin, 1890.

Inoue Nobutaka 井上順孝. *Kindai Nihon no shūkyōka 101* 近代日本の宗教家 *101*. Tōkyō: Shinshokan, 2007.

Inoue Shūten 井上秀天. *Indo jijō* 印度事情. Tainan, Taiwan: Tainan Gijuku Zōhan, 1903.

Inoue Zenjō 井上禅定. 2009. *Shaku Sōen den* 釈宗演伝. Kyoto: Zen Bunka Kenkyūjo.

Inoue Zenjō 井上禅定, Masaki Akira 正木晃, and Yamada Tomonobu 山田智信, eds. *<Shin'yaku> Shaku Sōen "Saiyū nikki"* ＜新訳＞釈宗演『西遊日記』. Tokyo: Daihōrinkaku, 2001.

Itō Chūta 伊東忠太. "Gokokutō no kenchiku" 護国塔の建築. *Nihon bijutsu*, no. 148 (June 1911): 1–4.

———. "Nirakusō no kenchiku" 二楽荘の建築. *Kenchiku kōgei sōshi* 建築工芸叢誌 20 (1913): 1.

———. *Itō Chūta kenchiku bunken* 伊東忠太建築文献. 6 vols. Tokyo: Ryūginsha, 1936.

Itō Hiromi 伊藤宏見, ed. *Unshō/Kōzen iboku shū* 雲照・興然遺墨集. Tokyo: Bunka Shobō Hakubun Sha, 1974.

Izawa Heizaemon 伊沢平左衛門. *Indo Busseki sanpai nisshi* 印度仏跡参拝日誌. Sendai: Izawa Heizaemon, 1927.

Izumi Hōkei 泉芳璟. "Meiji jidai ni okeru toin no Bukkyōto" 明治時代に於ける渡印の仏教徒. *Gendai Bukkyō* 105 (1933): 162–70.

Jacquet, Benoît. "Itō Chūta et son *Étude Architecturale du Hōryūji* (1893): comment et pourquoi Intégrer l'architecture japonaise dans l'histoire mondiale." *Ebisu* 52 (2015): 89–115.

Jaffe, Richard. M. "Shakuson o sagashite: Kindai Nihon Bukkyō no tanjō to sekai ryokō" 釈尊をさがして—近代日本仏教の誕生と世界旅行. Translated by Maeda Ken'ichi 前川健一. *Shisō* 943 (2002): 64–87.

———. "Seeking Śākyamuni: Travel and the Reconstruction of Japanese Buddhism." *Journal of Japanese Studies* 30, no. 1 (2004): 65–96.

———. "Buddhist Material Culture, Indianism, and the Construction of Pan-Asian Buddhism in Pre-War Japan." *Material Religion* 2, no. 3 (2006): 266–93.

———. "Senzen Nihon ni okeru Bukkyōteki busshitsu bunka, 'Indo shumi,' oyobi han Ajia Bukkyō no keisei" 戦前日本に於ける仏教的物質文化、＜インド趣味＞、及び汎アジア仏教の形成. Translated by Kirihara Kenshin 桐原健真 and Orion Klautau. *Tōhoku shūkyōgaku* 4 (2008): 157–89.

Jiun Onkō 慈雲飲光. "Nankai kiki naihōden geransho" 南海寄帰内法伝解纜鈔. In *Jiun Sonja zenshū* 慈雲尊者全集, edited by Hase Hōshū 長谷宝秀, 441–580. Kyoto: Shibunkaku, 1974.

Johnson, K. Paul. *The Masters Revealed: Madame Blavatsky and the Myth of the Great White Lodge*. SUNY Series in Western Esoteric Traditions. Albany: State University of New York Press, 1994.

Kamekawa Shōshi 亀川正史. *Honganji omoshiro sanpo* 本願寺おもしろ散歩. 1985. Reprint, Kyoto: Honganji Shuppansha, 2000.

Kanokogi Kazunobu 鹿子木員信. *Busseki junrei kō* 仏跡巡礼行. Tokyo: Daitōkaku, 1920.

———. *Sumera Ajia* すめらあじあ. Tokyo: Dōbun Shoin, 1937.

Karl, Rebecca E. "Creating Asia: China in the World at the Beginning of the Twentieth Century." *American Historical Review* 103, no. 4 (1998): 1096–1118.

Katomanzu Honganji カトマンズ本願寺. "Katomanzu Honganji カトマンズ本願寺." http://www.kathmanduhongwanji.org. Accessed February 8, 2018.

Katō Tatsuaki 加藤竜明. *Hohoemi no hakutō: Shakuson shinkotsu hōan hyakushūnen* 微笑みの白塔—釈尊真骨奉安百周年. Nagoya: Chūnichi Shinbunsha Shuppan Kaihatsu Kyoku, 2000.

Kawaguchi Akira 川口正. *Kawaguchi Ekai: Nihon saisho no Chibetto nyūkokusha* 河口慧海—日本最初のチベット入国者. Tokyo: Shunjūsha, 2000.

Kawaguchi Ekai 河口慧海. "Bokokuteki shisōka to shite no Tagōru" 亡国てき思想家としてのタゴール. In *Kawaguchi Ekai chosakushū* 15: 526–31. Originally published 1915.

———. *Bukkyō nikka* 仏教日課. Tokyo: Zaike Bukkyō Shugyō Dan, 1940. First published 1922, Bukkyō Sen'yō Kai.

———. "Bukkyō no konponteki kakumei" 仏教の根本的革命. In *Kawaguchi Ekai chosakushū* 16: 166. Originally published 1926.

Kawaguchi Ekai 河口慧海, and Okuyama Naoji 奥山直司. *Kawaguchi Ekai nikki: Himaraya/Chibetto no tabi* 河口慧海日記—ヒマラヤ・チベットの旅. Tokyo: Kōdansha, 2007.

Kawahara Hidetoshi 河原英俊. "Setagaya Yoda ni okeru Kawaguchi Ekai 世田谷代田における河口慧海." *Setagai* せたがい 51 (2000): 52–57.

Kemper, Steven. *Rescued from the Nation: Anagarika Dharmapala and the Buddhist World*. Buddhism and Modernity. Chicago: University of Chicago Press, 2015.

Ketelaar, James Edward. *Of Heretics and Martyrs in Meiji Japan*. Princeton, NJ: Princeton University Press, 1990.

Kimura Nichiki 木村日紀. "Daijō Shōjō to iu meimeigi no rekishiteki kenkyū" 大乗小乗とい ふ名名義の歴史的研究. *Ōsaki gakuhō* 81 (1932): 76–114.

———. "Aiku Ō no kyōhō" 阿育王の教法. *Ōsaki gakuhō* 83 (1933): 113–40.

———. *Indo gendai shichō* 印度現代思潮. Tokyo: Iwanami Shoten, 1935.

Kimura, Nikki. "My Memory about the Late Rash Behari Bose." In *Rash Behari Basu, His Struggle for India's Independence*, edited by Rash Behari Bose, Radhanath Rath and Sābitri Prasanna Chatterjee, 38–49. Calcutta: Biplabi Mahanayak Rash Behari Basu Smarak Samity, 1963.

Kimura Nikki. 木村日紀. *Hokekyō kōwa: Nichiren Shōnin to Hokekyō* 法華經講話：日蓮上人 と法華經. Tokyo: Kimura Masawo 木村まさを, 1966.

Kimura Ryūkan 木村竜寛. "Indo kenbun dan" インド見聞談. *Hokke* 2, no. 5 (1915).

———. *Upanishaddo monogatari* 優波尼沙土物語. Tokyo: Shinchōsha, 1916.

———. "Nichiren shugi o shiru mae ni Hokekyō o shirubeshi, Nichiren Shōnin o shiru mae ni Budda o shirubeshi" 日蓮主義を知る前に法華経を知る可し,日蓮聖人を知る前に仏 陀を知る可し. *Hokke* 7, no. 3 (March 1920).

———. "Indo no saishi girei ni tsuite" 印度の祭祀儀礼に就いて. *Ōsaki gakuhō* 30 (November 1930): 74–80.

———. "Konpon Bukkyō yori Hokekyō made" 根本仏教より法華経まで. *Ōsaki gakuhō*, Nichiren Shōnin roppyaku gojū onki kinen tokushū gō 日蓮上人六百五十遠忌記念特輯号 (December 1931): 229–302.

Kimura, Ryukan. *The Fundamental Doctrine of Gautama Buddha and Its Position in Indian Thought*. Tokyo: International Buddhist Society, n.d.

———. *The Original and Developed Doctrines of Indian Buddhism in Charts*. Calcutta: University of Calcutta, 1920.

———. *Introduction to the History of Early Buddhist Schools*. Calcutta: Calcutta University Press, 1925. https://dds.crl.edu/crldelivery/29678 .

———. *A Historical Study of the Terms Hinayāna and Mahāyāna and the Origin of Mahāyāna Buddhism*. Patna: Indological Book Corp., 1978. Orig. ed., 1927.

King, Richard. *Orientalism and Religion: Postcolonial Theory, India and "the Mystic East."* London Routledge, 1999.

Kinnard, Jacob. "When is The Buddha not The Buddha? The Hindu-Buddhist Battle over Bodh Gayā and Its Buddha Image." *Journal of the American Academy of Religion* 68, no. 4 (1998): 817–39.

Kirby, M. T. "The Spirit of the Mahayana." *Mahayanist* 1, no. 3 (1915): 18–19.

Kirihara Kenshin 桐原健真. "Kawaguchi Ekai: Kyūhō no michi no shūchakuten" 河口慧 海—求法の道の終着点. In *Ajia taiken to shisō no hen'yō, kindai Nihon no Bukkyōsha* ア ジア体験と思想の変容, 近代日本の仏教者, edited by Ogawara Masamichi 小川原正 道 and Koyama Satoko 小山聡子, 245–75. Tokyo: Keiō Gijuku Daigaku Shuppankai, 2010.

Kisala, Robert. *Prophets of Peace: Pacifism and Cultural Identity in Japan's New Religions*. Honolulu: University of Hawai'i Press, 1999.

Kitabatake Dōryū 北畠道竜. *Tenjiku kōroji shoken* 天竺行路次所見. Tokyo: Aranami Heijirō, 1886.

Kitabatake Dōryū Kenshō Kai 北畠道竜顕彰会. *Gōsō Kitabatake Dōryū* 豪僧北畠道竜. Wakayama, Japan: Kitabatake Dōryū Kenshō Kai, 1956.

Kitagawa, Joseph M. "Kawaguchi Ekai: A Pious Adventurer and Tibet." In *Reflections on Tibetan*

Culture: Essays in Memory of Turrell V. Wylie, edited by Turrell V. Wylie, Lawrence Epstein, and Richard Sherburne, 279–94. Lewiston, NY: Edward Mellen Press, 1990.

Kitao Harumichi 北尾春道. *Tsukiji Honganji* 築地本願寺. Tokyo: Kōyō Sha, 1934.

Kokusai Bukkyō Kyōkai 国際仏教協会. "Dai Go Kai Nanpō Budda Matsuri" 第五回南方仏陀祭. Tokyo: Kokusai Bukkyō Kyōkai, 1945.

Kokusai Bukkyō Kōryū Kyōkai 国際仏教興隆協会. "About Us." http://www.ibba.jp/協会について/about-us. Accessed February 8, 2018.

Komuro Shigehiro 小室重弘, ed. *<Shakuson goigyō> Denraishi* ＜釈尊御遺形＞伝来史. Nagoya: Okabe Toyokichi, 1903.

Kosambi, Dharmananda, and Meera Kosambi. *Dharmanand Kosambi: The Essential Writings*. Ranikhet, Bangalore: Permanent Black, 2010.

Krämer, Hans Martin. *Shimaji Mokurai and the Reconception of Religion and the Secular in Modern Japan*. Honolulu: University of Hawaiʻi Press, 2015.

Kumar, Nita. "Sanskrit Pandits and the Modernisation of Sanskrit Education in the Nineteenth to Twentieth Centuries." In *Swami Vivekananda and the Modernization of Hinduism*, edited by William Radice, 36–60. Delhi: Oxford University Press, 1998.

Kurakata Shunsuke 倉方俊輔. "Itō Chūta no sekkei shisō: yōkai to shite no kenchiku" 伊東忠太の設計思想—妖怪としての建築. In *Itō Chūta o shitte imasu ka* 伊東忠太を知っていますか, edited by Suzuki Hiroyuki 鈴木博之, 86–136. Tokyo: Ōkoku Sha, 2003.

Kuruma Takudō 来馬琢道. *<Mokusen Zenji> Nangoku junrei ki* ＜黙仙禅師＞南国巡礼記. Tokyo: Nangoku Junrei Ki Hensanjo, 1916.

———. "Shōrai no Bukkyō kenchiku" 将来の仏教建築. 1925. In Kuruma Takudō, *Gaitō no Bukkyō*, 131–33.

Kuruma Takudō 来馬琢道, ed. *<Zenteki taiken> Gaitō no Bukkyō* ＜禅的体験＞街頭の仏教. Tokyo: Bukkyōsha, 1934.

Leoshko, Janice. *Sacred Traces: British Explorations of Buddhism in South Asia*. Histories of Vision. Aldershot: Ashgate, 2003.

Lockwood, William W. *The Economic Development of Japan: Growth and Structural Change, 1868–1938*. Princeton, NJ: Princeton University Press, 1954.

Lopez, Donald S., ed. *A Modern Buddhist Bible: Essential Readings from East and West*. Boston: Beacon Press, 2002.

Maejima Shinji 前嶋信次. *Indogaku no akebono* インド学の曙. Tokyo: Sekai Seiten Kankō Kyōkai, 1985.

Malalgoda, Kitsiri. *Buddhism in Sinhalese Society, 1750–1900: A Study of Religious Revival and Change*. Berkeley: University of California Press, 1976.

Markovits, Claude, Jacques Pouchepadass, and Sanjay Subrahmanyam. *Society and Circulation: Mobile People and Itinerant Cultures in South Asia, 1750–1950*. Delhi: Permanent Black, 2003.

Masuda, Jiryō. "Early Indian Buddhist Schools." *Journal of the Department of Letters, University of Calcutta* 1 (1920).

———. "Origin and Doctrines of Early Indian Buddhist Schools: A Translation of Hsüan-Chwang's Version of Vasumitra's Treatise." *Asia Major* 2 (1925): 1–78.

Masuzawa, Tomoko. *The Invention of World Religions, or, How European Universalism was Preserved in the Language of Pluralism*. Chicago: University of Chicago Press, 2005.

Matsumoto, Shirō. "The Doctrine of the Tathāgata-garbha Is Not Buddhist." In *Pruning the Bodhi Tree: The Storm over Critical Buddhism*, edited by Jamie Hubbard and Paul L. Swanson, 165–73. Honolulu: University of Hawaiʻi Press, 1997.

Measuring Worth. "Seven Ways to Compute the Relative Value of a U.S. Dollar Amount—1774 to Present." MeasuringWorth.com. https://www.measuringworth.com/uscompare. Accessed June 13, 2017.

Metcalf, Thomas R. *An Imperial Vision: Indian Architecture and Britain's Raj*. Berkeley: University of California Press, 1989.

Meyer, Karl E., and Shareen Blair Brysac. *Tournament of Shadows: The Great Game and the Race for Empire in Central Asia*. Washington, DC: Counterpoint, 1999.

Miyata Emi 宮田恵美. "Oji Kawaguchi Ekai to sono omoide" 伯父河口慧海とその思い出. *Setagai* せたがい 58 (2006): 40–59.

Mizuno Kōgen 水野弘元. "Review of 'Gedatsu dōron to Shōjō dōron no hikakaku kenkyū': P. V. Vapat [*sic*], Vimutti-magga and Visuddhi-magga, a comparative study" 『解脱道論と清浄道論の比較研究』. *Bukkyō kenkyū* 3, no. 3 (1939): 114–37.

Mohr, Michel. "Imagining Indian Zen: Tōrei's Commentary on the *Ta-mo-to-lo ching* and the Rediscovery of Meditation Techniques during the Tokugawa Era." In *Zen Classics: Formative Texts in the History of Zen Buddhism*, edited by Steven Heine and Dale S. Wright, 215–46. New York: Oxford University Press. 2006.

Morgan, David, and Sally M. Promey. *The Visual Culture of American Religions*. Berkeley: University of California Press, 2001.

Morrell, Robert E. "Passage to India Denied: Zeami's Kasuga Ryūjin." *Monumenta Nipponica* 37, no. 2 (1982): 179–200.

Müller, F. Max. *Biographical Essays*. London: Longmans Green, 1884.

Murakami Mamoru 村上護. *Shimaji Mokurai den: ken o taishita itan no hijiri* 島地黙雷伝—剣を帯した異端の聖. Kyoto: Mineruva Shobō, 2011.

Murakami Myōsei 村上妙清. *Nyūjiku bikuni* 入竺比丘尼. Kyoto: Zennenji, 1944.

Murphy, Anne. "Mindfulness-based Therapy in Modern Psychology: Convergence and Divergence from Early Buddhist Thought." *Contemporary Buddhism* 17, no. 2 (2016): 275–325.

Nagai, Makoto. "The Vimuttimagga: The 'Way to Deliverance.'" *Journal of the Pali Text Society* (1917–19): 69–80.

Nagai Makoto 長井真琴. "Gedatsu dōron ni tsuite" 解脱道論に就いて. *Tetsugaku zasshi* (July 1919).

———. "Gedatsu dōron to Visudimagga to no taishō kenkyū" 解脱道論と「ヴィスディマッガ」との対照研究. In *Konpon Butten no kenkyū* 根本仏典の研究, edited by Nagai Makoto 長井真琴, 237–50. Tokyo: Tenchi Shobō, 1922.

Nakajima Takeshi 中島岳志. *Nakamura-ya no Bōsu: Indo dokuritsu undō to kindai Nihon no Ajia shugi* 中村屋のボース: インド独立運動と近代日本のアジア主義. Tokyo: Hakusuisha, 2005.

Nakanishi Naoki 中西直樹, and Yoshinaga Shin'ichi 吉永進一. *Bukkyō kokusai nettowāku no genryū: Kaigai Senkyōkai (1888-nen—1893-nen) no hikari to kage* 仏教国際ネットワークの源流: 海外宣教会 (1888年—1893年) の光と影. Ryūkoku Sōsho. Kyoto: Sannin Sha, 2015.

Nakanishi Naoki 中西直樹, Yoshinaga Shin'ichi 吉永進一, and Kaigai Senkyōkai 海外宣教會. *Kaigai Bukkyō jijō. The Bijou of Asia* 海外仏教事情. Fukkokuban. 3 vols. Kyoto: Sanjin Sha, 2014–15.

Nakatsuji Masanobu 中辻正信. *Indo ryokō ki* 印度旅行記. Tokyo: Fujitani Sūbunkan, 1942.

Naniwa Senmyō 浪花宣明, ed. *Gedatsu dōron* 解脱道論. Shin Kokuyaku Daizōkyō, Vol. 19 (Ronshūbu 論宗部 5). Tokyo: Kōei Bunka Sha, 2001.

Nanjō Bun'yū 南条文雄. *Indo kikō* 印度紀行. Kyoto: Sano Masamichi, 1887.

Nethercot, Arthur H. *The Last Four Lives of Annie Besant*. Chicago: University of Chicago Press, 1963.

Nichiren. *The Awakening to the Truth or "Kaimokushō."* Translated by N. R. M. Ehara assisted by Bhikkhu Soma and Bhikkhu Kheminda. Tokyo: International Buddhist Society, 1941.

Nihon Yūsen Kabushiki Kaisha日本郵船株式会社. *Golden Jubilee History of Nippon Yusen Kaisha, 1885–1935*. Tokyo: Nippon Yusen Kaisha, 1935.

———. *Shichijūnenshi* 七十年史. Tokyo: Nippon Yūsen Kabushiki Kaisha, 1956.

Nishino Junjirō 西野順次郎. *Nichi-Tai yonhyakunen shi* 日・泰四百年史. Tokyo: Jiji Tsūshinsha, 1978.

Noguchi Fukudō 野口復堂. *Shaku Kōzen to Shakuson Shōfū Kai* 釈興然と釈尊正風会. Kanagawa, Japan: Sanneji, 1920.

Nomoto Towa 野本永久. *Akegarasu Haya den* 暁烏敏伝. Tokyo: Daiwa Shobō, 1974.

Nosu, Kosetsu, and Basil Woodward Crump. *Mulagandhakuti Vihara Wall Paintings*. Sarnath: Benares, 1940.

Nosu Kōsetsu 野生司香雪. *Shakuson eden* 釈尊絵伝. Kawasaki: Numata Yehan, 1960.

Ōbaku Bunka Kenkyūsho 黄檗文化研究所. <*Ōbakusan Manpukuji Bunkaden Heisei Jūnendo Shūki Tokubetsuten*> *Kawaguchi Ekai Nepāru-Chibetto nyūkoku hyakushūnen kinen: sono sho kōkai shiryo to Ōbakusan no meihō* <黄檗山萬福寺文化殿平成十年度秋季特別展＞河口慧海ネパール・チベット入国百周年記念—その初公開資料と黄檗山の名宝, edited by Ōbakusan Manpukuji Bunkaden. Uji, Japan: Ōbakusan Bunkaden, 1998.

Ober, Douglas Fairchild. "Reinventing Buddhism: Conversations and Encounters in Modern India, 1839–1956." PhD diss., University of British Columbia, 2016.

Oda Tokunō 織田得能. *Shamu Bukkyō jijō* 暹羅仏教事情. Tokyo: Shinshū Hōwa Shuppan, 1891.

Ogawara Masamichi 小川原正道, and Koyama Satoko 小山聡子. *Ajia taiken to shisō no hen'yō, kindai Nihon no bukkyōsha* アジア体験と思想の変容, 近代日本の仏教者. Tokyo: Keiō Gijuku Daigaku Shuppankai, 2010.

Oikawa Shigeru 及川茂. *Kore zo Kyōsai! ten* これぞ暁斎！展, edited by Bunkamura Museum of Art, Kochi Museum of Art, Museum "Eki" Kyoto, Ishikawa Prefectural Museum of Art and Tokyo Shimbun. Tokyo: Tokyo Shimbun, 2017.

Okada Masahiko. "Vision and Reality: Buddhist Cosmographic Discourse in Nineteenth-Century Japan." PhD diss., Stanford University, 1997.

Oka Kyōtsui 岡教邃. *Indo Busseki shashin chō* 印度仏蹟写真帖. Tokyo: Oka Kyōtsui, 1918.

Okamoto, Yoshiko. "An Asian Religion Conference Imagined: Okakura Kakuzō, Swami Vivekananda, and Unwoven Religious Ties in Early Twentieth-Century Asia." *Japanese Religions* 42, nos. 1 & 2 (2016): 1–24.

Ōkawa Shūmei 大川周明. *Indo ni okeru kokuminteki undō no genjō oyobi sono yurai* 印度に於ける国民的運動の現状及び其の由来. Tokyo: Ōkawa Shūmei, 1916.

Ōkubo Ryōjun 大久保良順, ed. *Studies in Indian Buddhist History by Jiryo Masuda*. Tokyo: Taisho University, 1986.

Okuyama Naoji 奥山直司. *Hyōden Kawaguchi Ekai* 評伝河口慧海. Tokyo: Chūō Kōron Shinsha, 2003.

———. "Rankā no hassō: Meiji nijyū nendai zenhan no Indo ryūgakusō no jiseki" ランカーの八僧—明治二十年代前半の印度留学僧の事績. In *Indo Gaku shoshisō to sono shūen: Bukkyō Bunka Gakkai Jisshūnen Hōjō Kenzō Hakushi koki kinen ronbunshū* インド学諸

思想とその周延—仏教文化学会十周年北條賢三博士古稀記念論文集, edited by Buk-kyō Bunka Gakkai, 89–106. Tokyo: Sankibō Busshorin 2004.

———. "Nihon Bukkyō to Seiron Bukkyō to no deai: Shaku Kōzen no ryūgaku o chūshin ni" 日本仏教とセイロン仏教との出会い—釈興然の留学を中心に. *Contact Zone* コンタクト・ゾーン 2 (2008): 23–36.

———. "The Tibet Fever among Japanese Buddhists of the Meiji Era." Translated by Rolf Giebel. In *Images of Tibet in the 19th and 20th Centuries*, edited by Monica Esposito, 203–22. Paris: École française d'Extrême-Orient, 2008.

———. "Pilgrimage to the Crystal Mountain in Dolpo by the Japanese Monk, Kawaguchi Ekai." In *International Conference on Esoteric Buddhist Studies*, edited by International Conference on Esoteric Buddhist Studies Editorial Board, 207–22. Koyasan University: International Conference on Esoteric Buddhist Studies, 2008.

———. "Meiji Indo ryūgakuseitachi ga mita 'Hiei' to 'Kongō' no kōkai" 明治インド留学生たちが見た「比叡」と「金剛」の航海. *Tōyō Daigaku Ajia Bunka Kenkyūsho kenkyū nenpō* 43 (2008): 65–81.

———. "Correspondence between Kumagusu and Dogi Hōryū: On the Newly Found Letters from Kumugusu to Dogi." *Centre for the Study of Japanese Religions Newsletter* 20–21 (2010): 20–23.

Olcott, Henry Steel, and Elliott Coues. *A Buddhist Catechism, According to the Canon of the Southern Church*. 1st American ed. Biogen Series No. 3. Boston: Estes & Lauriat, 1887.

Olcott, Henry Steel, and Hikkaduve Sri Sumangala. *A Buddhist Catechism According to the Canon of the Southern Church*. Colombo, Ceylon: Theosophical Society, Buddhist Section, 1881.

Oldham, C. E. A. W. "David Brainerd Spooner." *Journal of the Royal Asiatic Society of Great Britain and Ireland* 2 (1925): 375–76.

Ōmiya Kōjun 大宮孝潤. *Busseki shihyō* 仏跡指標. n.d.

Ōsaka Kurashi no Konjaku Kan 大阪くらしの今昔館. "Tōyō + Seiyō = Itō Chūta: Yomigaeta Nishi Honganji 'Dendōin'" 東洋＋西洋＝伊東忠太—よみがえた西本願寺「伝道院」, edited by Ōsaka Kurashi no Konjaku Kan. Osaka: Ōsaka Kurashi no Konjaku Kan, 2012.

Ōsawa Kōji 大澤広嗣. "Pari Bunka Gakuin no taigai katsudō: senjiki ni okeru shūkyō senbu kōsaku no ichirei to shite" 巴利文化学院の対外活動—戦時期における宗教宣撫工作の一例として. *Kindai Bukkyō* 14 (2007): 51–81.

———. "Senjiki Furansuryō Indoshina ni okeru shūkyō kōsaku: Utsuki Nishū to Kuno Hōryū no genchi chōsa" 戦時期フランス領インドシナにおける宗教工作—宇津木二秀と久野芳隆の現地調査. *Tōyō bunka kenkyū* 15 (2013): 81–114.

———. *Senjika no Nihon Bukkyō to Nanpō chiiki* 戦時下の日本仏教と南方地域. Kyoto: Hōzōkan, 2015.

———. *Bukkyō o meguru Nihon to Tōnan Ajia chiiki* 仏教をめぐる日本と東南アジア地域. Ajia Yūgaku. Tokyo: Bensei Shuppan, 2016.

Ōshio Dokuzan 大塩毒山. *Indo Bukkyō shi chizu narabi [ni] sakuin* 印度仏教史地図並[二]索引. Tokyo: Daiyūkaku Shobō. 1924.

Ōtani Ei'ichi 大谷栄一, Yoshinaga Shin'ichi 吉永進一, and Kondō Shuntarō 近藤俊太郎, eds. *Kindai Bukkyō sutadīzu* 近代仏教スタディーズ. Kyoto: Hōzōkan, 2016.

Parmanand, M. A. *Mahāmanā Madan Mohan Malaviya: An Historical Biography*. 1st ed. 2 vols., Mahamana granthamala. Varanasi: Malaviya Adhyayan Sansthan, Banaras Hindu University, 1985.

Patil, D. R. *Kuśīnagara*. 2nd ed. New Delhi: Archaeological Survey of India, 1981.

Peleggi, Maurizio. *Lords of Things: The Fashioning of the Siamese Monarchy's Modern Image*. Honolulu: University of Hawai'i Press, 2002.

Pemaratana, Soorakkulame. "Promotion of the Ritual of Venerating the Buddha in Colonial Sri Lanka." Buddhism in the Global Eye: Beyond East and West, University of British Columbia, August 10–12, 2016.

———. "Bringing the Buddha Closer: The Role of Venerating the Buddha in the Modernization of Buddhism in Sri Lanka." PhD diss., Religious Studies, University of Pittsburgh, 2017.

Peppé, William, and Claxton and Vincent Arthur Smith. "The Piprāhwā Stūpa, Containing Relics of Buddha. *Journal of the Royal Asiatic Society of Great Britain and Ireland* (1898): 573–88.

Perreira, Todd LeRoy. "Whence Theravāda? The Modern Genealogy of an Ancient Term." In *How Theravāda is Theravāda? Exploring Buddhist Identities*, edited by Peter Skilling, Jason A. Carbine, Claudio Cicuzza, and Santi Pakdeekham, 443–571. Chiang Mai, Thailand: Silkworm Books, 2012.

Popplewell, Richard J. *Intelligence and Imperial Defence: British Intelligence and the Defence of the Indian Empire, 1904–1924*. Cass Series—Studies in Intelligence. London; Portland, OR: F. Cass, 1995.

Pōru Kērasu ポウル・ケーラス [Paul Carus]. *Budda no fukuin* 仏陀の福音. Translated by Suzuki Daisetsu 鈴木大拙. Tokyo: Satō Shigenobu, 1895.

Prothero, Stephen R. *The White Buddhist: The Asian Odyssey of Henry Steel Olcott*. Religion in North America. Bloomington: Indiana University Press, 1996.

Pruden, Leo M. "Some Notes on the *Fan-Wang-Ching*." *Indogaku Bukkyōgaku kenkyū* 15, no. 2 (1962): 915–25.

Pulle, V. E. P. "Buddhism in Ceylon." *Ōsaki gakuhō* 87 (December 1935): 2–6 (Left-Right).

Rambelli, Fabio. "The Idea of Tenjiku (India) in Pre-modern Japan: Issues of Signification and Representation in the Buddhist Translation of Cultures." In *Buddhism across Asia: Networks of Material, Intellectual, and Cultural Exchange*, edited by Tansen Sen, 259–90. Singapore: Institute of Southeast Asian Studies, 2014.

Rhodes, Robert. "Soga Ryōjin: Life and Thought." In *Cultivating Spirituality: A Modern Shin Buddhist Anthology*, edited by Mark Laurence Blum and Robert Franklin Rhodes, 104–5. Albany: State University of New York Press, 2011.

Rhys Davids, C. A. F. "Review of 'A Historical Study of the Terms Hinayāna and Mahāyāna and the Origin of Mahāyāna Buddhism' by Ryukan Kimura." *Bulletin of the School of Oriental Studies (London)* 4, no. 4 (1928): 856–57.

Ritzinger, Justin R. "Original Buddhism and Its Discontents: The Chinese Buddhist Exchange Monks and the Search for the Pure Dharma in Ceylon." *Journal of Chinese Religions* 44, no. 2 (2016): 149–73.

Ryūkoku Daigaku Ryūkoku Myūjiamu 龍谷大学龍谷ミュージアム, ed. *Bukkyō no kita michi: Shiruku Rōdo tanken no tabi* 仏教の来た道—シルクロード探検の旅, edited by Ryūkoku Museum. Kyoto: Ryūkoku Daigaku Ryūkoku Myūjiamu, 2012.

———, ed. *Nirakusō to Ōtani tankentai: Shirukurōdo kenkyū no genten to taiintachi no omoi: tokubetsuten* 二楽荘と大谷探検隊：シルクロード研究の原点と隊員たちの思い：特別展. Kyoto: Ryūkoku Daigaku Ryūkoku Myūjiamu, 2014.

Sakai-shi Hakubutsukan 堺市博物館, ed. *<Shūki tokubetsu ten> Kawaguchi Ekai: Bukkyō no genten o motometa hito* <秋季特別展>河口慧海—仏教の原点を求めた人. Sakai: Sakai-shi Hakubutsukan, 1993.

Sakya, Anil. "King Mongkut's Invention of a Universal Pali Script." In *How Theravāda is Theravāda? Exploring Buddhist Identities*, edited by Peter Skilling, Jason A. Carbine, Claudio Cicuzza, and Santi Pakdeekham, 401–13. Chiang Mai, Thailand: Silkworm Books, 2012.

Sandilyayana, Rastrapala. "Buddhism and Its Influence on Japanese Culture." *Young East* 8, no. 2 (1939): 22–29.

———. *A Short History of Japanese Buddhism*. Tokyo: International Buddhist Society, 1940.

Śāntideva, Kate Crosby, and Andrew Skilton. *The Bodhicaryāvatāra*. World's Classics. New York: Oxford University Press, 1996.

Satō Tetsurō 佐藤哲郎. *Daiajia shisō katsugeki: Bukkyō ga musunda, mō hitotsu no kindai shi* 大アジア思想活劇―仏教が結んだ、もうひとつの近代史. Tokyo: Saṃgha, 2008.

Sawada, Janine Anderson. *Practical Pursuits: Religion, Politics, and Personal Cultivation in Nineteenth-century Japan*. Honolulu: University of Hawai'i Press, 2004.

Seager, Richard Hughes. *The World's Parliament of Religions: The East/West Encounter, Chicago, 1893*. Religion in North America. Bloomington: Indiana University Press, 1995.

Seki Rokō 關露香. *Honpa Honganji Hosshu Ōtani Kōzui Haku Indo Tanken* 本派本願寺法主大谷光瑞伯印度探検. Tokyo: Hakubunkan, 1913.

Seki Seisetsu 関清拙. *Tenjiku angya* 天竺行脚. Kyoto: Baiyō Shoin, 1922.

Shaku Daishin 釈大眞. *Toin nisshi* 渡印日誌. Kyoto: Shaku Daishin, 1911.

Shaku Kaiyū 釈快祐, and Shaku Kōzen 釈興然. *Tenjiku Shakamuni Butsuzō oyobi sanzō shōgyō shōrai no en'yu* 天竺釈迦牟尼仏像及三藏聖経請来の縁由. Kanagawa: Shōfū Kai, 1909.

Shaku Kōzen 釈興然. *Shakuson shōfū* 釈尊正風. Toriyama: Sanneji, 1900.

———. *Shakuson shōfū o kakuchō suru no shui* 釈尊正風ヲ拡張スルノ趣意. Yokohama: Sanneji, 1893.

———. *Sanneji jihō narabi kyōyō ninka kisoku* 三會寺寺法並教養認可規則. Kanagawa: Sanneji, 1908.

Shaku Sōen 釈宗演. *Seinan no Bukkyō* 西南の仏教. Tokyo: Hakubunkan, 1889.

———. *Seirontō shi* 錫崘島志. Tokyo: Gukyō Shoin, 1890.

———. *Saiyū nikki* 西遊日記. Kamakura: Kamakura Matsugaoka Tōkeiji, 1941.

Shaku, Soyen (Shaku Sōen). "The Law of Cause and Effect, As Taught by Buddha." In *The World's Parliament of Religions; An Illustrated and Popular Story of the World's First Parliament of Religions, Held in Chicago in Connection with the Columbian Exposition of 1893*, edited by John Henry Barrows, 829–31. Chicago: Parliament Publishing Company, 1893.

Shibata Mikio 柴田幹夫. *Ōtani Kōzui no kenkyū: Ajia kōiki ni okeru sho katsudō* 大谷光瑞の研究―アジア広域における諸活動. Tokyo: Bensei Shuppan, 2014.

Shimaji Mokurai 島地黙雷, and Oda Tokunō 織田得能. *Sangoku Bukkyō ryakushi* 三国仏教略史. Tokyo: Kōmeisha, 1890.

Shimizu, Isamu. "Takaoka, Priest Imperial Prince Shinnyo." *Transactions of the Asiatic Society of Japan* Third Series 5 (1957): 1–35.

Shimizu Mokuji 清水黙爾. "Nepāru tanken nikki shō" 尼波羅探検日記抄. In *Shin Seiikiki: Ōtanike zōban* 新西域記 : 大谷家蔵版, edited by Uehara Yoshitarō 上原芳太郎. Tokyo: Yūkōsha, 1937.

Shirasu Jōshin 白須浄信. *Ōtani tankentai to sono jidai* 大谷探検隊とその時代. Tokyo: Bensei Shuppan, 2002.

Shōji Ichirō 荘司一郎. *Izawa Ryōan Ō den* 伊沢亮庵翁伝. Sendai: Izawa Ryōan Ō Den Kankōkai, 1935.

Silk, Jonathan A. "The Victorian Creation of Buddhism: Review of The British Discovery of Buddhism by Philip C. Almond." *Journal of Indian Philosophy* 22, no. 1 (1994): 171–96.

Skilling, Peter, Jason A. Carbine, Claudio Cicuzza, and Santi Pakdeekham eds. *How Thera-vāda is Theravāda? Exploring Buddhist Identities.* Chiang Mai, Thailand: Silkworm Books, 2012.

Snodgrass, Judith. *Presenting Japanese Buddhism to the West: Orientalism, Occidentalism, and the Columbian Exposition.* Chapel Hill: University of North Carolina Press, 2003.

Sōhonzan Chishakuin 総本山智積院. "Rekidai keshu" 歴代化主. Chishakuin 智積院. http://www.chisan.or.jp/about/rekidai. 2016. Accessed June 30, 2017.

Sōtōshū Shūmuchō. *Standard Observances of the Sōtō School.* Translated by T. Griffith Foulk. 2 vols. Tokyo: Sōtōshū Shūmuchō, 2010.

Spooner, D. Brainerd. "Welcoming the Buddha's Most Holy Bones." *Overland Monthly* 37, no. 1 (1901): 585–92.

Stede, W. "Review of 'A Historical Study of the Terms Hinayāna and Mahāyāna and the Origin of Mahāyāna Buddhism' by Ryukan Kimura." *Journal of the Royal Asiatic Society of Great Britain and Ireland* 4 (1928): 950–52.

Stender, Daniel. "Preliminary Survey of Sanskrit Texts of the *Bodhicaryāvatāra*." In *Puṣpikā: Tracing Ancient India through Texts and Traditions: Contributions to Current Research in Indology,* edited by Giovanni Ciotti, Alastair Gornall, and Paolo Visigalli, 147–69. Oxford: Oxbow Books, 2014.

Subrahmanyam, Sanjay. "Connected Histories: Notes towards a Reconfiguration of Early Modern Eurasia." *Modern Asian Studies* 31, no. 3 (1997): 735–62.

Surendran, Gitanjali. "'The Indian Discovery of Buddhism': Buddhist Revival in India, c. 1890–1956." PhD diss., Harvard University, 2013.

Szpilman, Christopher W. A. "Kanokogi Kazunobu: 'Imperial Asia,' 1937." In *Pan-Asianism: A Documentary History,* edited by Sven Saaler and Christopher W. A. Szpilman, 149–53. Lanham, MD: Rowman & Littlefield, 2011.

Takagai Shunshi 鷹谷俊之. *Tōzai Bukkyō gakusha den* 東西仏教学者伝. Karin Bukkyōgaku Sōsho. Ube: Karinbunko, 1970.

Takakusu, J. "Pali Elements in Chinese Buddhism: A Translation of Buddhaghosa's Samanta-pasadika, a Commentary on the Vinaya, found in the Chinese Tripitaka." *Journal of the Royal Asiatic Society* (July 1896): 415–39.

Takakusu, Junjiro. "India and Japan." *Young East* 1, no. 2 (1925): 35–39.

Takakusu Junjirō 高楠順次郎, Wada Sanzō 和田三造, and Kumagaya Kunizō 熊谷国造. *Indo Busseki jissha* 印度仏跡実写. Tokyo: Kōgeisha, 1926.

Takashina Rōsen 高階瓏仙 and Kuruma Takudō 来馬琢道. *Hioki Mokusen Zenji den* 日置黙仙禅師伝. Tokyo: Hioki Mokuzen Zenji Denki Kankōkai, 1962.

Takayama Aya 高山文. "Zenpukuji shin kenchiku to kindai Kōbe jiin" 善福寺新建築と近代神戸寺院. *Chūgai nippō.* November 23, 1930, 2.

Takayama Ryūzō 高山龍三. "Kawaguchi Ekai kenjō no zōkyō o motomete: 1998 nen Nepāru hōkoku" 河口慧海献上の蔵教を求めて――一九九八年ネパール報告. *Ōbaku bunka* 黄檗文華 118 (1998–99): 14–27.

――――. *Tenbō Kawaguchi Ekai ron* 展望河口慧海論. Kyoto: Hōzōkan, 2002.

――――. *Sekai o kakeru Kawaguchi Ekai* 世界を駆ける河口慧海. Uji: Ōbakushū Seinensō no Kai, 2006.

Tanabe, George J., Jr. *Myōe the Dreamkeeper: Fantasy and Knowledge in Early Kamakura Buddhism.* Cambridge, MA: Harvard University Press, 1992.

――――. "Grafting Identity: The Hawaiian Branches of the Bodhi Tree." Unpublished paper, 2002.

――――. "Śākyamuni for Modern Japan, Hawai'i, and California." When Modernity Hits Hard:

Buddhism's Search for a New Identity in Meiji-Taishō-Early Shōwa Japan, Berkeley, CA, April 17–18, 2015.

Tani Dōgen 渓道元. *Tani Dōgen Nan'a ryokō ki: hanseiki mae no Nan'a musen ryokō ki* 渓道元南亜旅行記—半世紀前の南亜無銭旅行記. Uji: Ōbakushū Kanchō, 1962.

Tarocco, Francesca. *The Cultural Practices of Modern Chinese Buddhism: Attuning the Dharma*. Routledge Critical Studies in Buddhism. London: Routledge, 2007.

Tashōzan Isshinji 太生山一心寺. "Indo bun'in ni tsuite" 印度分院について. http://tashozan-isshinji.org/indiabunin.html. Accessed February 8, 2018.

Tavakoli-Targhi, Mohamad. "Orientalism's Genesis Amnesia." *Comparative Studies of South Asia, Africa and the Middle East* 16 (1996): 1–14.

Terasawa Genshū 寺沢玄宗. *Shakuson goigyō denraishi—Kakuōzan Nittaiji hōantō no yurai* 釈尊御遺形伝来史—覚王山日泰寺奉安塔の由来. Nagoya: Kakuōzan Nittaiji, 1981.

Thomas, Edward J. *The Life of the Buddha as Legend and History*. London: Routledge & Kegan Paul, 1927.

Tillotson, Giles H. "Orientalizing the Raj: Indo-Saracenic Fantasies." In *Architecture in Victorian and Edwardian India*, edited by Christopher W. London, 15–34. Bombay: Marg Publications, 1994.

Trainor, Kevin. "Buddhism in a Nutshell: The Uses of *Dhammapada* 183." In *Embedded Languages: Studies of Sri Lankan and Buddhist Cultures: Essays in Honor of W. S. Karunatillake*, edited by Carol S. Anderson, Suzanne Mrozik, R. M. W. Rajapakse, and W. M. Wijeratne, 109–48. Colombo, Sri Lanka: Godage International Publishers, 2009.

Trevithick, Alan Michael. "A Jerusalem of the Buddhists in British India: 1874–1949." PhD diss., Harvard University, 1988.

———. "British Archaeologists, Hindu Abbots, and Burmese Buddhists: The Mahabodhi Temple at Bodh Gaya, 1811–1877." *Modern Asian Studies* 33, no. 3 (1999): 635–56.

Tseng, Alice Yu-Ting. "Styling Japan: The Case of Josiah Conder and the Museum at Ueno, Tokyo." *Journal of the Society of Architectural Historians* 63, no. 4 (December 2004): 473–97.

———. *The Imperial Museums of Meiji Japan: Architecture and the Art of the Nation*. Seattle: University of Washington Press, 2008.

Tsukiji Honganji 築地本願寺. "Katomanzu Honganji to Nepāru/Indo Busseki junpai: Shakuson shichidai seichi no tabi" カトマンズ本願寺とネパール・インド仏跡巡拝「釈尊七大聖地の旅」. Tsukiji Honganji. http://tsukijihongwanji.jp/news/「カトマンズ本願寺とネパール・インド仏跡巡拝. Accessed February 9, 2018.

Tuttle, Gray. *Tibetan Buddhists in the Making of Modern China*. New York: Columbia University Press, 2005.

Tweed, Thomas A., ed. *Retelling U.S. Religious History*. Berkeley: University of California Press, 1997.

Uehara Sadao 上原貞雄. "Kitabatake Dōryū ni okeru L. V. Shutain to no shisō kōryū: omo ni shūkyō to seiji, shūkyō to kyōiku no mondai ni kakawatte" 北畠道竜におけるL。V。シュタインとの思想交流—おもに宗教と政治、宗教と教育の問題にかかわって. *Gifu Seitoku Gakuen Daigaku Kyōiku Gakubu Gaikokugo Gakubu kiyō* 37 (1999): 133–56.

Uehara Yoshitarō 上原芳太郎. *Shin seiikiki: Ōtanike zōban* 新西域記—大谷家蔵版. 2 vols. Tokyo: Yūkōsha, 1937.

Ukai Chōsaburō 鵜飼長三郎. "Nirakusō kenchiku kōji gaiyō" 二楽荘建築工事概要. *Kenchiku kōgei sōshi* 20 (1913): 2–6.

Unebe Toshiya 畝部俊也. Taikoku watto/Rajyashiddaramu jiin hoka shozō shahon ni motozuku zōgai Butten no kenkyū タイ国ワット・ラジャシッダラム寺院他所蔵写本に基づく蔵外仏典の研究. Grants-in-Aid for Scientific Research. Nagoya: Nagoya University, 2012.

Umezawa Megumi 梅沢恵, and Tokura Takeyuki 都倉武之, eds. *Shaku Sōen to kindai Nihon—wakaki Zensō, sekai o kakeru* 釈宗演と近代日本—若き禅僧、世界を駆ける. Kita-Kamakura: Engakuji, 2018.

Upatissa. *The Path of Freedom (Vimuttimagga).* Translated by N. R. M. Ehara, Soma Thera, and Kheminda Thera. Kandy, Sri Lanka: Buddhist Publication Society, 1995. Orig. ed., 1961, reprinted 1975; 1995.

Vedanta Society of Japan. "History of the Vedanta Society of Japan." https://www.vedantajp-en.com/society-s-history/. Accessed February 8, 2018.

Walker, Brett L. *A Concise History of Japan.* Cambridge Concise Histories. Cambridge: Cambridge University Press, 2015.

Walleser, Max. *Die Sekten des alten Buddhismus, His: Die buddhistische Philosophie in ihrer geschichtlichen Entwicklung.* 4 vols. Heidelberg: C Winter, 1927.

Watanabe, Toshio. "Japanese Imperial Architecture: From Thomas Roger Smith to Itō Chūta." In *Challenging Past and Present: The Metamorphosis of Nineteenth-Century Japanese Art,* edited by Ellen P. Conant, 239–53. Honolulu: University of Hawai'i Press, 2006.

Watt, Paul Brooks. "Jiun Sonja (1718–1804): Life and Thought." PhD diss., Columbia University, 1982.

Wattles, Miriam. "The 1909 *Ryūtō* and the Aesthetics of Affectivity." *Art Journal* 55, no. 3 (1996): 48–56.

Welbon, Guy Richard. *The Buddhist Nirvāṇa and Its Western Interpreters.* Chicago: University of Chicago Press, 1968.

Wendelken, Cherie. "The Tectonics of Japanese Style: Architect and Carpenter in the Late Meiji Period." *Art Journal* 55, no. 3 (1996): 28–37.

———. "Pan-Asianism and the Pure Japanese Thing: Japanese Identity and Architecture in the Late 1930s." *positions* 8, no. 3 (2000): 819–28.

Yagirala Śrī Prajñānanda. *Śrī Sumaṅgala caritaya dvitīya bhāgaya.* Colombo: Lake House Publishing, 1947.

Yamada Kyōta 山田協太. "Kindai Bukkyō kenchiku no Higashi Ajia—Minami Ajia ōkan" 近代仏教建築の東アジア—南アジア往還. In *Bukkyō o meguru Nihon to Tōnan Ajia chiiki* 仏教をめぐる日本と東南アジア地域, edited by Ōsawa Kōji 大澤広嗣, 87–105. Tokyo: Bensei Shuppan, 2016.

Yamagami Tadashi 山上貞, ed. *Suirō zuiha* 遂浪随波. Tokyo: Kanagawa Shinbunsha, 1957.

Yamakami Sōgen 山上曹源. *Konnichi no Indo* 今日の印度. Tokyo: Genkōsha, 1915.

———. *Hagakure bushi no seishin* 葉隠武士の精神. Tokyo: San'yū Sha, 1942.

Yamakami, Sōgen. *Systems of Buddhistic Thought.* Calcutta: University of Calcutta, 1912.

Yonezawa Kikuji 米沢菊二. *Dai Tōa sensō to Indo no chii* 大東亜戦争と印度の地位. Tokyo: Kokubō Keizai Kyōkai, 1942.

Yonezawa Yoshiyasu 米沢嘉康, "Kaisetsu" 解説, in *Kawaguchi Ekai chosakushū* 5: 1–2.

Yoshinaga Shin'ichi 吉永進一. "Hirai Kinza ni okeru Meiji Bukkyō no kokusaika ni kansuru shūkyōshi/bunkashiteki kenkyū" 平井金三における明治仏教の国際化に関する宗教史・文化史的研究 [Hirai Kinza and the Globalization of Japanese Buddhism in the Meiji Era, a Cultural and Religio-Historical Study]. Grants-in-Aid for Scientific Research (Category C). Kyoto, 2007.

Index

Page numbers in italics refer to figures and tables.